# composers
## who changed history

# composers
## who changed history

**Penguin Random House**

**SECOND EDITION**
**Toucan Books Ltd.**
**Editorial Director** Ellen Dupont
**Art Editor** Thomas Keenes
**Editor** Dorothy Stannard
**Picture Research** Sharon Southren
**Consultant on Second Edition** Dr Christina Reitz
**Additional text** Joanne Bourne, Tiffany Jackson, Maisie Lewis,
Christina Reitz, Mike Robbins, Michael Yonchak

**DK London**
**Editor** Kathryn Hill
**Senior Art Editor** Helen Spencer
**Senior US Editor** Megan Douglass
**Managing Editor** Gareth Jones
**Senior Managing Art Editor** Lee Griffiths
**Production Editor** Robert Dunn
**Production Controller** Nancy-Jane Maun
**Senior Jackets Designer** Surabhi Wadhwa-Gandhi
**Jacket Design Development Manager** Sophia MTT

**DK Delhi**
**Jacket Designer** Vidushi Chaudhry
**Senior DTP Designer** Harish Aggarwal
**Senior Jackets Coordinator** Priyanka Sharma Saddi

**FIRST EDITION**
**Senior Editor** Laura Sandford
**Senior Art Editor** Helen Spencer
**Editor** Victoria Heyworth-Dunne
**US Editor** Megan Douglass
**Managing Editor** Gareth Jones
**Senior Managing Art Editor** Lee Griffiths
**Jacket Designers** Surabhi Wadhwa-Gandhi, Suhita Dharamjit
**Jacket Design Development Manager** Sophia MTT
**Pre-production Producers** Kavita Varma, Gillian Reid
**Senior Producer** Rachel Ng
**Associate Publishing Director** Liz Wheeler
**Publishing Director** Jonathan Metcalf
**Art Director** Karen Self

**Produced for DK by**
**cobaltid**
www.cobaltid.co.uk

**Art Editors** Paul Reid, Darren Bland, Rebecca Johns
**Editors** Marek Walisiewicz, Diana Loxley,
Johnny Murray, Kirsty Seymour-Ure

This American Edition, 2024
First American Edition, 2020
Published in the United States by DK Publishing
1745 Broadway, 20th Floor, New York, NY 10019

Copyright © 2020, 2024 Dorling Kindersley Limited
DK, a Division of Penguin Random House LLC
24 25 26 27 28   10 9 8 7 6 5 4 3 2 1
001–339248–Feb/2024

A catalog record for this book
is available from the Library of Congress.
ISBN: 978-0-7440-9280-6

DK books are available at special discounts when purchased
in bulk for sales promotions, premiums, fund-raising, or
educational use. For details, contact DK Publishing Special
Markets, 1745 Broadway, 20th Floor, New York, NY 10019
SpecialSales@dk.com

Printed in China

**www.dk.com**

# CONTRIBUTORS

**Jessica Duchen**
studied music at Cambridge and has worked in
music journalism and criticism for national
newspapers and specialist magazines across
30 years. Her output also includes numerous
books, opera libretti, and stage works.

**R. G. Grant**
has written extensively in the fields of history,
biography, and culture. His recent works include
*Sentinels of the Sea* and contributions to *Music:
The Definitive Visual History* and *Writers Who
Changed History*.

**Malcolm Hayes**
is a composer and writer. His Violin Concerto
was performed at the 2016 BBC Proms; his
books include biographies of Liszt and Webern,
and an edition of the *Selected Letters of
William Walton*.

**Diana Loxley**
is a freelance editor and writer, and a former
managing editor of a publishing company in
London. She has a doctorate in literature.

**Andrew Stewart**
studied musicology at King's College London and
has written about classical music as a journalist
and author for more than 30 years. He is an
experienced choir trainer and conductor.

**Marcus Weeks**
is a writer and musician. He studied music,
philosophy, and musical instrument technology
and worked as a teacher before embarking on
a career as an author. He has written and
contributed to many books on philosophy,
literature, and the arts.

**Richard Wigmore**
is a music writer, lecturer, and broadcaster
specializing in opera and Lieder. His works
include *Schubert: The Complete Song Texts*, the
*Faber Pocket Guide to Haydn*, and many articles
for music dictionaries and encyclopedias.

**Iain Zaczek**
studied French and history at Wadham College,
Oxford University. He has written more than
30 books on various aspects of culture, history,
and art.

◁◁◁ **PAGE 1  GRAND PIANO BY MANUEL
ANTUNES, LISBON, 1767**

◁◁ **PAGE 2  ISABELLA ANGELA COLBRAN,
JOHANN HEINRICH SCHMIDT, 1817**

◁ **PAGE 3** *THE FIVE SENSES: HEARING,*
**ABRAHAM BOSSE, c. 1635**

▷ *LA BARRE AND OTHER MUSICIANS,*
**ANDRÉ BOUYS, c. 1710**

CONTENTS

## CHAPTER 5
# Early 20th Century

## CHAPTER 6
# Late 20th & 21st Centuries

# Preface

Around the year 600, the great scholar St. Isidore of Seville lamented that "unless sounds are remembered by man, they perish, for they cannot be written down." In fact, the Babylonians and the Ancient Greeks had independently invented systems of musical notation more than a thousand years earlier, but after the decay of their civilizations these methods had been completely forgotten. This meant that for many centuries, the only way of preserving a musical composition was through a continuous tradition of performance, passing it on from generation to generation.

However, a century or so after St. Isidore's time, monks started experimenting with ways of making a written record of the chants they sang, and in the 11th century the most important of these pioneers, Guido d'Arezzo, laid the basis of the system of notation we use today. This gives him such a momentous role in musical history that he features as the first subject in this book. There had been composers before Guido, but it is only after him that their works and personalities really survive.

Like Guido, several of the early composers included here were Italians, and another concentration of musical genius was found in France and neighboring Flanders. England, too, had an impressive musical tradition in the late Middle Ages and Renaissance. In the 18th century, the balance of power decisively shifted, with Germany and Austria seeing a glorious sequence of illustrious composers, from Bach onward, that is unmatched anywhere else, while Vienna emerged as the undisputed musical capital of the world.

During the 19th century, the range of countries producing outstanding composers expanded greatly, with Russia, eastern Europe, and Scandinavia all coming to the fore; and from the 20th century, the distribution has become truly worldwide, with the US prominent and such diverse places as Australia, Brazil, Canada, and Japan figuring among the two dozen countries whose composers are represented in this book.

Just as the geographical spread of composers has increased enormously over the centuries, so the type of work they produce has become much more varied. In the Middle Ages, the Catholic Church was the most widespread and influential institution in the Western world; music—like the visual arts—was dominated by religion, and many leading composers devoted themselves mainly to settings of the words of the Mass, the central church ceremony commemorating the death and resurrection of Christ. However, the Renaissance brought increasing secularization to the arts, expressed in new forms such as opera, which was born in Italy around 1600, and subsequently the scope of music has expanded not only in genre but also in style and in the range of instruments and other sound sources used.

The lives of some of the earlier figures covered in this book are sparsely documented, but for many others there is a rich fund of biographical information. The popular "Hollywood" image of the great composer has been created largely by a handful of the giants of 19th-century music whose lives are the stuff of legend: Beethoven, the proud, rebellious outsider, increasingly isolated by deafness; Berlioz, pouring his unrequited passion for a beautiful actress into one of the most original of all symphonies; Chopin, the exquisite poet of the piano whose career was blighted by debilitating illness; Tchaikovsky, whose turbulent personal life and puzzling death continue to inspire speculation; and Wagner, whose colossal ego was matched by his colossal creative energy and originality.

Not all composers have been such memorable personalities, of course, but there are nevertheless many remarkable characters among them—the lesser-known figures as well as the household names. They include Carlo Gesualdo, the Italian nobleman who brutally murdered his wife and her lover but escaped punishment for the crime; Erik Satie, regarded as a kind of patron saint of eccentricity; and the formidable Ethel Smyth, a feminist heroine not only because she achieved success in a male-dominated world but also because she was a prominent figure in the suffragette movement and was imprisoned for her activism.

Some composers have sought solitude, but others have lived their lives on the public stage—for example, Mendelssohn, the prototype of the modern international star musician, who numbered Queen Victoria and Prince Albert among his friends. Several have been directly affected by political events: William Byrd and Thomas Tallis had to steer careful courses through the dangerous waters of the English Reformation, and both Prokofiev and Shostakovich were forced to toe the party line in Stalin's repressive Soviet Union.

Some of this book's subjects had lamentably short careers, notably Lili Boulanger, who suffered ill health from infancy and was only 24 when she died. The deaths of several other composers are known or believed to have been hastened by syphilis (Delius, Donizetti, Schubert, and Smetana among them), and Mussorgsky is perhaps the most famous example of a composer whose life was cut short by alcoholism. At the opposite extreme are those who ended their days at a ripe age and loaded with honors: Rodrigo and Tippett lived well into their nineties, and Saint-Saëns, Stravinsky, and Verdi into their late eighties.

The varied lives and achievements of these extraordinary men and women are celebrated in this book and set within wider historical and cultural contexts. Their friendships, loves, rivalries, key influences, and working methods are all part of the stories of how they created the masterpieces that speak to us so eloquently across the centuries.

# BEFORE
# 1600

**CHAPTER 1**

▷ **GUIDO D'AREZZO, FRESCO**
This 19th-century fresco in the Chigiana Music Academy in Tuscany, Italy, shows the famous Italian monk and music theorist as an inspirational teacher.

# Guido d'Arezzo

### c. 991–c. 1050, ITALIAN

While serving as a Benedictine monk, Guido developed innovative methods for learning the chants of the services, as well as a system of writing music on which modern Western notation is based.

Born in the city-state of Arezzo, some 50 miles (80 km) south of Florence, in about 990 CE, Guido Monaco became known as Guido d'Arezzo as his fame spread throughout the world of Italian church music. Little is known about his family or early life, except that he was educated at the Benedictine abbey of Pomposa on the northeast coast of Italy, and served there as a monk when he was young.

## Solving problems

At Pomposa, Guido showed great musical talent and, noticing the difficulties the monks had in learning the plainsong melodies, gained a reputation as an inspirational teacher. He also studied music theory and developed ways to improve the singers' ability to learn the chants by heart, using a sketchy system of notation as a study aid.

Guido realized that this arduous process could be made considerably simpler by employing mnemonics—assigning each note of the scale a name (associated with the melody of a hymn to John the Baptist that he composed specially for the purpose). He also visualized these names as if mapped on the joints of a hand, dramatically shortening the time it took to learn new chants, and devised a way of writing music as marks on the staff or stave (a system of parallel horizontal lines), indicating the precise pitch of each note.

### ON TECHNIQUE
### From neumes to staff notation

The numerous chants of the Catholic Church were originally learned by rote by the monks and then passed on orally. However, from around the 9th century, graphic symbols, known as neumes, began to appear above the texts to suggest the shape of the melody. In time, these were placed on a horizontal line representing a pitch, such as C or F. Guido is credited with the idea of using four lines (which were later expanded to the familiar five-line staff) to identify the precise pitch of each note.

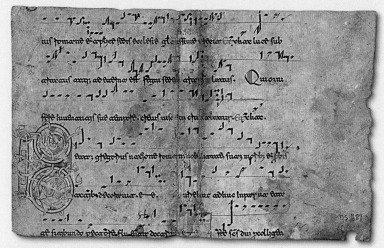

**12TH-CENTURY MUSIC NOTATION SHOWING DIASTEMATIC OR HEIGHTENED NEUMES AND A SINGLE-LINE STAFF**

Although these new techniques made learning and performing easier, many of the monks at Pomposa disliked Guido's innovation, and he left the abbey in about 1025. He returned to Arezzo, where the bishop appointed him as a teacher to the choristers of the cathedral, and commissioned him to write a treatise on the principles of his musical theories and to compile a collection of antiphons to present to Pope John XIX.

Guido completed his *Micrologus de disciplina artis musicae* (*Treatise on the teaching of the art of music*) in about 1026—it soon became the standard text for music theory and education in the Middle Ages. His reputation spread, and he was invited by the pope to Rome in 1028, but ill health restricted his activities until his death in about 1050.

## Legacy and influence

Guido was not, strictly speaking, a significant composer (his only known original work is the hymn that he used as a teaching aid), but his principles of musical education and the development of staff notation had profound influence. With a system of precise notation, musicians could perform more complex music, and even produce original compositions, knowing that these could be accurately reproduced. A written record of the music meant that it was possible to distribute ideas widely and quickly. It is no exaggeration to say that Guido ushered in the age of Western classical composers.

◁ **AERIAL VIEW OF POMPOSA ABBEY**
The imposing bell tower of Pomposa Abbey, where Guido spent several years of his life, dominates the spectacular Codigoro landscape in northeast Italy.

▽ **16TH-CENTURY GUIDONIAN HAND**
Guido created his notated-hand system so that, in his words, "any intelligent and diligent person" could learn a chant. This 16th-century example is complete with solmization syllables (*re, mi, fa*, for example)—syllables that are attributed to the notes in a musical scale.

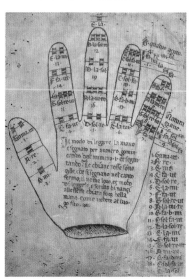

# Hildegard of Bingen

## 1098–1179, GERMAN

A mystic, composer, scholar, theologian, preacher, and scientist, Hildegard was an astonishingly gifted woman, whose musical works are hailed as among the most accomplished of the Middle Ages.

Hildegard of Bingen—also known as St. Hildegard and the Sibyl of the Rhine—was born in 1098 in a small village in the Rhineland (now Western Germany), possibly Bermersheim, to a noble, although not hugely wealthy, landowning family. She is thought to have been the last of 10 children.

Even as a child, Hildegard was exceptional. From the age of five she began to have visions that, many years later, came to assume great spiritual significance in her life (see p.16), and that she eventually documented via her own striking illustrations, music, and a series of accomplished theological works.

### A life of devotion

In 1106, at the age of eight, Hildegard was placed under the guidance of Jutta of Spanheim (1092–1136), a hugely devout young noblewoman, who taught her Latin and the Psalms. The decision to place Hildegard in Jutta's care was doubtless as much a financial as an educational or religious decision on the part of her parents, who did not have great

capital—unlike the Spanheims, who were an extremely wealthy, influential family in the region. The placement helped to secure their daughter's future stability.

In 1112, after living together for six years, the two young women began a highly reclusive, intensely religious life at the (male) Benedictine monastery of Disibodenberg at Odernheim (see box, below), which soon after extended to include a small nunnery, or convent, where Jutta became abbess. The nuns

lived in small stone cells, isolated from the monks. By 1115, Hildegard had taken her vows and, on Jutta's death in 1136, succeeded Jutta as abbess. Hildegard spent almost half her life at Disibodenberg.

Her assistant there was the learned Volmar, a monk and scribe who, in accordance with standard monastic practice, became her secretary and helped to document her visions. He was also her spiritual guide, confessor, and companion. His death in 1173,

△ **MONASTERY OF DISIBODENBERG**
Hildegard began her life of religious devotion at the Disibodenberg monastery in the Rhineland when she was just 14 years old. She stayed there for 40 years.

◁ **HILDEGARD OF BINGEN**
Hildegard challenged patriarchy via the Church, her music, and her books on topics from theology and the natural world to medicine and sexuality.

### IN CONTEXT
### Challenging elite monasticism

Monasteries were hugely influential institutions in Europe at the time of Hildegard's birth and had exerted their impact on economic, political, and spiritual life. Monks and nuns were often from privileged families and wielded tremendous power in the region, which led to corruption and excessive wealth. Challenges to this system emerged in the 12th century by, for example, the Cistercians—a religious order that advocated manual labor for monks and nuns—and by the religious leader Peter Waldo, who renounced his wealth, calling for voluntary poverty.

CISTERCIAN MONKS AND NUNS LABORING IN THE FIELDS

> "[**Music** is] the **sacred sound** through which **all creation resounds**."
>
> HILDEGARD OF BINGEN

△ **THE UNIVERSE AND COSMIC MAN**
This 13th-century illustration of a human astride the spheres that form the universe is from Hildegard's *Book of Divine Works* (1163–1174). In this text, she set out, among other things, her theories of man and the cosmos—all of which spring from the basic (early Greek) premise that humans are composed of the same elements that form the world: earth, water, air, and fire.

six years before her own, would have been a great personal and professional loss for her.

In 1141 Hildegard recorded a vision of a "... mass of fiery light of the greatest brightness pouring down from the heavens. It enveloped my brain and my heart was kindled with a flame that ... warmed me as the sun warms the earth." This powerful experience, which she claimed to be divine intervention, prompted her to make public her visions—in part, via her theological texts. The most acclaimed of these are: *Scivias* (*Know the Way*, 1141–1151), thought to have been illustrated by Hildegard herself, which discusses creation, redemption, and salvation; the *Book of Life's Merits* (1158–1163), an exchange between virtue and vice; and her last great visionary text, *Book of Divine Works* (1163–1174), which outlines the author's theories on cosmology.

### New directions

The revelations about her visions brought Hildegard considerable fame and numerous converts, inspiring her to found her own convent at Rupertsberg near Bingen (from where her name is derived) around 1148. She also later founded a second monastery, at Eibingen, on the hillside above Rüdesheim on the east bank of the Rhine, but never lived there.

▷ **HILDEGARD RECEIVING A VISION**
In this illustration from *Scivias*, Hildegard of Bingen is depicted (left), during one of her visionary experiences, receiving divine inspiration. She is accompanied by her assistant, the scribe and prior Volmar. A shaft of bright light from Heaven is shown descending on her head as she documents the extraordinary experience on a tablet.

At the age of 60, Hildegard began a series of preaching tours in Germany that focused on her visions and spiritual insights—a bold and courageous decision for a woman of that period in a ferociously patriarchal world. Among Hildegard's passions and numerous talents was music: paradise, for her, was to be filled with it. She maintained that her compositions "completed" her visions. Her pieces always combine music and words—she perceived the two to be inextricably connected: "The words symbolize the body, and the ... music indicates the spirit."

Music was fundamental to life in the cloisters and Hildegard would have been familiar with chant genres, including Gregorian chant (the plainsong or liturgical chant of medieval church music), and may have been exposed to some secular music (see box, opposite). She would also probably have been aware of the work of the 11th-century German composers and theorists Hermanus

> "I am the **fiery life** of divine substance, **I blaze** above... the fields, **I shine** in the waters, **I burn** in the sun, moon, and stars."
>
> HILDEGARD OF BINGEN

Contractus and Berno of Reichenau. However, as Hildegard indicates in her writings, she was largely uneducated and had never studied music, form, or composition. Her work, by all accounts, was propelled by her visionary experiences. The literary scholar and linguist Mark Atherton has suggested that Hildegard's technique departs substantially from the accepted conventions of Gregorian plainsong: "Her melody often ranges over two octaves, frequently leaping suddenly from a low note to a high, varying its short phrases and motifs, and lingering on one syllable as it ascends and descends."

Hildegard's compositions extend from flamboyant early works and sensual pieces to the more restrained chants of later years. Rooted in liturgical practice and dated between c.1140 and c.1160, they include devotional songs, antiphons, elaborate responsories, hymns, and sequences for the Mass. Her most famous compositions are her version of opera, *Ordo virtutum* (*Order of the Virtues*, c.1150)—a morality play set to music, with 82 melodies—and her 77 liturgical chants, *Symphonia armonie celestium revelationum* (*Symphony of the Harmony of Heavenly Revelations*, c.1158).

According to Christopher Page, a scholar of medieval music, "We don't know if Hildegard is sitting

△ **RUPERTSBERG MONASTERY**
The monastery at Rupertsberg in Bingen, on the junction of the Rhine and Nahe rivers, was founded by Hildegard in c.1148. It was destroyed in 1632 by the Swedish army in the Thirty Years' War.

and humming the songs, or if she's perhaps humming and writing them down on a white tablet, with a final version then being written by someone else on slate or parchment ... We don't know if the words come first, or if the words and the music grow together in an organic development."

### A pioneering woman

Hildegard of Bingen died in 1179 at her monastery in Rupertsberg. She was canonized by Pope Benedict XVI in 2012. During her lifetime, she was revered as a visionary prophet, but her extreme seclusion and the fact that she was a woman meant that her music received

little attention—it is only since the 1980s that Hildegard's pioneering achievements in this field have been recognized. Her legacy also extends to an impressive body of writing on medicine, science, cosmology, and the natural world. She has acquired almost iconic status in some circles, particularly within feminism, and is the subject of great popular and scholarly interest.

**Poet-musicians of the 12th century**

As well as her undoubted knowledge of Gregorian chant and the religious music of the day, Hildegard may have been familiar with the *trouvères*, aristocratic poet-composers, who were active in northern France in the 12th century, and whose lyrics were sung, often by the poets themselves, sometimes with an instrumental accompaniment. Hildegard would also certainly have heard of the *minnesänger*, or minnesingers, traveling singers of northern Europe, and of their famous composer-performer Walther von der Vogelweide (c.1170–c.1230), who wrote poems on politics and love, and whose delightful and best-known work, "Under the Linden Tree," resembles the song of a nightingale.

**MINSTRELS, FROM THE CODEX OF THE *CANTIGAS DE SANTA MARIA*, c.1280**

## KEY WORKS

**1141–51**
Writes *Scivias* (*Know the Way*), her first remarkable visionary and theological manuscript.

**c.1150**
Composes a type of opera, *Ordo virtutum* (*Order of the Virtues*), a play set to music.

**c.1158**
Composes *Symphonia armonie celestium revelationum* (*Symphony of the Harmony of Heavenly Revelations*).

**1158–63**
Writes the *Book of Life's Merits*, which stages a dialogue between good and evil.

**1163–74**
Compiles her masterpiece, *Book of Divine Works*, the final text on her visions.

# Guillaume Dufay

## c.1397–1474, FRENCH

The foremost composer of the Burgundian School in the 15th century, Dufay perfected his craft while working in Italy, developing an elegant style that bridged the transition from medieval to Renaissance.

The illegitimate son of a priest, Guillaume Dufay was probably born in 1397 in Beersel, near Brussels (then in the Burgundian Netherlands). His father's identity remains unknown. Guillaume was brought up by his mother, and adopted her name of Du Fayt, later also spelled Du Fay or Dufay.

While Guillaume was still a child, he moved with his mother to Cambrai to live with a relative who was a canon at the cathedral. In 1409, through this connection, he became a cathedral chorister and began his musical education in earnest. He rose through the ranks of the clergy to become a subdeacon.

### Travels in Italy

In 1420, Dufay traveled to Italy to take up a post in the service of the Malatesta family in Rimini. This allowed him to further his career in the Church and to broaden his musical horizons, coming into contact with the latest developments of the nascent Italian Renaissance musical style.

From Rimini, he moved to Bologna, where he was ordained as a priest in 1428, and then went on to Rome to join the papal choir. By this time, he had made a name for himself as a composer and managed to secure a series of prestigious posts: *maître de*

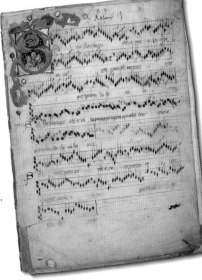

△ **MUSICAL CODEX, 1420s**
An early-15th-century illuminated page from a manuscript written by Dufay that is an important source for his early works.

*chapelle* (choirmaster) in the court of Savoy, under Duke Amédée VIII (later Antipope Felix V); then at the papal chapel in Florence; and finally in the service of the Este family in Ferrara.

Throughout the 1430s, political turmoil between the papacy and the Council of Basel rocked the Catholic Church, and Dufay's position in Italy became insecure. In about 1440, he returned to Cambrai to supervise music at the cathedral, and also made connections with the court of Philip the Good of Burgundy (see box, right).

### A new style of music

Dufay was considered to be one of the finest composers in Europe at that time, known for both his sacred and his secular compositions. He pioneered the composition of complete Masses based on a single chant or melody ("cyclical" Masses)—often the tune of a popular secular song, or one of his own *chansons*. With his colleague Gilles Binchois, he established a highly distinctive Burgundian early-Renaissance style, moving away from the austerity of medieval music and introducing the lyricism of Italian melodies, as well as the *contenance angloise*, or "English manner"—the sweeter harmonies of English composers such as John Dunstaple.

Dufay still had hopes of settling in Italy, and in 1449 he went back to Turin and Savoy in search of a post for his retirement years. However, the political situation was still volatile, so he returned to the Burgundy court in Cambrai again in 1458 and, thanks to a degree in canon law conferred on him by the pope while in Turin, he was also made a canon at Cambrai cathedral. Dufay then remained in Cambrai until his death in 1474.

*PHILIP III OF BURGUNDY*, AFTER ROGIER VAN DER WEYDEN, c.1445

▷ **PORTRAIT OF A YOUNG MAN**
This portrait by the Flemish artist Jan van Eyck, c.1432, is generally believed to be of Dufay when he was in his thirties.

> "If **my face** is **pale, the cause** is **love.**"

GUILLAUME DUFAY, IN THE SONG "IF MY FACE IS PALE"

▷ **THOMAS TALLIS**
Tallis, the foremost composer of English choral music in the 16th century, worked for both Catholics and Protestants during the Reformation. As a member of the Chapel Royal (an institution rather than a building), he wrote music that met the changing spiritual needs of the royal family. Tallis is depicted here in a stained-glass window at St. Alfege Church at Greenwich in London.

# Thomas Tallis

## c. 1505–1585, ENGLISH

Tallis was a leading composer of church music during the Tudor period. He steered a difficult course through the Reformation, but maintained his status as a distinguished member of the Chapel Royal.

Little is known about Thomas Tallis's early life. There are claims that he came from Leicestershire or Kent, but the first known record dates from 1532, when he was an organist at Dover Priory. By 1537, Tallis had moved to the parish church of St. Mary-at-Hill in London. A year later, he transferred to Waltham Abbey, outside the capital.

This was probably a shrewd move. Religious houses were already being suppressed as part of Henry VIII's plan to take control of the Church of England, but the severance pay was generous. When Waltham was dissolved in 1540, Tallis received 20 shillings in back-pay and a further 20 shillings "reward."

## The Chapel Royal

For many journeyman musicians, the Dissolution of the Monasteries was a disaster (see box, below), but Tallis's talent and ambition helped secure his future. He soon found another job, as one of the "singing men" at Canterbury Cathedral. Two years later, in 1543, he landed his dream job in the Chapel Royal—an elite group of clergy and musicians attached to the royal household, who played wherever the monarch required. For a composer of sacred music, this was the absolute pinnacle of the profession—a secure, well-paid job, working with the finest musicians. Not surprisingly, Tallis remained with the group until he retired.

## Change and adaptation

The composer's greatest asset was his adaptability as he negotiated the tumultuous changes during the Reformation: services were held in English rather than Latin; and the chantries—where "soul-priests" sang Masses for the dead—were abolished, along with special services on saints' feast-days. There was less music and it was more direct and simple. Elaborate polyphony was replaced by greater emphasis on psalms and anthems. Yet these changes were not permanent. Catholicism was revived during the reigns of Edward VI (1547–1553) and Mary (1553–1558), before Protestantism returned under Elizabeth I.

Tallis switched from one musical idiom to another with assurance. *Videte miraculum* is a graceful, six-part antiphon for the Virgin Mary, while the anthem *If ye love me* is a fine example of his simpler "reformed" style.

Tallis's masterpiece, however, is the monumental *Spem in alium*, a motet sung by eight five-part choirs arranged in a circle. The audience sits in the center, as the voices eddy back and forth around them. There was a rumor that Tallis composed this extraordinarily intricate piece in response to a challenge from the duke of Norfolk, but this cannot be verified.

In his later years, Tallis worked with his pupil William Byrd (see pp.26–27). The pair were granted an exclusive license by Elizabeth I to print and sell music, and in 1575 they produced a book of motets, *Cantiones sacrae* (*Sacred Songs*).

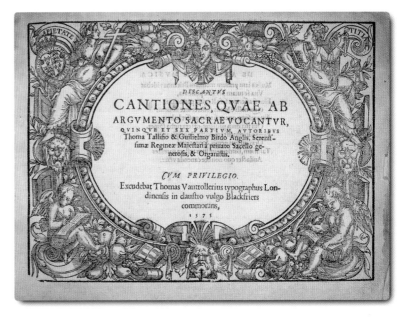

△ **SCORE OF *CANTIONES SACRAE***
In 1575, the composers Thomas Tallis and William Byrd together published, under special license, *Cantiones sacrae* (*Sacred Songs*). The cover of the original manuscript is shown here.

WALTHAM ABBEY, ESSEX, ENGLAND

△ **HENRY VIII**
England's Tudor king (reigned 1509–1547) imposed a series of repressive measures on religious houses that had a grave impact on the welfare of some musicians.

# Giovanni da Palestrina

## c. 1525–1594, ITALIAN

Palestrina is best known for his spiritually uplifting vocal music for church services. He achieved a serene purity of expression through his mastery of the complex interweaving of voices.

Born Giovanni Pierluigi around 1525, the composer became known as Palestrina after the name of the town of his birth, just outside Rome. As a child, he sang in the choir at Rome's prestigious basilica of Santa Maria Maggiore. By the age of 20, he had been appointed director of music at Palestrina cathedral, and six or so years later, he was invited by Pope Julius III to head the choir at St. Peter's Basilica, which involved writing sacred music and directing its performance. Palestrina's first book of Masses was published in 1554.

### A change of fortune

Julius III was not concerned that Palestrina was married (the holder of the post was supposed to be celibate) or that his religious works were interspersed with secular madrigals. However, after Julius's death in 1555 and the brief reign of Pope Marcellus II—to whom Palestrina dedicated his most famous Mass, *Missa Papae Marcelli*—the more austere Paul IV was installed in the Vatican. The new pope dismissed Palestrina.

◁ **POPE JULIUS III**
Julius III (depicted here by the sculptor Fulvio Signorini) spotted Palestrina's talent when the young composer was director of music at Palestrina cathedral.

Nevertheless, the composer's talent and reputation ensured him work at other Roman churches. By the time he was reinstated as papal choirmaster in 1571, he had adapted his style to the demands of the Counter-Reformation (see box, right), describing his new works as "music written ... in accordance with the views of the most serious and religious-minded persons in high places."

In the 1570s, plague raged in Rome. Palestrina suffered the deaths of his wife and two of his three sons. In 1581, however, he married a second time, the widow of a Roman fur trader, and took over running her former husband's business, which he handled very profitably. Alongside this commercial activity he continued to write a stream of Masses and other sacred music, including settings of the Song of Solomon published in 1584 and the *Stabat Mater* for eight voices, dating from around 1590. By the time of his death in 1594, his total output amounted to 105 Masses, more than 300 motets, and hundreds of other works, both religious and secular.

### Music from Heaven

Palestrina was famous in his lifetime and his reputation remained high through the succeeding centuries. His works were widely studied as perfect technical examples of polyphony and were admired by composers from Bach (see pp.56–61) to Mendelssohn (see pp.116–119), who claimed that Palestrina's music sounded "as if it came direct from Heaven."

(see pp.56–61) (see pp.116–119)

### IN CONTEXT
### Palestrina and the Counter-Reformation

In the 16th century, provoked by the Protestant Reformation, the Catholic Church embarked on a Counter-Reformation to remedy lax practices and reinvigorate the faith. In the early 1560s, Catholic divines meeting at the Council of Trent discussed banning music from church services, arguing that it distracted worshippers with sensual pleasure. There is a legend that a performance of Palestrina's *Missa Papae Marcelli* so moved the church dignitaries that they changed their minds. Although the legend itself is not true, Palestrina's music did in the long run satisfy the Church that chaste spiritual music could indeed reinforce Catholic faith.

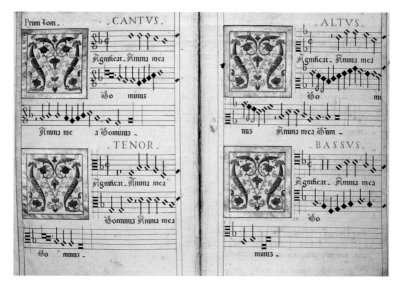

◁ **SCORE OF MAGNIFICAT**
This illuminated 16th-century manuscript is the first double page of Palestrina's score of one of his settings for the *Magnificat*, or the hymn of praise by Mary, as found in the Bible.

▷ **GIOVANNI DA PALESTRINA**
The Italian Renaissance composer is shown here holding the score of his famous Mass *Missa Papae Marcelli* (1562). According to Palestrina, "Music should give a zest to divine worship ... delighting in voices blending in harmony."

# Orlande de Lassus

## c.1532–1594, FLEMISH

A late-Renaissance composer, Lassus was in his day the most popular songwriter in Europe. Writing exclusively for voices, he was tirelessly prolific, composing more than 2,000 pieces of secular and sacred music.

Orlande de Lassus was born at Mons in the Hapsburg-ruled Netherlands (now Belgium), an area renowned for Renaissance music. Much about his origins is uncertain. His birth may have occurred in 1530 or 1532; nothing is known of his parents. His name never achieved a definite form, with variants ranging from Orlando di Lasso to Roland de Lattre.

### Early days

As a child, Lassus is said to have had such a beautiful voice that he was kidnapped three times by rival choirs. Around the age of 12, he joined the entourage of a Hapsburg general, Ferrante Gonzaga, who took him to Italy. Lassus is then thought to have begun composing during his stays in Mantua, Palermo, Naples, and Milan. By 1553, he was director of music at the cathedral of St. John Lateran in Rome—an elevated post for a man in his early twenties.

In 1555, Lassus returned to the Netherlands, and his first book, a collection of his madrigals, motets, and songs, was published in Antwerp.

△ **PATROCINIUM MUSICES**
This is the title page from 1589 for Lassus's Masses for Five Voices in his *Patrocinium Musices* (1573–1580). The illustration at the bottom of the page shows musicians around a table.

◁ **ORLANDE DE LASSUS**
An anonymous Flemish School portrait shows Lassus formally dressed and unsmiling. The composer is said to have suffered from depression in his later life.

### A Renaissance sensation

Lassus supplied secular music for the court and sacred music for its chapel. Some of his music was reserved for the duke's exclusive enjoyment—Lassus was not allowed to publish his much-admired *Penitential Psalms* until after the duke's death. But a large part of the composer's prodigious output appeared in print. It has been estimated that more than half of all the music published in Europe in the second half of the 16th century was by Lassus. Some of his works gained popularity well beyond the restricted circle of royal courts. He traveled widely, recruiting singers for the Munich establishment and supervising performances of his work. Lassus's appearance at the court of the French king Charles IX in 1571 caused such a sensation that he was invited back twice. The Holy Roman Emperor elevated him to noble status and, in 1574, Pope Gregory XIII made him a knight of the Golden Spur.

The death of Albrecht V in 1579 was followed by cuts in the costly Bavarian musical establishment. Lassus's last collection of madrigals, the haunting *Lagrime di San Pietro*, was completed just before his death in 1594. Some of his most famous works, including the *Prophetiae Sibyllarum* motets, were published posthumously by his sons.

His name came to the attention of Albrecht V of Bavaria (see box, right), who invited him to his court in Munich. Lassus's first official position was as a tenor singer, but by 1563 he was the duke's head of music, a post he would hold for the rest of his life. He married a maid of honor at the court, Regina Wäckinger; their two sons would both grow up to be composers.

**ALBRECHT V OF BAVARIA WITH A LION, HANS MIELICH, 1556**

"**All** were **forced ...** to **respect** [Lassus] in his **presence** and to **praise him** in his **absence.**"

SAMUEL VAN QUICKELBERG, 1566

▷ **WILLIAM BYRD, c. 1580**
The talented composer, who wrote more than 500 works, was initially trained, at London's Chapel Royal, in singing by Richard Bower and in keyboard and composition by Thomas Tallis. Years later, he was described by the Chapel Royal as "a Father of Musick."

# William Byrd

## c. 1540–1623, ENGLISH

A prolific and versatile composer of vocal and instrumental music, both sacred and secular, Byrd maintained his popularity despite his conversion to Catholicism during the English Reformation.

William Byrd is thought to have been born in London in about 1540, although this date is disputed. What can be assumed is that he had a thorough musical education, and was most likely a chorister at London's Chapel Royal, where he was a pupil of Thomas Tallis (see pp.20–21).

In 1563, he was appointed organist and choirmaster at Lincoln Cathedral, a post that he held for nine years. In Lincoln, he married Julian Birley—it was a happy marriage that lasted from 1568 to her death in the 1580s.

## A growing reputation

During his time in Lincoln, Byrd's reputation as a performer and composer was growing, and in 1570 he was honored with the title of Gentleman of the Chapel Royal. There were, however, signs of friction between him and the rather Puritan Church authorities, probably because of his penchant for writing ornate church music.

Nevertheless, his compositions were appreciated by the musical establishment and by many of the nobility, and in 1575 he began sharing the post of organist with Tallis at the Chapel Royal. Elizabeth I overlooked Byrd's tendency to the elaborate ritual of high Anglicanism, granting him and Tallis a patent to print and sell music and ruled manuscript paper—consort music and part-songs were a popular pastime among the English middle-classes, and Byrd received a sizable income from the franchise.

## Catholic composer

Around this time, he converted to Catholicism and, taking advantage of the queen's endorsement, composed music for the Catholic services as well as for the Anglican Church. But in the 1580s, attitudes toward Catholics began to harden, and he and his family were under suspicion because of their connections with prominent Catholic families. Despite repeated accusations of recusancy—refusing to attend Anglican services—Byrd continued to compose for both the Church of England and the Catholic rites, but rather cynically curried favor with the Protestant nobility by dedicating many of his compositions to them. These included, as well as the two collections of motets, known as *Cantiones sacrae*, a large number of pieces for instrumental consorts, two English song-books, and *My Lady Nevells Booke* for keyboard— all of which were written with the popular market in mind.

Byrd remarried after his wife's death, and in 1593 or 1594 moved with his family to Stondon Massey in Essex, where he had Catholic friends, including his patron, Sir John Petre. This gave him the opportunity to compose the cycles of Catholic Masses for three, four, and five voices, and the two sets of motets, the *Gradualia*. These were his last major works before his retirement.

◁ **SCORE OF *SING JOYFULLY***
The late work *Sing joyfully unto God our strength* is a church anthem for six voices. It is widely hailed as one of Byrd's finest anthems.

## IN CONTEXT
## The English Reformation

**PORTRAIT OF ELIZABETH I BY NICHOLAS HILLIARD**

Following Henry VIII's controversial establishment of the Protestant Church of England, there was a long period of sectarian turmoil, which characterized the English Reformation. Despite the Church's renunciation of papal authority, many people, including Henry's daughter Mary, clung to Catholic beliefs. As queen of England, Mary attempted to reverse her father's reforms. When she was succeeded by the Protestant Elizabeth I, Catholicism again became a covert religion.

Byrd was about 18 years old and a Protestant when Elizabeth came to the throne in 1558, but he converted to Catholicism in the 1570s, halfway through her reign. Perhaps because Elizabeth was more tolerant than some of her Puritan subjects, and a music-lover, too, Byrd did not suffer undue persecution, and he lived to enjoy the more liberal attitudes of her successor, James I, the son of Mary, Queen of Scots.

◁ **LINCOLN CATHEDRAL**
Byrd was appointed choirmaster and organist at the magnificent cathedral in Lincoln in 1563, succeeding the composer Thomas Appleby. It was during Byrd's time there that his reputation as an outstanding composer and performer was established. He left Lincoln in 1572.

# Carlo Gesualdo

## 1566–1613, ITALIAN

Known as much for the notorious murder of his wife and her lover as for his richly expressive music, Gesualdo devoted his life to his art. He spent his final years dogged by depression in isolation on his estate.

Carlo Gesualdo's highly expressive and personal style of composing, especially in his madrigals and sacred vocal music, reflected the mood of his turbulent life.

He was born into a noble family that had recently become rulers of the principality of Venosa in southern Italy, and when his elder brother died in 1584, Carlo became heir to the principality. It was expected of him to marry and produce a family to carry on the line of succession. Although this ruined his plans to become a priest, it did give him the opportunity to spend even more of his time on his particular passion for music.

### Dangerous liaisons

Carlo married his cousin Maria d'Avalos in 1586, but within a very short time she became dissatisfied with his complete lack of attention to her, and sought her pleasures elsewhere. For some years, she carried on an affair with another nobleman, Fabrizio Carafa, and although the relationship was common knowledge throughout the region, Gesualdo seemed unaware of the betrayal. That is, until one night in October 1590, when he discovered the couple *in flagrante*, and, with the help of his servants, murdered them in their bed. It was, by all accounts,

a gruesome and bloody crime of passion, with the lovers being stabbed, shot, and mutilated. Gesualdo ordered that the bodies be displayed outside the palace to make their shame public.

Because of the circumstances of the murder and the aristocratic status of the perpetrator, the case was dismissed, and Gesualdo remained a free man. But, of course, the incident had a profound effect on him. He succeeded as prince of Venosa when his father died the following year, and in 1594 he arranged a second marriage, to the noblewoman Leonora d'Este. This was not a love match but a marriage of convenience, and appears to have been prompted by Gesualdo's wish to spend time in her home town of Ferrara, which was renowned for fostering composers and performers of madrigals.

Over the following few years, he established a similar musical set-up in his castle at Gesualdo in Avellino, and began composing in earnest.

### Devotion and isolation

The first of Gesualdo's books of madrigals was written in Ferrara, and was followed by five further volumes and two sets of *Sacrae cantiones*.

His devotion to composition led to the breakdown of his marriage, with Leonora spending increasingly long periods with her brother, especially after the death of their son, Alfonsino, in 1600. Gesualdo became ever more reclusive, never leaving his estate, and suffered constant depression, which drove him to acts of self-flagellation. The death of his son Emanuele by his first marriage appears to have been the final straw, as he died only three weeks after him, in 1613.

△ **SACRAE CANTIONES**
Two volumes of Gesualdo's collection of motets, *Sacrae cantiones* (*Sacred Songs*), were published in 1603—the illustrated and tinted title page of one of them is shown here.

◁ **CARLO GESUALDO**
This portrait by Francesco Mancini depicts the composer-prince wearing clothes that suggest his aristocratic status, but gives no hint of Gesualdo's unhappy, deeply turbulent life or of his melancholy temperament.

## ON TECHNIQUE
### Expressive harmony

Perhaps the most striking aspect of Gesualdo's music is his extraordinary use of chromatic harmonies—that is, harmonies that are unrelated to the key in which the piece is written. Gesualdo used such unexpected and exotic chords for dramatic effect, to express the extremes of emotion and pain in his madrigals and sacred music. This idiosyncratic and often unsettling style distinguishes his compositions as among the most intensely personal music of the Italian late Renaissance period.

**MADRIGAL SINGERS WITH LUTE AND SCORE, VENETIAN, 16TH CENTURY**

▷ **JOHN DOWLAND**
Dowland is shown here, lute and quill in hand, with the sad and doleful expression for which, by all accounts, he was well known. Indeed, many of his darker works tap into the vogue for melancholy that was characteristic of his age. This was not considered to be a negative emotion, but an indicator of deep and meaningful thought.

# John Dowland
## 1563–1626, ENGLISH

Dowland was an outstanding lutenist and songwriter. His immense talent was reflected in the plaintive, bittersweet melodies for which he became famous throughout Renaissance Europe.

◁ **PAGES FROM *THE FIRSTE BOOKE OF SONGES OR AYRES***
The original, 1597 edition of John Dowland's highly successful *Firste Booke of Songes or Ayres* is shown here, with its innovative "table layout."

## IN CONTEXT
### A climate of treason

In 1570, Pope Pius V excommunicated Elizabeth I, releasing her Catholic subjects from allegiance to her. This sparked plots against her life, among them the Ridolfi Plot (1571) and the Babington Plot (1586). In response, Elizabeth employed secret agents to help unearth possible conspirators, at home and abroad. These activities were supervised by her "spymaster," Francis Walsingham, and secretary of state, Robert Cecil. It was to Cecil that Dowland wrote when, following an incident in Italy, he became fearful that he would be accused of treason.

**ROBERT CECIL, 1ST EARL OF SALISBURY**

Nothing is known for certain about John Dowland's early days. He is first documented in 1580, when he was in Paris, serving as a retainer in the household of the English ambassador, Sir Henry Cobham. John had probably already learned to play the lute in an aristocratic household of this kind. While in France, he took the fateful step of converting to Catholicism— a move that would have a profound effect on his future career.

### Home and abroad
Dowland returned to England in the mid-1580s and earned a music degree at Oxford University. He also married and had a son. In music circles, his reputation was growing. Some of his songs were performed at royal entertainments and, in 1594, he felt confident enough to apply for a vacant post as a court lutenist. He was rejected, however—apparently because of his faith. Dowland was downhearted at this and, leaving his family behind in England, he decided to seek his fortune abroad.

Dowland's travels took him to princely courts in Germany and Italy, where he was received enthusiastically and showered with expensive gifts to send to his wife—a gold chain and clothing from the duke of Brunswick; a gold ring and cup from the landgrave of Hesse. In Italy, though, he ran into a group of disaffected Catholics, who seemed to be plotting against Elizabeth I (see box, right). Dowland immediately took fright. He wrote a long, rambling letter to Robert Cecil, the secretary of state, assuring him of his loyalty to Elizabeth and offering his services as a spy. What the authorities made of this somewhat paranoid missive is not recorded, but it certainly did not help Dowland's job prospects.

He returned to England in 1597, still hoping for royal preferment, but once again he was overlooked. Dowland profited from the visit, however, by publishing his groundbreaking collection, *The Firste Booke of Songes or Ayres*. This proved hugely popular, in part because of its ingenious "table layout," which enabled musicians or singers to stand around a small table and read their parts from a single text.

### A novel combination
The songs themselves were equally novel. Dowland blended elements from the madrigal, the consort song, and the broadside ballad to create exquisitely plaintive melodies. These display a bittersweet melancholy that was then highly fashionable, typified by titles such as "In darkness let me dwell" and "Welcome, black night" (a wedding song). Dowland published three books of his songs, along with the extraordinary *Lachrimae* (*Tears*, 1604). The latter features seven variations of his most famous song, "Flow, my tears."

These books helped make Dowland one of the most famous musicians in Renaissance Europe. He was particularly successful as the court lutenist in Denmark, where Christian IV paid him an exorbitant salary. Dowland was never valued as highly in his homeland, although he did belatedly receive a royal appointment from James I in 1612.

▽ **ELSINORE, DENMARK, c. 1600**
Dowland was in Denmark from 1598 to 1606, when relations between England and Denmark were tense, especially on the issue of fishing rights. He was hired not only as a lutenist, but as a negotiator and messenger between the two countries.

# Directory

## Beatriz de Dia

### 1140–1212, FRENCH

Very little is known about the life of the Comtessa de Dia, whom historians believe was called Beatriz. Working as a *trobairitz*, or female troubadour, she composed, wrote verses, and performed for the Occitan noble courts. *Trobairitz* are some of the first documented female composers of Western secular music. De Dia's song *"A chantar m'er de so qu'eu no volria"*, written in old Occitan, is the only *canso* (a form of song commonly composed by troubadours) by a trobairitz to survive with its music.

**KEY WORK:** *"A chantar m'er de so qu'eu no volria"*

## Pérotin

### ACTIVE c.1200, FRENCH

Pérotin (sometimes known by the Latin form, Perotinus) is an obscure figure, but the information that survives suggests that he was one of the most significant musicians of his time. He is thought to have worked at Notre-Dame Cathedral, Paris, and all his music is religious. He may have been a pioneer of polyphony: music in which several melodic lines blend or weave in and out harmoniously, a development associated with the composers of the Notre Dame school. Some earlier works had used a plainchant melody sung against another melodic line, but Pérotin composed pieces in three and four parts.

**KEY WORKS:** *Viderunt omnes* (*Everyone Saw*); *Sederunt principes* (*The Princes Sat*); *Alleluia Pascha nostrum* (*Alleluia, Our Passover* [Easter hymn]); dates unknown

## ▽ Guillaume de Machaut

### c.1300–1377, FRENCH

A poet as well as a composer, Machaut was one of the outstanding cultural figures of his time, with a reputation that extended throughout Europe. A large amount of his music survives (well over 100 works), more than for any other composer of his time. Although he held various minor positions in the Church, most of his music is secular (the main exception is his *Mass of Our Lady*, the first surviving complete Mass setting by a single composer). He is most famous for his songs, many on the theme of courtly love. They introduced a new variety and complexity to the genre.

**KEY WORKS:** "Rose, liz, printemps, verdure" ("Rose, Lily, Spring, Greenery"), c.1340s; *Messe de Nostre Dame* (*Mass of Our Lady*), c.1360; "Ma fin est mon commencement" ("My End is My Beginning"), c.1370

## John Dunstaple

### c.1390–1453, ENGLISH

Little is known about Dunstaple's life, but in his own time he was recognized as a major figure, and he is now acknowledged as the outstanding English composer of the 15th century. There is evidence that he worked for several high-ranking patrons, but the details are obscure. About 60 musical compositions attributed to him survive, almost all of them religious, including two complete Masses and various other settings of sacred Latin texts. His style is notable for its melodic freshness and sweetness. He was highly regarded in Europe—indeed, he has been described as "the most influential English composer outside England before the Beatles."

**KEY WORKS:** *Missa Rex seculorum* (*Mass of the King of Ages*); *Salve Regina, mater misericordiae* (*Hail Queen, Mother of Mercy*); *O crux gloriosa* (*O glorious cross*); dates unknown

△ GUILLAUME DE MACHAUT, FRANCE, 14TH CENTURY

△ JACOB OBRECHT, HANS MEMLING

## Johannes Ockeghem

c.1410–1497, FRANCO-FLEMISH

Ockeghem was Flemish but he spent most of his career working at the French court. The political geography of the time was complex and places of origin are often uncertain, so he is one of a number of composers whose nationality is characterized by the broad term Franco-Flemish. He composed secular music, including songs, but his work is mainly religious: there are 14 surviving Masses by him, among them the earliest known polyphonic Requiem Mass. His style is sophisticated, with intricate textures and harmonies.

KEY WORKS: *Missa pro defunctis* (*Mass for the Dead*); *Missa cuiusvis toni* (*Mass in Any Mode*); *Ma bouche rit* (*My Lips Are Smiling*); dates unknown

## Josquin des Prez

c.1450–1521, FRANCO-FLEMISH

Josquin was one of the most highly acclaimed musicians of his time and, in the generation after his death, he became widely regarded as the supreme composer of the age. His fame was spread by the invention of printing: the first collection of printed music devoted to a single composer was a volume of his Masses published in Venice in 1502, and two other such collections followed in his lifetime. His early career was spent mainly in Italy, where he worked for two popes and the dukes of Ferrara and Milan. From 1504 until his death he was provost of the church of Notre-Dame (famed for its music) at Condé-sur-l'Escaut in northern France. Josquin was a singer and virtually all his large output consists of vocal music, both sacred and secular. His work is varied and highly inventive—he rarely repeated himself.

KEY WORKS: *Adieu, mes amours* (*Farewell, My Love Affairs*), c.1480; *Missa Hercules dux Ferrariae* (*Mass of Hercules* [i.e. *Ercole d'Este*], *Duke of Ferrara*), c.1505; *Missa de Beata Virgine* (*Mass of the Blessed Virgin*), c.1510

## ◁ Jacob Obrecht

c.1457–1505, FRANCO-FLEMISH

During his own time, Obrecht was a celebrated figure, and among the Franco-Flemish musicians of his period, he now ranks second only to Josquin des Prez. The son of a city trumpeter in Ghent, he was primarily a religious composer, holding positions in churches and cathedrals in Antwerp, Bruges, and elsewhere. (Some of these posts were short-lived and he seems to have been rather restless in his movements.) However, he also wrote secular music and he ended his career working at the court of Duke Ercole d'Este in Ferrara, where he died of plague. Obrecht excelled chiefly as a composer of Masses—about 30 by him survive, showing a style that is fluid, graceful, and sonorous. His secular works include numerous songs in Dutch, ranging from the lighthearted to the serious.

KEY WORKS: *Missa Fortuna desperata* (*Desperate Fate Mass*), c.1490; *Missa Sub tuum praesidium* (*Mass Under Thy Protection*), c.1500; *Missa Maria zart* (*Mass for Gentle Mary*), c.1500–1505

## John Taverner

c.1490–1545, ENGLISH

Although his career was fairly brief (most of his music was probably written in the 1520s), Taverner is regarded as the outstanding English composer of his time. In 1526, he became director of the choir at Cardinal Wolsey's magnificent new foundation in Oxford, Cardinal College (now called Christ Church). However, soon after Wolsey's downfall in 1529, Taverner returned to his native Lincolnshire and became a member of the choir at St. Botolph's Church. He seems to have retired from church music by 1537 and then lived the life of a prosperous gentleman. He wrote a few songs and instrumental pieces, but his music consists mainly of religious works, particularly Masses. His style has florid elements that link him to the Middle Ages, but also a sweeping sense of melody that is forward-looking.

KEY WORKS: *Western Wynde Mass*; *Missa Corona spinea* (*Crown of Thorns Mass*); *Missa Gloria tibi Trinitas* (*Glory to You, O Trinity Mass*); dates unknown

## Tomás Luis de Victoria

1548–1611, SPANISH

Victoria was the towering figure of Spanish music of his period. He began his musical career as a choirboy at Avila Cathedral. After his voice broke, he went to Rome, where he spent about 20 years (c.1565–c.1586). He was ordained a priest in 1575 and held various church appointments as well as publishing several collections of his musical works. After his return to Spain, he served as chaplain to Philip II's sister, the dowager empress Maria, who lived at the Convent of the Descalzas Reales in Madrid. Following her death in 1603, Victoria stayed at the convent as organist until his own death. All his music is religious. It is remarkable for its emotional intensity, with a mystical flavor that is thought to be quintessentially Spanish. He has been seen as a musical counterpart to El Greco, his great contemporary among Spanish painters.

KEY WORKS: *Officium Hebdomadae Sanctae* (*Music for Holy Week*), 1585; *Veni, Sancte Spiritus* (*Come, Holy Spirit*), 1600; *Officium defunctorum* (*Office [rite] of the Dead*), 1605

# 17th & 18th
# CENTURIES

CHAPTER 2

# Claudio Monteverdi

## 1567–1643, ITALIAN

Working in Mantua and Venice, Monteverdi wrote the earliest operas still regularly performed today. He is also admired for the expressiveness of his many madrigals and the ornate brilliance of his *Vespers*.

The son of an apothecary, Claudio Giovanni Antonio Monteverdi was born in the small city of Cremona in northern Italy in 1567. There is no evidence whatsoever of music-making in his family background, although the young Claudio must somehow have revealed a significant aptitude for music, for he was taken on as a pupil by Marcantonio Ingegneri, director of music at Cremona cathedral.

### Rising through the ranks

Ingegneri was an accomplished composer in the Renaissance tradition of polyphony, in which all the parts in a work are independent and accorded equal status. By the age of 15, Monteverdi had sufficiently absorbed Ingegneri's lessons to be able to publish his own conventional three-voice compositions. He also developed into a skilled player of string instruments such as the viol.

Living in Cremona through the 1580s, Monteverdi attracted attention as a promising young composer, his published works including two books

△ **CREMONA CATHEDRAL**
Monteverdi's long and successful career in music began when, as a teenager, he was invited to be a pupil of the director of music at Cremona cathedral.

of secular madrigals. In 1590, he secured a post at the prestigious court of the duchy of Mantua. Although he was aware of Monteverdi's talent for composition, Mantua's ruler Duke Vincenzo I Gonzaga (see box, below) took him on as a viol player.

The composer had to work his way up through the court's musical hierarchy. He was frustrated not to be appointed Mantua's director of music on the death of the incumbent in 1596 but he nonetheless received many signs of ducal favor, as when he was chosen to lead the musicians accompanying Vincenzo to Hungary on a military expedition against the Turks in 1595. Monteverdi was joined at court by his younger brother Giulio Cesare, also a musician, and in 1599 married a singer, Claudia Cattaneo,

daughter of a fellow court musician, with the duke's blessing. Cattaneo may have been one of the duke's mistresses whom he had tired of and wished to set up with a suitable husband, but evidence on this is scant.

### Public controversy

Through this time, Monteverdi had continued to publish books of madrigals that were sufficiently innovative to provoke notable public controversy. In 1600, conservative music scholar Giovanni Artusi launched an outspoken attack on "the imperfections of modern music," accusing Monteverdi in particular of crude dissonance and violation of the proper rules of musical composition. The supporters of "modern music," including the composer himself,

◁ **CLAUDIO MONTEVERDI, c. 1630**
This portrait by Bernardo Strozzi shows Monteverdi in later life. When in his seventies, the composer produced a magnificent final flowering of creativity that crowned his life's achievement.

### IN CONTEXT
### Mantua under the Gonzagas

Monteverdi's patrons, the Gonzaga family, ruled the city of Mantua for almost 400 years. In the 15th and 16th centuries, their palace was a major center of Renaissance culture, attracting artists such as Andrea Mantegna, who depicted the Gonzagas in the murals of the palace's Camera degli Sposi (1465–1474). Isabella d'Este, married into the family in 1490, was among the most renowned patrons of Renaissance art. When Monteverdi arrived in Mantua in 1591, the court was still at the height of its splendor and prestige, but the 17th century brought rapid decline. Gonzaga rule ended in 1708.

LUDOVICO GONZAGA (LEFT) WITH HIS FAMILY, FRESCO BY MANTEGNA, c. 1474

△ **FRONTISPIECE OF *L'ORFEO***
Monteverdi's *L'Orfeo* is one of the world's first operas. This frontispiece is from a 1609 edition, published two years after the work was written.

responded by identifying two equally valid musical "practices." The first, which had predominated in the previous century, followed strict rules of polyphony, irrespective of the text being sung. The new "seconda pratica," which Monteverdi had been criticized for following, gave precedence to the emotional implications of the text, using dissonance and other departures from traditional musical rules to bring out the sense and feeling of the words.

Monteverdi was finally accorded the coveted post of director of music at Mantua in 1601 and in the following year he was honored with Mantuan citizenship. In 1607, the duke's son Francesco Gonzaga commissioned Monteverdi to create a theatrical entertainment for the carnival season in Mantua. Such works, later called operas (see box, below), had been performed in other Italian cities, so the Gonzagas were keeping up with fashion. A variant on the Greek myth of Orpheus and Eurydice, Monteverdi's *L'Orfeo* combined orchestral and choral writing with long recitatives and arias to powerful effect. His first large-scale work, it was an immediate success. He wrote a second opera, *L'Arianna*, the following year. The only section of this work to have survived is the dramatic recitative known as the "Lamento d'Arianna."

### Troubled times

Although Monteverdi was at the peak of his musical powers, his life had entered a difficult phase. The death of his wife after a painful illness in September 1607 left him grief-stricken and solely responsible for three children. Forced into overwork on lavish court entertainments the following year—including the stressful production of *L'Arianna*—he suffered some kind of nervous breakdown and for a time withdrew from Mantua. His relations with the Gonzagas never fully recovered. He wrote querulous letters expressing his dissatisfaction with his pay and his status at court. When Francesco Gonzaga succeeded his spendthrift father in 1612, financial cuts were the order of the day. The troublesome Monteverdi and his brother were fired.

△ **ST. MARK'S BASILICA, VENICE**
Monteverdi was appointed director of music at the magnificent basilica in Venice when he was in his mid-forties and stayed there for the rest of his life.

Monteverdi then turned his focus on patronage of the Church. In 1610, he published a volume of sacred music, comprising a polyphonic Mass and the *Vespers for the Blessed Virgin*, a dramatic and complex work in the "modern" style combining solo songs, duets, and instrumental interludes. Dedicated to Pope Paul V, this dazzling volume was virtually a job application, showing how his talents could adapt to religious purposes. In 1613, he was appointed director of music at St. Mark's Basilica in Venice.

Monteverdi appears to have been more content in Venice than at the Mantuan court. He conscientiously executed his duties, writing music for church services and directing the basilica choir. He also continued to write secular music and to explore fresh ways of expressing emotion and linking music to words. His most impressive experiment was a setting of part of Torquato Tasso's epic poem

---

## IN PROFILE
## Jacopo Peri

Toward the end of the 16th century, Florentine humanists, obsessed with recovering the art and learning of the Ancient world, sought to recreate Ancient Greek drama, which was known to have included music. In 1598, in keeping with the spirit of this pursuit, the composer and singer Jacopo Peri (1561–1633) produced *La Dafne*, which is generally considered to be the first opera. He followed this up two years later with *Euridice*, the first opera whose score has survived to this day. The new fashion spread rapidly to other Italian cities, leading to Monteverdi writing *L'Orfeo* in Mantua in 1607.

**JACOPO PERI, ALSO KNOWN AS Il ZAZZERINO**

"The **end of** all good **music** is to **affect the soul**."

CLAUDIO MONTEVERDI

Jerusalem Liberated. First performed at a private palace in Venice in 1624, *Il combattimento di Tancredi e Clorinda* is considered the first oratorio and included the first use of pizzicato—the strings imitating striking swords.

Monteverdi took holy orders in 1632, but never ruled out a return to secular patronage. He seriously considered a post at the royal court of Poland and sought to attract the attention of the Holy Roman Emperor in Vienna. However, in the end he remained at St. Mark's for the rest of his days, constantly muttering about inadequate pay and worrying about an unpaid pension he was owed from Mantua.

### New horizons

Remarkably, in his seventies, a crotchety old man, Monteverdi produced a late flowering of creativity, with his last two operas exploring new frontiers in musical theater. They followed from the opening of the world's first public opera houses in Venice at the end of the 1630s.

The operas that Monteverdi wrote to be staged at the Teatro Santi Giovanni e Paolo, *Il ritorno d'Ulisse in patria* (*The Return of Ulysses to his Homeland*) and *L'incoronazione di Poppea* (*The Coronation of Poppea*), were dramatic masterpieces that exhibited a range of distinctive characters in emotionally realistic situations. Immediately successful, they undoubtedly did more than any other works to establish opera as a major genre of the future.

When Monteverdi died in 1643, he was honored with a tomb in Venice's splendid Frari church. After falling from favor, his music was rediscovered in the 20th century, along with the techniques and instruments that were required to perform it authentically. A bridge between the Renaissance period and the Baroque, his work is enjoyed by modern listeners for its emotional intensity and sheer beauty of sound.

△ **L'INCORONAZIONE DI POPPEA**
Monteverdi's last opera, *L'incoronazione di Poppea* (1643), tells the story of Emperor Nero's love for his mistress. The production shown here is from a 2017 performance at the Staatsoper in Berlin, Germany. The performance was notable for, among other things, its lavish Baroque-style costumes.

## KEY WORKS

**1587**
Monteverdi's first book of secular madrigals is printed—the last book (of eight) came in 1638.

**1607**
*L'Orfeo*, one of the earliest operas and Monteverdi's version of the Orpheus legend, is staged at the court in Mantua.

**1610**
*Vespers for the Blessed Virgin*, Monteverdi's most complex work of sacred music, is published.

**1624**
*Combattimento*, from Tasso's epic poem *Jerusalem Delivered*, premieres at Venice's Palazzo Mocenigo.

**1640**
*Il ritorno d'Ulisse in patria*, his first work written for a public opera house, is performed in Venice.

**1643**
Writes *L'incoronazione di Poppea*, his last opera. He dies later that year.
.

# Francesca Caccini

## 1587–AFTER 1641, ITALIAN

A highly paid court musician and the first woman to write an opera, Caccini was an immensely gifted composer and singer. She wrote numerous works, mainly for voice, only a few of which survive.

Francesca Caccini was born into a musical family in Florence in 1587. Her mother, brother, and younger sister were singers; her father Giulio Caccini, a celebrated composer and teacher, was one of the leading musicians of his day who had links to influential figures via his employment at the court of the Medicis, Europe's most powerful family.

### A family ensemble

When Francesca was six, her mother died and her father was left with three young children and a teenage son. The following year, 1594, he married another singer, 18-year-old Margherita della Scalain. The women of the household (Francesca, her younger sister, Settimia, and her stepmother) began singing professionally in a family ensemble. Francesca made her first professional, public appearance with this group in 1600, at the age of 13, in Jacopo Peri's opera *Euridice*.

A gifted, hugely intelligent child (and with a career as a musician clearly in the sights of her ambitious family),

Francesca had been trained in guitar, lute, harp, keyboard, voice, and composition at an early age—to significant effect: in 1605, she was offered lucrative work as a singer by the court of Henry IV. However, Grand Duke Ferdinand of Tuscany, keen to retain her exceptional talent within the Medici court, refused her permission to leave Florence.

Confined in this way, Caccini had little option but to follow the career path of her father. In 1607, she started work at the Medici court, where she was to remain for the next 20 years as a teacher, singer, and composer of chamber and stage music (see box, right). Within seven years, she had become the court's best-paid musician. In the same year as joining the Medicis, Francesca married Giovanni Battista Signorina, another court singer. The couple went on to have one child, Margherita, in 1622.

In 1618, the year of her father's death, she published *Il primo libro delle musiche* (*The First Book of Madrigals*), comprising 32 solo songs and four

duets setting both sacred and secular texts. However, Caccini is most famous for being the first woman to write an opera: *La liberazione di Ruggiero dall'isola d'Alcina* (*The Liberation of Ruggiero from Alcina's Island*), which was published in 1625 and adapted from an episode in Ludovico Ariosto's epic poem *Orlando furioso* (1516), focuses on a struggle between two sorceresses—one good, one evil—over the warrior Ruggiero.

### Altered landscapes

In 1626, Caccini's husband died and about a year later, after moving to Lucca, she married an aristocrat (thus elevating her social standing), with whom she had a son, Tommaso. She was, however, widowed again by 1630. Three years later, now wealthy and a landowner, she returned to Florence to work once again for the Medici family, but retired from the post around 1637, or possibly later.

Caccini composed hundreds of works throughout her life, including songs and incidental music for the theater, most of which are now lost. A poet as well as a composer, she wrote the lyrics for many of her works. The reason for and date of her death are uncertain, although Tommaso is known to have been placed in his uncle's care in 1645.

▷ **FRANCESCA CACCINI**
There are very few verified depictions of Caccini, but this portrait by Italian artist Jacopo Palma is often thought to be of the composer as a young woman.

◁ **FLORENCE, c. 1650**
This painting shows Florence as it would have looked in Caccini's day. It was here that the composer was born, grew up, and spent many years of her life.

# Barbara Strozzi

## c. 1619–1677, ITALIAN

Born into the male world of 17th-century Venice, Strozzi was the most-published composer of secular vocal music in her day and a key figure in the rise of the cantata and aria.

Born in Venice around 1619, Barbara Strozzi was the illegitimate child and adopted daughter of the poet Giulio Strozzi. Her mother, Isabella Garzoni, was a servant and possibly also a courtesan (a high-class sex worker) of Giulio's. A member of the Accademia degli Incogniti (Academy of the Unknowns, see box, right), Giulio used his elite connections to promote his daughter's musical talents, and sent her off to study with the prominent composer and pioneer of opera Francesco Cavalli.

### A woman's work

By 1637, aged 18, Strozzi had made a name for herself as a virtuoso singer, and in 1644 she launched her career as a female composer with the publication of her *First Book of Madrigals* for two to four voices.

By her early thirties, she had four children. Their father was probably Giovanni Vidman, patron of the arts and a friend of her father. However, Strozzi was a single mother and never married. Unsubstantiated accounts suggest she was also a courtesan.

◁ **BARBARA STROZZI**
This portrait of Strozzi with a breast exposed has divided critics: for some, it confirms her status as a courtesan; for others, it indicates her maternal role.

◁ **CANTATA BY STROZZI**
The original score shown here is in Barbara Strozzi's own handwriting—the composer was an important figure in the development of the Italian cantata.

to the private sphere of writing and performing, in the very limited genres of secular vocal and chamber music, to small, elite circles of men (see box).

### Finding a voice

Nonetheless, her work was popular in England, Austria, and Germany, as well as Venice. Her success as a prolific female composer was due to her tenacity, shrewdness in business, and scant regard for what was deemed respectable for women of her day. Far from concealing her identity behind a male pseudonym—a tactic used by many women who wanted their voices to be heard—she put her name to all her works.

Strozzi lived most of her life in Venice but died in Padua in 1677. Her popularity waned after her death and the details of her life and work were largely relegated to obscurity until the 1990s, when they were recuperated by feminist scholars interested in understanding her achievements in the context of the uncompromisingly patriarchal environment of 17th-century Venice.

Following the death of her father in 1652, Strozzi published numerous works (no doubt for financial reasons): more than 100 pieces of secular vocal music—ariettas, arias, and lengthy, complex cantatas—and a book of sacred songs. Most of her music is for solo soprano and focuses on themes of love and desire. Her work is notable for her sensitivity to text and to sound.

Conspicuously absent from Strozzi's compositions and performances is opera, despite the fact that it was such a fashionable new genre. As scholars Diane Jezic and Elizabeth Wood have suggested, her gender confined her

**GIULIO STROZZI, BARBARA'S FATHER, c.1620s**

"Being **a woman** I am concerned about **publishing** this **work**. Would that it ... **not be** endangered by the **swords of slander**."

BARBARA STROZZI, ON THE PUBLICATION OF HER *FIRST BOOK OF MADRIGALS* IN 1644

# Arcangelo Corelli

## 1653–1713, ITALIAN

Hailed by music theorist Angelo Berardi as "the new Orpheus of our days," Corelli helped to define the Italian instrumental sonata and concerto. Despite a modest output, he was influential throughout Europe.

Among the many notable musicians who were drawn to Rome in the 17th century, Arcangelo Corelli was famed for his expressive violin-playing and exemplary compositions. Although he was by all accounts a serene and modest man, his performances were said often to be fiery and dynamic.

Arcangelo was born in Fusignano in February 1653 into a family of wealthy landowners. His father died just before he was born, so he and his four siblings were raised solely by their mother. He probably received his first music lessons from a priest and, in 1666, aged 13, was sent to Bologna to continue his studies. An exceptional violin-player, he was soon accepted as a member of Bologna's recently founded Accademia Filarmonica.

### From strength to strength

Corelli flourished after moving to Rome in the mid-1670s. Propelled by family connections and talent, he moved up the ranks to become a chamber musician to Christina, the former ruler of Sweden, who had lived in the city since abdicating in 1654. Christina had been raised as a prince and crowned king. Corelli dedicated his Op. 1 collection of church sonatas to them and, while working for other members of Rome's elite, performed for Christina until their death in 1689.

Cardinal Benedetto Pamphili, a great patron of the arts and a competent composer himself, lured Corelli to play in the Sunday concerts at his palace in Rome, and later appointed him as his music master. "Il Bolognese," as Corelli was known, also attracted the patronage of Cardinal Pietro Ottoboni, to whom he dedicated his Op. 4 collection of chamber trios. The young Ottoboni, the last in a controversial line of cardinal-nephews appointed by the pope, treated Corelli as a friend, as evident in his letters to the composer.

### Ingenuity and originality

The ample orchestras belonging to the two cardinals served as musical laboratories for Corelli. He used them to test his concertos for strings. These were strikingly inventive works that influenced other musicians in Rome, including Handel, and traveled beyond the Alps after Corelli signed a publishing deal with Estienne Roger of Amsterdam in 1712. Bach and Tartini were among those who based original compositions on themes by Corelli, a trend that was revived in the 20th century by Rachmaninoff and Tippett.

Corelli's Op. 6 collection, published in 1714, a year after his death, contains 12 *concerti grossi*: eight in the so-called church style, four in the chamber style. Europe's music-lovers were captivated by their ingenuity—not least the lilting Largo from Op. 6, No. 8, the "Christmas Concerto"—and by the great economy and ease of Corelli's writing. His six publications went through multiple editions and remained in the repertoire throughout the 18th century, rare in an age that was hungry for the latest fashions.

△ **CARDINAL PIETRO OTTOBONI**
A musician himself (and also a librettist), Ottoboni was one of Corelli's patrons. This portrait, c.1689, shows the cardinal in his early twenties.

▷ **ARCANGELO CORELLI**
Corelli was born in Fusignano into a wealthy family who waged an abortive campaign to rule the town. His success, although derived from immense talent, was certainly aided by family connections.

### ON TECHNIQUE
### The *concerto grosso*

Corelli published only six volumes of works, devoted to solo sonatas, trio sonatas, and concertos for strings. He made significant contributions to each genre, setting high artistic standards and accommodating a rich variety of moods. Corelli's *concerti grossi*, conceived for the large ensembles engaged by his rich Roman patrons, served as models of independent instrumental music, set free from the human voice and poetic texts. They exploit contrasts of volume and dramatic intensity between a small group of instruments, or *concertino*, and a larger company of players, the *ripieno* or "full" band.

SCORE FROM *CONCERTO GROSSO* IN G MINOR, ARCANGELO CORELLI, 1675

▷ **HENRY PURCELL, c. 1695**
This portrait of Henry Purcell was painted by John Closterman in the year of the great composer's tragically early death in 1695. He was just 36 and at the peak of his career. The illness that caused his death is unknown, although there is speculation that it was tuberculosis. There is also speculation that he died from a chill, which he caught when he came home drunk one night and his wife locked him out of the house.

# Henry Purcell

## 1659–1695, ENGLISH

Famed, above all, for *Dido and Aeneas*—the first true English opera—Purcell was one of the greatest and most versatile composers of the Baroque period.

During his brief yet hectic lifetime, Henry Purcell was acknowledged as unequaled among English composers. After his premature death at the age of 36, he was hailed by contemporary commentators as "our all-pleasing Britain's Orpheus" and "the Delight of the Nation and the Wonder of the World." A century later, he had become "our musical Shakespeare." None of the composers of his day matched his melodic genius or his inspired eclecticism, which absorbed the fashionable continental styles of Lully (see p.55) and Corelli (see pp.44–45) without sacrificing a quintessential Englishness. His great sensitivity to the rhythms of the English language remains unsurpassed.

Yet the biography of the composer who became a national icon remains fragmentary. What is certain is that he was born into a family of court musicians in 1659, grew up in the shadow of Westminster Abbey, London, and was one of 12 boy trebles in the Chapel Royal.

At the age of 18, he was appointed "composer-in-ordinary for the king's violins." In 1679, he became organist of Westminster Abbey, and a year or two later he married Frances Peters.

### Building a career
For the next decade, Purcell's career centered on court and chapel, with the production of verse anthems, royal odes, royal welcome songs (in which the music repeatedly transcends the sycophantic texts), and, in 1685, coronation anthems for James II. His sets of viol fantasias and the Italianate sonatas in three and four parts reveal his genius, not least in their rich chromatic harmonies. The poignantly concise *Dido and Aeneas* (c.1683–1689) tells the story of the love between Aeneas, hero of Virgil's epic poem the *Aeneid*, and the Carthaginian queen Dido, who dies by suicide when Aeneas is tricked into abandoning her.

After James II was overthrown in 1688, Purcell's creative activities broadened. From 1689, he provided

▷ **SCORE FROM *THE FAIRY-QUEEN***
This handwritten score is of the aria "Thrice Happy Lovers" from Act 5 of Purcell's semi-opera *The Fairy-Queen* of 1692. The piece cautions against jealousy and the "anxious Care and Strife,/That attends a married Life."

◁ **_DIDO AND AENEAS_, SET DESIGN**
Illustration of the set for Purcell's opera *Dido and Aeneas*, designed by Francesco da Bibiena in 1712. Bibiena, an architect, not only built theaters, but was famous for his spectacular set designs.

birthday odes for Queen Mary II (see box, right). But with the militaristic William III opposed to elaborate church music, he now began to write for a broader middle-class audience: in the published sets of "choyce ayres and songs," in incidental music for plays, and in the "semi-operas" (as the contemporary writer Roger North dubbed them) for the Dorset Garden Theatre, off Fleet Street. Purcell the court composer had morphed into a composer for the commercial stage.

All-sung opera, that dangerously exotic Italian import, was still deemed alien to the "robust" English temperament. The recipe for public success was to take an existing play, fillet it, and stuff it with music, dance, and spectacular scenic effects. These multi-media extravaganzas, involving separate casts of actors, dancers, and singers, present a serious challenge to today's producers and are therefore rarely performed. Yet the four semi-operas—*Dioclesian*, *King Arthur*, *The Fairy-Queen*, and *The Indian Queen*—from Purcell's final years contain some of his most atmospheric and melodically alluring music.

# Antonio Vivaldi

## 1678–1741, ITALIAN

Versatile and highly prolific, Vivaldi was the outstanding Italian composer of his time as well as a celebrated violinist. However, after his death, he was virtually forgotten and not rediscovered until the 20th century.

◁ **VENICE, FRANCESCO GUARDI**
This 18th-century painting of Venice is a contemporary view of the city so closely associated with Vivaldi. He was born, ordained, and fêted there for much of his life, leaving just a year before his death.

### IN CONTEXT
### St. Mark's, Venice

Vivaldi's first known appearance as a musician came at the age of 18, when he performed alongside his father as a violinist in St. Mark's, Venice's most important church. It was built mainly in the late 11th century and has a long tradition in music. The eminent composers associated with it include Giovanni Gabrieli, who was principal organist in 1585–1612, and Claudio Monteverdi, who was music director in 1613–1643. Music featured not only inside the church but also in religious processions in St. Mark's Square.

Vivaldi's name is inseparable from his most famous work, *The Four Seasons*, one of the most frequently performed and recorded pieces in the classical repertoire. However, these four violin concertos represent only a tiny part of his output. In addition to about 500 concertos (almost half of them for his own instrument, the violin), he wrote 50 or so operas, of which 16 survive complete and others in part, a large amount of sacred music, numerous sonatas for one or two instruments, and various other compositions. Critics have accused him of overproduction and repetition, but his finest creations rank among the greatest of their time.

Vivaldi was born in Venice and although he traveled a good deal, within Italy and elsewhere, he spent most of his life in the city. His father, who started out as a barber, was such an good amateur violinist that he was able to turn professional, and in 1685 he began working as a musician at St. Mark's Church.

### Music and religion

Vivaldi inherited his father's talent on the violin, so a musical career beckoned, but religion was also to play an important role in his life. In 1693, he began training for the priesthood, perhaps influenced by an uncle who was a priest at the family's parish church.

◁ **ANTONIO VIVALDI**
The heavy wig that Vivaldi wears in this anonymous contemporary portrait hides his red hair, which earned him the nickname *il prete rosso* ("the red priest").

**THE NAVE OF ST. MARK'S CHURCH, VENICE, ITALY**

> " I have **heard him boast** of **composing a concerto** faster than **a copyist** could **write it down**. "

CHARLES DE BROSSES, FRENCH VISITOR TO VENICE, 1739

## KEY WORKS

**1711**
L'estro armonico, a set of 12 concertos, is published in Amsterdam and has a wide influence.

**1713**
Vivaldi's first opera, Ottone in villa ([Emperor] Otto at his Villa), has its premiere in Vicenza.

**c.1715**
Writes Gloria, his most famous piece of choral music; it is lost after his death and not performed again until 1939.

**1725**
The Four Seasons is published in Amsterdam in a set of 12 concertos entitled The Contest Between Harmony and Invention.

**1735**
Griselda, an opera in which Vivaldi collaborates with the playwright Carlo Goldoni, has its premiere in Venice.

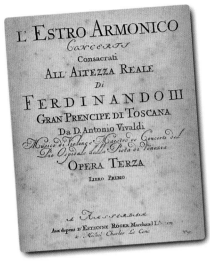

△ **L'ESTRO ARMONICO**

The title page of Vivaldi's *Harmonic Inspiration*, published in 1711, shows a dedication to Ferdinand, Grand Prince of Tuscany, a great patron of the arts, and of music in particular. Ferdinand's villa at Poggio a Caiano near Florence was the venue for many musical performances.

▷ **SCORE FOR OPUS 9, LA CETRA**

Antonio Vivaldi dedicated his set of 12 concertos for the violin, entitled *La cetra* (named after a lyre-like instrument), to Charles VI and presented the emperor with a manuscript copy.

Vivaldi was ordained a priest in March 1703, at the age of 25. Six months later, he was appointed violin teacher at the Ospedale della Pietà (Hospital of Mercy), a home for orphaned and abandoned girls—one of four such institutions in Venice. Music was part of the curriculum at these homes and by Vivaldi's time, the Pietà in particular was famous for the quality of its choir and orchestra. Leading composers wrote music especially for them and their concerts were eagerly attended.

In addition to teaching, Vivaldi's duties at the Pietà came to include composing, conducting, and buying instruments. He kept his association with the home almost until the end of his life. However, his other activities and travels meant that his services could not be exclusive, and his character seems at times to have caused conflict with the institution's administrators. He was notorious for his vanity, boastfulness, and touchiness about criticism, and some contemporaries thought that his worldliness conflicted with his status as a priest.

### International fame

Vivaldi's music was first published in Venice in 1705, but more significantly, in 1711 Estienne Roger, a Frenchman working in Amsterdam, published a collection of 12 of his concertos collectively entitled *L'estro armonico* (*Harmonic Inspiration*). Roger was the most important music publisher in Europe, partly because of the quality of his engraving and printing, but mainly because he had a highly efficient distribution network, with agents in Berlin, London, Paris, and other cities. He played a key role in securing Vivaldi's international reputation.

Vivaldi's own travels also helped spread his fame. His first opera was produced in Vicenza in 1713 and in 1718–1720 he lived in Mantua—a city subject to the Holy Roman Empire—where he wrote several works for the court of the music-loving governor, Prince Philip of Hesse-Darmstadt. In the early 1720s, he spent much of his time in Rome, where several of his operas were performed (he was the impresario as well as composer). From late 1729 to early 1731, he traveled in central Europe with his elderly father, visiting Vienna and perhaps also Prague.

Vivaldi's operas brought him into contact with an attractive young singer called Anna Girò (or Giraud), who regularly appeared in them, usually in a leading role, from 1726 to 1739. Although she was about 30 years younger than Vivaldi, there was gossip that they were lovers. The rumors were probably groundless, but they damaged Vivaldi's career. In particular, in 1738 the archbishop of Ferrara forbade him to enter the city and this led to canceled performances of his operas there.

### A late move to Vienna

By this time, Vivaldi's music had in any case passed the peak of its popularity in Italy and in 1740 he moved to Vienna, hoping to win further patronage from the emperor Charles VI (the two had first met in 1728 and Charles—an accomplished amateur musician—had treated him generously). However, soon

"Such playing has **not been heard** before and can **never be equaled ...**"

J.F.A. VON UFFENBACH, ON HEARING VIVALDI PLAYING A SOLO, 1715

after Vivaldi arrived, Charles died unexpectedly and the composer's career petered out. He died in Vienna the following year and was given a very modest funeral, which suggests that he was short of money. Although he had earned a considerable amount throughout his career, he also spent profusely, not least on producing his operas.

After his death, Vivaldi's reputation declined and he remained virtually forgotten throughout the 19th century. Scholarly interest in the composer emerged in the early 20th century and in 1926 was given a boost by the discovery of a large collection of his scores, including hundreds of previously unknown works.

However, Vivaldi's popular fame did not develop significantly until the 1950s, closely linked with the rise of LP records, which first appeared in 1948. *The Four Seasons* seemed tailor-made for the new format (with two concertos fitting neatly on each side) and the work soon caught the public imagination.

## Concerto legacy

Although Vivaldi set great store by his operas, they are now little known and his reputation rests mainly on his concertos. They are full of exuberant, inventive music and notable for the three-movement pattern that Vivaldi established and that was copied by countless others: a slow, lyrical middle movement between two much quicker ones—the first one typically majestic and the third more playful. *The Four Seasons* is also one of the earliest and greatest examples of program music—that is, music expressing a narrative or pictorial idea: barking dogs, rustic bagpipes, and icy landscapes are among the vivid images that Vivaldi conjures.

## ON TECHNIQUE
### The Baroque violin

The violins used in Vivaldi's time are superficially similar to today's models, but there are significant differences in their design. There is no chin rest on the Baroque violin, because early instrumentalists played it in a lower position than the one familiar today, and the fingerboard is shorter. Strings are made of organic materials (sheep intestines) rather than the metal or synthetic materials that superseded them. The sound produced is typically lighter and more intimate than that of the modern violin. Specialist performers of early music often use Baroque violins, either original instruments or replicas.

**BAROQUE VIOLIN, 1750**

◁ **CHARLES VI OF AUSTRIA**
Vivaldi met Charles VI—depicted here in a painting by Josef Kiss and Friedrich Mayrhofer—while the emperor was visiting Trieste. Charles became a great admirer of Vivaldi's work, conferring on him the title of knight.

# Georg P. Telemann

### 1681–1767, GERMAN

Open to every major style of composition, Telemann was a creative powerhouse. He produced, among other treasures, some of the world's finest late-Baroque instrumental works.

During his lifetime, Georg Philipp Telemann was Germany's leading composer. His output was vast: he wrote almost 40 operas, more than 1,000 church cantatas, around 125 overture-suites, at least the same number of concertos, 50 sonatas, 40 quartets, a mountain of chamber music, and about 250 pieces for solo keyboard. He harmonized 500 hymns and published several dozen songs. Yet Telemann was celebrated not for the quantity but for the quality of his work, for his innovation and invention, his genius for combining diverse musical styles, and his ability to keep pace with changing tastes.

## A secret passion

Telemann was born in Magdeburg (see box, below) in 1681. His father died soon after his birth. Although the young Georg received singing lessons and basic keyboard training, he was essentially a self-taught musician and composer. His mother disapproved of his passion for music, and confiscated all his instruments; like Handel, who was 50 miles (80 km) south in Halle, he practiced and composed in secret.

Family pressure and personal ambition nudged Telemann to study law at Leipzig University. After his setting of Psalm 6 was performed at St. Thomas's, Leipzig's mayor invited him to write works for St. Thomas's and for New Church. Telemann formed a student band soon after, became musical director of Leipzig's opera and organist of New Church, and fell out with the envious Johann Kuhnau, St. Thomas's overworked cantor.

During his Leipzig apprenticeship and later in service to the Count of Promnitz, Telemann mastered the major European musical styles while absorbing Polish and Moravian folk music. He took jobs in Eisenach, Bach's hometown, and in Frankfurt, where he made a rich living as city director of music and church musician. In 1721, he accepted an invitation to become cantor of Hamburg's famous Johanneum and the musical director of its five main churches; he increased his workload the following year by becoming director of the city's Gänsemarkt Oper, Germany's first public opera house.

## Marital issues and workload

Telemann's first wife had died in 1711. His second wife, his junior by 17 years, with whom he had eight sons and one daughter, had an affair with a Swedish military official that was satirized in a Hamburg marionette play in 1724.

She also racked up heavy gambling debts, paid off with help from her husband's friends, before finally leaving home in 1736.

Telemann's productivity in Hamburg alone was superhuman. But he still found time to freelance for the Bayreuth and Eisenach courts; write three autobiographies; maintain friendships with Bach and Handel; create the first German-language music periodical; correspond with talented young composers, including his godson C.P.E. Bach; teach composition; write poetry; broaden the bounds of what a musician could be; and even take up gardening. He remained active as a composer into his eighties and was still exploring the latest musical styles shortly before his death in 1767.

After his death, Telemann was airbrushed from history, partly because he was overshadowed by Bach and Handel. However, in recent years, performers have revived select pieces from his *Tafelmusik* (*Table Music*) of 1733—a vast survey of almost every instrumental genre of the day—and championed works such as *Hamburger Ebb und Fluht* (known as *Water Music*) and his heart-rending *Brockes-Passion*.

△ **SCORE, SACRED CANTATA**
This autographed score for Telemann's Sacred Cantata shows the section for the first violin. It is one of more than 1,000 church cantatas that he wrote.

## IN CONTEXT
### The Thirty Years' War

Magdeburg, devastated during the Thirty Years' War (1618–1648), was in ruins when Telemann was a boy. Memories of bloodshed and famine, the legacy of the Protestant city's destruction by Catholic forces in 1631, haunted its people. The shadow of civil war focused German minds on promoting national and international peace via commerce and the arts.

German composers contributed to the harmony of nations by creating what became known as the "mixed taste," a union of different styles. Telemann proved a musical alchemist, able to transform what he called "French liveliness ... Italian flattery ... and the British and Polish jesting".

**THE FALL OF MAGDEBURG IN 1631, DURING THE THIRTY YEARS' WAR**

# Jean-Philippe Rameau

## 1683–1764, FRENCH

Having always nursed ambitions to succeed on the stage, Rameau produced his first opera at the age of 50. He never looked back, becoming a highly distinguished Baroque composer and music theorist.

Jean-Philippe Rameau was born in Dijon to a musical family. His father was a church organist; Jean-Philippe took a similar path, holding a series of posts as an organist, which he combined with writing and teaching.

It was Rameau's writing that first drew him to the public's attention. His *Treatise on Harmony* (1722) caused a stir and became highly influential. Two years later, a book of harpsichord pieces cemented his reputation. He continued to compose, concentrating mainly on sacred music, but a major breakthrough still eluded him. In part, this may have been due to Rameau's prickly temperament (the writer Voltaire was among those with whom he had a tempestuous relationship). Eventually, he found a patron in the

◁ **JEAN-PHILIPPE RAMEAU, c. 1728**
Rameau's musical career was launched after having taken a trip to Italy as a young man and playing "as first fiddle" with a group of traveling musicians.

financier Le Riche de la Pouplinière, who enabled him to stage his opera *Hippolyte et Aricie* in 1733. (The work later divided the critics: devotees of the operatic composer Jean-Baptiste Lully found it too brash, too "Italian," but it also won many admirers.)

◁ **TITLE PAGE, *CODE OF MUSIC PRACTICE***
Rameau's *Code of Music Practice*, published in 1760, was a leading work of music theory in the 18th century.

### Seizing opportunity

Rameau took advantage of this opportunity. During the 1730s, he composed a series of operas, including *Castor et Pollux* and *Les Indes Galantes*, which became two of his most popular productions. He retained Lully's varied format, with its mix of spectacles, transformation scenes, and ballet interludes—Lully's works comprise lyric tragedy, the opera-ballet, and the comedy-ballet. Rameau favored a more dynamic approach. He expanded Lully's string orchestra—adding flutes, bassoons, oboes, trumpets, and drums—and created complex harmonic interplays between his choruses and his soloists. "Lully needs actors," he proclaimed, "but I need singers."

### Altered perceptions

Rameau eventually achieved the same renown as Lully. Many of his later productions were staged at the Paris Opéra or in royal palaces and, in old age, Louis XV honored him with a title, a pension, and the office of royal composer. With the rise of Italian comic opera, however, there was an ironic turnaround in his reputation. In his youth, the critics had dubbed Rameau too Italian (too ornate), but during the "War of the Buffoons" (see box, right), pamphleteers mocked him for not being Italian enough, for being a staid representative of the old French school. His reputation was restored in the 20th century.

◁ ***HIPPOLYTE ET ARICIE***
Rameau's first opera was the lyric tragedy *Hippolyte et Aricie*, shown here at a performance in Toulouse in 2009. Although written late in life, the work propelled him to fame.

# Johann Sebastian Bach

## 1685–1750, GERMAN

Hailed by many as the greatest Baroque composer, Bach created music ranging from oratorios to intimate keyboard pieces. His composition combines mathematical complexity with profound humanity.

◁ BACH HOUSE, EISENACH
The half-timbered house in Eisenach, once mistakenly thought to be Bach's birthplace, now serves as a museum to his life and work. It contains several of the instruments he owned and played.

at the age of 15, his vocal ability won him a place at the prestigious Michaeliskirche school in Lüneburg, near Hamburg in northern Germany. There, his interest in the organ grew under the influence of composer Georg Böhm, the organist at Lüneburg's Johanniskirche.

### Disgruntled employee

Bach finished his education at the age of 17 and set out to earn a living. After a spell in a minor post at the court of the duke of Weimar, in 1703 he became church organist, first at Arnstadt, then Mühlhausen, both towns in Thuringia. However, with his exuberant talents harnessed to mundane work, he proved to be a troublesome employee. The church authorities in Arnstadt were annoyed that he spent a long leave of absence in distant Lübeck, where he had traveled to hear performances by Dieterich Buxtehude, then at the cutting edge of German music. They also claimed that his accompaniments to chorales were far too elaborate.

The last of eight children, Johann Sebastian Bach was born in the town of Eisenach in Thuringia, Germany, in March 1685. Members of his family had been musicians since the 16th century: his father, Johann Ambrosius, was a talented string player prominent in Eisenach's small-town musical life; several uncles were organists; and a cousin, Johann Christoph Bach, had achieved some renown as a composer.

Johann Sebastian learned to play and compose early in life, immersed in his family's rich musical tradition as well as its Lutheran Protestantism. He was orphaned at the age of nine, his father dying nine months after his mother, and was sent to live with his eldest brother, Christoph, at nearby Ohrdurf. Christoph was an organist who had been a pupil of the celebrated composer Johann Pachelbel (see p.85) and Johann Sebastian's informal musical education was able to continue under his brother's gaze. It may have been at Ohrdurf that he first learned to play the organ, and he certainly sang in the church choir as,

### ON TECHNIQUE
### Lutheran church music

Music was an integral element of Lutheran church services. By the 18th century, the singing of chorales (hymns) by the congregation was accompanied and harmonized by an organist, who might provide solo preludes and interludes. Cantatas—more elaborate performances by solo singers, choir, and instrumentalists—were also integrated into the service. The musical element of a service might last an hour or more. Sunday services were the main musical performances available in German cities, although some Lutherans felt that music distracted from worship.

GERMAN BAROQUE ORGAN MADE IN THURINGIA IN AROUND 1650

"One **can't fake** things **in Bach**, and if one gets all of them to work, **the music sings.** "

HILARY HAHN, VIOLINIST

▷ JOHANN SEBASTIAN BACH, 1746
This portrait by the German artist Elias Gottlob Haussmann depicts Bach at the age of around 60, holding his famous six-voice puzzle canon.

## IN PROFILE
## Anna Magdalena Bach

Bach's second wife, born Anna Magdalena Wülcken in 1701, was the daughter of a trumpeter. Before they married, she was a singer at the Köthen court. She gave birth to the first of 13 children in 1723. Anna Magdalena was a competent musician who copied scores for her husband, but claims she wrote some of his music are spurious. The *Anna Magdalena Notebooks*, collections of music assembled by Bach for his wife, testify to her role in domestic music-making. After Bach's death, Anna Magdalena was left destitute. She died a beggar in 1760 and was buried in a pauper's grave.

PAGE FROM THE *CHACONNE* IN BACH'S PARTITA IN D MINOR FOR SOLO VIOLIN, HANDWRITTEN BY ANNA MAGDALENA

## Early recognition

By this time, the quality of Bach's organ-playing had begun to attract attention and some of his noteworthy compositions had also emerged. The cantata *Gott ist mein König* (*God is My King*), his first published work, was printed while he was at Mühlhausen in 1707. He may also have composed the Toccata and Fugue in D minor— one of his most celebrated organ works—around this time.

Bach followed a strict Lutheran code of sexual morality. The only early evidence of interest in women was a complaint from church authorities that he had allowed a "strange maiden" into the Arnstadt organ loft. In 1707, buoyed by a small inheritance from his maternal uncle, he married his second cousin, Maria Barbara. They had seven children, only four of whom survived infancy. Most of these births took place at the ducal court at Weimar, where, from 1708, Bach was an organist and later a concertmaster.

## Weimar influences

The wider connections of a dukedom brought Bach into contact with current musical trends outside Germany,

△ **THE DUKE OF SAXE-WEIMAR**
In 1708, Bach took a position as chamber musician in the court of Duke Wilhelm Ernst of Saxe-Weimar, who ruled over the duchy with his brother, Johann Ernst.

notably the work of Italian composer Antonio Vivaldi. It also spread Bach's reputation as a virtuoso. He was reportedly invited to Dresden to take part in a contest with French organist Louis Marchand; the Frenchman failed to turn up, implicitly conceding defeat. Although less constraining, and considerably better paid, than being a Thuringian church organist, Bach's position as a servant of the capricious duke of Weimar was never wholly comfortable. In 1717, he sought permission to accept the post of musical director at another German court, that of Prince Leopold of Köthen. Outraged by this disloyalty, the duke imprisoned Bach for a month, before reluctantly letting him go.

Prince Leopold was a keen amateur musician who maintained a small orchestra, and Köthen provided

Bach in turn grumbled about the wide-ranging duties he had been given, which distracted him from the organ and his composition. He had no patience with the poor quality of local musicians, and once engaged in a violent brawl with a young bassoonist whose abilities he had insulted.

◁ **BACH CHURCH, ARNSTADT**
Bach served as the organist in the Neue Kirche (New Church) in Arnstadt, Thuringia, in 1703–1707. It was renamed Johann-Sebastian-Bach-Kirche in his honor in 1935.

fertile ground for Bach's lively imagination. His focus shifted from organ music and cantatas to works for harpsichord, violin, and cello, and for the chamber orchestra.

### The Köthen years

Although it is notoriously difficult to date many of Bach's compositions, it was probably at Köthen that he wrote such masterpieces as the Concerto for Two Violins, the Suites for Solo Cello, and the Sonatas and Partitas for Solo Violin. The *Brandenburg Concertos*, six

works based on the Italian *concerto grosso* style in which soloists play together with a small orchestra, were written in 1721, and the first book of the *Well-Tempered Clavier*—24 preludes and fugues in the full range of major and minor keys—was completed the following year.

The period at Köthen was generally a happy time for Bach, but was marred by family tragedy in 1720. While Bach was accompanying the prince to the spa at Carlsbad, his wife Maria Barbara unexpectedly

fell ill and died. He returned too late for the funeral. A year later, Bach married the 20-year-old singer Anna Magdalena Wülcken (see box, p.58).

### A decisive move to Leipzig

Whether unsettled by these events or by changes at court, the prince married a woman who was utterly uninterested in music, and Bach started looking for an alternative post and a new challenge. In 1723, a vacancy appeared in the Saxon city of Leipzig, a thriving center of

△ **THE THOMASSCHULE, 1840**
Bach lived in Leipzig at the Thomas School, which was affiliated with Thomaskirche, the Lutheran church where he was musical director. This sketch of the school was made by Felix Mendelssohn, who lived in a building opposite from 1835 to 1847. It was Mendelssohn who helped revive interest in Bach's works in the 19th century.

"The **sole end** and **aim** of **all music** should be the **glory of God** and the **recreation of the mind**."

J.S. BACH

△ **BACH AND HIS SONS, 1730**
This painting by German portraitist Balthasar Denner is thought to depict Bach, holding a cello, with three of his sons; some historians, however, dispute that it shows the family of Bach.

commerce and culture. A "cantor" was needed, who would be responsible for the music in the Thomaskirche and other major churches in the city. Having failed to recruit their desired candidate, the prominent composer Georg Philipp Telemann, the city authorities reluctantly took on Bach—

as one councilor put it, "when the best man cannot be obtained, mediocre ones have to be accepted." Bach had to promise that his music would "not last too long," nor be "operatic" in style. Despite this unpromising beginning, Bach had found a post he was to fill for the rest of his life.

Bach's creative energy in his early years in Leipzig was astonishing. Responsible for the music at four churches, he wrote new cantatas at an average rate of one a week, plus larger-scale works for the high points of the church year—the *Magnificat* for Christmas 1723, the *St. John Passion*

## KEY WORKS

**1721**
Writes the six *Brandenburg Concertos* for the Köthen court orchestra. They are dedicated to the Margrave of Brandenburg.

**1722**
*The Well-Tempered Clavier*, Bach's first book of 24 keyboard preludes and fugues, is published. A second book follows.

**1724**
Bach's *St. John Passion* is premiered at Easter in his first year as director of church music in Leipzig.

**1727**
The *St. Matthew Passion* is performed at Easter at Leipzig's Thomaskirche.

**1734–35**
The *Christmas Oratorio*, a work in six parts, is performed at Leipzig's Nikolaikirche.

**1741**
Writes 30 keyboard variations—called the *Goldberg Variations*—for the Russian ambassador to Saxony in Dresden.

**1747**
Writes *The Musical Offering*, elaborate fugal variations on a tune provided by Prussian King Frederick II.

**1749**
Completes his Mass in B Minor, a choral work, begun in 1733. It is not performed in his lifetime.

◁ **ST. MATTHEW PASSION**
In the *St. Matthew Passion*, sung in German and shown here in a handwritten score from the 1740s, Bach's music stresses the terrible anguish of the Crucifixion.

for Easter 1724, and the *St. Matthew Passion* for Easter 1727. Nor was his output by any means restricted to sacred music. Some of his best-loved keyboard pieces, including the Partitas, *English Suites*, and *French Suites*, date from this period. In 1729, he became director of Leipzig's Collegium Musicum, which staged weekly performances of secular music at the Zimmerman coffeehouse.

## Home life and family

Bach's home became a center of music-making, in which the entire family participated. The composer wrote many works for domestic performance or as learners' pieces for his numerous offspring. Anna Magdalena gave birth to 13 children between 1723 and 1742, of whom only six survived infancy; however, the constant round of births and deaths does not appear to have interrupted Bach's productivity, nor to have disturbed what was a mutually contented marriage.

In contrast, Bach's relations with his Leipzig employers were always difficult. There were endless conflicts over pay and status, and over the nonmusical teaching duties that he was supposed to have performed but often did not. In 1736, he secured an additional post as court composer to the elector of Saxony in Dresden, a prestigious position that made

him largely immune to any further criticism from the Leipzig authorities. It was at the Dresden court that Bach received a commission from the Russian ambassador, Count Keyserlingk, to write a soothing piece of music for harpsichordist Gottlieb Goldberg to play to help the count sleep at night—the work now known as the *Goldberg Variations*.

## Travels and troubles

Bach did not follow musical fashions. In 1737, he was strongly attacked by the young music critic Johann Adolf Scheibe for his allegedly "bombastic

◁ **FREDERICK II OF PRUSSIA**
Bach dedicated his *Musical Offering* to the Prussian king, though the work is now seen as the composer's critique of Frederick's religious and aesthetic values.

and confused style" that offended contemporary tastes for simplicity and clarity of melody and harmony. However, Bach's later music only served to reaffirm his old-fashioned commitment to dense counterpoint, or the intertwining of two or more melodic lines.

In 1747, on a visit to Berlin, he was invited to play in front of the Prussian king, Frederick the Great, who was employing Bach's son Carl Philipp Emmanuel (see box, right) as a court musician. The king presented Bach with an original theme on which—for the royal amusement—he spontaneously improvised a three-part fugue at the pianoforte. Back in Leipzig, he used the same theme to create *The Musical Offering*, a set of contrapuntal pieces including a six-part fugue. Up to his death, he was working on his *Art of Fugue*, an exhaustive exploration of the possibilities of contrapuntal writing that was a monumental tribute to a disappearing musical world.

## Final works

In 1749, Bach went blind. He died the following year, possibly of diabetes, and was buried in an unmarked grave. His work as a composer was soon largely forgotten, but interest revived in the 19th century, especially after Mendelssohn's performance of the *St. Matthew Passion* in Berlin in 1829.

By the century's end, Bach had become famous enough for his body to be dug up and reburied in a stone sarcophagus. His remains now lie in Leipzig's Thomaskirche.

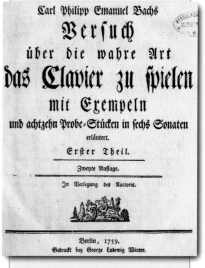

**TITLE PAGE OF C.P.E. BACH'S *TREATISE ON THE HARPSICHORD*, 1759**

" **Bach** was the **most prodigious organist** and **keyboard player** that there has **ever been**. "

BACH'S OBITUARY, IN THE *MUSIKALISCHE BIBLIOTHEK*, 1754

# Domenico Scarlatti

## 1685–1757, ITALIAN

Italian Scarlatti wrote his most famous works in Spain. His fiery keyboard sonatas, incorporating elements of Spanish popular music, defied the rules of composition and extended the range of keyboard technique.

Giuseppe Domenico Scarlatti was born in Naples in 1685—an auspicious year that also saw the birth of J.S. Bach and Handel. He was a child of opera composer Alessandro Scarlatti (see box, right), who had his son appointed organist at the Neapolitan royal chapel at the age of 15. Although Domenico showed exceptional ability as a keyboard player, his father insisted he write vocal music, and his first opera was performed in Naples in 1703.

In 1709, Scarlatti obtained a post as in-house composer for Queen Maria Casimira of Poland, who was living in exile in Rome. Over the following five years, he wrote seven operas for the queen's theater and also established a reputation as a harpsichord virtuoso.

### Royal duties

In 1715, Scarlatti was appointed *maestro di cappella* at St. Peter's, the position Palestrina had once held (see p.22), but he was increasingly frustrated by his subjection to his father's authority and by being forced to focus on vocal music.

◁ **BARBARA OF PORTUGAL**
Scarlatti wrote pieces for his talented keyboard student, Princess María Bárbara de Bragança.

In 1719, he accepted an invitation to join the royal court of Portuguese King Joao V in Lisbon. One of his duties was to teach music to the king's nine-year-old daughter, Princess María Bárbara de Bragança. When she married the future king of Spain in 1729, Scarlatti accompanied her to Seville and then to Madrid, where he lived at the court for the rest of his life.

### Keyboard innovation

On a visit to Rome, Scarlatti married 16-year-old Maria Caterina Gentili in 1728. The couple had six children before she died in 1739. The composer fathered four more offspring with a second wife, Anastasia Maxarti Ximenes, the last born when he was 64.

During his years in Spain, Scarlatti wrote the 555 single-movement keyboard sonatas for which he is renowned. Mostly intended for the harpsichord, they reveled in unexpected modulation and harmonic dissonance, exploiting a wide range of innovative techniques including the crossing of hands. Many of their original effects were inspired by Spanish folk music, with echoes of guitar-strumming, castanets, stamping dance rhythms, and flamenco song. The publication of 30 sonatas under the title *Exercises* in 1638 established Scarlatti's Europe-wide reputation, but little more of his music was published in his lifetime.

Since Scarlatti's death in Madrid in 1757, the rest of the keyboard works have been gradually rediscovered. Although little of his vocal music is highly rated today, Scarlatti's sonatas have an idiosyncratic "modern" feel that guarantees their popular place in the repertoire.

**SCORE OF ALESSANDRO SCARLATTI'S**
*LA CADUTA DE' DECEMVIRI* (1682–1683)

▷ **DOMENICO SCARLATTI**
This portrait made by Domingo Antonio Velasco in 1739 commemorates Scarlatti's initiation into the Spanish Order of Santiago the previous year.

▷ **HARPSICHORD FROM 1725**
Scarlatti was a master of the harpsichord. In a keyboard competition with Handel in Rome, judges estimated Handel to be superior at the organ but Scarlatti the better harpsichordist. One contemporary described his playing "as if ten hundred devils had been at the instrument."

# George Frideric Handel

**1685–1759, GERMAN-BRITISH**

Handel wrote Italian operas, English-language oratorios, and lively orchestral suites in Georgian London. Direct, vigorous, and unsentimental, his music exemplified the finest qualities of the Baroque era.

◁ **ALMIRA, 2014**
Handel's first opera, *Almira*, premiered in Hamburg, Germany, in 1705. The production shown here was staged by the Hamburg State Opera in 2014.

◁ **GEORGE FRIDERIC HANDEL**
This portrait of Handel by Balthasar Denner, c.1726, shows the composer in his early forties—prosperous, celebrated, and at the height of his career.

Georg Friederich Händel was born in the German town of Halle, near Leipzig, in 1685. He later anglicized his name to George Frideric Handel. His father served as barber-surgeon to the local aristocracy and his mother was the daughter of a Lutheran pastor. Prosperous members of the middle class, they intended Georg to make a career as a lawyer and were not especially pleased when, from an early age, he displayed an exceptional gift for music. After his talent on the organ was noticed by a local nobleman, the parents were persuaded to pay for music lessons with the organist at their parish church, the Marienkirche. Apart from this induction, Handel was self-taught, learning through imitating other people's compositions.

Handel was a young man of robust temperament—sociable, energetic, enterprising, gifted, with boundless self-confidence. At 18, he left Halle for the port city of Hamburg, where he was employed as an instrumentalist at the city's opera house, the Gänsemarkt theater. According to a famous anecdote, his life nearly ended there when a quarrel with a colleague led to a duel in which the point of his opponent's sword was parried only by a button on Handel's coat.

## Italian adventures

Following the success of his first attempt at opera, *Almira*, staged at the Hamburg opera house in 1705 to great acclaim, Handel traveled to Italy, Europe's leading center of vocal music, in 1707. He mixed in the fashionable society of Florence, Rome, Venice, and Naples, exciting great admiration with his virtuoso performances on the organ. He may have conducted a love affair with a Florentine singer, Vittoria Tarquini; if true, this was his only known liaison.

Musically, his stay in Italy completed his education; he learned to compose operas in the current Italian style, designed to showcase the virtuosity of castrati (see box, right) and sopranos. His *Agrippina*, performed in Venice in 1709–1710, was a triumphant success.

**PORTRAIT OF FARINELLI, CORRADO GIAQUINTO, c.1753**

> "**Never** has **perfection** in **any art** been **combined** in the **same man** with such **fertility** of **production**."

ANTOINE PREVOST, ON HANDEL, 1733

FIREWORKS IN GREEN PARK, 1749

named Royal Academy of Music, at the King's Theatre in Haymarket, touring Europe to recruit the most famous singers, including castrato Senesino (see box, p.65), soprano Francesca Cuzzoni, and mezzo-soprano Faustina Bordoni. Managing these superstars was never easy. It is said that once, frustrated by her refusal to sing an aria he had written, Handel threatened to throw Cuzzoni out of a window. But the performances Handel put on at the King's Theatre became, for a time, the most fashionable entertainments in London. His celebrated operas of this period include *Ottone* (1723), *Giulio Cesare* (1724), and *Tamerlano* (1724).

### A move to London

In 1710, Handel moved back to Germany, accepting the post of music director at the court of Hanover. This small, ambitious state had a special relationship with Britain, because its prince had been designated as Protestant heir to the British throne. Almost immediately, Handel took a long leave of absence in London and soon abandoned the Hanoverian court altogether, seduced by the musical and financial opportunities the British capital offered. He was to live there for the rest of his life.

In London, Italian opera was the height of fashion and Handel's *Rinaldo*, staged at the Queen's Theatre in 1711, introduced him to his new country as a master of the genre. The composer ingratiated himself with the British aristocracy, earning the patronage of

the earl of Burlington and the duke of Chandos. He also curried favor with Queen Anne, receiving a royal pension after writing music for the celebration of the Peace of Utrecht that ended war with France in 1714.

Anne's death in the same year brought the accession of Handel's Hanoverian employer as King George I. This was a potentially tricky moment for Handel, since he had abandoned Hanover without permission, but the king did not bear a grudge. In 1717, Londoners were treated to the spectacle of King George drifting down the Thames accompanied by 50 musicians in a barge playing music specially composed by Handel for the occasion—the three suites known as the *Water Music*.

### The Royal Academy of Music

Establishing himself in a new town house in London's Brook Street, Handel set out not just to write operas—15 in the decade of the 1720s—but to run an opera company. Backed by wealthy investors, he set up the pretentiously

### From operas to oratorios

In the late 1720s, Handel's operatic enterprise ran into problems. The popular success of John Gay's lively English-language music drama *The Beggar's Opera*, staged in 1728, deflated the vogue for Italian opera. Bankrupted by the huge fees paid to its star singers, the Royal Academy of Music folded. In 1734, Handel abandoned the theatrical business, although he continued to write operas, mostly staged at the new Covent Garden theater, until 1741.

The decline in the fashion for Italian opera led Handel to move into writing oratorios. These large-scale sacred concert pieces for soloists, orchestra, and choir proved hugely popular. Selecting biblical themes and setting English-language texts, he appealed to British patriotism and Protestantism. *Esther*, presented as part of the opera season in 1732, was followed by more than 20 oratorios over the next two decades. The most famous, *Messiah*, was first performed in 1742 in Dublin, where Handel had been invited to organize a concert season by the British Lord Lieutenant of Ireland.

## "Go to him to learn how to achieve great effects, by such simple means."

LUDWIG VAN BEETHOVEN, ON HANDEL

## KEY WORKS

**1711**
*Rinaldo*, the first of Handel's operas performed in London, is an outstanding success.

**1717**
Three instrumental suites, *Water Music*, are played on a barge on the Thames to entertain King George I.

**1727**
*Zadok the Priest* is written for and performed at the coronation of George II.

**1739**
Publishes *Concerti grossi*, 12 works for small instrumental ensembles.

**1742**
*Messiah*, Handel's most famous oratorio, is performed for the first time, in Dublin.

**1749**
*Music for the Royal Fireworks* is written for the celebration of the peace of Aix-la-Chapelle.

Despite objections from some critics and audiences about using such a sacred subject as Jesus in a concert performance, *Messiah* was soon well on its way to becoming a British institution, as was Handel himself.

Although disliked by some members of the royal family, Handel served, in effect, as the Hanoverian monarchy's official composer, called upon to write music to celebrate a peace or a victory. His status as a national icon was reflected in a statue of Handel

by French sculptor Louis-François Roubiliac erected in the Vauxhall Pleasure Gardens in 1738.

In the early 1750s, Handel lost his sight. His last oratorio, *Jephtha*, was performed at Covent Garden in 1752, the composer conducting despite being almost blind. He became more pious and socially concerned in his later years, mounting performances of *Messiah* at the Foundling Hospital in Bloomsbury to raise money for its work with abandoned children.

Throughout his life, Handel had desired wealth and fame: he died in 1759 having achieved both. His funeral in Westminster Abbey was attended by thousands. He had been adopted by the British as one of their own; his oratorios were idolized, becoming the focus of a specifically British choral tradition. Although a revival of interest in his operas had to wait until the second half of the 20th century, he has always been internationally recognized as one of the great composers.

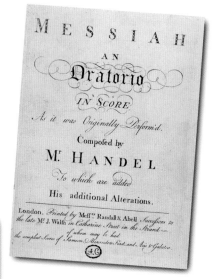

△ **HANDEL'S *MESSIAH***
This score for the *Messiah* dates from 1747, five years after its premiere in Dublin. The composer continued working on the oratorio until 1754, when he arrived at the version known today.

◁ **THE CORONATION OF GEORGE II**
Handel wrote his glorious anthem *Zadok the Priest* for the coronation of George II in 1727. It has been played at every British coronation since.

▷ **CHRISTOPH GLUCK, 1775**
This portrait of Gluck was made when the composer was in his early sixties, during the final years of his career. Despite his humble beginnings, and opposition from his family at his choice of career, Gluck rose to enjoy great wealth and fame.

# Christoph W. Gluck

**1714–1787, AUSTRIAN**

Revered by Mozart, Berlioz, and Wagner, Gluck deserves more credit than any other composer for purging opera of virtuoso display in favor of emotional directness and dramatic truth.

Born in the small town of Erasbach, Bavaria, in 1714, Christoph Willibald Gluck was determined to become a musician, despite opposition from his father, who was a forester for the Bohemian nobility. At the age of 13, he ran away to Prague, surviving by singing and playing the Jew's harp.

In his early twenties, Gluck went via Vienna to Milan, where he composed his earliest opera, *Artaserse* (1741). Its success prompted further works in the then fashionable genre of *opera seria*. After visiting London (where he met Handel) in 1745, Gluck settled in Vienna in 1752. That year, he composed his most boldly inventive *opera seria* to date, *La clemenza di Tito* (*The Clemency of Titus*) to a Metastasio libretto that was later set by Mozart.

## Increasing success

During the 1750s and early 1760s, Gluck also wrote on mythological themes for the imperial court, and composed several French *opéras comiques*. These culminated in *La Rencontre imprévue*, whose plot and Turkish harem setting influenced Mozart's *Die Entführung aus dem Serail*. But the two key events of these years were the revolutionary ballet *Don Juan* (1761) and the

opera *Orfeo ed Euridice* (1762), his first collaboration with the librettist Ranieri de' Calzabigi (see box, right), and a milestone in operatic history.

Then came two more operas whose classical plots and integration of solos, chorus, and ballet unified Gluck's and Calzabigi's dramatic principles. The aim of *Alceste* (1767)—according to its foreword—was to achieve "simplicity, truth, and naturalness" in form, plot, and language. In *Paride ed Elena* (1770), Gluck avowedly depicted "the different characters of two nations, Phrygia and Sparta, by

◁ **IPHIGENIE EN TAURIDE**
This is the title page of the first edition of Gluck's *Iphigénie en Tauride*, arguably the composer's finest work, which was published in Paris in May 1779.

contrasting the rude, savage nature of the one [Sparta] with all that is delicate and soft in the other."

The last years of Gluck's career centered on Paris. Beginning with *Iphigénie en Aulide* (premiered in 1774), he applied his revolutionary dramatic principles to a series of powerful works for the Parisian stage: an expanded version of *Orfeo* as *Orphée et Eurydice* (1774) and a radical French reworking of *Alceste* (1776). This was followed by the romantically colored *Armide* (1777) and *Iphigénie en Tauride* (1779), arguably his supreme masterpiece, and, like *Orfeo*, a key influence on Mozart's *Idomeneo*.

Gluck's final French opera, *Echo et Narcisse*, was a dismal failure. This was due in part to squabbling claques (the supporters of Gluck versus those of the Italian Niccolò Piccinni) and because Gluck's French operas had accustomed his audiences to sterner stuff. In poor health, Gluck left Paris in October 1779 and spent his last years enjoying his wealth and fame in Vienna. He died, aged 73, in 1787.

◁ **ORPHEE ET EURYDICE**
In this rehearsal of Gluck's highly acclaimed opera, the Russian singer Dmitry Korchak (center), here playing Orphée, is shown surrounded by dancers of the ballet ensemble. The production was staged by US choreographer and director John Neumeier, under the musical direction of Alessandro De Marchi, and premiered in February 2019 at the Hamburg State Opera, Germany.

# Joseph Haydn

## 1732–1809, AUSTRIAN

Highly prolific, Haydn wrote more than a hundred symphonies and a host of chamber works that founded the Classical era in Western music. His works were a major influence on Mozart and more especially on Beethoven.

Franz Joseph Haydn was born in 1732 in the village of Rohrau, near the border between Austria and Hungary, the son of a wagonmaker and a cook. Neither of his parents was musically literate, but an uncle was responsible for the music at a church in the nearby town of Hainburg. At the age of five, Haydn was sent to live in this relative's house and join in the church music-making. There he was spotted by the choirmaster from Vienna's St. Stephen's Cathedral and recruited to the cathedral choir. From the age of eight, he endured the casual ill-treatment—poor food, frequent flogging—visited upon 18th-century choristers, but picked up valuable practical musical experience.

### From cathedral to street

By the age of 17, Haydn had lost the pure treble voice required of choirboys. An incident in which he allegedly cut off the pigtail of a fellow chorister was used as a pretext for his dismissal. Thrown out with only the clothes on his back, he survived as a busker, singing serenades on street corners.

From this unpromising start, with determination, luck, and irrepressible talent, he built a musical career. While scratching a living in Vienna, he taught himself the basics of composition from manuals and the study of other people's music, notably the keyboard works of C.P.E. Bach. Exploiting a chance encounter, he made himself a useful servant to Italian composer and teacher Nicola Porpora, receiving in return advice on composition and contacts with potential patrons among the aristocracy.

### Court life

Around the age of 27, Haydn secured his first full-time employment as musical director at the modest court of Count Ferdinand Maximilian von Morzin. It was for Count Morzin's small orchestra that he wrote his first symphonies. At last enjoying a regular income, he rushed into a marriage with Maria Anna Keller, the daughter of a hairdresser. The couple proved incompatible—Haydn had really been in love with Maria Anna's sister—and endured an acrimonious childless union, from which both sought relief with other lovers, until Maria Anna's death in 1800.

◁ **ST. STEPHEN'S CATHEDRAL**
Vienna's imposing cathedral, one of the city's most symbolic buildings, is where Joseph Haydn and his younger brother Michael served as choristers.

**The Esterházy princes**

The Esterházys were a Hungarian noble family, princes of the Holy Roman Empire, and among the largest landowners in Europe. They were loyal subjects of the Hapsburg emperors in Vienna, although often wealthier than the Hapsburgs themselves. Their Esterháza palace, begun in the 1760s, was on such a grand scale it was known as the "Hungarian Versailles." It earned Haydn's main patron, Prince Nikolaus Esterházy (1714–1790), the sobriquet "the Magnificent." Prince Nikolaus II (1765–1833) was also a patron of music, commissioning Beethoven's Mass in C in 1807, but the family's fortunes never recovered from his profligacy and debauchery.

NIKOLAUS I, WEARING THE UNIFORM OF HIS HUNGARIAN INFANTRY REGIMENT

▷ **JOSEPH HAYDN**
In this 18th-century portrait, Haydn is shown hard at work and elegantly dressed in clothes that suggest his considerable success. From humble beginnings, he built himself an impressive and lucrative career.

△ **ESTERHAZA PALACE**
In 1766–1790, Haydn lived in a four-room apartment in servant's quarters near the main Esterháza palace. The remoteness of the palace led to boredom among his musicians, but allowed Haydn time to develop his compositions.

In 1761, Haydn moved his services to a far grander establishment, the princely court of the Hungarian Esterházy family (see box, p.70). By 1766, he was the Esterházy's director of music, in control of an orchestra of more than 20 players—large for its time—and of an opera house at the newly built Esterháza palace. Technically he was only a senior palace servant, but he in fact enjoyed an enviable degree of independence. He was in effect permitted to use the court musicians as a testbed for his compositions and could, as he later said, "be as bold as I pleased." His only significant constraint was the need to write many pieces for the baryton (a now extinct instrument related to the cello), which Prince Nikolaus Esterházy liked to play.

▷ **BARYTON, c. 1720**
At the request of his employer, Haydn composed around 200 pieces (mostly trios) for the baryton, an instrument that had both plucked and bowed strings.

## Classical innovation

Haydn met the requirements of the court for operas and concerts to entertain the household and its guests, who sometimes included the Austrian empress, Maria Theresa. His operas are now largely forgotten, but the orchestral and chamber music he wrote at this time founded the Classical style in Western music. He established the four-movement symphony as the standard orchestral work and virtually invented the string quartet and piano trio. In his hands, formal musical structures, such as the sonata and rondo, revealed their rich potential for variety of expression and dramatic effect.

Later critics have identified a *Sturm und Drang* (storm and stress) period in his music of the early 1770s, allegedly reflecting a wider cultural turn toward troubled emotion. But Haydn did not fit the profile of an anguished Romantic; he was a man of sanguine temperament who peppered his works with musical jokes and surprises. He knew how to evoke grave sadness, gentle melancholy, and aching beauty, but his works always resolved into a bracing display of energy and joy in life.

## International reputation

Haydn labored in relative isolation at the Esterháza palace, but enjoyed mounting fame in the wider world as his works filtered into print. From 1779, the Esterházys allowed him to publish for his own profit and he began to write for the international market. His Paris symphonies, written in 1785–1786, were commissioned for performance in the French capital.

He was allowed to spend more time in Vienna, where he met Mozart, forming a relationship of mutual admiration and influence. Meanwhile court life was enhanced by a sexual liaison with a young Italian mezzo-soprano, Luigia Polzelli, carried on with the connivance of her husband.

In 1790, Prince Nikolaus Esterházy died and his successor, Prince Anton, was uninterested in maintaining an expensive musical establishment. Although still on the Esterházy payroll, Haydn found himself with

# KEY WORKS

**1761**
Writes Symphonies No. 6–8—his first trio of symphonies for the Esterházy court.

**1772**
Writes "Trauer" Symphony No. 44, in a more emotional style typical of his *Sturm und Drang* period.

**1781**
Begins writing works such as String Quartets Op. 33 for a music publisher rather than for his employer.

**1791–95**
Writes 12 symphonies, the "London" Symphonies No. 93–104, for his two visits to Britain.

**1796**
Writes the Trumpet Concerto, which will become his most popular concerto, for trumpet virtuoso Anton Weidinger.

**1798**
*The Creation*, the first of Haydn's two great oratorios, is performed in Vienna.

no orchestra and little to do. Musical impresario Johann Peter Salomon (see box, right) was eager to engage a composer whose work was famous but who had never been seen by the public. He enlisted Haydn for a series of concerts in London in 1791.

## Triumph in London

Haydn's arrival in music-mad London caused "a great sensation." He was wined and dined, met the king, went to the races, received an honorary doctorate from Oxford University, and conducted a romance with a widow, Rebecca Schröter. His concerts, for which he wrote six new symphonies, were a triumph. Known today as his "London" Symphonies, they are among his best-loved works. Haydn

went again to England, in 1794–1795, composing six more symphonies for the occasion. The London concerts were a success financially as well as musically. He was now a wealthy man.

The accession of a new Esterházy prince, Nikolaus II, in 1794 led to a partial resumption of Haydn's duties. He produced a series of Masses and in 1797 wrote a patriotic anthem for the Austrian Empire, then engaged in desperate warfare against the armies of the French Revolution. Partly through the influence of the young Beethoven, Haydn explored new musical territory. Composed in 1797–1798, his final set of string quartets, Op. 76, and his last piano trios exceed any of his previous chamber works in intensity and expressive range.

Two oratorios, *The Creation* (1798) and *The Seasons* (1801), formed the climax of his creative life. Inspired by Handel's oratorios that Haydn had seen in London, they set libretti by Gottfried van Swieten (based respectively on the Book of Genesis and the poetry of James Thomson). *The Creation* in particular inspired fervent enthusiasm in its audiences. It was given more than 80 performances in Haydn's lifetime, both in Vienna and abroad.

Aging and ill, Haydn retired in 1802. His last appearance was at a performance of *The Creation* given in his honor in 1808. He died the following year in Vienna. His final days were not peaceful, coinciding with a major defeat of his beloved Austria by French forces in the Napoleonic Wars.

### IN PROFILE
### Johann Peter Salomon

Born in Bonn, German musician Johann Salomon (1745–1815) was the son of an oboist. He moved to London in 1781, becoming a leading figure in the city's musical life as an admired violinist, composer, and conductor. He is most remembered, however, as the musical impresario who brought Haydn to Britain in the 1790s. He was later one of the founders of the Royal Philharmonic Society, which created the first permanent orchestra in London in 1813. He is buried in Westminster Abbey.

JOHANN PETER SALOMON, THOMAS HARDY, 1790–1792

◁ **VIENNA BOMBARDED**
During Haydn's terminal illness in May 1809, French troops besieging Vienna bombarded the district where he lived with explosive shells. By the time the composer died on the last day of the month, the French had occupied the city.

## "**God** has bestowed **a talent** upon me and **I thank him** for it. "

JOSEPH HAYDN, c. 1800

# Joseph Bologne

## 1745–1799, FRENCH

A virtuoso violinist and composer, Joseph Bologne, also known as Chevalier de Saint-Georges, was the first European of African descent to receive widespread praise for concertos, symphonies, and operas.

Joseph Bologne was born to George Bologne, a wealthy planter on the island of Guadeloupe in the French Caribbean, and Nanon, an enslaved Senegalese woman. Shortly after Joseph's birth, his father was wrongly accused of murder, prompting him to flee to France with his family, including Nanon and Joseph. George adopted the surname "de Saint-Georges," but the nobility it implied was not officially bestowed until 1757.

At the age of 13, Joseph showed exceptional talent in fencing, honing his skills under Parisian fencing master Nicolas Texier La Boëssière. At the end of his training, he earned the title *Gendarme de la Garde du Roi* (King's Guard), was nicknamed "Chevalier" (Knight), and entered French high society.

### Musical achievements

In addition to displaying dazzling skills as a swordsman, Bologne excelled in music. Pursuing a musical career, he received training from composers such as François-Joseph Gossec and Antonio Lolli, becoming the leader of Gossec's orchestra, the Concert des Amateurs (*amateurs* here meaning music lovers), in 1769. Three years later, Bologne debuted as a solo violinist, captivating audiences with his virtuosic playing of his first two violin

concertos. Initially, Bologne composed mainly instrumental works, but later focused on vocal works.

In 1776, King Louis XVI was on the verge of making Bologne director of the Paris Opéra, but four singers delivered a racially motivated petition to Queen Marie Antoinette disputing the appointment of "a mulatto." The king nationalized the opera to avoid scandal, and halted the appointment. Undeterred, Bologne became music director at the home theater of Madame de Montesson, wife of the Duc d'Orléans, and was also put in charge of her husband's hunting estate. Following two successful opera

◁ **SIX QUARTETS**
Bologne wrote 18 string quartets (three sets of six), including Six Quartetto Concertans, written in 1777. His string quartets are considered his finest work and helped popularize the musical form in France.

premiers at estate theaters, he founded the Concert de la Loge Olympique in 1781. Here, he commissioned Joseph Haydn's Paris symphonies at the request of cellist Claude-François-Marie Rigoley, the Comte d'Ogny.

### Military role and politics

In 1788, Bologne joined the *Société des Amis des Noirs* (the Society of the Friends of the Blacks), dedicated to stopping French involvement in the slave trade. At the same time, he served as a commissioned colonel in the revolutionary French National Guard, and in 1792 was appointed commander of a legion of "citizens of color." A year later, during the period of the French Revolution known as the "Reign of Terror," he was accused of misconduct and imprisoned for 18 months, but he eventually cleared his name. After his release, he petitioned in vain to regain his regimental station. Tragically, he died in 1799 due to problems with an ulcerated bladder.

### ON TECHNIQUE
#### The Tourte bow

Bologne's style of writing in his first two violin concertos pushed the instrument to its limits and involved some extended techniques. These feats, and the range of expression they created, were made possible by the development of the Tourte bow.

Invented and refined through a collaboration of former watchmaker François Tourte and Italian violin virtuoso Giovanni Battista Viotti between 1785 and 1790, the new style of bow intentionally moved away from the traditional method of constructing bows from simply cutting the appropriate wood and using heat to bend it to the desired shape. These new bows were noticeably heavier and included a screw at the frog that allowed the player to adjust the bow hairs to the desired tension. In addition, a small "spreader block" flattened the hairs to prevent them from tangling. Seized upon by violin virtuosos at the time, the Tourte bow is the standard violin bow to this day.

**MODERN VIOLIN BOW**

> "[Saint-Georges] is the most **accomplished man in Europe** in Riding, Running, Shooting, **Fencing**, Dancing, **Musick**."
>
> JOHN ADAMS, US STATESMAN, 1799

▷ **JOSEPH BOLOGNE**
In 1787, Bologne was invited to London, where he gave fencing demonstrations. Impressed by his superb skills, the Prince of Wales commissioned this portrait of Bologne by American artist Mather Brown.

# Muzio Clementi

## 1752–1832, ANGLO-ITALIAN

Hailed as the father of the pianoforte, Clementi was one of Europe's
most influential musicians. He is best known for his sonatas for piano
and was a key figure in the development of the form.

Born in Rome to a humble family in 1752, Muzio Clementi studied music from an early age. By 1766, aged 14, he was an organist at the church of San Lorenzo in Damaso, Rome. Later that year, his keyboard skills were spotted by a wealthy English traveler to Rome, Sir Peter Beckford, who took the talented young musician to his estate in Dorset, England.

Here, in rural isolation and under Beckford's sponsorship, Clementi spent the next seven years practicing harpsichord and studying music. His Six Sonatas for the Harpsichord or Pianoforte, Op. 1, date from this period.

## London and abroad

In 1774, aged 22 and now free of his seven-year indenture with Beckford, Clementi moved to London, where he worked initially as a "keyboard conductor" at the King's Theatre. In 1779, he published his Three Sonatas, Op. 2, which are widely considered to have been a major breakthrough in keyboard-writing—his reputation as a dazzling composer-performer grew. Success inspired him to embark on a promotional tour of France, Germany, and Austria—this was the first of

many visits to Europe. In Vienna, he was honored in 1781 with an invitation from Emperor Joseph II to play at the imperial court, where he met Mozart (see box, right).

After 1781, on his return to his home base in London, Clementi's focus turned from the harpsichord to a newly invented instrument, the piano. In 1782, Clementi's Three Piano Sonatas, Op. 40, boosted his career as a composer-performer. By his early thirties he was famous in Europe, reaching his professional peak between 1785 and 1790,

◁ *GRADUS AD PARNASSUM*
This is the title page of the Offenbach edition (c. 1870) of Clementi's *Gradus ad Parnassum, or The Art of Playing the Piano* (1817–1826).

the year in which his innovative Sonata in F-sharp minor, Op. 25, No. 5, appeared—introducing, in parts, a slower, more introspective mood into the music of the period.

With a shrewd eye to a potentially lucrative market, in 1798 Clementi invested in a music publishing and piano manufacturing company, known as Clementi & Co. from 1800, which proved immensely successful.

## A life dedicated to the piano

Clementi's practical treatise *The Introduction to the Art of Playing on the Piano Forte* was published under his own imprint in 1801 and went on to appear in various languages and with several reprints. Clementi was also famous as a teacher and as cofounder, in 1813, of the Philharmonic Society of London, which, a century later, became the Royal Philharmonic Society. He is, however, probably best known for his monumental studies for piano technique, *Gradus ad Parnassum*, which was published in three volumes between 1817 and 1826.

Clementi wrote more than 50 sonatas and numerous other keyboard works, six symphonies, and two overtures, as well as chamber music, vocal works, and a piano concerto. With his tremendous originality, his whirlwind keyboard runs, and the formidable technical complexity of his work, he was hailed as the first true piano virtuoso. Clementi married three times and is thought to have had four children. He died in March 1832, after a brief illness, and was buried at Westminster Abbey in London.

EMPEROR JOSEPH II (DETAIL), ANTON VON MARON, 1775

△ **A CLEMENTI SQUARE PIANO**
This square piano was made in 1813 by Clementi's flourishing piano manufacturing company, Clementi & Co., which was active until 1830. Clementi pianos have a reputation for being a joy to play—highly responsive and with a light touch.

# Wolfgang Amadeus Mozart

## 1756–1791, AUSTRIAN

Mozart is a towering figure in Western classical music. He died at the age of 35, having composed in his short life more than 600 works, including 22 operas, 23 piano concertos, and 41 symphonies.

Wolfgang Amadeus Mozart was born in Salzburg on January 27, 1756. His father, Leopold, was employed as a musician at the court of Salzburg's ruling prince-archbishop. Leopold was a competent composer who attained some renown as the author of a manual on violin technique, but the family was both short of money and low in status, living in a rented apartment above a grocery shop.

### Musical prodigy

Wolfgang Amadeus was the seventh and last child in the family, and the second to survive. His sister Maria Anna, known as Nannerl, was four years his senior. Taught by their father, both children proved exceptionally gifted, but Wolfgang exceeded his sister in talent and precocity. He could play pieces on the keyboard at the age of four and created his first simple compositions at age five. Realizing that his son was a prodigy, Leopold embarked on a campaign to exploit the opportunity this presented for immediate financial gain and for the child's longer-term success in life.

◁ **WOLFGANG AMADEUS MOZART**
This posthumous portrait was made in 1819 by Viennese painter Barbara Krafft. Mozart's sister, Nannerl, thought it to be a good likeness of the composer.

In 1762, the Mozarts set off on the first of a series of show tours that were to continue for more than a decade. Leopold took both children to perform in Munich and then in Vienna, where they were exhibited to the formidable Austrian Hapsburg empress Maria Theresa at the Schönbrunn Palace. Showing a disregard for social distances that was to last through his life, Wolfgang spontaneously kissed the empress. Royals, nobles, and ambassadors were suitably impressed by the children's precocious musical skills but, whether because of Wolfgang's inappropriate embrace or Leopold's upstart pushiness, they did not win the empress's patronage.

### Tours and triumphs

Returning to Salzburg in 1763, Leopold was promoted to deputy master of the chapel at the prince-archbishop's court and immediately took another, longer leave of absence. The family traveled to Paris, where the children performed in front of the

△ **FIRST VIOLIN**
Mozart's first violin was a workmanlike instrument made in Salzburg in the 1740s by Andreas Ferdinand Mayr, luthier to the archbishop's court and a musician colleague of Leopold Mozart.

### IN CONTEXT
### Salzburg

In Mozart's day, the city of Salzburg was ruled by its archbishop as an independent state, although it was part of the wider Hapsburg-ruled Holy Roman Empire, with its capital at Vienna. With a population of less than 20,000, the city supported elaborate court and ecclesiastical life and was embellished with fine Baroque architecture. Despite its many splendors, Mozart despised Salzburg as a backwater, deriding its court musicians as "coarse, slovenly, dissolute." In 1803, the city lost its independence and eventually became part of Austria.

**SALZBURG BENEATH THE GREEN DOMES OF ITS BAROQUE CATHEDRAL**

> " The **poor little fellow** plays marvelously, he is a child of **spirit, lively, charming ...** "

COUNT KARL VON ZINZENDORF, ON MOZART AT AGE SIX, 1762

△ **FAMILY GROUP**
A 1781 painting by the Austrian artist Johann Nepomuk della Croce shows Leopold Mozart holding a violin, with his children Wolfgang and Nannerl seated at the piano. A portrait of their deceased mother hangs on the wall.

French king Louis XV, and then on to London, where they stayed for over a year in 1764–1765, giving many public concerts. They were befriended by composer Johann Christian Bach, a son of Johann Sebastian Bach who was a prominent figure on London's music scene. J.C. Bach's lucid but dramatic and emotional compositional style was to be a major influence on Mozart's development.

Back in Salzburg from late 1766, the family made another foray to Vienna only nine months later, again in search of elusive imperial patronage. The family's constant journeying, mostly by coach on poor quality roads, was arduous and hazardous. Both of the children contracted serious illnesses, Wolfgang coming close to dying of rheumatic fever in 1767. Moreover, the costs of travel and lodging used up much of the money gained from public performances. But Leopold's will and ambition were implacable—the second journey to Vienna had been undertaken despite a smallpox epidemic gripping the city.

Mozart's last tours as a paraded prodigy were three circuits of Italy with his father between 1770 and 1773. The first was triumphant: he was made a member of the musical academy in Bologna; in Rome the pope created him a knight of the Golden Spur; and he wrote an Italian opera, *Mitridate, re di Ponto*, which was staged in Milan just before he turned 15. However, his second two visits to Italy were met with less enthusiasm; by 1773, he was simply too old to be marketed as a prodigy.

"**Music** should **never be painful** to the ear but should **flatter** and **charm** it. "

MOZART, LETTER TO HIS FATHER, SEPTEMBER 26, 1781

# "[His works] are **clear**, **transparent**, and **joyful as a spring** ... "

WANDA LANDOWSKA, ON MOZART

Wolfgang had been accorded the post of concert master at the Salzburg prince-archbishop's court at age 13 and his stipend—together with that of his father—enabled the family to move into better accommodations. They became celebrities in the town in which many of Mozart's new compositions were performed. However, the accession of a new prince-archbishop, who was less well disposed toward music, made their position at court more precarious.

## An independent spirit

In 1778, at his father's urging, Mozart again embarked on his travels in search of wealthy patronage. Leopold stayed in Salzburg, worried he might lose his post if he went away again, and Mozart was instead accompanied by his mother. In Paris—a foreign city in which they were friendless and isolated—disaster struck: Mozart's mother died of a sudden illness. His father irrationally blamed Wolfgang, who returned to Salzburg. From this point, Mozart became set on escaping from his father's controlling influence.

Mozart's personality, warped by the adulation he had received as a child, lacked the balance and elevated qualities found in his music. He had many affairs with young women and his letters display a scatological sense of humor. He was tactlessly arrogant and never troubled to conceal his sense of superiority. Being treated as a paid servant—the effective status of a musician at that time—made him furious. In 1781, after a row with a Salzburg court official and Mozart's subsequent dismissal with an undignified kick in the behind for his insolence, he decided to try to make his living in Vienna as a freelance composer, piano performer, and music teacher.

## Marriage and finances

Having lost his regular income, Mozart compounded his financial worries by marrying a woman without money. He had been pursuing Aloysia Weber, a soprano who was the daughter of a poor bass player. When she jilted him, he turned his attention to her younger sister Constanze. Under pressure from

the Weber family, who threatened him with legal action, in 1782 he formalized the liaison. Children soon followed—Constanze eventually bore six offspring, of whom two survived infancy. The marriage was a success emotionally but placed demands on Mozart's finances that were often hard to meet.

△ **MITRIDATE, RE DI PONTO**
This page of sheet music for Mozart's early opera dates from its first performance in 1770. The work was a huge success at the Milan carnival and was given a further 21 performances— a powerful endorsement of the composer's talent.

---

## IN CONTEXT
### Freemasonry

**Freemasonry was fashionable in the 18th century. Aristocrats and royalty became Masons. Mozart was admitted to a Masonic lodge in 1784 and his late opera *The Magic Flute* allegedly contains Masonic symbolism and expresses Masonic ideals of universal brotherhood. From the late 18th century, Catholics and monarchists in Europe came to view the Masons as a dangerous organization, subversive of the authority of the Church and kings. It is not known whether it had such political significance for Mozart.**

**MASONIC INITIATION WITH MOZART SEATED ON THE FAR LEFT**

△ **CONSTANZE MOZART, 1802**
A portrait by Danish painter Hans Hansen depicts Mozart's wife. The composer's marriage brought him happiness but also his father's strong disapproval.

## KEY WORKS

**1778**
Symphony No. 31 ("Paris" Symphony) is first performed in public during Mozart's second visit to Paris.

**1782**
The German-language opera *Die Entführung aus dem Serail* is a major success when first staged in Vienna.

**1784–86**
Writes 12 piano concertos in three years, including the dramatic Concerto No. 24.

**1785**
Six Mozart string quartets dedicated to Haydn are published.

**1786**
Mozart's most famous comic opera, *The Marriage of Figaro*, is performed at the Burgtheater in Vienna.

**1787**
*Don Giovanni*, Mozart's serio-comic masterpiece, is staged for the first time in Prague.

**1788**
Composes his last three major orchestral works, Symphonies No. 39 to 41, between June and August.

**1791**
His final opera, *The Magic Flute*, premieres three months before his death.

### △ *IDOMENEO*, FIRST PRINT, 1781

Mozart's *Idomeneo*, perhaps his greatest "serious opera," tells of King Idomeneo's promise to Neptune, god of the sea, to sacrifice the first person he sees in return for safe passage over the ocean. The first person Idomeneo sees is his very own son, Idamante—but in a change of heart, Neptune agrees to spare him if Idomeneo gives up his throne to the young man.

### ▽ PRAGUE PIANO

During his visits to Prague, Mozart is believed to have stayed at Bertramka, home of the Czech composer František Dušek. It is likely that he played this piano at the house, and may have composed parts of *Don Giovanni* on the instrument.

### Creative intensity

In the first half of the 1780s, Mozart's compositional output flourished. After his opera *Idomeneo* was a success in Munich in 1781, he wrote the German-language *Singspiel* (opera with dialogue) *Die Entführung aus dem Serail* for performance at Vienna's Burgtheater, an institution sponsored by Maria Theresa's successor, Emperor Joseph II. Opening in 1782, *Die Entführung* proved a major triumph. It tells the story of the hero Belmonte's attempt to rescue his beloved Constanze from a harem. Mozart's other works in this fruitful period include some of his finest piano concertos, a notable series of six string quartets dedicated to Haydn, and two of his best-known symphonies, the "Haffner" (1782) and the "Linz" (1783).

After a lengthy search for the right follow-up to *Die Entführung*, Mozart found his ideal librettist in the Italian poet Lorenzo da Ponte (see box, above). The result was *Le nozze di Figaro* (*The Marriage of Figaro*). First performed in the Burgtheater in 1786, it raised opera to a new level with the realism of its characterization subtly expressed in music. A tale of class and sexual politics, *Le nozze* chimed with Mozart's rebellion against aristocratic arrogance. It was very well received, but failed to match the success of *Die Entführung* in Mozart's lifetime.

In 1787, Mozart made his first visit to Prague, a city that took him to its heart. His second collaboration with da Ponte, *Don Giovanni*, was written for performance at Prague's Estates Theatre, where it premiered in October. Performances in Vienna followed in 1788, although Emperor Joseph was again worried by the complexity of the music, which he declared "too difficult for the singers."

### Late works

When Leopold Mozart died in May 1787, Wolfgang's compositional powers were at their peak. The three great symphonies he wrote in the summer of 1788 (Nos. 39, 40, and 41)

### IN PROFILE
### Lorenzo da Ponte

The librettist for three of Mozart's finest operas, da Ponte was born of Jewish parents in Venice in 1749. After converting to Catholicism, he was ordained a priest in 1773 and became a poet. By 1785, when he first worked with Mozart, he held a post at the imperial court in Vienna. In total, he wrote the libretti for 28 operas by 11 composers, including Mozart. In the 1790s, he migrated first to Britain and then to the US. Settled in New York, he became the first professor of Italian literature at Columbia College and opened the city's first opera house. He died in New York in 1838.

LORENZO DA PONTE, 1759

were the crowning achievement of his orchestral writing. The comic opera *Così fan tutte*, first staged in 1790, completed his trio of successful collaborations with da Ponte. *La clemenza di Tito*, a rapidly written *opera seria*, was performed in Prague in 1791 as part of the official celebrations of the coronation of a new emperor, Leopold II.

Although sometimes seriously short of ready money, Mozart was a star in the musical firmament and had no reason to despair of future patronage. His last completed masterpiece,

*Die Zauberflöte* (*The Magic Flute*), premiered at a popular suburban Viennese theater in September 1791. It was a triumph, drawing impressive crowds.

### Death and legacy

Mozart was at work on a Requiem Mass, commissioned by an Austrian aristocrat, when a fever confined him to bed. He died on December 5, 1791, hastened to the tomb by the fatal attentions of ignorant doctors. His burial followed the common custom of his time and place—a shared,

unmarked grave and no mourners. Fanciful accounts of Mozart's death began appearing soon after the event, but no evidence exists to support such fantasies as his alleged poisoning by court musician and jealous rival Antonio Salieri. His music surged in popularity after his death and was a major influence on Beethoven, among many others. In the Romantic period, his music partially fell out of favor but his standing revived in the 20th century. On his bicentenary in 1991, he was hailed by many commentators as the greatest composer of all time.

△ **BURGTHEATER, VIENNA**
Created in 1741 by the Hapsburg empress Maria Theresa, the Burgtheater was directly connected to her home in the Hofburg Palace. Three of Mozart's operas premiered at the theater, which moved to larger premises in 1888.

" **Death** is the **key** which **unlocks the door** to our **true happiness**. "

MOZART, LETTER TO HIS FATHER

# Directory

## Girolamo Frescobaldi

### 1583–1643, ITALIAN

Frescobaldi was one of the first great keyboard virtuosos (he played organ and harpsichord, as well as being a fine singer) and the first eminent composer to focus on music for an unaccompanied keyboard. He was born in Ferrara and spent most of his career in Rome, where he was organist at St. Peter's for most of the period from 1608 until his death (he had an interlude working at the Medici court in Florence from 1628 to 1634). During his lifetime, he was internationally famous, and his music continued to be admired and influential for several decades afterward (it was, for example, studied by the young J.S. Bach some 60 years later). His style was lively and inventive, often showing dramatic changes of tempo. In addition to keyboard works, he wrote sacred and secular vocal music and compositions for instrumental ensembles.

**KEY WORKS:** *Toccate e partite... libro primo* (*First Book of Toccatas and Partitas*), 1615; *Ego sum panis vivus* (*I Am the Living Bread* [vocal]), 1621; *Fiori musicali* (*Musical Flowers* [a collection of sacred organ music]), 1635

## ▷ Heinrich Schütz

### 1585–1672, GERMAN

More than anyone else, Schütz put German music on the map, giving it an importance that it had never previously enjoyed and establishing high intellectual and technical standards that became characteristic of the country's composers. He spent most of his long career at the court in Dresden, but he also worked elsewhere in Germany and he made two lengthy visits to Venice and two to Copenhagen. His large output (there are more than 500 surviving works) is highly varied. Most of his music is religious, but he also wrote, for example, the first German opera, *Dafne* (1627), although this does not survive. His early work was much influenced by the ornate style of Italian music, but it became a lot more austere, probably in part because the devastation caused by the Thirty Years War (1618–1648) discouraged extravagance in the arts.

**KEY WORKS:** *Psalmen Davids* (*Psalms of David*), 1619; *Symphoniae sacrae 1* (*Sacred Symphonies, Book One*), 1629; *Musikalische Exequien* (*Funeral Music*), 1636; *Historia der Geburt Jesu Christi* (*Story of the Birth of Jesus Christ*, popularly known as *Weihnachtshistorie*, *Christmas Story*), 1660

△ **HEINRICH SCHÜTZ, c.1650**

## Isabella Leonarda

### 1620–1704, ITALIAN

At the age of 16, Isabella Leonarda, a member of a local aristocratic family, entered a convent in Novara, northwest Italy, where she spent the rest of her life. During this period of almost 70 years she became head of the convent and one of the leading female composers of her time, with about 200 works to her credit. They are mainly sacred vocal works of various kinds, but she also wrote secular instrumental pieces, including a set of four sonatas that are thought to be the first sonatas ever published by a woman (the majority of her work was published in handsome editions during her lifetime, mainly in Bologna but also sometimes in Milan and Venice). Leonarda confined her composing to periods allocated to rest so that it did not distract her from her normal duties as a nun.

**KEY WORKS:** *Ave suavis dilectio* (*Hail, Sweet Love*), 1676; *Ave Regina caelorum* (*Hail, Queen of Heaven*), 1684; *Sonata for Solo Violin and Continuo*, 1693

## Dieterich Buxtehude

### c.1637–1707, DANISH-GERMAN

The date and exact place of Buxtehude's birth are uncertain. Reflecting the complex, shifting political geography of the time, he is sometimes described as Danish and sometimes as German. His early career was spent in what is now Denmark, and from 1668 until his death he held the highly prestigious post of organist at the Marienkirche (St. Mary's Church) in Lübeck (now in Germany), a huge and wealthy church with an outstanding musical tradition. In effect, he was music director for the whole city. He was acclaimed as one of the greatest organists of his time and his compositions for the instrument form the most important body of such work before those of

J.S. Bach. Buxtehude also wrote a good deal of sacred (and some secular) vocal music and instrumental music for various combinations of instruments, mainly strings.

**KEY WORKS:** *Membra Jesu nostri* (*The Limbs of our Jesus* [oratorio]), 1680; Seven Trio Sonatas (for violin, viola da gamba, and harpsichord), 1696; *Passacaglia in D minor*, c.1690–1700

## Marc-Antoine Charpentier

1643–1704, FRENCH

Charpentier spent most of his life in Paris, where he enjoyed a busy and varied career. The bulk of his large output is devoted to sacred music, which he wrote for churches, convents, and private patrons, notably Marie of Lorraine, Duchess of Guise (known as Mademoiselle de Guise), who was devoted to both religion and music. These works include Masses, psalm settings, and various other types of composition. Charpentier also wrote chamber music and work for the stage, sometimes in collaboration with the great dramatist Molière. His most famous composition today is the majestic, uplifting instrumental prelude to his *Te Deum*. This work was lost until 1953, but the year after its rediscovery the prelude was adopted as the theme music of the European Broadcasting Union, used to precede programs such as the Eurovision Song Contest.

**KEY WORKS:** *Mass for Four Choirs*, c.1670–1675; *The Denial of St. Peter* (oratorio) c.1680–1700; *Andromeda* (music for Pierre Corneille's play), 1682; *Te Deum*, c.1692

## Johann Pachelbel

1653–1706, GERMAN

One of the leading German musicians of his time, Johann Pachelbel was distinguished as an organist and

△ **THOMAS ARNE, c.1760**

teacher as well as a composer. He was born and died in Nuremberg, but he also worked in a number of other places in Germany and Austria, including Erfurt, Stuttgart, and Vienna, and his reputation as an organist was such that he was offered—but declined—a post in Oxford. In addition to his notable organ compositions, Pachelbel's large output includes chamber music, pieces for harpsichord, and vocal works of various kinds. Following his death in 1706, he was little known except to musical scholars, and he did not achieve widespread fame until the 1970s, when his serene but joyous *Canon in D major* became a surprise hit, being recorded again and again, featuring as background music in film and television, and inspiring adaptations in pop music.

**KEY WORKS:** *Canon and Gigue for 3 Violins and Basso Continuo* (*Canon in D major*), c.1680–1690; *Musicalische Ergötzung* (*Musical Delight* [collection of chamber music]), c.1691; *Hexachordum Apollinis* (*Six Strings of Apollo* [arias for organ or harpsichord]), 1699

## Tomaso Albinoni

1671–1751, ITALIAN

Albinoni was Vivaldi's leading contemporary among Venetian composers and almost as prolific. He is believed to have written about 80 operas (although few of them have survived in complete form), which he successfully staged in Venice over a period of almost half a century—a remarkable

achievement at a time of rapidly changing fashions, and a reflection of his gift for appealing melody. They also won acclaim outside Italy. Albinoni's other works include numerous concertos (notably for oboe) and sonatas (likewise internationally successful in his time) and some church music. Curiously, the piece most closely associated with his name—the dreamily mellifluous "Albinoni's Adagio"—is not actually by him. In 1958, the musicologist Remo Giazotto published an Adagio in G minor as a work that was based on a supposed fragment of manuscript by Albinoni, but it is now thought to be almost entirely by Giazotto.

**KEY WORKS:** 12 Trio Sonatas (his first published works), 1694; *Pimpinone* (opera), 1708; Concerto in D minor for Oboe, 1722

## ◁ Thomas Arne

1710–1778, BRITISH

Although he wrote music of various types (including Masses—he was a Catholic), Arne specialized in work for the stage (his sister was an actress and his wife a singer). He had long associations with two major London theaters (Covent Garden and Drury Lane) and also with Vauxhall Gardens, a leading center of popular entertainment. His large output includes operas, oratorios, masques, and incidental music for plays. Much of his work is routine, but at his best he had a memorable gift for melody, as in his most famous piece, the stirring though now controversial song "Rule, Britannia!" It was originally part of Arne's patriotic masque *Alfred* (about Alfred the Great), but it quickly achieved an independent life. His other famous songs include "Where the Bee Sucks," sung by Ariel in Shakespeare's *The Tempest*.

**KEY WORKS:** *Comus*, 1738; *Alfred*, 1740; *Music for The Tempest*, 1740, *Artaxerxes*, 1762; *Love in a Village*, 1762

# EARLY 19th CENTURY

CHAPTER 3

# Luigi Cherubini
## 1760–1842, ITALIAN

A towering composer in his day, Cherubini is best known for his powerful operas and majestic sacred music. In 1814, he was awarded the Legion of Honor, France's highest tribute.

Luigi Cherubini was born in Florence in 1760 and began learning music at the age of six; by the time he was 13 years old, he was composing his own works. In 1778, aged 18, Cherubini began a three-year apprenticeship with Giuseppe Sarti in Bologna and Milan, where he learned counterpoint and dramatic composition. His first opera, *Quinto Fabio*, appeared in 1780 and led to opera commissions throughout Italy. Then, in 1784, he was contracted as a house composer at the King's Theatre in London, where he presented four operas, the first of which was *Demetrio* (premiered 1785).

### A major move
The following year Cherubini moved to Paris, where he was to remain for the rest of his life. During his first six years in the capital, he shared an apartment with the violinist Giovanni Battista Viotti, who introduced him to Queen Marie Antoinette and to leading musicians of the day. His first commission for the Paris Opéra was *Démophon* (1788), written the year before the French Revolution brought turmoil to the city (see box, right).

Cherubini soon became a major figure in Paris—as a conductor and teacher as well as a composer. His works of the revolutionary period were often somber and austere. But in 1791

his *Lodoïska*, a form of *opéra comique*, premiered at the Théâtre Feydeau in Paris. Mixing comic and serious themes, and featuring ordinary people, its depiction of heroism captured the revolutionary spirit and was an early example of "rescue opera" (here, the heroine is rescued from a castle by a servant). Outstandingly popular, it became his first international success, securing more than 200 performances in the first year alone and inspiring Beethoven's opera *Fidelio* (1805).

Following the storming of Paris's Tuileries Palace in August 1792, Cherubini moved to Rouen. On his return to the French capital in 1794, he married Anne-Cécile Tourette; the couple had three children. Three years later, he produced *Médée*, or *Medea*, his most famous work, and in 1800 another immense success, *Les Deux Journées*—based on an event during the so-called Reign of Terror, when revolutionaries took over the government—which was popular throughout the 19th century.

In 1806, after a year-long stay in Vienna for work, Cherubini fell into a deep depression and, turning away from composition, developed an interest in botany and painting. He resumed writing in 1808, but from 1816 composed mainly religious music, notably *Requiem in C minor* (1816)—praised by other musicians and played at Beethoven's funeral—and *Requiem in D minor* (1836).

In 1822, Cherubini became director of the Paris Conservatoire. He wrote his book *Cours de contrepoint et de fugue* in 1835. The composer died in Paris in 1842, aged 81, and was buried in Père Lachaise cemetery.

△ **SCORE OF *MEDEA*, FIRST EDITION**
Cherubini's opera *Medea* is a passionate and brutal revenge story based on a tragedy by Greek dramatist Euripides. The story focuses on Medea's terrifying plot against her husband, who has abandoned her. The first, 1797, edition of Cherubini's score is shown here.

◁ ***LUIGI CHERUBINI AND THE MUSE OF LYRIC POETRY*, 1842**
In Jean Auguste Dominique Ingres's allegorical portrait of his friend, a young muse towers above the weary octogenarian composer, whose tiny red bud of the ribbon of the Legion of Honor sings out from his somber black robes.

## IN CONTEXT
### Political background

During the turbulent revolutionary period, Cherubini was keen to hide his links with the Ancien Régime, but he was adept at navigating allegiances, seeming to align himself at times with revolutionaries, at other times with monarchists—in 1797, for example, he wrote a funeral cantata honoring a revolutionary hero, only to rework it in 1820 to honor a royalist. Cherubini would have been witness to major historical events such as the storming of the Bastille, the execution of Louis XVI, and the rise of Napoleon (with whom he had a rocky relationship). The return of monarchical rule in 1814 made his life much easier.

**EXECUTION OF LOUIS XVI OF FRANCE IN JANUARY 1793**

# Ludwig van Beethoven

## 1770–1827, GERMAN

Although stone deaf for years, Beethoven was a genius of the Classical era and a pioneer of the new Romantic age—his work, which bridges a gap between the two, includes nine symphonies and 32 piano sonatas.

Ludwig van Beethoven was born in 1770 in Bonn, Germany, then part of the Holy Roman Empire. His family was of Flemish origin—hence the "van" in his name. His father, Johann van Beethoven, was a chorister at the court of the archbishop elector of Cologne in Bonn, where Ludwig's grandfather had been musical director before him. Ludwig's talent was recognized and encouraged from an early age, his father imposing a draconian routine of lessons and practice. The young Ludwig excelled at the keyboard and performed in court music-making, but a half-hearted attempt by his father to promote him as a child prodigy failed.

### Travels to Vienna

Beethoven's family did not provide a secure emotional environment. His father was an unhappily married alcoholic who presided over failing family finances. But Beethoven nonetheless received plentiful support for his musical ambitions. The court organist, Christian Neefe, helped him with composition and arranged for his first work, *Nine Variations for Piano on a March*, to be published when he was only 12 years old. The archbishop elector sent Beethoven, aged 17, to Vienna to develop his talents. He probably took a few lessons with

Wolfgang Amadeus Mozart before his mother's death brought him back to Bonn to handle the family's affairs as his father's condition deteriorated.

### Romantic influences

Working as a musician at the Bonn court for five more years, Beethoven was drawn into the cultured social circle around Helene von Breuning, the widow of a senior official. There he was introduced to the literary and

philosophical ideas of nascent German Romanticism, with its belief in the transcendent value of art and the artist—a belief he took as his own and applied to the art of music. For the first time he experienced failure in love, hopelessly adoring Breuning's daughter Lorchen. He also made an important friend in the music-loving Viennese aristocrat Count Ferdinand von Waldstein, to whom Beethoven dedicated many works, including the

△ **BEETHOVEN HOUSE, BONN**
The composer's desk and belongings are preserved at the museum now occupying the house at Bonngasse 20, where Beethoven was born. Many other court musicians lived near the Beethovens.

## ON TECHNIQUE
### Beethoven's pianos

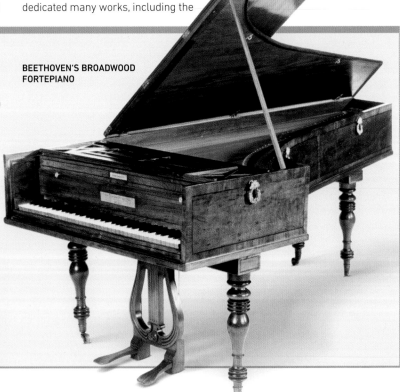

BEETHOVEN'S BROADWOOD FORTEPIANO

The pianoforte evolved significantly during Beethoven's lifetime. He began performing on five-octave pianos (which were different from modern pianos that span over seven octaves). These wood-framed instruments were delicate and lacked power and durability; they often broke under the stress of Beethoven's muscular high-octane playing. In 1803, he adopted an Erard piano because he admired the effects achieved by its "una corda" soft pedal. Later in Beethoven's life, pianos were made that were closer to his ideal, such as the six-and-a-half octave Broadwood sent to him from England by Thomas Broadwood, head of the company, in 1818. His last works exploited the full range of tone and pitch that such an instrument allows.

> "What is in **my heart** must **come out** and so I **write it down.**"
>
> LUDWIG VAN BEETHOVEN

▷ **LUDWIG VAN BEETHOVEN, 1820**
This work by Joseph Karl Stieler is one of many portraits of Beethoven, but reportedly the only one painted from live sittings with the composer.

△ **STRING QUARTETS**
The Takács Quartet performs the full cycle of Beethoven's 16 string quartets at Alice Tully Hall, New York, in 2005. Beethoven's quartets show his mastery of the Classical string quartet form.

"Waldstein" Piano Sonata. In 1790, Joseph Haydn visited Bonn. A plan was hatched for Beethoven to make another trip to Vienna to take lessons with Haydn in order, in Waldstein's words, to "receive Mozart's spirit from Haydn's hands." He set off in 1792.

However, before the year ended, Beethoven's father died and the French Revolutionary Wars put Bonn in a war zone (see box, p.94). In 1794, the French annexed the city and the archbishop elector's court was abolished. The small world in which Beethoven grew up had been erased while he flourished in Vienna.

The lessons with Haydn did not last long but, armed with introductions from Waldstein, Beethoven was patronized by some of the city's leading aristocratic music-lovers. Lodging at the palace of Prince Karl Lichnowsky, a patron of the arts in Vienna, the composer quickly won recognition as an outstanding piano virtuoso, giving performances in private salons and at public concerts

of the Vienna Philharmonic Society. Listeners were astonished by his extraordinary skills.

## Musical innovation

Beethoven's early compositions were predominantly piano works that he performed himself, but the publication of his Opus 1 Piano Trios in 1795 proved a commercial success and he was soon responding to a flood of commissions for new works from music publishers and aristocratic patrons. He wrote piano sonatas, including the famous "Pathétique" published in 1799; began composing string quartets from 1798; and in 1800 premiered his First Symphony at Vienna's Burgtheater. His music of this early period was still rooted

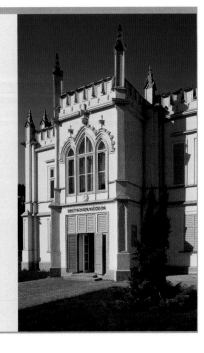

## IN PROFILE
### Josephine von Brunsvik

A countess from Hungary, Josephine von Brunsvik took piano lessons with Beethoven in 1799, shortly before her marriage to Count Joseph Deym. After the count's death in 1804, Beethoven expressed his love for Josephine in a series of passionate letters. In 1810, she married Estonian nobleman Cristoph von Stackelberg. The marriage soon broke up in mutual acrimony. Josephine was probably the "Immortal Beloved" referred to by Beethoven in a letter in 1811, and they may have met for the last time as late as 1816. After miserable final years of illness and isolation, Josephine died in 1821 aged 42.

**BRUNSVIK CASTLE NEAR BUDAPEST, HOME OF JOSEPHINE**

doctors. It was probably for her that he wrote the piano piece confusingly known as *Für Elise*. This infatuation also came to nothing.

### A peak of creativity

Between 1802 and 1812, Beethoven produced a stream of masterpieces that revealed his creative ambition. He never broke with the established Classical forms of the late 18th century—sonatas and rondos, symphonies and string quartets—but stretched them beyond all previous emotional and formal limits. His Third Symphony, the "Eroica," which premiered in 1805, is often taken as the initiation of a new musical era. It was far longer than any previous symphony, but also more complex, vigorous, and emotionally draining.

His expansion of the possibilities of orchestral writing continued with the tragic and triumphant Fifth Symphony (1808) and the irrepressibly energetic Seventh Symphony (1812). The three "Razumovsky" String Quartets of 1806 carried his new range and ambition into chamber music. For the piano, peaks included the "Waldstein" and "Appassionata" Sonatas (1804 and 1807) and the "Emperor" Concerto (1811). Although initial response to his works varied—his only opera, *Fidelio*, was coolly received in 1805—Beethoven benefited from the open-minded enthusiasm of his Viennese public and patrons.

### Fame and status

The first composer to think of himself as an artistic genius, Beethoven did not accept the lowly place in the social hierarchy traditionally accorded to even the most gifted musicians. In his dealings with the upper class, he bluntly refused to observe the usual deference and in 1806 had a violent quarrel with Prince Lichnowsky that ended their relationship. Yet, just like earlier composers, he continued to thrive on the generosity of the music-besotted liberal Viennese aristocracy. In 1808, a group of them clubbed together to provide him with a generous annuity— an income for life.

### Empire and revolution

Beethoven's staunchly independent attitude is often associated with the changes that were brought about by the French Revolution of 1789, which overthrew aristocratic and monarchical power in France. The "Eroica" Symphony was initially dedicated to Napoleon Bonaparte, the general of the Revolutionary armies; Beethoven erased this dedication when Napoleon declared himself emperor of the French in 1804, presumably because this assumption

△ **"MOONLIGHT" SONATA**
This score of Beethoven's Piano Sonata No. 14 is in the composer's own hand. It was later named the "Moonlight" Sonata after the German critic Ludwig Rellstab compared its first movement to the sight of moonlight reflected in Lake Lucerne.

▽ **THE MALFATTI FAMILY**
Therese Malfatti, shown seated at the piano surrounded by her family, was the object of Beethoven's affection around 1810. Some historians speculate that he proposed marriage to her.

in the past, showing the influence of both Mozart and Haydn, but it was already recognized by contemporaries as daringly innovative. Beethoven was also in demand as a music teacher, his famous pupils including Carl Czerny, who would later premiere two of his master's piano concertos. He was distressingly prone to falling in love with his female pupils, including Josephine von Brunsvik (see box, opposite), whom he taught from 1799, and Giulietta Guicciardi, to whom the "Moonlight" Sonata was dedicated in 1802. These were women of high birth, never likely to marry a piano teacher, however distinguished.

Around 1810, Beethoven courted Therese Malfatti, an Austrian musician and daughter of one of the composer's

"You who **think** or **say** that I am **malevolent**, **stubborn**, or **misanthropic**, how **greatly** do you **wrong** me! "

LUDWIG VAN BEETHOVEN, 1802

*NAPOLEON AT THE BATTLE OF AUSTERLITZ*, FRANCOIS GERARD, 1805

of an imperial throne was a betrayal of the principles of the Revolution. Yet Beethoven was no revolutionary republican. He also dedicated major works to Archduke Rudolf, a son of the emperor of Austria who was both his patron and his friend. In 1813, Beethoven wrote the patriotic *Wellington's Victory* (known as the

◁ **ARCHDUKE RUDOLF OF AUSTRIA**
Rudolf (1788–1831) was a nobleman and cardinal. He took lessons from Beethoven and became his friend and patron. Beethoven dedicated many works to him.

"Battle Symphony") to celebrate a victory of imperial Austria's British allies over the French in Spain.

## Deafness and isolation

It is a bitter irony that during this period of supreme musical achievement, Beethoven was losing his hearing. The medical reason for this is unknown. As early as 1802, he wrote that he was avoiding company because people might notice his deafness and that he felt "driven to despair." A series of quack treatments failed to alleviate his condition.

From around 1812, there was a sharp, but temporary, falling off in his creativity and he had to give up performance. By 1818, he could only converse in writing. The advance of

deafness led to increasing isolation and unstable behavior. Rooms in which he lived or worked degenerated into disorderly squalor. He was often described as ill-mannered, unkempt, and bad-tempered. After the death of his brother Kaspar in 1815, he became involved in a vicious dispute with his sister-in-law Johanna over the fate of his nine-year-old nephew, Karl. A custody battle in the courts lasted until 1820, with the child suffering long-term emotional damage.

## Late masterpieces

Despite his deafness, Beethoven delivered a glorious "late period" of innovative, intellectually demanding music. It was heralded by the "Hammerklavier" Sonata in 1818, one of the most technically and emotionally challenging works in the entire piano repertoire. Other masterpieces followed, including the three last piano sonatas, written between 1820 and 1822, and the

## KEY WORKS

**1795**
Beethoven's first commercially successful work, the Three Op. 1 Piano Trios, are published.

**1802**
Writes Piano Sonatas No. 16–18, a set of boldly experimental sonatas heralding his fertile "middle period."

**1805**
Symphony No. 3, "Eroica," receives its first public performance in Vienna.

**1806**
String Quartets Op. 59, the "Razumovsky" Quartets, are written for the Russian ambassador to Vienna.

**1808**
Symphony No. 5 is premiered in the same concert as the "Pastorale" Symphony No. 6.

**1812**
Writes the final masterpiece of his "middle period," Symphony No. 7.

**1818**
Piano Sonata No. 29, the mighty "Hammerklavier" Sonata, initiates Beethoven's "late period."

**1824**
Beethoven's choral Symphony No. 9 receives its triumphant first performance.

# "I shall **hear** in **heaven**."

LUDWIG VAN BEETHOVEN, REPORTED AS HIS LAST WORDS, MARCH 1827

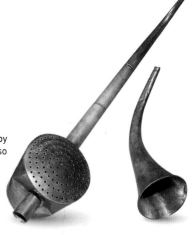

magnificent choral *Missa Solemnis*, completed in 1823. Part of the *Missa Solemnis* was performed at the same concert that premiered Beethoven's Ninth Symphony in Vienna in May 1824. Unprecedented orchestral forces had been assembled for the occasion, along with the choir and soloists for the symphony's last-movement setting of Friedrich Schiller's "Ode to Joy." The concert was a triumph, although Beethoven himself could hear neither the music nor the rapturous applause.

The reception of the Ninth Symphony showed the considerable status that Beethoven still enjoyed. However, he was no longer the composer of the moment—rather, a revered figure from the past. Even the most advanced connoisseurs were prone to dismiss his late string quartets, which were composed in the midst of terminal illness in 1825–1826, as incomprehensible. Nonetheless, these quartets would later come to be recognized as prophetic works of supreme power and invention.

▷ **HEARING AIDS**
Beethoven tried to mitigate his failing hearing using ear trumpets designed by his friend Johann Nepomuk Mälzel, also the inventor of the metronome.

After a long illness, Beethoven died in Vienna in March 1827. His funeral was attended by some 20,000 people. In an oration at Währing Cemetery, poet Franz Grillparzer said: "He whom you mourn is now among the greatest men of all time, unassailable for ever."

▽ **BEETHOVEN'S FUNERAL**
Thousands of admirers lined the streets of Vienna at the composer's funeral. Famous musicians, including Franz Schubert and Carl Czerny, served as pallbearers.

▷ **NICCOLO PAGANINI**
An anonymous portrait shows Paganini gaunt and with furrowed brow, wearing his trademark black suit. Chronic illness, for which he took lethal doses of mercury and opium, plagued much of his life. The composer was said to be a gambler (a habit learned from his father), on at least one occasion pawning his violin to pay off his debts; he was also an inveterate adulterer who, according to rumor, had been imprisoned for murdering one of his conquests.

# Niccolò Paganini

### 1782–1840, ITALIAN

A legendary, thrilling violinist-composer, Paganini was one of the most popular and radical musicians of his day. His success and increasing wealth sparked a passion for drinking, gambling, and womanizing.

◁ **THE FIRST TRIUMPH OF PAGANINI**
This painting by Annibale Gatti, c.1890, is thought to show the young composer at one of his performances at the court in Lucca at the start of the 19th century.

One of six children, Paganini was born in the port city of Genoa in 1782. His father, probably a dock worker, was an amateur musician who taught his son to play the mandolin and the guitar. By the age of eight, Niccolò was also learning to play the violin and composing his own work; he gave his first concert aged 11 and soon after this went on his first tour.

### Pursuit of fame and glory

Niccolò had studied violin briefly in Genoa; in Parma, the celebrated violinist Alessandro Rolla said the boy was so talented that there was little he could teach him. But Paganini's desire for fame was such that he subjected himself to a grueling routine, often practicing his own compositions on the violin for many hours a day.

In 1801, aged 19, Paganini began composing his *24 Caprices for Solo Violin* (not published until 1820)—which became his most celebrated work—and four years later accepted the post of music director for the princess of Lucca, Napoleon's sister.

He left the court appointment in 1809 to become a traveling solo performer-composer. His fame spread from the early 1800s, along with his reputation for adultery and indulging in drink.

In 1820 Paganini developed serious health issues, including a persistent cough, for which he was prescribed opium. Around three years later, syphilis was diagnosed (probably contracted when he was just 22), which was treated, according to him, with "murderous doses" of mercury—after which, his teeth loosened and eventually fell out, his eyesight and handwriting began to fail, and he suffered gastrointestinal problems as well as a host of other horrific maladies that worsened with age. But

▷ **THE "CANNON" VIOLIN**
Made by luthier Giuseppe Guarneri, this powerful violin was one of a magnificent collection of instruments owned by Niccolò Paganini.

in 1824, he fell in love with the singer Antonia Bianchi and the following year they had a son, Achille. The relationship lasted just four years; Antonia was handsomely paid off, and Achille stayed with his father.

### Success, wealth, and tragedy

That same year, 1828, aged 46, the composer set off on a European tour to Austria, Bohemia, Germany, France, and England. The shows were astonishing for the musician's energy, technical wizardry, and lightning-fast passages (Berlioz referred to him as a "comet")—by all accounts, he could play 12 notes a second and never followed sheet music. These sensational performances of his own works thrilled audiences, fueling speculation that he was in league with the devil (see box, right). But in 1834, ill health brought an end to his tours. He died in Nice six years later from throat cancer.

His fortune was left to Achille. Paganini revolutionized violin-playing and was particularly famous for radical techniques such as *spiccato* and left-hand pizzicato. Apart from his magnificent instrumental *24 Caprices*, his other compositions include chamber music (sonatas and guitar quartets) and orchestral music, with scores for mandolin and guitar as well as violin. Many of Paganini's works were not published until after his death in 1840.

### IN CONTEXT
### The devil myth

Paganini's breathtaking, almost superhuman virtuoso violin-playing led to the popular belief that he was "the devil's fiddler." A slick showman and astute businessman, the composer was quick to cultivate a demonic persona. Skeletal, with long hair, pale skin, sinewy hands, and sunken cheeks (exaggerated after losing his teeth in 1828), he would appear on stage dressed from head to toe in black, often with a single spotlight accentuating his bizarre appearance. Sometimes, he would ride in a black carriage drawn by black horses. The diabolic associations greatly boosted box-office sales. However, it has been claimed that Paganini's appearance and dexterity may have been partly due to Marfan and Ehlers-Danlos syndromes—conditions leading to long, thin limbs and joints and ultra-flexibility. Whatever the cause, such was the power of the myth that the Catholic Church refused to bury him.

**DAGUERREOTYPE, BELIEVED TO BE OF PAGANINI**

"This **Satan** who **ruled** over the **lush dreams** of the **female sex**. "
KLAUS KINSKI, IN HIS FILM *PAGANINI*, 1989

# Gioachino Rossini

## 1792–1868, ITALIAN

Dominating the first quarter of the 19th century, Rossini's operas enjoyed a long run of success, culminating in the magnificent *William Tell*. However, at the age of 37, Rossini retired and never wrote another opera.

Gioachino Rossini was born in Pesaro, on the northeastern coast of Italy. His parents were professional musicians: his father held the post of town trumpeter and played the horn in a local orchestra; his mother was a singer. Under their influence, Gioachino developed musical skills at a very early age. He had already started composing by the time he entered the *liceo musicale* (music college) in Bologna at the age of just 14.

### Early career

Before his voice broke, Rossini earned some money singing in churches and theaters, although composition remained his chief focus. By 1810, he had completed his first two-act operatic score, *Demetrio e Polibio* (premiered 1812). Later in 1810, he achieved the first public staging of one of his operas—*La cambiale di matrimonio* (*The Marriage Contract*), a one-act *farsa comica* (blend of farce and opera), which appeared at a small theater in Venice.

*La cambiale* was well received and this, coupled with further successes in the following years, convinced Rossini of his career path. He left the *liceo*, even though his tutors urged him to stay, and began churning out operas in rapid succession. By the age of 21, nine of his operas had been staged.

Rossini moved to Venice, since this was the main operatic center in the northeast. Several of his early operas were performed there but, as his name became better known, he was lured to other cities. This was not just a case of provincial rivalry. Italy had not yet been unified, so these cities belonged to separate states. To

◁ **THE MARRIAGE CONTRACT**
*The Marriage Contract* was the first of Rossini's operas to be publicly staged—it premiered in 1810. The work is more usually called *La cambiale di matrimonio*.

complicate matters, Rossini's career coincided with the Napoleonic Wars, when France and Austria were competing for control of the peninsula. Venice, for example, changed hands four times between 1797, when it was conquered by Bonaparte, and 1814, when it was ceded to the Austrians.

Rossini could not fail to be affected by some of these issues. His father had been imprisoned briefly on two occasions for political activities and he had come under suspicion from the Austrian police after penning a hymn to independence in 1815. More often, though, any patriotic sentiments were subsumed into the fiction of his compositions. In *L'italiana in Algeri* (*The Italian Girl in Algiers*), Isabella leads a group of enslaved Italians to freedom

### ON TECHNIQUE
### Cutting corners

Urged on by impatient theater promoters, Rossini was constantly pushed to work at a furious pace. In order to meet their punishing schedules, the composer took a number of shortcuts. He reused some overtures—the overture to *The Barber of Seville*, for example, had already featured in two of his earlier operas (*Elizabeth, Queen of England* and *Aureliano*). Rossini also adopted the practice of using *arie di baule* (luggage arias)—individual arias borrowed from other operas, even if they were irrelevant to the plot. Similarly, he farmed out some less significant sections to other composers, including Giovanni Tadolini. Rossini outsourced much of the recitative of *Cinderella*, as well as reusing earlier arias, in order to get the opera ready in time for the Christmas season.

◁ **GIOACHINO ROSSINI**
The Italian composer, depicted here by G.P. da Fano, retired at the age of just 37, reducing his workload to live a life of luxury and indulge his passion for food.

▷ **THE FRENCH ENTER VENICE**
Rossini's career overlapped with the Napoleonic Wars. This painting shows the French takeover of Venice in May 1797, headed by Napoleon Bonaparte.

> "Give me a **laundry list** and I will set it to **music**."
> GIOACHINO ROSSINI

## KEY WORKS

**1816**

Rossini's comic masterpiece, *The Barber of Seville*, receives its premiere in Rome. The composer claimed to have written the music in just 13 days.

**1817**

*La Cenerentola* is Rossini's version of the Cinderella story. Although the commission was written at breakneck speed, it was a great success.

**1819**

Adapted from the novel by Sir Walter Scott, Rossini composes *The Lady of the Lake* for his future wife, Isabella Colbran.

**1823**

Rossini's last Italian opera, *Semiramide*, is based on a tragedy by Voltaire. It is staged initially in Venice, where it meets with great acclaim.

**1829**

Composes *William Tell*, his grandiose tale of Romantic heroism, based on a play by Schiller. This will be his final opera.

### IN PROFILE
### Domenico Barbaja

Rossini's dealings with Barbaja (1778–1841), the most dynamic impresario of the age, played a major part in his career. Described by contemporaries as disreputable, Barbaja made his first fortune with a gambling empire, which exploited the passion for the new game of roulette. He subsequently acquired theaters in Naples, Milan, and Vienna. Barbaja had a keen eye for talent, but he worked his composers ruthlessly. Rossini was contracted to deliver two operas a year, as well as assisting with the staging of other productions. "If he could, he would have had me working in the kitchen as well," Rossini noted ruefully.

DOMENICO BARBAJA IN NAPLES IN THE 1820s

with a famous aria, "Pensa alla patria" ("Think of the homeland"), following a sly musical reference to the French national anthem, the Marseillaise. Similarly, the plot of *William Tell* revolves around the efforts of a heroic Swiss revolutionary to free his land from its Austrian occupiers.

### Breakthrough and success

Rossini's early operas were rather repetitive, but with *Tancredi* he came of age. Set in 11th-century Syracuse, this *opera seria* placed a tender love story against the backdrop of a war between Sicily and its Saracen enemies. *Tancredi* was a slow starter at the box office, but Rossini's melodies soon caught on. One aria in particular, "Di tanti palpiti" ("After such palpitations"), became a favorite with the gondoliers, who helped to spread its fame far and wide.

If *Tancredi* was his breakthrough, *L'italiana in Algeri* was his first runaway success. Written at a furious pace to help out an impresario who had an unexpected gap in his schedule, the opera was premiered in Venice in 1813. It featured a mix of drama with madcap comedy, some of which was clearly inspired by the clownish antics of the *commedia dell'arte* (traditional Italian street theater). Rossini felt galvanized by the need for speed—"nothing spurs

inspiration more than necessity," he commented—though he also farmed out the recitative and at least one of the arias to an unknown assistant.

Rossini's success drew the attention of other promoters. Domenico Barbaja (see box, left) was the most influential of these and, in 1815, he persuaded the composer to move to Naples, where Rossini became musical director of the royal theaters.

Rossini also found time to write for other theaters. *The Barber of Seville*, for example, was first performed in

Rome. It had a stormy opening night, partly because of demonstrations from supporters of a rival production and partly because a stray cat wandered onto the stage. But from the second night onward, *The Barber* was a triumph and has since become Rossini's most popular creation.

▽ **THE BARBER OF SEVILLE**

This page from the Introduction, Act I, of Rossini's most popular opera, *The Barber of Seville* (premiered in 1816), shows the composer's handwriting.

"**Delight** must be **the basis** and **aim** of this art. Simple **melody** – clear **rhythm**!"

GIOACHINO ROSSINI, LETTER, 1868

By this stage, the composer had developed many of his most familiar trademarks. He dispensed entirely with unaccompanied recitative, enabling his music to flow smoothly and continuously. He noted all vocal embellishments in the score, rather than allowing his singers to improvise. Rossini himself excelled at dazzling passages of coloratura, as well as dramatic crescendos. The latter were very simple and direct, built around relentless chord progressions, although some critics found them too predictable. He also liked to employ "patter-songs"—melodies that are sung at high speed for purely comic effect. These were particularly useful in sections where the narrative was flagging.

## Romance and Paris

Rossini composed a number of more serious operas for the prima donna Isabella Colbran, among them *Othello* and *The Lady of the Lake*. When the pair first met, she was Barbaja's mistress, but she soon transferred her affections to Rossini and the couple were eventually married in 1822. Two years later, they moved to Paris, where Gioachino reached the pinnacle of his career. The French capital was regarded as the center of the operatic world and Rossini was greeted there like a conquering hero. He was appointed director of the Théâtre-Italien, commissioned to produce work for the Opéra, and honored by the French king. Rossini responded by composing his crowning masterpiece, *William Tell*.

With its famous overture (used as the theme tune for the television series *The Lone Ranger*) and its monumental scale (it lasts over four hours), *William Tell* was a landmark in the development of grand opera.

It boasted magnificent sets, huge choruses, graceful ballets, and some of Rossini's most stirring melodies. Opening in 1829, the piece was enthusiastically received and also frequently revived, clocking up some 500 performances in the course of the composer's lifetime.

*William Tell* was also Rossini's swan song. Although aged just 37, he never wrote another opera in the remaining 39 years of his life. The reasons for his retirement are unclear: he suffered from various ailments, so health may have been a cause; or he may have sensed that his style was going out of fashion. In any event, Rossini spent his final years composing some religious music—including the ironically titled *Petite Messe solennelle* (1863), which was neither "little" nor "solemn"— indulging his love of good food, and enjoying the well-earned celebrity that his music had brought him.

▷ **ISABELLA COLBRAN, c. 1835**
The sensational Spanish soprano's voice was described as "sweet and mellow, with a rich middle register able to conjure touching lyricism." She and Rossini were married in 1822. This portrait of her, aged about 50, is by Johann Baptist Reiter.

# Franz Schubert

## 1797–1828, AUSTRIAN

A master of melody, Schubert was renowned for his song settings of German poetry. His genius in symphonies and chamber and piano works was cut tragically short by his death at the age of just 31.

Franz Peter Schubert was born in Vienna in 1797, the twelfth of a family of 14 children, only five of whom survived beyond infancy. His father was a schoolmaster and a cellist (though a poor one); music was often played in the household, and Franz's outstanding talent was soon noticed. In 1808, he won a scholarship to sing in the Austrian Imperial Court Chapel choir, which carried with it the right to be educated as a boarder at the prestigious Royal Seminary school.

### A society figure

Schubert's elite education brought him into contact with pupils from a higher social class, some of whom would remain his friends throughout his life. He took lessons in composition from the court composer Antonio Salieri (1750–1825)—notorious for his earlier rivalry with Mozart (see p.83)—and composed with extraordinary facility by early adolescence. By the time he left the Seminary in 1813, Schubert had already written songs, dances, choral works, chamber music, and even his First Symphony.

Following the death of his mother, he returned home to become a reluctant assistant teacher at his father's school, but the flow of compositions continued. In the space of a single year in 1815 he wrote almost 150 songs, including a dramatic setting of Johann Wolfgang von Goethe's ballad "Erlkönig" that was to become one of his most popular works.

Schubert found an escape from teaching through his circle of friends. With the support of young aristocrats, including the wealthy literary dilettante Franz von Schober and Joseph von Spaun, a friend from the Seminary days, he was able to leave the family home and adopt an artistic bohemian lifestyle, devoted to music, café talk, and drinking—which he often did to excess. A good-natured, gregarious individual, nicknamed *Schwammerl* (literally "little mushroom") because of his diminutive chubby figure, Schubert was soon established as a minor celebrity in the tight-knit world of Viennese musical enthusiasts.

His wide group of literary and artistic friends celebrated his gifts through private gatherings dubbed *Schubertiades*, at which selections of his music were performed. Schubert attracted the attention and admiration of a famous singer of an older generation, Johann Vogl (1768–1840), whose performances introduced his songs to a wider public.

Schubert's extravagant life put some strains on his finances, but these were largely alleviated by the well-paid summers he spent at the rural estate of the Hungarian aristocrat Count Esterházy, giving lessons in singing and piano to the count's two daughters. Much of the music Schubert wrote during this period, such as the famous "Trout" Quintet of 1819, breathes happiness and tranquillity.

△ **THE RED CRAB**
Schubert was born in a house called *Zum roten Krebsen* (The Red Crab) in the Viennese suburb Himmelpfortgrund. He lived in the family apartment for nearly five years; the living space was modest, consisting of one room and a kitchen.

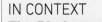

◁ **FRANZ PETER SCHUBERT**
This oil portrait was made by Austrian painter Wilhelm August Rieder in 1875 from an earlier watercolor. Rieder was the son of composer Ambros Rieder, and became a close friend of Schubert.

## IN CONTEXT
### The Biedermeier period

In 1814–1815, Schubert's native city hosted a conference, the Congress of Vienna, that marked the end of the long Napoleonic Wars. In the years that followed, known as the Biedermeier period, tastes were dominated by the middle classes, who reacted against the preceding turmoil by embracing domestic life. There was a rapid growth in music-making in the home and a strong market for sheet music, especially dances and songs. This was the form in which Schubert's music was mostly known to the public in his lifetime.

MAHOGANY BIEDERMEIER TABLE PIANO

## KEY WORKS

**1814**
Conducts his Mass in F major at Lichtental church in Vienna; it is his first significant work to be performed.

**1821**
Schubert's dramatic song "Erlkönig," which he composed in 1815, is performed and hailed by critics in Vienna.

**1822**
Writes the only two movements of his "Unfinished" Symphony in B minor, which are not performed until 1865.

**1823**
Schubert's first song cycle, *Die schöne Müllerin*, is published. It consists of 20 settings of poems by Wilhelm Müller.

**1824–27**
Writes his finest orchestral piece, the "Great" C major Symphony; it is not performed in public until 1839.

**1828**
Schubert's second song cycle, *Winterreise*, also settings of poems by Müller, is published a month after his death.

△ **THERESE GROB**
In his teens, Schubert developed an affection for baker's daughter Therese Grob. It is thought that he presented her with a collection of his songs (along with one of her own compositions) on her 18th birthday.

According to some accounts, in around 1814 Schubert fell in love with a young soprano, Therese Grob, a childhood friend. Prevented from marrying her because of his poverty, he could never love another woman. Yet solid evidence for this relationship, beyond the fact that she performed some of his music, is scant. Lack of evidence for any romantic attachments to women has led to speculation that Schubert was gay—and it is certain that close male friendships were at the heart of his way of life. It is clear at least that he had a sex life, for in 1822 he contracted syphilis, suffering a severe bout of the illness which disabled him for over a year and from which he may never have completely recovered.

### Illness and adversity
Several other factors, in addition to illness, darkened Schubert's life in the 1820s. Paranoid about political subversion in the wake of the French Revolution, the Austrian authorities regarded all unconventional groups of young people with suspicion. In 1820, Schubert and four of his friends were arrested by Viennese police for allegedly insulting imperial officials. Schubert escaped with a reprimand but one of his friends was exiled.

Meanwhile, other members of his group were deserting carefree bohemianism for the security of paid jobs. Schubert continued to make a modest living out of music, but despite a growing reputation as a popular songwriter he found publishers reluctant to print his work and failed to break into the lucrative field of opera. One of his friends, the writer and dramatist Eduard von Bauernfeld, later spoke of "a black-winged demon of sorrow and melancholy" that at times overshadowed the sunnier side of his nature. Somber premonitions of mortality dominate the powerful "Death and the Maiden" String Quartet written in 1824.

### Creative impetus
Although even Schubert's admirers tended to see him as primarily a composer of songs, dances, and charming short piano pieces, his deepest ambition was to emulate the monumental achievements of Beethoven, the towering musical genius of his day. But his efforts to assert himself as an orchestral composer met with frustration. The true story of his "Unfinished" Symphony, written in 1822, has never been established—it is uncertain whether he only completed the first two movements and the opening bars of the third movement or whether the rest of the symphony has simply been lost. Either way, this innovative work was never performed in Schubert's lifetime. His "Great" Symphony in C major, now considered one of the supreme pieces in the concert repertoire, was accepted for rehearsal by the orchestra of Vienna's Society of Friends of Music in 1827, but then declared too difficult to perform.

Despite such setbacks, Schubert's creative drive was at full strength in his final years. Works such as his last three piano sonatas, written in 1828, were complex achievements,

### ON TECHNIQUE
### Song cycles

A song cycle is a group of individual songs, each capable of standing alone but usually performed together in a fixed order, because they make emotional and dramatic sense as a sequence. Schubert was not the first composer to create cycles of German art songs (known as *Lied*, plural *Lieder*), but his masterpieces *Die schöne Müllerin* and *Winterreise* established the genre's major status. Their themes include unrequited love, melancholy, and isolation. Robert Schumann and Gustav Mahler were among the composers who continued the German song-cycle tradition.

AUTOGRAPH SCORE OF "GUTE NACHT" FROM SCHUBERT'S *WINTERREISE*, 1827

harnessing a supreme lyrical gift for melody to an individual handling of large-scale musical structure. The late songs of the *Winterreise* cycle and the song collection *Schwanengesang*, both also from 1828, have a depth and range of feeling that announce the full onset of Romanticism. Schubert was only now beginning to receive the degree of recognition he craved. In March 1828, he gave a public concert of his works that was both a critical and a financial success. His renown at last began to spread beyond Vienna.

### Death and legacy

Schubert died in 1828, possibly from typhoid, having allegedly requested a performance of Beethoven's String Quartet No. 14 on his deathbed. His death was an unexpected shock.

Schubert was buried in Vienna's Währing Cemetery, close to where Beethoven had been interred only a year before. There were laudatory obituaries in the press. His admirers regretted the loss of the works he might have created in the future, but none truly realized the scale of his achievement. As work after work received its posthumous first performance, the following decades saw his reputation rise to stellar heights. Championed by Romantic composers Robert Schumann and Felix Mendelssohn, his "Great" C major Symphony was first performed in 1839 and the rediscovered "Unfinished" Symphony in 1865. Schubert's total output turned out to be vast—about a thousand of his works are now cataloged and he has taken his place in the pantheon of great composers alongside Beethoven, Haydn, and Mozart.

△ **SCHUBERTIADE**
One of Schubert's obituaries described him as a man who had "lived solely for art and ... [his] circle of friends." The latter hosted gatherings, or *Schubertiades*, in their homes, where his new works were staged. This sketch, showing Schubert at the piano, depicts one such evening.

## "Whenever I attempted to **sing** of **love**, it **turned to pain**."

FRANZ SCHUBERT, *MY DREAM*, 1822

# Gaetano Donizetti

## 1797–1848, ITALIAN

Equally adept at producing comic and serious works, Donizetti succeeded Rossini to become the leading composer of Italian opera at the beginning of the 19th century.

> "*Lucia di Lammermoor* has been **performed**, and kindly **permit me** to ... tell you the **truth**. It has ... **pleased** very much."

GAETANO DONIZETTI, LETTER TO THE PUBLISHER GIOVANNI RICORDI, 1835

◁ **GIUDITTA PASTA**
Donizetti wrote for several prominent singers, including Giuditta Pasta (née Negri, 1797–1865), for whom he composed the title role of *Anna Bolena*.

Extreme poverty shaped Gaetano Donizetti's early childhood. Born in Bergamo in September 1797, the fifth of six children, he was raised in the dismal basement of an apartment block. In 1806, the family's situation improved somewhat with a move to better lodgings; young Gaetano, meanwhile, received a scholarship to attend choir school under Simon Mayr, the Bavarian-born *maestro di cappella* at Bergamo's cathedral and a prolific composer of opera.

### Road to success

Mayr's lessons set foundations for Donizetti's career. He arranged for his pupil to attend Bologna's Liceo Filarmonico Comunale and, after completion of his studies in 1817, for an opera commission in Venice. Mayr also promoted Donizetti's cause in Rome, which led, in 1821, to his first commission for a major opera house, the Teatro Argentina, where Rossini's *The Barber of Seville* had premiered five years earlier.

Domenico Barbaja, the impresario of Neapolitan theaters, struck by Donizetti's Roman debut, invited the young composer to produce operas for him in Naples. Donizetti's first hit with the Neapolitan public, *La zingara*, enchanted Vincenzo Bellini, a student at Naples' Royal College of Music. A flop at Milan's La Scala and failures in Palermo were followed by a run of successful and well-paid works for Naples, and commissions elsewhere. With this new-found financial security he married Virginia Vasselli in 1828.

### Prolific output

Between 1822 and 1843, Donizetti created three or four operas a year, an output that was not rare at the time but was made outstanding by the high quality of his music. Works such as *Elisabetta al castello di Kenilworth*, *Anna Bolena*, and *Maria Stuarda* satisfied the Italian public's appetite for British history and legend. *L'elisir d'amore*, created for Milan in 1832; *La Fille du régiment;* and *Don Pasquale*, first staged in Paris in 1843 (see box, below), proved the composer's mastery of comic opera, while his well-judged blend of Classicism and Romanticism brought distinction to his tragic drama *Lucia di Lammermoor* and *La Favorite*, a four-act work for the Paris Opéra.

Donizetti completed 65 operas, written for such excellent singers as Giuditta Pasta and the tenor Giovanni Rubini, a fellow native of Bergamo, known for his high notes and expressive voice. While many of Donizetti's operas were performed for decades after his death from syphilis on April 8, 1848, most fell into obscurity. Yet *Don Pasquale*, *La Fille du régiment*, *Lucia di Lammermoor*, *La Favorite*, and *Lucrezia Borgia* held their place in the international repertoire, and many others have been revived and recorded over the past half century.

△ **ANNA BOLENA, TITLE PAGE**
Title page of the score for *Anna Bolena*, Donizetti's tragic opera in two acts. It was this work, which premiered in Milan in 1830, that brought the Italian composer international acclaim.

THEATRE ITALIEN, PARIS, WHERE DONIZETTI'S *DON PASQUALE* PREMIERED IN 1843

# Vincenzo Bellini

## 1801–1835, ITALIAN

With meticulous care for words and music, Bellini brought the turbulent emotions of Romanticism to Italian opera. He was the master of *bel canto* and inspired many composers.

△ **WAR HYMN IN *NORMA***
This is the musical score in Bellini's own handwriting for the war hymn in Act II of *Norma* (1831), one of his 10 operas and considered a masterpiece.

Vincenzo Bellini was born in Catania, Sicily, on November 3, 1801. In the summer of that year, his island home had been attacked by Tunisian pirates eager to enslave people for the lucrative market in north Africa—an event that sparked a three-year war.

The theme of sea battles with pirates was to reemerge in Bellini's life many years later in the form of one of his earliest works, *Il pirata*. Also among his formative experiences were the Sicilian and Neapolitan folk songs and theater tunes that he had heard as a boy.

Bellini's childhood, like much of his short life, was dressed in myth by early biographers (see box, right), who portrayed the boy as a doomed genius: "blond as the cornfields, sweet as the angels," in one account.

◁ **VINCENZO BELLINI**
Bellini's bright blue eyes, good looks, brief but dazzling career, and death at the age of just 33 later contributed to the creation of his near cult-like status.

Bellini was the eldest of seven children; his father and grandfather were musicians. He wrote his first piece of music at the age of six and became his grandfather's musical apprentice soon after. In 1819, he won a scholarship to the Royal College of Music in Naples, where he honed his skills as a composer for the voice.

He supplemented his training in harmony and counterpoint with lessons learned during visits to the vast San Carlo Theater in Naples to hear works by Rossini, Mayr, Donizetti, Mercadante, and Spontini. He crowned his studies with his opera *Adelson e Salvini* (1825), which led to a commission for San Carlo: *Bianca e Fernando*, first performed in May 1826. This launched the composer's professional career. The following April, Bellini moved north to Milan to work at the Teatro alla Scala, which was one of Italy's finest opera houses. His first work for La Scala, *Il pirata* (1827), was a triumph and was promptly staged in Naples and Vienna.

Opera was the most lucrative outlet for the work of Italian composers in the early 1800s. The peninsula's assorted kingdoms and city-states supported a great network of opera houses, each serving audiences that were hungry for new pieces.

### Success cut short

While many of his contemporaries wrote three or more operas a year, the perfectionist Bellini rarely wrote more than one. His painstaking approach (he paid as much attention to the words as to the notes) at its best produced *La sonnambula* (1831), *Norma* (1831), and *I puritani* (1835), masterworks that secured Bellini's status as one of the highest-earning composers of the age.

In demand in both London and Paris, Bellini wrote *I puritani* for the French capital. He died of dysentery in the Paris suburbs in September 1835, nine months after the opera's premiere at the Théâtre Italien.

According to Bellini, "opera must make people weep, feel horrified, die through singing." The observation, which encapsulates his vision for the art form, is clear in its commitment to strong emotions, bold dramatic gestures, and the projection of tempestuous psychological states.

◁ **TEATRO DI SAN CARLO**
The spectacular interior of the San Carlo Theater in Naples—where Bellini's *Bianca e Fernando* premiered in 1826, launching his career—is represented in this work, c.1830, by Cetteo de Stefano. The San Carlo is Europe's oldest opera house.

# Hector Berlioz

**1803–1869, FRENCH**

In many ways the archetypal Romantic composer, Berlioz took up music against his family's wishes and was undervalued in his country. His most famous work, *Symphonie fantastique*, emerged out of an obsessive love.

Born in a village near Grenoble, Hector Berlioz was the eldest of six children. His father, Louis, a highly respected country doctor, was one of the first Westerners to use acupuncture in his treatments. He took a keen interest in his son's upbringing, educating him at home. Under his guidance, Hector developed an abiding love for classical literature and culture.

## Conflicting paths

Hector's education was wide-ranging, but it was geared to preparing him for the medical profession, so music had a minor role. The boy learned to play his father's flageolet (a woodwind instrument) and was given some lessons on the flute and the guitar. Unusually for a composer, he had no formal training on the piano and was never particularly proficient on any instrument, although he did become a very fine conductor. With typical bullishness, Berlioz chose to put a positive spin on this. He believed that he had been "saved from the tyranny of keyboard habits, so dangerous to thought, and from the lure of conventional harmonies." Instead, it would be the orchestra that formed the basis of his compositional outlook.

Hector worked hard, earning the grades he needed for admission to medical school. He managed this in spite of the distractions of falling in love. Throughout his teenage years, he was obsessed with a girl in the neighborhood, Estelle Duboeuf, who was seven years his senior. This could easily have been dismissed as an adolescent crush, but Hector never forgot her and renewed their friendship in the 1860s.

In 1821, Berlioz began his studies at the medical school in Paris. He did his best to follow his parents' wishes, but a clash of wills became inevitable. For the most part, this was down to Hector's genuine distaste for the horrors of the dissection room. At the same time, his commitment to music grew rapidly, as he enjoyed the cultural benefits of living in the capital. He visited the Opéra and the theater and, from 1822, he began to frequent the library of the Conservatoire.

Berlioz graduated from medical school in 1824, when he was finally compelled to inform his parents that he was going to make his career in music. They already suspected this, but were still horrified. His father cut

△ **BATON**

This conductor's baton belonged to Hector Berlioz. It is now on display at the museum dedicated to the composer in the house where he was born in La Côte-Saint-André, Isère, southeastern France.

## IN CONTEXT
### The Romantic movement

Berlioz's life coincided with the rise of the Romantic movement, which affected literature, painting, and music. Reacting to the rationalism of the Enlightenment, there arose a taste for conveying themes that were bizarre, unusual, violent, or macabre. Berlioz was drawn to such subjects. His winning entry for the Prix de Rome was a cantata, *The Death of Sardanapalus*—a scene of butchery made notorious in a painting by Eugène Delacroix. Similarly, Berlioz's *Symphonie fantastique* climaxes in a witches' sabbath, a favorite theme of Spanish painter Francisco Goya.

*THE DEATH OF SARDANAPALUS*, EUGENE DELACROIX, 1827

" ... characteristics of my music are **passionate** expression, **intense** ardor, **rhythmical** animation, and **unexpected** turns. "

HECTOR BERLIOZ, *MEMOIRS*, 1865

▷ **HECTOR BERLIOZ**

A portrait by Alexis-Marie Lahaye shows Berlioz dressed in black, the red ribbon of the Legion of Honor, awarded to him in 1839, prominent on his chest. But for most of his career, he was held in higher regard abroad than at home in France.

" No one who hears **this symphony** ... played by Berlioz's orchestra, can help believing that he is hearing **a marvel without precedent**. "

RICHARD WAGNER, ON BERLIOZ'S *SYMPHONIE FANTASTIQUE*

PORTRAIT OF IRISH ACTRESS HARRIET SMITHSON, c.1829

his allowance, while his puritanical mother even laid a curse on him. By this stage, Berlioz had already started composing, supplementing his meager income with some music criticism. His first significant production was his *Messe solennelle* (*Solemn Mass*). Written in 1824, it was performed the following year. The score was subsequently lost and rediscovered only in 1991.

### Obsessive love

In addition to opera, Berlioz also enjoyed drama, developing a great fondness for Shakespeare's plays. In September 1827, he visited the Odéon, where he witnessed productions of *Hamlet* and *Romeo and Juliet* by an English theatrical company. Berlioz was transfixed, falling desperately in love with the leading lady, Harriet Smithson (see box, left). There was an obsessive quality about his passion for this beautiful stranger. Letters to her went unanswered and he moved into lodgings across the street from hers, only for her to promptly move out. Fortunately, Berlioz found a practical outlet for this fixation, using it as inspiration for his most famous creation, *Symphonie fantastique*.

Completed in 1830, this masterpiece is one of the most memorable landmarks of the Romantic movement. It has been hailed as a pioneering example of "program music"—

▷ **A BERLIOZ CONCERT**
A caricature of Hector Berlioz published by Austrian journal *Wiener Theaterzeitung* in 1846 shows the composer conducting a deafening concert with an exploding cannon, and chaos and panic in the crowd; formally dressed concert-goers cover their ears against the terrible din.

a musical piece expressing themes and ideas that lie outside the scope of music itself and that are explained in program notes for the audience. Berlioz constructed his symphony in five movements, conveying the hopeless, unrequited love of a young musician. Plunged into despair, he takes opium, resulting in a series of outlandish visions, culminating in a march to the scaffold and an orgy at a witches' sabbath. The object of the musician's affections, his *idée fixe*, is represented by a melodic theme, which recurs in differing forms throughout the piece.

Harriet Smithson eventually heard a performance of the *Symphonie* in 1832 and, learning that it was about her, agreed to meet Berlioz.

Romance blossomed and the couple were married in 1833. There was, however, no happy ending. Harriet gave birth to their son in 1834, but her own career was on the slide and the marriage soon turned sour. She became jealous and resentful of Hector's growing success and turned increasingly to drink. They eventually parted and Berlioz took a new mistress, Marie Recio.

During the course of the 1830s, Berlioz achieved professional recognition, although lack of money always remained a problem. In 1834, at the request of Niccolò Paganini, he composed *Harold in Italy*, a symphony with solo viola. Paganini never performed the work, but the composers remained on friendly

terms and Paganini later gave Berlioz 20,000 francs to finance one of his other projects.

## Challenges and reputation

Berlioz also received a state commission for his *Requiem* (1837), which commemorates victims of the 1830 Revolution. This was a vast undertaking, involving more than 400 performers. A tremendous success, it was always cited by the composer as the achievement of which he was most proud.

The fate of Berlioz's first opera, *Benvenuto Cellini* (1838), was rather less auspicious. The first night was a disaster and it closed after four performances. Critics have praised the verve and imagination of some sections, but the composer's ambition undermined the overall effect. Berlioz was intent on cramming in so much variety, which was often delivered at a frenetic pace and demanded such virtuosity from his musicians, that the opera was not only technically difficult to perform but also challenging for an audience to process.

Similar problems were apparent in Berlioz's most celebrated opera, *Les Troyens* (*The Trojans*, 1856–1858). Its original running time was well over five hours and the many, complex scene changes made it a nightmare to produce. As a result, he was obliged to divide it into two separate operas. The first full staging of the entire work did not take place until a production at Covent Garden in London in 1957.

Berlioz was awarded the Legion of Honor in 1839 and appointed curator of the Conservatoire library, but was passed over for many more important official posts. He was generally held in higher esteem outside France—his concert tours as conductor in England, Germany, and Russia, for example, were a triumph. Berlioz's reputation in his home country grew after his death, aided greatly by the publication of his sparkling *Memoirs* (1865), and he is now revered as one of the nation's greatest Romantic composers.

## KEY WORKS

**1830**
Creates the *Symphonie fantastique*, his hallucinatory vision of his love for his future wife, Harriet Smithson.

**1834**
Inspired by a poem by Lord Byron, Berlioz composes *Harold in Italy*, a symphony in four movements.

**1838**
*Benvenuto Cellini*, inspired by the memoirs of a Florentine sculptor, premieres in Paris, the first of his three operas.

**1841**
Composes *Les Nuits d'été* (*Summer Nights*), a song cycle for single voice and piano.

**1846**
Described by Berlioz as a "dramatic legend," *The Damnation of Faust* is a box-office failure.

**1858**
Completes *Les Troyens* (*The Trojans*). It is so long that it is initially staged as two separate operas.

# Fanny Mendelssohn

## 1805–1847, GERMAN

Although she has long been overshadowed by her famous brother, Felix, Fanny Mendelssohn is now recognized as a significant figure in her own right and her substantial body of work is being rediscovered.

Fanny Mendelssohn was born in Hamburg, the eldest of four children of a wealthy, cultivated family. She enjoyed the same privileged upbringing as her brother Felix, with the best tutors available in every subject. Like Felix, she was intellectually accomplished and her talent for music seemed on par with his. However, the social conventions of the time prevented her from giving full expression to her gifts. She was a superb pianist, but her father thought a concert career to be unseemly and she performed only once in public, at a charity benefit concert in 1838. Although Felix

◁ **SCORE FOR FOUR SONGS FOR PIANOFORTE, 1846**
Fanny did not start publishing her music until the year before her death. These four works formed her Op. 2.

was devoted to his sister, he thought the commercial side of music was unsuitable for an upper-class lady, and for these reasons, Fanny published almost none of her work during her lifetime.

### Home performances

Fanny spent most of her life in Berlin, where in 1829 she married the painter Wilhelm Hensel (see box, right). Her musical life revolved around performances of her own and others' work that she organized in her home. Attendance at these prestigious social events was by invitation only, but audiences reportedly numbered up

to 200. The guests sometimes included members of the Prussian royal family, and among the visiting performers were such luminaries as Franz Liszt and Clara Schumann.

### Death and rediscovery

In May 1847, while she was rehearsing for one of these events, Fanny's hands went numb and moments later she suffered a massive stroke. She died the following day, aged only 41. When he heard the news, Felix screamed in anguish and then fainted. For many years, Fanny was little more than a footnote in musical history, but from the later 20th century her work has been gradually rediscovered. About 500 compositions by her are known, including piano music, songs, chamber works, and choral pieces—always beautifully crafted, often lyrical in mood but sometimes stormy.

Discoveries continue to be made. The manuscript of a piano piece known as the "Easter Sonata," found in a bookstore in France in 1970, is signed "F. Mendelssohn" and is a work of such distinction that it was assumed to be by Felix. However, in 2010, a US musicologist proved that the manuscript had been cut from an album of Fanny's compositions, and in 2012 it was performed for the first time as her work.

◁ **FANNY MENDELSSOHN**
This portrait of Fanny Mendelssohn was painted in 1842 by Moritz Oppenheim, a long-standing friend of Fanny's husband, Wilhelm Hensel.

◁ **THREE SONGS, 2015**
To this day, relatively few of Fanny Mendelssohn's works have been presented in public. Here, Anna Lucia Richter performs her Three Songs with the Budapest Festival Orchestra.

### IN PROFILE
### Wilhelm Hensel

Although his work is little known today, Fanny's husband, Wilhelm Hensel, had a fairly successful career as an artist. In 1829, he was appointed court painter by Frederick William III of Prussia. He was best known in his lifetime as a portraitist, but he also produced religious and historical pictures. Hensel had no particular interest in music, but he was devoted to Fanny, had great respect for her talents, and was hugely supportive of her career and ambitions. Her sudden death was a devastating blow from which he never fully recovered.

**WILHELM HENSEL, SELF-PORTRAIT, 1829**

# Felix Mendelssohn

**1809–1847, GERMAN**

Multi-talented and extraordinarily hardworking, Mendelssohn packed a huge amount into his short life. Famed as a composer, pianist, organist, conductor, and administrator, he stood at the forefront of European music.

△ **A MIDSUMMER NIGHT'S DREAM**
In 1842, 16 years after he composed his youthful *Overture to A Midsummer Night's Dream*, Mendelssohn wrote incidental music for the play. It includes the famous *Wedding March*, and also a lively scherzo, in this edition arranged for piano.

Felix Mendelssohn was born into a wealthy, loving, culturally enlightened family that unstintingly fostered his talents. He was handsome and graceful, had a magnetic personality, and was so gifted that he would probably have excelled in any field. His happy childhood was followed by a happy married life, with a beautiful wife and five children. However, fate dealt him cruel blows in later life with the unexpected death of his beloved sister and, soon afterward, his own death at the age of 38.

## A precocious talent

Mendelssohn came from a Jewish family whose most notable member was philosopher Moses Mendelssohn, his paternal grandfather. His father was a banker and his mother, an excellent amateur pianist, also came from a banking family. In 1822, his parents converted from Judaism to Protestantism; to show their new allegiance, they added the name "Bartholdy" (from a Christian branch of the family) to their own. Thus the composer is sometimes known as Felix Mendelssohn-Bartholdy.

Felix was born in 1809 in Hamburg, the second of four children, and grew up in Berlin. All four children were highly intelligent and had great musical talent, but Felix and his elder sister, Fanny (see pp.114–115), were exceptional in this regard, seeming to master all aspects of the subject with ease. Felix gave his first public performance as a pianist at the age of nine, and he also excelled on the organ and violin. By his teens, he was pouring out compositions in various genres, including chamber music and symphonies; his parents even hired an orchestra so he could try out his works. At 16, he wrote his first acknowledged masterpiece, the String Octet, and at 17 the famous Overture to *A Midsummer Night's Dream*, which captures the fairy magic of Shakespeare's play with gossamer lightness. The history of music is full of prodigies, but not even Mozart wrote anything so memorable, original, and completely mature at this tender age.

## A star of the podium

In addition to gaining a reputation as a composer and pianist, Mendelssohn also quickly made a mark as a conductor; this specialist role was still new and Mendelssohn became one of

---

### IN CONTEXT
### The Gewandhaus

From 1835 to his death, Mendelssohn was musical director of Leipzig's Gewandhaus Orchestra, one of the oldest and most acclaimed in the world. It was founded in 1743 and in 1781 began holding its concerts in part of the Gewandhaus ("garment house"), a building used by cloth merchants, from which it takes its name. A new concert hall, opened in 1884, was destroyed during World War II and the present building, famed for its fine acoustics, opened in 1981. The orchestra also often performs in Leipzig's St. Thomas's Church, which is closely associated with J.S. Bach.

**MONUMENT TO MENDELSSOHN OUTSIDE THE GEWANDHAUS , 1911**

---

" This year [is] an **important segment** in our family life. **Felix, our soul**, is **going away.** "

FANNY MENDELSSOHN, DIARY ENTRY, JANUARY 1, 1829

▷ **FELIX MENDELSSOHN, 1834–1835**
This portrait by German artist Theodor Hildebrandt conveys the genial character of Mendelssohn. He is depicted as a prosperous gentleman but his tousled hair suggests his artistic nature.

"There is **one god—Bach—**and **Mendelssohn** is his **prophet.** "

HECTOR BERLIOZ

the first real "stars" of the podium. Most notably, in 1829, aged 20, he organized and conducted the first performance of Bach's *St. Matthew Passion* since the composer's death, thus inaugurating a major revival of interest in Bach's music.

### Travels and meetings

Soon after this triumph, Mendelssohn embarked on his first independent journey abroad, to England. He later made nine more visits to the country, where he felt at home (he spoke the language fluently) and was much acclaimed. During this first stay, which lasted from April to November 1829, he also spent a week in Wales

and made a more extensive tour of Scotland, his sightseeing including a boat trip to the uninhabited island of Staffa in the Inner Hebrides. This inspired him to write his overture *The Hebrides*, also known—from the most remarkable feature of the island—as "Fingal's Cave." It is one of the first notable examples of a "concert overture": one that is freestanding rather than used as an introduction to a ballet, opera, or other performance.

A leg injury in a carriage accident delayed Mendelssohn's return to Germany and caused him to miss Fanny's wedding, which was held in Berlin on October 3, 1829. The following year, although he was still

only 21, he was offered the position of head of the music department at Berlin University. However, he turned it down as he wanted to continue seeing the world, and he spent much of the next two years traveling—in Austria, Italy, Switzerland, France, and England again. During this time he met several famous musicians, including Berlioz in Rome and Chopin in Paris.

In 1833, Mendelssohn was appointed municipal music director in Düsseldorf, then two years later he took up the more prestigious post of director of the Gewandhaus Orchestra in Leipzig (see box, p.116). This city was to be his home for the remainder of his life. However, he continued to travel and

▽ **FINGAL'S CAVE**
The sight of the octagonal basalt columns of Fingal's Cave on the island of Staffa in the Inner Hebrides inspired the famous opening theme of Mendelssohn's overture *The Hebrides*, a work he dedicated to Frederick William IV of Prussia.

◁ *AM AMALFI MAI*, 1831
A talented artist, Mendelssohn made many drawings and watercolors on his travels, including this one of the Amalfi coast in Italy.

## Changing reputations

Mendelssohn's stellar reputation declined after his death. In the age of Romanticism, his music was thought by some to be over-polite and sentimental. This mainly applied to his religious music. His oratorios *St. Paul* (1836) and *Elijah* (1846) were popular when first performed, but 50 years later Irish writer George Bernard Shaw referred to Mendelssohn's "despicable oratorio-mongering."

Mendelssohn had endured anti-Semitic attacks in his life, and these increased after his death, with the banning of his music in Nazi Germany and the removal of his statue in front of the Gewandhaus in 1936 (a replacement was unveiled in 1993).

Some detractors claim he reached his peak as a composer by the age of 21 and that his later music lacks range and depth. But one of his final works, the Violin Concerto, is among his greatest—highly original in form and rich in feeling. The celebrated violinist Joseph Joachim described it as "the heart's jewel." And despite Bernard Shaw's damning indictment, *Elijah* has now risen to become one of the composer's most popular works.

Mendelssohn does not have the near god-like status he held in his lifetime, but his position as a leading figure in 19th-century culture is undoubted.

◁ *ELIJAH*, **HANDWRITTEN SCORE**, 1846
Mendelssohn wrote this oratorio, based on the life of the prophet and miracle-worker Elijah, for the triennial Birmingham Festival.

### IN PROFILE
### Prince Albert

Queen Victoria's husband (1819–1861) was passionate about music and his enthusiasm for Mendelssohn—a fellow German—underlined the composer's success in Britain. Albert was an accomplished pianist and organist, a good singer, and an occasional composer (mainly of songs but also of religious music). He expanded Victoria's court band into a full-size orchestra and made proposals for a National Training School for Music, which was eventually founded in 1873 (replaced by the Royal College of Music in 1882).

**MENDELSSOHN PLAYS FOR QUEEN VICTORIA AND PRINCE ALBERT, 1842**

work elsewhere, organizing festivals in various German cities and also in Birmingham. He was extremely successful as the Gewandhaus's director, raising its standards, improving conditions for its members, and using innovative programming in which the work of past giants, such as Beethoven and Mozart, mixed with contemporary pieces. In 1843, he also founded a conservatory in Leipzig; this became the leading music school in Germany.

### Royal patronage and tragedy

Mendelssohn's brilliant career brought him into contact with many notable people, among them King Frederick William IV of Prussia. In 1842, the king gave him a letter to deliver to his cousin Prince Albert in England and in this way Mendelssohn met the British royal family. Queen Victoria and Prince Albert (see box, right) were great admirers of his work and the three of them became friends, making music together in Buckingham Palace on several occasions.

Mendelssohn's grueling workload took a toll on his health and by the beginning of 1847 he was visibly ill.

When Fanny died suddenly in May that year, it was a shattering blow, and he survived her by only a few months, dying—after suffering a series of strokes—in Leipzig on November 4, aged 38. His body was taken by train to Berlin where it was buried alongside his sister's. Tragedy struck again six years later when Mendelssohn's widow, Cécile—a clergyman's daughter whom he had married in 1837—died of tuberculosis, leaving their orphaned children to be brought up by relatives.

## KEY WORKS

**1825**
Writes the String Octet, his first masterpiece, at the age of 16. It was dedicated to his teacher, Edward Ritz.

**1833**
In London, conducts the premiere of his Symphony No. 4, "Italian."

**1842**
Conducts the premiere of his Symphony No. 3, "Scottish," in Leipzig. He dedicates the work to Queen Victoria.

**1844**
Completes his Violin Concerto in E minor; it has its premiere the following year in Leipzig.

**1846**
In Birmingham, conducts the premiere of *Elijah*, his most famous oratorio.

# Frédéric Chopin

## 1810–1849, POLISH

Chopin was one of the archetypal tragic heroes of Romanticism: his life embraced exile from his war-torn homeland, a love affair with a scandalous woman, and an extraordinary talent betrayed by a frail body.

No composer is more intimately associated with the piano than Chopin. All his compositions involve the instrument, on which he was a superlative performer. They are mainly solo pieces, although he also wrote orchestral works (notably two sparkling piano concertos), some chamber music, and a few songs. His work is deeply personal and full of heartfelt emotion, but there is never any of the exhibitionism sometimes associated with Romanticism. Instead, it displays exquisite taste and craftsmanship—an expression of his own fastidious personality.

### A musical prodigy

Frédéric François Chopin (Polish: Fryderyk Franciszek Szopen) was born at Zelazowa Wola, near Warsaw, where his French-born father, Nicolas, was tutor to the children of a local aristocrat. Six months later, the family moved to Warsaw, where Nicolas got a job teaching French— the second language of the Polish aristocracy—at the recently founded Lyceum. At this time, Poland was not

◁ **FREDERIC CHOPIN, 1838**
This portrait by Eugène Delacroix was part of an unfinished painting of Chopin and his lover and muse, George Sand, which was later cut into two parts.

an independent country. It had been fought over for much of the previous century and after the Napoleonic Wars ended in 1815 it effectively became part of the Russian Empire—a situation that fostered a strong movement for national freedom.

The young Frédéric had a weak constitution and although he grew to average height for the time, he remained very slight in build and suffered ill health throughout his life. From an early age, he showed musical interests, in which he was encouraged by his loving, cultured family: he began serious piano lessons when he was

◁ **PIANO CONCERTO NO. 1**
Chopin composed this concerto in 1830 and was the soloist at its first performance on October 11. He was immediately celebrated as a national hero in his native Poland.

six, had his first compositions published when he was seven, and made his public debut as a performer when he was eight. Soon he had a reputation as a boy wonder.

### Early successes

From 1826 to 1829, Chopin studied at the Warsaw Academy of Music, where his final report described him as a "musical genius." He had indeed already shown remarkable gifts as a composer and pianist. The most important compositions of his youth are his two piano concertos, both written by the time he was 20. He was the soloist at their first performances, in Warsaw's National Theater in March and October 1830. They won great acclaim, but Warsaw was considered provincial in musical terms and Chopin was already thinking beyond Poland. He had briefly visited Berlin in 1828 and Vienna in 1829, and in November 1830, following the success of his piano concertos, he set out to make a longer stay in Vienna—the musical capital of Europe.

## ON TECHNIQUE
### Chopin's pianos

For most of his career, Chopin used pianos by the two leading French manufacturers, Erard and Pleyel. Erard pianos produced a bigger, richer sound, but Chopin generally preferred the bright, silvery tone of Pleyels: "When I am not in the mood, I play on the Erard piano, where I find the ready tone easily. But when I am full of vigor and strong enough to find my very own tone, I need a Pleyel." During his stay in Britain he also enjoyed using the "very sweet instruments" produced by the firm of Broadwood.

CHOPIN'S PLEYEL PIANO IN HIS APARTMENT IN PARIS

> " **Mold** the **keyboard** with a **velvet hand** and **feel** the **key** rather than **striking it**. "

FREDERIC CHOPIN (ADVICE TO HIS PUPILS)

# "Chopin ... made **a single instrument** speak a **language of infinity**."

GEORGE SAND

A week after he arrived in Vienna, news came that a rebellion against the Russians had broken out in Warsaw. Chopin was advised by his parents not to return home but to stay away from the bloodshed. Lonely and homesick, he made little headway in Vienna, so decided to move to Paris, arriving in September 1831. On the journey, he heard that Warsaw had been captured by the Russians, an event said to have inspired one of his most turbulent pieces, the "Revolutionary" Etude, which packs a torrent of emotion into less than three minutes of music.

## Life in Paris

Paris was to be Chopin's home for the rest of his life. He never saw Poland again, but his music often reflected his heritage and his patriotism. He wrote more than 20 polonaises, a type of composition based on a court dance of the Polish aristocracy, and more than 50 mazurkas, based on a Polish peasant dance. Other groups of his works include nocturnes and waltzes. These are all essentially miniatures,

▷ **GEORGE SAND, 1864**
Famous for her novels that explored the lives and loves of the rural poor, George Sand was also a prodigious dramatist campaigner, and one of the first modern, liberated women. She became Chopin's lover, muse, and nurse until their relationship ended in 1847.

lasting only a few minutes each, but they show inexhaustible melodic invention and have a freedom of construction, a feeling for color and texture, and a wealth of expressive nuance that opened up new paths for piano music.

Chopin's intimate music and his delicate keyboard style were better suited to the drawing room than the concert hall. He made his living in Paris mainly by playing in aristocratic houses and giving lessons to wealthy pupils. This suited his character, for he was a dandy with impeccable manners and also something of a social climber. He earned well, but spent most of his money maintaining an extravagant lifestyle appropriate to the circles in which he moved.

It was a lifestyle that brought Chopin into contact with many attractive young women. He had various tepid youthful romances (one of which ended with a broken engagement), but they were all overshadowed by his affair with the novelist Aurore Dudevant (1804–1876), better known by her pen name George Sand. When she met Chopin in 1836, she was already famous because of her writings and unconventional life: separated from her husband, with two children, she had numerous lovers, wore men's clothing, and smoked cigars. Her affair with Chopin began in earnest in 1838 and they spent the winter of 1838–1839 together on the island of Majorca.

The relationship lasted almost a decade before ending acrimoniously in 1847. By this time Chopin's health

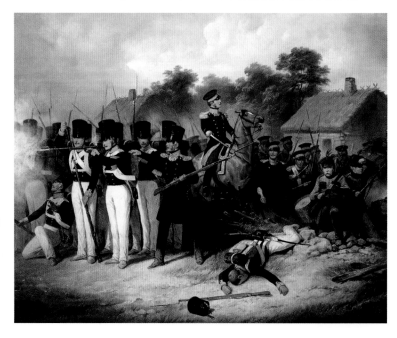

▷ **THE NOVEMBER UPRISING**
This painting of the Polish rebellion against Russian rule is by Polish artist January Suchodolski, who fought in what became known as the November Uprising (1830–1831). The rebellion was brutally crushed by the superior Russian forces. For Chopin, this defeat meant that, as a Polish nationalist, he was prevented from returning to his native Poland. His yearning for his homeland, and deep dismay at the failure of the rebellion, is reflected in several of his works.

was in decline, he was short of money, and Paris was an uncomfortable place to be, with revolution in the air after King Louis Philippe was deposed in February 1848. Chopin escaped by staying in England and Scotland from April to November. He gave public concerts in London, Manchester, Edinburgh, and Glasgow, but mainly performed in aristocratic homes—in London (where Queen Victoria was guest of honor on one occasion) and in Scotland (in country houses belonging to friends and relatives of his Scottish pupil Jane Stirling; see box, p.122). By now he was so ill that he looked like a walking corpse. He could no longer climb stairs and had to be carried up by his servant, but he could still produce magic at the piano.

## A final return

Back in Paris, Chopin continued to deteriorate and he died—probably of tuberculosis—on October 17, 1849, aged 39. In his final days he was visited by a host of friends and acquaintances, one of whom (the singer Pauline Viardot) remarked cynically that all the great ladies of Paris came to his rooms to faint.

After a funeral service attended by 3,000 people at the church of the Madeleine, its facade draped in black velvet, Chopin was buried in Père Lachaise Cemetery. However, at his request, his heart was removed and taken back to Poland, where it rests beneath a monument to him in the church of the Holy Cross, Warsaw.

△ **PLAYING FOR NOBILITY**
In this scene painted by Henryk Siemiradzki in 1887, Chopin plays in the salon of his patron, Prince Antoni Radziwiłł, at the prince's palace in Berlin.

▽ **POLONAISE "HEROIQUE"**
Chopin wrote his Polonaise in A-flat major in 1842. This solo piano piece is one of his most acclaimed works.

## KEY WORKS

### 1830
The premiere of Piano Concerto No. 2 is followed by Piano Concerto No. 1 (the numbers indicate the order of publication).

### 1833
Publishes first set of Nocturnes; seven more sets are published in his lifetime, containing 18 Nocturnes in all.

### 1839
Completes Piano Sonata No. 2, the third movement of which is the celebrated funeral march.

### 1846
Completes the Sonata for Piano and Cello, his most ambitious piece of chamber music.

# Robert Schumann

## 1810–1856, GERMAN

Schumann wrote some of the most intense, innovative music of the Romantic era, notably in his works for piano and his songs. His career was cruelly terminated by the onset of severe mental illness.

Born in 1810 in Zwickau, Saxony, Robert Schumann was encouraged in his interest in literature and music by his father, a bookseller and publisher. Robert learned the basics of music and how to play the piano from one of his school teachers, soon showing an exceptional gift for composition and improvisation.

### Charting a course

Into adolescence he still imagined that his vocation might lie in literature. Imitating his heroes, the writers of the German Romantic movement, he had written poetry and a novel by the time he was 16 years old—neither of them showing any great promise. In 1825, Schumann's elder sister Emilie died

by suicide, throwing herself into a river. Ten months later his father died. His mother, who had always disapproved of her son's interest in music, sent him to study law at university, first in Leipzig and later at Heidelberg.

Schumann was not diligent in his studies, devoting his days to the piano and his nights to drinking and adultery. In 1828, he met Friedrich Wieck, a Leipzig musician famed for

◁ **FRONTISPIECE, *PAPILLONS***
Schumann's *Papillons*, Op. 2 for piano, was an adaptation of the concluding chapter of the novel *Flegeljahre* (*The Awkward Age*, 1804–1805), by German Romantic writer Jean Paul.

◁ **CLARA WIECK**
Wieck met Schumann at the age of 11 and was in love with him throughout her teens. They married after a battle with her father, who tried to block the union.

his unique method of teaching piano. Wieck provided Schumann with an escape from a legal career by promising Schumann's mother he would turn him into a great piano virtuoso. In 1830, Schumann moved into Wieck's house in Leipzig as a live-in pupil, joining a household that included Wieck's 11-year-old daughter Clara, a musical child prodigy.

Schumann's pursuit of a career as a piano virtuoso was short-lived. Through experimenting with a mechanical device to strengthen his fingers, he permanently damaged his hand. The accident left him free to focus on composition.

### Building a career

The *Abegg Variations*, published as his Opus 1 in 1831, was the first of a series of remarkable works for solo piano that expressed his complex mind and strikingly original musical sensibility, from *Papillons* (1832) and *Carnaval* (1835) to the *Davidsbündlertänze* (1837) and *Kreisleriana* (1838). Free in form, innovative in harmony, and often

*WANDERER ABOVE THE SEA OF FOG,*
CASPAR DAVID FRIEDRICH, 1817

▷ **ROBERT SCHUMANN, 1839**
Between 1832 and 1839, Schumann composed almost entirely for piano. But in 1840 he wrote almost 140 songs, including the famous *Dichterliebe*.

> "To **send light** into the **depths** of the **human heart**—this is the **artist's calling**."
> ROBERT SCHUMANN

## Romantic complications

In Schumann's personal life, a long, romantic attachment to an older woman was followed in 1834 by his betrothal to Ernestine von Fricken, whom he believed to be the daughter of a wealthy nobleman. He ended the engagement after discovering that she was illegitimate and penniless. This left him free to fall in love with Clara Wieck. His feelings for her probably informed the passionate piano solo *Fantasie in C*, composed in 1836.

Schumann proposed marriage in 1837, but Clara's father refused permission and banned Schumann from the house. This was hardly an irrational reaction, given that Clara was a highly gifted 18-year-old with a fine career ahead of her and Schumann a man of evident emotional instability and uncertain financial prospects. There followed a long period of clandestine meetings and exchange of love letters. The young couple's struggle to marry against the father's veto ended up in the courts, where a judge eventually ruled in their favor. They married in 1840 and the first of their eight children was born the following year.

## The year of song

For Schumann the composer, 1840 was the "year of song." He wrote almost 140 songs, including *Dichterliebe*, a worthy successor to the song cycles of his hero Schubert. Clara encouraged her husband to embark on orchestral works, leading to the First Symphony, premiered with Felix Mendelssohn conducting in 1841, and the famous Piano Concerto, completed in 1845. Schumann considered his secular oratorio *Paradise and the Peri*, written in 1843 and based on the Irish poet Thomas Moore's *Lalla-Rookh*, to be his finest work. He also produced much chamber music during this period, including the exuberant Piano Quintet of 1842. But his style did not appeal to contemporary taste and he failed to attract a popular following.

Mendelssohn found Schumann a teaching post at the Leipzig Conservatory to supplement his income from journalism, but Clara was undoubtedly the family's chief breadwinner, her piano performances attracting large audiences. When the couple undertook a concert tour of Russian cities in early 1844, Clara was the star, not her husband.

## Mental suffering

In fall 1844, Schumann moved with his family from Leipzig to Dresden, abandoning his editorial role on the *New Journal for Music*. It was in Dresden that he began to suffer from aural hallucinations, as well as anxieties, phobias, and depression. This did not stop him producing a steady stream of new compositions, including the *Manfred* Overture, written in 1848, which was destined to become his most frequently performed orchestral piece. He placed great hopes in his opera *Genoveva*, but this was poorly received when premiered in 1850.

That year, Schumann took up a post as musical director in Düsseldorf on the Rhine. The new location provoked a burst of creativity, both his "Rhenish" Symphony and his Cello Concerto, written in the first few months after arrival. However, Schumann's mental condition soon began to deteriorate

---

### ON TECHNIQUE
### Musical cryptograms

A musical cryptogram is a theme that uses the letter names for notes in order to encode a word, most often a person's name. Various devices give letters other than A to G—in German the letter "H" indicates B natural and E flat can be "Es" or "S".

First used by Baroque composers, this technique was taken much further by Schumann. In his *Carnaval*, for example, a recurrent theme (A, E flat, C, B) spells the word "Asch," the name of the town in which his betrothed, Ernestine von Fricken, was born. Schumann is represented by the notes E flat, C, B, A—spelling the abbreviation "Scha."

---

literary in inspiration, these suites expressed a wide range of mercurial moods, while also abounding in personal references and musical cryptograms (see box, left). In this same period, Schumann established himself as a leading music journalist, and founded the influential *New Journal for Music* in 1834. In his writings, he invented contrasting personae to represent opposed sides of his personality—the virile and assertive Florestan and the dreamy, reflective Eusebius.

Schumann was an excellent music critic, being the first in Germany to acknowledge the genius of Chopin as well as a key contributor to the discovery of Schubert's late works (see p.103).

---

" What would I not do **for love of you**, my own **Clara**! "

ROBERT SCHUMANN, LETTER TO CLARA WIECK, 1838

## KEY WORKS

**1831**
The early piano suite *Papillons* is inspired by a masked ball in Jean Paul's novel *Flegeljahre*.

**1838**
Touchingly depicts childhood innocence in *Kinderszenen*, 13 short piano pieces.

**1840**
*Dichterliebe*, Schumann's finest song cycle, is a setting of poems by Heinrich Heine.

**1845**
The Piano Concerto is premiered in Dresden with Clara Schumann as soloist.

**1851**
Symphony No. 3 in E-flat major, known as the "Rhenish," has its first performance in Düsseldorf.

△ **NEW JOURNAL FOR MUSIC,**1834
Schumann founded the *New Journal for Music* in Leipzig in 1834, which positioned him as a respected music journalist. The first edition of the journal is shown here.

alarmingly. He was plagued by a cacophony of musical notes and voices in his ears and saw visions of angels and devils. His duties as musical director included conducting an orchestra and choir. By 1853, his eccentric performances on the podium had caused a storm of local criticism and he was forced to resign.

▽ **SCHUMANN'S STUDIO**
In 1852, Schumann moved to Düsseldorf; the studio in his house is shown here. The move initially sparked creativity in him, but by 1853 he was suffering mental instability and the next year attempted suicide by hurling himself into the Rhine.

### A tragic finale

In September of that year, the unknown 20-year-old composer Johannes Brahms turned up at the Schumanns' door. Immediately adopted as a family friend and hailed by Schumann in print as a genius of the future, Brahms was a witness to the tragic finale to Schumann's life. Plagued by hallucinations, on February 27, 1854, Schumann fled his home and threw himself into the Rhine. He was rescued and taken at his own request to an asylum for the mentally ill at Endenich, near Bonn. There he descended into terminal mental and physical decline.

Numerous theories have been proposed concerning Schumann's condition, including that he was suffering the long-term effects of poisoning by mercury, administered as a cure for syphilis. What is more certain, however, is that there is clear evidence of mental instability in his family and that the composer exhibited many of the symptoms of schizophrenia and bipolar disorder. Robert Schumann eventually died on July 29, 1856. Championed by Brahms and performed by Clara, his oeuvre came to be recognized as among the crowning achievements of German Romanticism.

**FRANZ LISZT, 1838**
The composer is captured here by Henri Lehmann in 1838, aged 27. Two years later, Liszt visited England; *The Birmingham Journal* reported: "He is a very good-looking young man ... with a fine forehead, good nose, and well-cut mouth, not a little resembling the portraits of Bonaparte ... He is plainly ... a man of great genius and originality." The strong resemblance to Napoleon had not gone unnoticed by the young (married) women of the Paris salons who, by all accounts, were equally enthralled by the young man's good looks and his musical genius.

# Franz Liszt

## 1811–1886, HUNGARIAN

One of the greatest composer-pianists of all time, Liszt raised the music of the Romantic era to a spectacular pinnacle. Retiring at the height of his fame, he later took minor orders in the Catholic Church.

Franz Liszt was born in 1811 in the eastern Austrian village of Raiding. His father, Adam Liszt, a manager on the local aristocratic Esterházy estate, was a cellist who had played in the Esterházy family's private orchestra when Haydn was its director. Adam's only child—named after the monastic order he had once joined—was baptized Franciscus, but became known as Franz. While still a small child, he showed a spellbinding gift as a pianist—he was remarkable for his ability to improvise at the keyboard with total fluency.

## Prodigy and virtuoso

Adam Liszt took his son to study in Vienna, where the famous piano teacher Carl Czerny put his charge through a tough technical program designed to channel his natural talent. For composition, Liszt studied under Antonio Salieri (see p.83).

In Vienna, Czerny took Liszt to play to Beethoven, who was as impressed as everyone else by the boy's amazing talent. The family then headed for Paris, the other great musical center of the day, where Liszt's pianism

△ **LISZT'S BIRTHPLACE**
Liszt was born in this house in Raiding, a village in the Austro-Hungarian Empire. There was some Hungarian ancestry on his father's side.

mesmerized concert audiences. His newly composed full-length opera, *Don Sanche*, was premiered there when he was just 13 years old.

Father and son were on tour in Boulogne when, in 1827, Adam Liszt died of typhoid, leaving his teenage son to organize his career for himself. Temporarily recoiling from life as a performing celebrity, he set himself up as a piano teacher. A love affair with a young pupil, Caroline de

Saint-Cricq, came to an abrupt end after she married someone else. Liszt turned to religion for consolation.

## Coming to life

An uprising in Paris in 1830 against the imperial government of Charles X jolted Liszt out of his introspection. He was a republican supporter and retained these political sympathies when the rebellion was suppressed. He also found himself to be the darling of the elite salon scene, where much of Paris's cultural life took place. And with his tall and slender figure, long hair, alluring looks, and astonishing piano-playing, Liszt soon attracted the attention of bored young wives with older husbands. A friendship with Chopin dates from this time, although some sources suggest that it was later soured by professional rivalry.

Then, in 1833, Liszt was introduced to Countess Marie d'Agoult—a much-admired beauty eight years his senior, the mother of two small children from a loveless marriage, and an aspiring writer. Shared artistic affinities soon deepened an instant emotional bond, and in 1835 the couple ran away to Geneva, Switzerland, where the first of their three children was born. Encouraged by Marie, Liszt read widely and began to compose his first

△ **COUNTESS MARIE D'AGOULT**
Liszt was captivated by the dazzling charm of the distinguished Marie when introduced to her in 1833. He ran off to Switzerland with her two years later.

## IN CONTEXT
## Romanticism and revolution

A key idea of European Romanticism was the drawing together of different art forms into a single work—as in Liszt's orchestral symphonic poems, with their portrayals of ideas and characters from, for example, literature (*Tasso: Lamento e trionfo* and *Hamlet*). Liszt was also deeply responsive to the radical political movements of his era. When the Hungarian nationalist revolution of 1849 was brutally put down by the ruling Hapsburg Empire, Liszt composed his tumultuous piano work *Funérailles* in memory of those who had died in the nationalist cause.

**DEFEAT OF THE HUNGARIAN REBELS AT VILAGOS, AUGUST 1849**

△ **PLAYING FOR FRANZ JOSEPH**
In this anonymous painting, Liszt is shown, in his later years, playing the piano for a charitable event. Emperor Franz Joseph and other members of the imperial family are seated before him.

◁ **DANTE SYMPHONY, 1859**
The 1859 frontispiece of the score for Liszt's *A Symphony to Dante's Divine Comedy*. The symphony consists of two movements, the first depicting Hell and the second Purgatory.

major works; among these was a piano collection, *Album d'un voyageur*, inspired by the local Alpine scenery, later revised as the first "year" of the great cycle *Années de pèlerinage (Years of Pilgrimage)*.

Next year came an equally fruitful visit to Italy (early versions of the mighty *Dante Sonata* date from this period). The trip was interrupted by news of the flooding of the Danube

valley in Hungary; suddenly identifying strongly with his Hungarian ancestry, Liszt gave a fundraising concert in Vienna, which marked the start of his career as a traveling virtuoso.

## Fame and mastery

For the next 12 years, Liszt criss-crossed Europe with his Erard grand piano strapped to the roof of a stage-coach—giving concert tours that stretched from Ireland to Istanbul, setting sensational new standards of virtuoso pianism, and attaining near-adulation.

Marie's unhappiness at the composer's protracted absences meant that the couple drifted apart;

and Liszt's relentless performing schedule allowed little time for him to compose. In 1847, following a concert in Kiev, he met the Ukrainian princess Carolyne Sayn-Wittgenstein, a married woman with a young daughter. Again, an instant attraction was deepened—this time, by a shared Catholic faith. Liszt abandoned his life as a traveling pianist and moved to Weimar with Carolyne and her daughter, Marie. There he became Kapellmeister in Extraordinary, a post created for him by Weimar's ruler, Grand Duke Carl Alexander.

The couple lived there for the next 12 years; Liszt conducted the local orchestra, taught piano pupils, and at

## KEY WORKS

| **1837–51** | **1852–53** | **1854–57** | **1861** | **1866–72** | **1877–82** |
|---|---|---|---|---|---|
| Liszt's *Etudes d'exécution transcendante* are among the most difficult piano works ever composed. | The Sonata in B minor combines the piano sonata's traditionally separate movements in a single movement. | Based on Goethe's play, the *Faust Symphony* features musical portraits of the three leading characters, plus a choral finale. | Depicting devilish Mephistopheles in *Faust*, *Mephisto Waltz No. 1* is a masterpiece of whirling keyboard virtuosity. | A huge three-part choral and orchestral oratorio, *Christus* is the major statement of Liszt's years in Rome. | In the final volume of the piano cycle *Années de pèlerinage*, the musical mood is sometimes radiant, sometimes dark. |

# "His **personal magnetism** is **immense**, and I can scarcely **bear it** when he **plays**. He can make me **cry** all he **chooses**."

AMY FAY, LISZT'S STUDENT AT A MASTERCLASS IN WEIMAR, 1873

◁ **PRINCESS CAROLYNE**
The noblewoman and writer Princess Carolyne Sayn-Wittgenstein met Liszt in Kiev in 1847. Her attempts to secure an annulment of her marriage so that she could marry Liszt were unsuccessful.

last had substantial time to compose. Brilliant revisions of his earlier piano music from the Swiss and Italian years produced Romantic masterworks in the first two books of *Années de pèlerinage*, the *Etudes d'exécution transcendante*, and a religiously inspired piano cycle, *Harmonies poétiques et religieuses*. New creations included the Sonata in B minor and an ongoing sequence, *Hungarian Rhapsodies*. And with an orchestra now at his disposal, Liszt completed a cycle of 12 symphonic poems, plus his *Faust Symphony* and *Dante Symphony*, and a choral Mass written for the newly built cathedral in the Hungarian city of Esztergom.

Although he gave the premiere of his First Piano Concerto in 1855, by this time he seldom played the piano in public, never for a fee, and usually only to support a charitable cause of his choosing.

## Abbé Liszt and the last years

In 1860, intending that she and Liszt should at last marry, Carolyne traveled to Rome to try to secure a papal annulment of her Catholic marriage to her aristocratic husband. Local intrigue had undermined Liszt's position in Weimar, and he resigned his post to join her in Rome. Then came a sequence of disasters. When Carolyne's annulment was repeatedly blocked, she suffered a breakdown, and lapsed into eccentricity, seldom leaving her apartment, where she spent the rest of her life writing a 24-volume religious tract. Liszt's son, Daniel, had died of tuberculosis in 1859; now his daughter Blandine died, too, of post-natal complications. His surviving daughter, Cosima, although already married, began a relationship with Wagner; despite a longstanding friendship with his fellow composer, Liszt at first deeply disapproved, until he realized that her divorce and second marriage were inevitable. For several years he lived in a cell in a local monastery, played at church services, and composed; in 1865 he took minor orders as a Catholic *abbé*.

From 1869, Liszt divided his time between Rome and Weimar (where he gave piano master classes), while also helping to establish the conservatoire in Budapest (known today as the Liszt Academy). In his later years, he preferred to use the Hungarian version of his first name, Ferencz. The loneliness and declining health of old age often darkened his music, some of which developed a dissonant harmonic language that seems to gaze ahead toward the 20th-century Modernism of Bartók or Schoenberg. In 1886, Liszt was visiting the Wagner Festival at Bayreuth (which was run by Cosima after Wagner's death), when he died, leaving a vast musical legacy remarkable for its radicalism, much of which remains little known or performed, even today.

▽ **LISZT AND THE WAGNERS**
Here, Liszt (seated, with gray hair) is shown with Richard Wagner (standing) and Cosima Wagner (Liszt's daughter and Wagner's wife), at the Wagners' house in Bayreuth, northern Bavaria, c.1880.

# Directory

## Franz Krommer

1759–1831, CZECH

In his day sometimes ranked with Beethoven, Krommer (also known as František Kramář) is noted for his writing for wind instruments and his numerous string quartets. Born in Kamenice, Moravia, then a part of the Austrian Empire, now in the Czech Republic, he studied violin and organ with his uncle, who was a choirmaster. His talents as an instrumentalist and composer earned him various musical posts at ducal courts and cathedrals. His compositions, appearing from the early 1790s, were chiefly influenced by Haydn and Mozart. In the early 1800s, he responded to demand for wind music by producing notable clarinet concertos and a series of partitas for wind bands.

From 1811, Krommer worked at the Austrian imperial court, attaining the post of court composer in 1818. He was prolific in his output, writing 77 string quartets, some of them strikingly innovative, as well as at least nine symphonies.

**KEY WORKS:** Symphony No. 1 in F major, Op. 12, 1797; Clarinet Concerto in E-flat major, Op. 36, 1803; Octet Partita for Winds in F major, Op. 57, 1807; Three String Quartets, Op. 103, 1821

△ JOHANN NEPOMUK HUMMEL

## Bernhard Crusell

1775–1838, FINNISH/SWEDISH

Clarinetist and composer Crusell was born in Uusikaupunki (Nystad) in Finland, then part of the kingdom of Sweden. His parents, impoverished bookbinders, were not interested in music, but he learned to play the clarinet and joined a regimental band. In 1792, he was recruited to the Royal Court Orchestra in Stockholm. He played clarinet with the orchestra for the next 40 years, while also winning international renown as a soloist. After studying composition with the German composer Abbé Vogler, he began writing his own works, at first chiefly for clarinet. His output included three clarinet concertos, as well as chamber works for wind instruments. He also wrote vocal music, notably settings of verse by Sweden's leading Romantic poet Esaias Tegnér. His opera *Lilla Slavinnam* (*The Little Slave Girl*), first staged in 1824, received 34 performances in his lifetime.

**KEY WORKS:** Sinfonia concertante in B-flat major, Op. 3, 1804; Clarinet Concerto in F minor, Op. 5, 1815; Divertimento for Oboe and Strings in C major, Op. 9, 1823; *Frithiofs Saga* (songs), 1826

## ◁ Johann Nepomuk Hummel

1778–1837, AUSTRIAN

A leading figure in the transition from the Classical to the Romantic era in European music, Hummel was born in Pressburg (Bratislava), then part of the Austrian Empire. The son of a prominent musician, he was a child prodigy on piano, embarking on his first international concert tour at age 10. Hummel received lessons from Mozart and Haydn, and as a piano virtuoso in Vienna in the 1790s was a rival of Beethoven. He succeeded Haydn as director of music for Prince Esterházy from 1804 to 1811. For the last 18 years of his life, he served as director of music at the Weimar court. His compositions included operas, masses, and chamber music, but he is best known for his piano works, which influenced Chopin and Schumann. He was also a conductor, piano teacher, and campaigner for musical copyright.

**KEY WORKS:** Trumpet Concerto in E major, 1803; Fantasy for Piano in E-flat major, Op. 18, 1805; Piano Concerto No. 2 in A minor, Op. 85, 1816; Piano Sonata in F-sharp major, Op. 81, 1819

## George Bridgetower

c.1778–1860, POLISH

A violinist and composer of mixed heritage—his father was of African descent, his mother European—Bridgetower was the inspiration and original dedicatee for Beethoven's *Kreutzer Sonata*. The dedication was changed after the former friends fell out. Born in Poland, and raised in Austria, Bridgetower was a violin prodigy, performing across Europe in his youth, including for the future George IV, who became his patron. He studied violin with François-Hippolyte Barthélemon, and composition and piano with Thomas Attwood—and perhaps Haydn, too. He received a music degree from Cambridge University and became a member of the Royal Philharmonic Society. Bridgetower later taught piano, and his most notable compositions are for that instrument.

**KEY WORKS:** *Henry: A Ballad for Voice and Piano*, c.1812; *Diatonica Armonica for the Pianoforte*, 1812.

## John Field

1782–1837, IRISH

A pianist and composer of music for piano, Field was the son and grandson of professional musicians. Taught music at home, he moved with his family from Dublin to London in 1793.

There he became a pupil of pianist-composer Muzio Clementi and a salesman for Clementi pianos. In 1802–1803 he traveled with Clementi to Europe, settling in St. Petersburg. Field lived in Russia for the remainder of his life and his music was influenced by Russian folk songs. As a pianist he was noted for his intimate style and singing tone. His compositions included seven piano concertos and 16 "Nocturnes," a genre that he invented. His expressive melodies and chromatic harmonies influenced many Romantic composers, most notably Chopin. Suffering from cancer, he died in Moscow in 1837.

**KEY WORKS:** Three Piano Sonatas, 1801; Piano Concerto No. 2 in A-flat major, 1811; Nocturnes Nos. 1–3, 1812; Nocturnes Nos. 4–5, 1817

△ MIKHAIL GLINKA, ILYA REPIN, 1887 (PAINTED 30 YEARS AFTER GLINKA'S DEATH)

## Carl Maria von Weber

1786–1826, GERMAN

Renowned as the founder of German Romantic opera, Weber was born into a theatrical and musical family—one of his cousins married Mozart. He was a sickly child but precociously gifted, publishing his first composition at the age of 12 and seeing his first opera performed at 14. He was an outstanding pianist; his keyboard works demand exceptional virtuosity. Often in financial difficulties, he was exiled from Württemberg after being imprisoned for embezzlement in 1810. As a conductor he brought a fresh perfectionism to performances at opera houses in Breslau, Prague, and finally Dresden, where he directed the German Opera from 1817. His magical opera *Der Freischütz*, written at Dresden, was an international success and has remained his most famous work. It was followed by *Euryanthe*, an opera seen as paving the way for Wagner.

**KEY WORKS:** *Invitation to the Dance* (piano solo), 1819; *Der Freischütz* (opera), 1821; *Euryanthe* (opera), 1823; *Oberon* (*Singspiel*), 1826

## Giacomo Meyerbeer

1791–1864, GERMAN

The most successful composer of Romantic grand opera, Meyerbeer was born Jakob Liebmann Beer, the son of wealthy, cultured Jewish parents in Berlin. He acquired an early reputation as a piano virtuoso but by age 20 was set on writing operas. From 1816 he lived in Italy. His Italian operas culminated in success with *Il crociato in Egitto* in 1824. Moving to Paris, he wrote the French grand operas *Robert le diable* and *Les Huguenots* that made him an international celebrity. In 1842 he returned to Berlin, serving for six years as director of music to the king of Prussia. Unashamedly wealthy and retaining his Jewish faith, Meyerbeer came under attack from jealous antisemitic critics, but *Le Prophète* was a triumph when staged in Paris in 1849. His final work, *L'Africaine*, was in rehearsal at the time of his death.

**KEY WORKS:** *Il crociato in Egitto* (opera), 1824; *Robert le diable* (opera), 1831; *Les Huguenots* (opera), 1836; *Le Prophète* (opera), 1849

## Franz Berwald

1796–1868, SWEDISH

Now considered Sweden's leading Romantic composer, Berwald was born into a family of musicians in Stockholm. Following in his father's footsteps, he became an orchestral violinist from the age of 14. His first known compositions date from 1816, but success eluded him. He earned a living as an orthopedist in Berlin in the 1830s, and from 1849 ran a glass factory at Sandö in Sweden. In his spare time he wrote ambitious music, including symphonies, tone poems, operas, and chamber works. Of his seven symphonies, only the first was performed in his lifetime. He enjoyed a belated success when his opera *Estrella de Soria* was applauded at its premiere in Stockholm in 1862. Two years before his death he became professor of composition at the Stockholm Conservatory.

**KEY WORKS:** Violin Concerto in C-sharp minor, 1820; *Estrella de Soria* (opera), 1841; Symphony No. 3 in C major, "Singulière," 1845; Piano Concerto in D major, 1855

## △ Mikhail Glinka

1804–1857, RUSSIAN

The founder of Russian musical nationalism, Glinka was born into a wealthy family in the Smolensk region of Russia. In his youth he had piano lessons from John Field, and at first wrote songs while working as a civil servant in St. Petersburg.

In 1830, Glinka went to live in Western Europe, enjoying the operas of Bellini and Donizetti in Italy and studying composition in Berlin. Returning to Russia in 1834, he embarked upon the opera *A Life for the Czar*, freshening up operatic conventions with references to Russian folk music. His second opera, *Ruslan and Lyudmila* (1842), showed greater originality but received a cool reception from critics. Glinka returned to Western Europe and died in Berlin in 1857. All subsequent Russian composers acknowledged his influence.

**KEY WORKS:** *A Life for the Czar* (opera), 1836; *Ruslan and Lyudmila* (opera), 1842; *Kamarinskya* (symphonic poem), 1848

# LATE 19th CENTURY

# Richard Wagner

## 1813–1883, GERMAN

An opera composer and librettist, Wagner was a controversial figure and a radical force in 19th-century culture. His idea of the "total work of art" found its fullest expression in the four operas of the *Ring* cycle.

The youngest of nine children, Richard Wagner was born in Leipzig in 1813. His father died when he was a baby, after which his mother lived with actor and painter Ludwig Geyer, who may have been Richard's biological father. Originally attracted to writing drama, around the age of 15 Wagner discovered his musical vocation, inspired by hearing Beethoven's Ninth Symphony. Studying composition in Leipzig, he wrote a juvenile symphony and various keyboard works, but his ambitions soon focused exclusively on opera. From the outset he wrote his own libretti, regarding himself as a dramatist as well as a composer.

### Turmoil and instability

Wagner had completed two unsuccessful operas, *Die Feen* and *Das Liebesverbot*, by 1836, when he married Minna Planer, an actress. She left him, briefly, for another man. Although they were reconciled, it was not an easy marriage. Wagner became music director at the opera house in Riga on the Baltic, but could not live on the income. In 1839, he and Minna fled to escape creditors—the stormy sea voyage inspired his ghost-ship opera *The Flying Dutchman*. Then came another two years of poverty and overspending in Paris, where he was again threatened with debtors' prison.

Wagner's breakthrough work was *Rienzi*, a conventional grand opera in the style of established composers such as Vincenzo Bellini and Giacomo Meyerbeer. It was rejected in Paris but, with Meyerbeer's backing, accepted for performance at the Dresden opera house in Wagner's native Saxony. The success of this production in 1842, and of *The Flying Dutchman* in 1843, led to his appointment as director of music at Saxony's royal court. There he wrote *Tannhäuser*, performed in Dresden in 1845, and *Lohengrin*, completed in 1848. Drawing on Germanic myth, these mature works established Wagner's originality as an operatic composer.

### Revolution and escape

Political upheaval prevented *Lohengrin* from being premiered in Dresden. In 1848, the German kingdoms, including Saxony, faced uprisings and demands for a unified German nation-state. Wagner sided with the revolutionaries, advocating a German national theater and embracing republicanism. In May 1849, after street fighting, the rebels

**JEAN DE RESZKE IN THE ROLE OF SIEGFRIED FROM THE *RING* CYCLE**

ON TECHNIQUE
**The leitmotif**

Richard Wagner sought to create operas that were unified dramas, rather than broken up into arias, choruses, and recitatives. Starting with *The Flying Dutchman*, which was composed in the early 1840s, he employed leitmotifs—recurring musical themes that are associated with specific characters or other elements of the drama.
   This technique was fully developed by the time Wagner wrote the first operas of his *Ring* cycle in the 1850s. Leitmotifs such as the horn call representing the heroic Siegfried constantly recur and transform, weaving a continuous musical web that underlies the work's dramatic action.

◁ **TANNHÄUSER POSTER**
This poster announces the premiere of Wagner's *Tannhäuser* at the Opéra de Paris in 1861. The opera touches on the conflict between sexual and spiritual love.

" The **oldest, truest,** most **beautiful organ** of **music** ... is the **human voice.** "

RICHARD WAGNER, *OPERA AND DRAMA*, 1851

▷ **RICHARD WAGNER, 1868**
Despite a life of profligacy, philandering, controversy, and exile, Wagner had a profound influence on Western music. This portrait by Franz von Lenbach shows the composer in his mid-fifties.

LUDWIG II (OR LOUIS II), KING OF BAVARIA, WILHELM TAUBNER, 1864

▷ *DIE WALKÜRE*
Shown here is a scene in Act III from an 1899 production of Wagner's *Die Walküre* (The Valkyrie), the second opera in his *Ring* cycle, featuring eight female warriors, or Valkyries (from the old Norse, meaning "chooser of the slain").

## KEY WORKS

**1842**
Achieves his first success with *Rienzi*, a five-act opera performed in Dresden.

**1845**
Based on German legend, the opera *Tannhäuser* contrasts sacred and profane love.

**1865**
Wagner's opera of doomed love, *Tristan und Isolde*, completed in 1859, belatedly premieres in Munich.

**1868**
*Die Meistersinger von Nürnberg*, Wagner's only mature comic opera, is hugely popular with German audiences.

**1876**
The first complete performance of the *Ring* cycle is given at the Bayreuth Festival.

**1882**
Wagner's mystical last opera, *Parsifal*, premieres at Bayreuth.

in Dresden were suppressed. Known for his revolutionary sympathies, Wagner fled to Switzerland to escape arrest, becoming a political exile banned from all German states.

### A total work of art

He produced a series of polemical writings—*Art and Revolution*, *The Art of the Future*, *Opera and Drama*—that described a program for a post-revolutionary culture. With capitalism overthrown, a "total work of art" would unify music, poetry, drama, and dance, and provide a focus for the people. The antisemitic Wagner left no place for Jews in his imaginary community, branding them "aliens" and decrying their influence on German music. He supported himself by borrowing large sums from adoring women.

By 1853, Wagner had written the text for *Der Ring des Nibelungen*, a cycle of four operas based on Nordic sagas. The music for the first two, *Das Rheingold* and *Die Walküre*, was completed by 1856. These works were aligned with his theoretical writing, which saw music as subordinate to the poetic text. But in the mid-1850s, he discovered the philosophy of Arthur Schopenhauer—Buddhist-influenced, and positing music as the highest of the arts. He also discovered Otto and Mathilde Wesendonck. Otto was a silk merchant who became another of Wagner's admiring benefactors; his wife, a poet, became the composer's muse and possibly his lover. He played her the singular compliment of setting her verse, rather than his own, in his *Wesendonck-Lieder* (1858). Above all,

she was the inspiration for *Tristan und Isolde*, his opera of love and death, completed during spells in Venice and Lucerne in 1858–1859. In *Tristan*, the passionate music dominates the drama. Its unresolved yearning harmonies, failing to establish a clear tonality, are often seen as the starting point of musical Modernism.

### Desperation and salvation

By the 1860s, Wagner's relationship with the Wesendoncks had broken up and the ban on his return to German territories had been lifted. After the staging of a revised version of *Tannhäuser* in Paris in 1861 proved a fiasco, his finances remained in a desperate state, his luxurious tastes far outreaching his income. Salvation arrived in 1864 in the person of

Ludwig II, the 18-year-old ruler of Bavaria (see box, opposite). A star-struck admirer of the composer, Ludwig cleared Wagner's debts and gave him a lavish annual income. At the same time, the composer's more intimate needs were met by Cosima von Bülow, Liszt's daughter and the wife of Hans von Bülow, a conductor who premiered several Wagner operas. She became Wagner's mistress and had three children before she obtained a divorce and married him in 1870 (Wagner's first wife died in 1866). Wagner wrote his *Siegfried Idyll* for Cosima's first birthday as his spouse and after the birth of their son Siegfried.

Wagner rode the wave of assertive German nationalism that came with the creation of the German Empire, under Prussian rule, between 1866 and 1871. His comic opera *Die Meistersinger von Nürnberg* was a triumph from its first performance in 1868, hailed as representing the true spirit of the resurgent German people. He resumed composition of the *Ring* cycle, abandoned since the 1850s, finishing the third opera, *Siegfried*, in 1871 and the final work in the sequence, *Götterdämmerung*, in 1874. With Ludwig II's backing, he built a theater at Bayreuth in northern Bavaria to stage his masterpiece. The first complete performance of the *Ring* cycle in 1876 was a major cultural event with a celebrity audience. The cycle has maintained its fascination ever since, its symbolism attracting diverse interpretations ranging from Marxist anti-capitalism to Freudian psychodrama.

## Later years

Wagner lived for the rest of his life at Wahnfried, the villa he had built by the Bayreuth theater. His final creative project was *Parsifal*, an operatic version of the legend of the Holy Grail, completed in 1882. He regarded it as a sacred work, to be performed exclusively at Bayreuth so it would not degenerate into an "entertainment." His apparent embrace of a mystical Christianity alienated some of his previous admirers, including the philosopher Friedrich Nietzsche. Other critics have viewed the opera as an expression of Wagner's racial theories and antisemitism.

Wagner's habits of a lifetime never changed. He still ran into debt and he was unfaithful to his wife. It was after a marital fight that he died of a heart attack in Venice in 1883. His body was brought back to Bayreuth for burial. Cosima Wagner became the self-appointed guardian of the purity of performances of Wagner's operas at the annual Bayreuth Festival, a role she maintained into the 20th century.

▷ **RICHARD AND COSIMA WAGNER**
Cosima (shown here c. 1875), illegitimate daughter of Liszt, divorced the conductor Hans von Bülow to marry Wagner, who was not faithful to her.

△ **BAYREUTH FESTIVAL, 1892**
Held annually since 1876, and with initial funding by Ludwig II, the festival and its theater (built 1871–1876) are devoted to the showcasing of Wagner's stage works. This late-19th-century painting is entitled *The Arrival of the Guests.*

" The most **terrible thing** of all is **happy love,** for then there is **fear in everything**. "

COSIMA WAGNER

# Giuseppe Verdi

## 1813–1901, ITALIAN

Verdi wrote operas in a popular style that blended high drama and emotion with memorable melodies. He was celebrated as a cultural hero by his Italian contemporaries engaged in a struggle for independent nationhood.

△ **MARGHERITA BAREZZI**
This portrait by Augusto Mussini depicts Verdi's first wife, Margherita. The couple met when Verdi lodged in the house of her father, Antonio, a wine merchant and music-lover who became Verdi's patron.

The son of an innkeeper, Giuseppe Verdi was born in 1813 in the village of Le Roncole, near Busseto, in northern Italy. He picked up the basics of music from the organist at the village church. When he was sent away to school in Busseto at the age of 10, his musical talent attracted the attention of a wealthy local businessman and amateur musician, Antonio Barezzi, who became Verdi's patron.

### The Barezzi family

When Verdi was 18, Barezzi sent him to Milan to study music at the Conservatory, but his untutored skills were inadequate to gain admission. Instead he took private lessons, funded by Barezzi, while learning about musical drama by attending performances at Milan's La Scala opera house. After two years in Milan, Verdi returned to Busseto to take up the post of director of municipal music and marry his patron's daughter, Margherita Barezzi. The couple had two children, both of whom died in infancy and were followed to the grave by their 26-year-old mother in 1840.

Through this time of personal tragedy, Verdi was founding his career as a composer. Using the contacts he had made in Milan, in 1839 he succeeded in having his first opera, *Oberto*, staged at La Scala, where it was well received. Accordingly he was commissioned to write three more operas; the first, *Un giorno di regno*, was a complete flop, pulled after a single performance. Verdi vowed never to compose another opera, but the La Scala management pressed upon him a Bible-based libretto by Temistocle Solera, relating the conquest and exile of the Jews by the king of Babylon. First staged in 1842, *Nabucco* was a sensational hit, running for 57 performances.

The high point of *Nabucco* for Milanese audiences was the chorus "Va, pensiero," a stirring lament for the conquered and enslaved Hebrews. It was adopted as a patriotic anthem by Italians resentful of the rule exercised by the Austrian Hapsburgs over northern Italy. Verdi's next opera, *I Lombardi*, staged in Milan in 1843 to a similarly enthusiastic reception, also had nationalist overtones and, like its predecessors, slipped past the Austrian censors.

## IN CONTEXT
### The Risorgimento

The 19th-century movement called the Risorgimento ("resurgence") turned Italy into a united nation state. In 1815, the Italian peninsula was politically fragmented, with different areas ruled by Austria, the pope, and various monarchs. Popular uprisings in 1848–1849 seeking to create an Italian republic failed. After a series of wars, including the invasion of Sicily and the south by the followers of Giuseppe Garibaldi in 1860–1861, the whole of Italy was united in 1870 under King Victor Emmanuel II. As Italy's leading composer, Verdi acted as a focus for nationalist sentiment throughout the Risorgimento.

GIUSEPPE GARIBALDI IS WELCOMED IN VICENZA ON MARCH 7, 1867

> " I am the **least erudite** among **past** and **present composers.** "
> GIUSEPPE VERDI

▷ **GIUSEPPE VERDI, 1886**
Verdi commissioned this lively painting of himself from the fashionable Italian portraitist Giovanni Boldini. The composer introduced the artist to the milieu of opera, where he gained a substantial number of lucrative commissions.

# "In the **theater** the **public** will stand for **anything but boredom**."

GIUSEPPE VERDI, LETTER, 1869

△ **LA TRAVIATA SCORE, 1853**
In Verdi's opera about passion and loss, Violetta is forced to give up her lover, Alfredo, by his father. The work was only successful after Verdi revised it in 1854.

## IN PROFILE
### Giuseppina Strepponi

Born in 1815, singer Giuseppina Strepponi was the daughter of a cathedral organist. After studying at the Milan Conservatory, she made her stage debut as a soprano in 1834 and was soon an international celebrity, singing lead roles in operas by Rossini, Bellini, and Donizetti. She performed in most of Verdi's early operas, including *Nabucco*, before her voice gave way under the strain of an excessive performance schedule. After her retirement, she became Verdi's lover in Paris in 1847. Married in 1859, they remained together happily until her death in 1897.

**STREPPONI WITH THE MUSIC SCORE OF**
*NABUCCO*, ANONYMOUS ARTIST

Although Verdi was sympathetic to the Italian nationalist cause, he took no part in political plots. After the success of *Ernani*, based on a play by Victor Hugo, his growing international reputation led him to spend long periods abroad and when Italy erupted in revolution in 1848, he was in Paris enjoying a love affair with the soprano Giuseppina Strepponi.

Verdi did, however, respond to a request for an opera from embattled Italian Republicans in Rome. The result was *La battaglia di Legnano*; Verdi visited Rome for its staging in January 1849. Its clear message of Italian resistance to foreign oppression was rapturously received, but the subsequent collapse of the Roman Republic temporarily dampened enthusiasm for revolution.

### Art meets life
Verdi's drive to fulfill the insatiable demand for his musical dramas in any case left little time for political activity. He took a thoroughly businesslike attitude to composition, seeking to maximize his earnings. Down-to-earth and unintellectual, he accepted that his job was to provide entertainment for audiences that appreciated melodrama and strong emotion rather than subtlety. By 1850, he had completed 15 operas, complaining that he had to work "like a galley slave."

In the early 1850s, Verdi wrote three masterpieces that have stood the test of time: *Rigoletto*, *La traviata*, and *Il trovatore*. These were works that built

on the *bel canto* (literally, "beautiful singing") tradition of his Italian predecessors Rossini, Bellini, and Donizetti, but with greater dramatic power and an element of social and political provocation. *Rigoletto* ran into trouble with the censors because it depicted a dissolute and wicked ruler, implicitly questioning monarchical authority. *La traviata*, based on Alexandre Dumas' recent novel *La Dame aux Camélias*, was considered shocking for its sympathy with a fallen woman "living in sin" with her lover.

The theme of *La traviata* was of direct relevance to the composer himself, who was sharing his life, unmarried, with Strepponi. In 1851, in line with his image of himself as a simple man of the people, he returned to his native countryside, where he began occupying a villa that he had built at Sant'Agata, just outside Busseto. The local people perceived Verdi's cohabitation with Strepponi as sinful. Utterly irreligious, he made plain his absolute contempt for their narrow-mindedness and when the municipality sought to profit from his celebrity by creating a theater named for him, Verdi refused to even step inside the building. However, he did eventually marry Strepponi in 1859.

Italy's adoption of Verdi as a hero of the Risorgimento (see box, p.140) gathered momentum as the unification of the country progressed. In 1859, nationalists adopted the slogan "Viva Verdi" as shorthand for "Viva Vittorio Emanuele Re d'Italia" ("Long Live Victor Emmanuel King of Italy").

### Fame and fortune
After the declaration of the Kingdom of Italy in 1861, Verdi was persuaded to accept election to parliament, though he rarely attended. He adopted the lifestyle of a country landowner, writing operas at a less frantic pace. Works such as *Un ballo in maschera*

▷ **VERDI THEATER, BUSSETO**
The theater named after Verdi was inaugurated on August 15, 1868, with performances of *Un ballo in maschera* and *Rigoletto*. Verdi himself refused to attend.

(1859) and *La forza del destino* (1862) showed a turn toward large-scale spectacle that reached its climax with *Aida*. This work was commissioned by Khedive Ismail, ruler of Egypt, who had built the Khedivial Opera House in Cairo to celebrate the opening of the Suez Canal in 1869. First performed in the Khedivial Opera House in 1871, *Aida* ensured its enduring popularity through the sumptuous exploitation of its foreign Ancient Egyptian setting.

Verdi did not compose a new opera for another 16 years. In 1874, he wrote his *Requiem* Mass for poet Alessandro Manzoni, which was described by

the conductor Hans von Bülow as "an opera in ecclesiastical robes." He also revamped older works and tinkered with plans, unfulfilled, for an operatic version of Shakespeare's *King Lear*.

### Shakespearean opera

It was finally a libretto for an opera based on *Othello*, written by poet Arrigo Boito, that drew Verdi out of retirement. *Otello* was followed by *Falstaff*, another Shakespeare-inspired opera, in 1893. These works showed Verdi's undimmed creative vitality and taste for innovation. Less straightforwardly tuneful than his

earlier operas, they are regarded by many critics as his finest creations. After the death of his wife in 1897, Verdi divided his time between Sant'Agata and a luxury suite at a hotel in Milan. It was while staying in Milan that he died of a stroke in January 1901. He was first buried in the city's Cimitero Monumentale and then moved, a month later, to lie alongside Giuseppina in the Casa di Riposo, a charitable home for aging musicians that he had funded. Both burials drew vast crowds, paying tribute to a man who had become a symbol of Italian national identity.

△ **AIDA, 2011**
Verdi's *Aida*—a story of conflict, love, and betrayal in Ancient Egypt—involves a love triangle between Aida, an enslaved Ethiopian princess; Radamès, a warrior; and Amneris, an Egyptian princess. It has become one of the most famous and widely performed of all operas. The production shown here was directed by Charles Roubaud and staged in Orange, France, in 2011.

## KEY WORKS

| **1842** | **1851** | **1853** | **1871** | **1874** | **1893** |
|---|---|---|---|---|---|
| Verdi's third opera, *Nabucco*, is a popular success when performed at La Scala in Milan. | *Rigoletto*, the first of Verdi's middle-period operas, premieres at La Fenice in Venice. | *Il trovatore* and *La traviata*—two of Verdi's most famous operas—appear in the same year. | Verdi's *Aida*, a spectacular opera set in the Egypt of the pharaohs, premieres in Cairo. | The *Requiem*, Verdi's only major nonoperatic work, is performed in Milan Cathedral. | The comedy *Falstaff*, Verdi's last opera, is staged at La Scala in Milan. |

# Clara Schumann

## 1819–1896, GERMAN

A leading 19th-century piano virtuoso, Clara Schumann was also a gifted composer. Her creative output, although impressive, was restricted by the expectations of a woman's role in a male-dominated society.

Clara Wieck was born in Leipzig in 1819. Her mother was a singer and her father a music teacher. In 1824, when Clara was five, her parents divorced, after which she was brought up by her father. Recognizing her natural musical talent, he subjected his young daughter to a rigorous routine of lessons and practice.

Clara became a child prodigy, embarking on her first concert tour as a solo pianist at the age of 11. She also composed, publishing her first short piano pieces in 1831 and performing her own Piano Concerto with the Leipzig Gewandhaus orchestra at the age of 16. Her solo piano concerts in Vienna in the winter of 1837–1838 were a popular and critical triumph. Praised for the sensitive musicality of her playing, in contrast to the showy technical virtuosity then in vogue, she was the first pianist to regularly perform from memory.

### Subordination and control

Clara met her future husband, Robert Schumann (see pp.124–127), nine years her senior, in 1828 when she was still a child. After they fell in love in 1835, Clara's controlling father did his best to block the relationship. The couple finally married in 1840 after a court ruled that her father's permission was not required. Their marriage was loving. Her concert performances continued, and were the family's chief source of income. Despite bearing eight children in 13 years, she found time to compose works such as her substantial Piano Trio of 1846. But her husband's creative ambitions took precedence, and the practical concerns of the household fell on her. When the family was caught up in a violent revolt in Dresden in 1849 (see box, right), it was Clara—pregnant as usual—who braved gunfire to rescue three of the children, who had been left in the care of a maid.

Clara's creative drive was above all undermined by a sense of isolation in a male-dominated sphere. "A woman must not desire to compose," she wrote, "there has never yet been one able to do it. Should I expect to be the one?" Her last significant composition, the *Three Romances for Violin and Piano*, was written in 1853. She was then engulfed in the tragic events of her husband's decline into insanity, which she endured with the support of young composer Johannes Brahms.

### Late performances

After Robert's death in 1856, Clara threw herself into concert tours, often performing with the violinist Joseph Joachim (see p.160), but she no longer composed. Clara is said to have given at least 1,300 performances before declining health curtailed her appearances from the mid-1870s. She outlived four of her children, her son Ludwig dying in an insane asylum like his father. Deaf and wheelchair-bound, she died in 1896 and was buried alongside her husband in Bonn.

◁ **CLARA SCHUMANN**
Despite her exceptional talent as both a pianist and composer, Clara put her own creative desires and ambitions to one side in order to ensure the success and well-being of her family and her husband.

**IN CONTEXT**
**Revolution in Europe**

The Schumann family lived through a period of great political turmoil. The upheavals of the French Revolution in 1789 and the Industrial Revolution in Europe and the US (1760–c.1840) gave rise, in 1848–1849, to a series of revolts across Europe sparked by mass social and economic discontent, and targeted at monarchical rule.

Revolutionary action began in Sicily and extended to France, Germany, Italy, and the Austrian Empire. The 1848 uprising in France was the only one to succeed and led to the downfall of the monarchy. The uprising in Dresden in May 1849 that Clara Schumann and her family became embroiled in was one of the last insurrectionary events of 1848–1849.

**POPULAR UPRISING IN DRESDEN'S ALTMARKT, MAY 1849**

◁ **HANDWRITTEN SCORE**
This handwritten score by Clara Schumann dates back to 1853. It is entitled *Variations for Pianoforte on a Theme by Robert Schumann*.

▷ **CESAR FRANCK, 1885**
Franck combined his conventional approach toward composition with a flair for improvisation and a readiness to explore new ideas. The composer is shown in this portrait by Jeanne Rongier at his organ, at the peak of his career, aged 63, just five years before he died. There is some speculation about the cause of his death, but it is widely thought to have been from a respiratory infection.

# César Franck

## 1822–1890, BELGIAN

Franck was a skilled public performer in his youth, but his immense talent for composition only truly blossomed in his final years. He went on to become an influential organist, composer, and teacher.

Born in Liège in 1822, César Auguste Franck spent most of his career in France, although his family background was part ly German. His father had a disappointing job as a bank clerk, sometimes unemployed, and transferred all his ambitions onto his children. So, when Franck and his younger brother showed early musical promise, they were swiftly enrolled at the Liège Conservatoire. By 1835, Franck had made sufficient progress to perform at public concerts in Brussels and Aachen, and the entire family moved to Paris to help promote the youngster's career.

### In search of recognition

Critics have questioned the wisdom of this push for success. Always a quiet lad, Franck was denied part of his childhood, and the pressure may have affected the development of his natural talent. He entered the Paris Conservatoire in 1837, where he won a number of awards, but the big prize, the Prix de Rome, eluded him.

Furthermore, Franck's earliest compositions met with little acclaim. His initial work, a set of trios for piano, violin, and cello (Op. 1), was published after winning the support of Chopin and Liszt, but his first large-scale composition, a biblical oratorio on Ruth, was greeted unenthusiastically at its premiere in January 1846.

Family tensions increased further when he fell in love with Félicité Saillot Desmousseaux, the daughter of two actors. His father opposed the match, but the couple married during the Paris riots of 1848. Guests clambered over barricades to reach the church: an omen, perhaps, of a marriage that was to have its stormy moments. But, finally freed from the tyrannical interference of his father, Franck

pursued a fresh course—the organ, rather than the piano, became his principal instrument, as he sought the security of a church organist's post.

### Interest and acclaim

Success followed rapidly as Franck became first the choirmaster (1853) and then the organist (1858) at the Basilica of St. Clotilde in Paris. This was extremely timely, as he was able to "christen" the church's brand new Cavaillé-Coll organ (see box, right). Franck soon became a virtuoso on this incredible instrument. Congregations would linger after the service to listen to his improvisations. The organ company was so impressed by his skills that it hired him as an artistic consultant, which meant he could give recitals on other Cavaillé-Coll organs.

Franck was also a notable teacher, becoming professor of organ at the Paris Conservatoire in 1871, where he also informally taught composition to a group of faithful students known as the *bande à Franck*. His jobs left him little time for his own composition, and it was only after retirement that he saw the celebrity status his father had hoped for. The *Six Pièces* (1859–1862) is probably his finest organ work, while the *Variations Symphoniques* (1885) and the Violin Sonata (1886) are generally seen as his masterpieces.

" It was said of Franck that **the discovery** of a single **new chord** was sufficient to make him **happy** for a **whole day**. "

NORMAN DEMUTH, ENGLISH COMPOSER AND MUSICOLOGIST, 1951

# Bedřich Smetana

## 1824–1884, CZECH

Smetana sounded a rallying call for Czech independence with a series of enchanting operas and his set of symphonic poems *Má vlast*, enduring symbols of national pride.

Bedřich Smetana was born in Litomyšl, Bohemia, on March 2, 1824. His father made a good living as a master brewer and played violin in his free time. Musically gifted, young Bedřich took violin lessons and excelled as a pianist, giving his first concert at the age of six.

Smetana attended several schools, including one in Bohemia's capital, Prague. In 1843, he continued his musical training with the blind pianist and composer Josef Proksch, and scraped a living as piano tutor to the five children of Count Leopold Thun.

The brief Prague Revolution that took place in June 1848, in which the city's residents rose up unsuccessfully against Bohemia's Hapsburg rulers, shaped Smetana's awareness of Bohemian nationalism. He wrote several patriotic works in response, including "Song of Freedom." That same year, he opened a Piano Institute in Prague, and in 1849 he married the pianist Kateřina Kolářová, whom he had known since his school days.

Despite developing a successful career as a pianist and composer, Smetana felt vastly underappreciated in Prague, and in 1856 left for Gothenburg, Sweden.

### Return to Prague

The Czech National Revival (see box, right) persuaded Smetana, who had remarried after his wife's death, to return home in 1862. He became conductor of Prague's new Provisional Theater—founded as a home for Czech opera—in 1866, and worked to develop its repertoire of Czech operas. Having been brought up speaking German, he now learned the Czech language, and set it with great eloquence in his mature operas. Over the next 20 years, he completed eight magnificent works based on national legend or comic tales, *The Bartered Bride* (1866), *Dalibor* (1867), and *The Kiss* (1876) among them.

◁ **DALIBOR**
Smetana's opera *Dalibor*, the title page of which is seen here, was first staged at the New Town Theater in Prague, in 1868.

However, numerous conservative critics disapproved of Smetana's Wagner-influenced style and tried to subvert his position. He resisted the campaign for his dismissal, but was forced to resign in 1874 after suffering from the onset of syphilis. That fall he became totally deaf.

Over the next few years, Smetana worked on six symphonic poems intended to embody the spirit of Czech nationalism. The cycle, *Má vlast* (*My Homeland*), first performed in 1882, became an emblem of Czech resurgence. Professional success countered the composer's depression and distracted him from great physical pain. Smetana's String Quartet No. 2 in D minor (1882–1883) may reflect his disturbed state of mind; certainly his physical and mental decline caused him to suffer immensely, provoking hallucinations and paranoia. He was admitted to Prague's asylum for the insane where he died on May 12, 1884.

**AUSTRIAN EMPEROR FRANZ JOSEF I IN UNIFORM**

◁ **LITOMYSL CASTLE**
This 16th-century Renaissance arcaded castle was Smetana's birthplace. Until 1831, his family lived in a ground-floor apartment in the castle brewery, where his father was brewer to Count Waldstein.

▷ **BEDRICH SMETANA**
Smetana, seen here in a painting by Per Sodermark, studied with the Hungarian composer Franz Liszt, whose works inspired and energized him. He visited Liszt several times in Weimar, Germany.

▷ **ANTON BRUCKNER, 1885**
The imposing yet stark portrait of Anton Bruckner by German painter Hermann von Kaulbach shows the composer in profile at the age of 61. At this stage in his career—the year after the triumphant premiere of his Seventh Symphony—Bruckner was enjoying notable success. In 1886, Franz Joseph I of Austria awarded him the Order of Franz Joseph.

# Anton Bruckner

## 1824–1896, AUSTRIAN

Deeply religious, and during his life known mainly as a church composer and organist, Bruckner was the creator of nine large-scale symphonies, a cycle today seen as one of the pinnacles of 19th-century music.

# "They want me to **write differently** ... I could, but **I must not**. **God** has ... given me this talent. It is to Him that I must **give account**."

ANTON BRUCKNER

Anton Bruckner was born in the small Upper Austrian village of Ansfelden, near the city of Linz. His father was the village schoolmaster and a part-time musician and organist; his mother had sung in the village church choir. He was the oldest of 11 children, several of whom died in infancy.

### Early years in rural Austria

Bruckner's father, a good-natured man, encouraged his son's musical talent: aged only 10, young "Tonerl" would deputize for him as organist at the church. There were early signs, too, of Bruckner's obsessive streak: he was capable of practicing the organ for 12 hours at a stretch. The defining event in his early life was when his parents first took him to the nearby Augustinian monastery of St. Florian, with its large and ornately decorated Baroque church, impressive organ,

and extensive cloisters and living quarters. For Bruckner, a devout Roman Catholic from his earliest years, St. Florian represented spiritual and musical paradise.

His fine treble voice enabled him to become a chorister there, and he studied the violin besides the organ. When the time came to leave, he decided to become a teacher like his father, and did a year's training in Linz. His first position was as assistant schoolmaster in the tiny village of Windhaag, where additional chores included spreading manure in the fields of his unlikeable superior's farm holding. The prior of St. Florian found him a happier post in the village of Kronstorf (where Bruckner wrote some early choral works), then in 1845 at St. Florian itself as assistant teacher. Bruckner stayed there for the next ten years, rising to the position of

principal organist, and developing his phenomenal skill as an improviser on the instrument.

### From Linz to Vienna

In 1855, the organist of Linz's Old Cathedral died. Diffident and self-effacing as ever, Bruckner had to be persuaded to turn up at an audition for the post, and was absorbed in prayer until the organ-tuner suggested he try for the job. Bruckner's mighty improvisation amazed everyone present, and the position was his. By this time, he was an experienced church composer of psalm settings, hymns, choral motets, and a complete Requiem Mass, mostly written for St. Florian. Although accomplished, these works conform to conservative local church-music tradition, and show little sign of the strikingly individual mastery that was to come.

◁ **ORGAN AT ST. FLORIAN CHURCH**
As a young man in his early twenties, Bruckner was the principal organist at the glorious Baroque church of St. Florian in Upper Austria. He played this magnificent organ, which has been known as the Bruckner Organ since the 1930s. The composer's body is interred in a tomb below it.

△ **SKETCH FOR SYMPHONY NO. 9**
The last years of Bruckner's life were largely given over to the composition of his Ninth Symphony, which was unfinished at the time of his death.

## ON TECHNIQUE
### Melody and harmony

The great purity of the interweaving melodic lines in the music of the Renaissance composer Palestrina was a quality greatly admired by Bruckner. In his Mass in E minor, commissioned for the inauguration of the Votive Chapel of the New Cathedral in Linz (which remained unfinished until 1924), the music recalls Palestrina's spiritual polyphony. Yet Bruckner was also influenced by the radical harmony of Wagner—tense, chromatic, exploratory, ambiguous, unstable, complex—which pushed the limits of convention. Bruckner found a way of drawing both elements together in a style that was entirely his own.

▽ **BRUCKNER'S HOUSE, BELVEDERE**
The year before Bruckner's death, the emperor of Austria, Franz Joseph, granted the aging musician rooms in the caretaker's wing of the historic building complex of Belvedere, Vienna, so that he did not have to climb stairs.

Musical life in Linz was much more wide-ranging than at St. Florian, and Bruckner now found himself encountering the concert-hall works of Beethoven and the other Classical masters. Deeply impressed and intimidated by Beethoven's music in particular, he enrolled in a musical correspondence course run by Simon Sechter in Vienna (see box, p.149), and worked on its various technical exercises so obsessively that Sechter warned him to slow down or risk mental problems. Two years after completing the course, Bruckner heard Wagner's music for the first time: a performance of *Tannhäuser* triggered a near-idolatrous admiration of the older composer and a search to find a way of responding to Wagner's advanced harmonic language within Bruckner's own style. The result, in 1864, was what he regarded as his first "official" piece, a choral and orchestral Mass in D minor, to be followed by two more in E minor and F minor.

Bruckner's eccentric streak had not been modified by years of professional life in Linz. He continued to engage with the world around him in the style of an Austrian countryman, retaining his rural accent and dialect. His desire to marry led him to propose to a sequence of teenage girls—thanks to a simple conviction that for marriage to be worthy in the eyes of God, his prospective bride should be a virgin, as he himself was. He would be told, often kindly: "But Herr Bruckner, you are too old!" These rebuffs, although always accepted, made him unhappy; one of them, combined with overwork, led in 1867 to a four-month nervous collapse. (Sechter's warning had been remarkably perceptive.)

### Mastery and misconception
When Sechter died in 1867, Bruckner was asked to apply to replace him as a professor at the Vienna Conservatory. After chronic indecision, he finally accepted the post, and gained a reputation as a fine teacher whose brand of unpretentious eccentricity was understood and (once they were used to it) generally liked by his pupils. Bruckner then began to appear more widely as an organist: the magnificence of his improvisations,

for example at Paris's Notre-Dame in 1869 and at London's Royal Albert Hall two years later, quickly passed into legend.

Bruckner was gradually developing into one of the greatest symphonists that classical music had ever known; his work introduced new aspects of depth, originality, grandeur, and audaciousness into the symphonic form. His official First Symphony had been completed in Linz in 1866. (A successor, dating from 1869 but then rejected by him, has—bizarrely—been given the posthumous designation No. 0.) The work was subsequently and repeatedly revised, like most of the great cycle to come—a process partly of self-criticism, but also often of Bruckner's taking on board advice from other musicians, advice that was usually well-meaning but often completely misguided. There was a perception that he was a Wagnerian

Anton Bruckner's Sterbehaus im Belvedere in Wien.

## KEY WORKS

**1851**
Receives his first major musical appointment, as principal organist at St. Florian, where he had been a boy chorister.

**1863**
A first encounter with Wagner's music, at a performance of *Tannhäuser* in Linz, radically influences Bruckner's conservative idiom.

**1865**
Travels to Munich for the premiere of Wagner's *Tristan und Isolde*, meeting the composer for the first time.

**1872**
A performance of the Mass in F minor is Bruckner's first Viennese success, impressing Brahms and Liszt, among many others.

**1884**
Arthur Nikisch conducts the triumphant premiere of Bruckner's Seventh Symphony in Leipzig.

**1886**
Played by the Vienna Philharmonic under Hans Richter, the Seventh Symphony is again a great success, although some press reviews are vitriolic.

**1894**
Completes the Adagio third movement of his Ninth Symphony.

symphonist, with little appreciation of the engaging spirit of Austrian country dance that he adopted in his work. There was also insufficient understanding of the fact that Bruckner's immense, powerful orchestral climaxes related more to the layered sonorities of the organ than to Wagner's sophisticated blending. Today, later Wagnerian-influenced "revisions" of the symphonies by others are rightly regarded as spurious.

## Legacy and reputation

In speaking of this great originality and the unorthodox nature of Bruckner's work, musicologist Deryck Cooke, writing in 1980, suggests that, initially, his "processes seemed so strange and unprecedented that they were taken as evidence of sheer incompetence ... [but now] it is recognized that ... Bruckner created a new and monumental type of symphonic organism ...," producing something profoundly different in music, "something elemental and metaphysical."

Although Bruckner's music was sometimes dismissed and ridiculed, it did have wonderful moments of success in his lifetime. His Fourth and Seventh Symphonies, his most lyrical in style, were much acclaimed, and now feature regularly in performances across the world. Much less often played are the monumental, more austere Fifth and often very beautiful Sixth. With their huge structures and exploratory, pre-Modernist harmony, the Eighth and unfinished Ninth Symphonies remain major undertakings. But while the style and scale of a Bruckner symphony is not to every concert-goer's taste, the stature of his achievement is today regarded as unassailable.

△ **BRUCKNER AT HIS PIANO**, c. 1894
The great composer sits beside his grand piano in his workroom in Vienna, a crucifix on the sideboard to the left. He is pictured here, a frail old man aged 70, shortly before his death.

" The **absolute victory** of **light** over **darkness**. "

HUGO WOLF, COMPOSER, ON A PERFORMANCE OF BRUCKNER'S EIGHTH SYMPHONY, 1892

# Johann Strauss II

## 1825–1899, AUSTRIAN

Praised by Wagner and admired by Berlioz and Brahms, Strauss attracted a significant cult following, earning worldwide fame as Vienna's "Waltz King."

Johann Strauss was born in 1825 in Ulrich, near Vienna, several years before his father (also named Johann), a prominent dance musician, launched his own orchestra. The young Johann spent much of his childhood at the magnificent Sperl ballroom—made famous by the Congress of Vienna (see box, below)—or listening to his father's band rehearse at home.

Johann's father wanted his oldest boy to train for a career in banking; his mother, however, secretly arranged for him to study violin with the leader of her husband's orchestra. He also received composition lessons from the future choirmaster of Vienna's St. Stephen's Cathedral.

### Launching a career

In 1834, Strauss abandoned commercial studies at the Polytechnic Institute in Vienna and applied for permission to give public concerts. He launched his career with a ball at Dommayer's Casino in October 1844, performing several of his own works, including the *Gunstwerber* waltz and *Herzenslust* polka.

Following his father's death in 1849, Strauss dominated Vienna's dance scene. He amalgamated his father's orchestra with his own, attracting a cult following as a composer of brilliant waltzes, polkas, marches, and quadrilles. His long collaboration with Vienna Men's Choral Association produced such immortal waltzes as *The Blue Danube* (1867) and *Wine, Women, and Song!* (1869).

### Worldwide fame

Strauss and his orchestra were in great demand overseas and toured regularly between 1856 and 1886. A trip to the US in 1872 secured Strauss's international fame, and a significant fortune.

In addition to writing dance music, Strauss composed 16 operettas, *The Gypsy Baron* and *Die Fledermaus* outstanding among them. Although the latter's "Champagne Song" drew criticism after the collapse of Vienna's stock market, its hugely uplifting party spirit and rousing beat guaranteed the work's lasting appeal.

In his dances, the commercially astute composer celebrated events such as the opening of buildings, royal occasions, the launch of technologies, and international exhibitions. Many of his finest pieces (including the *Tritsch-Tratsch-Polka*, the *Egyptian March*, and, with his brother Josef, the *Pizzicato-Polka*) were written for the summer seasons that he conducted from 1856 to 1865 at the Vauxhall Pavilion at Pavlovsk.

From 1887, Strauss's third wife rekindled the composer's creative fire after his divorce from actress Angelika Dittrich. In the decade before his death in 1899, works such as *A Night in Venice* and the *Emperor Waltz* were added to his list of enduring hits.

△ **THE BLUE DANUBE, COVER**
Strauss's famous waltz was first performed in Vienna in 1867 as a choral work, but drew far greater acclaim when an orchestral version premiered in Paris later the same year.

◁ **AN EVENING WITH STRAUSS, 1894**
Franz von Bayros's work shows Strauss at his piano, flanked by his third wife, Adele (left), Brahms (right), and other high-society friends. Bayros married Strauss's stepdaughter, Alice, two years after painting this work.

### IN CONTEXT
#### The Congress of Vienna

The economic shock of the Napoleonic Wars (1805–1813) and the repressive measures imposed to unify Europe after the Battle of Waterloo (1815) cast a shadow over the 19th century. From November 1814 to June 1815, Vienna—the seat of the Hapsburg dynasty—hosted a conference of major European powers. Away from the negotiating table, delegates at the Congress of Vienna displayed their wealth at a series of parties and balls. Reports of dancing aristocrats and of court ladies wrapped in silver cloth and covered in diamonds fueled a dance craze among the imperial city's rapidly expanding middle class.

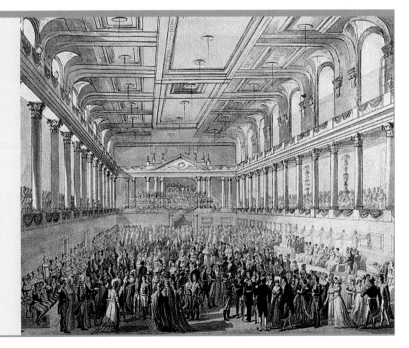

EXTRAVAGANT BALL HELD DURING THE CONGRESS OF VIENNA, c.1815

▷ **ALEXANDER BORODIN**
Borodin worked on his magnum opus, the opera *Prince Igor*—a forceful depiction of medieval Russia—for almost 18 years. However, he wrote music only as a hobby: he was a chemist by training and is said to have been one of the first scientists to link high cholesterol to heart disease.

# Alexander Borodin

## 1833–1887, RUSSIAN

A chemist by profession, Borodin rose to fame as one of The Five, a group of composers eager to establish a uniquely Russian school of music. He is most famous for his String Quartet No. 2 and his opera *Prince Igor*.

The illegitimate son of an aging Armenian prince, Luka Gedianov, and his mistress, Alexander Borodin was born in 1833 and baptized as the son of one of his father's serfs. Prince Gedianov stood by the boy and his mother, Avdotya Antonova: he lived with them in St. Petersburg during Alexander's childhood. In 1839, he arranged for Avdotya to marry a medic; and, just before his death, freed his son from serfdom (see box, right).

Alexander's home education included flute lessons but his musical interests expanded after Mikhail Shchiglev joined the household as a boarder: Borodin taught himself to play the cello, Shchiglev the violin.

## Science and music

In 1849, Borodin published three salon pieces, and the following year he entered St. Petersburg's prestigious Medical-Surgical Academy to pursue his passion for chemistry. Despite his chemistry professor's disapproval, he continued to compose and perform while working for his PhD, which was awarded in 1858 for a dissertation, entitled "On the Analogy of Arsenic Acid with Phosphoric Acid in Chemical and Toxicological Behavior."

After moving to Heidelberg in 1859 for advanced studies in chemistry, Borodin immersed himself in the city's musical life and met his future wife, Ekaterina Protopopova, a pianist who was in Germany to receive treatment

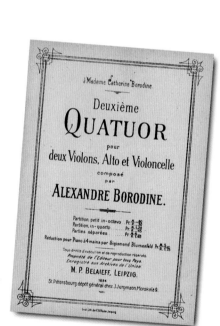

### IN CONTEXT
### Russian serfdom

Russia's peasants had been exploited for centuries before a system of full serfdom was adopted in the 1600s—according to which, landowners took control of those who worked their land. Rules were often breached, but serfs could not be bought or sold independent of the land. They were bonded to their owners for life in return for tenancy of small plots of land. The system delivered social stability, economic stagnation, and appalling injustice. All Russian serfs were finally emancipated in 1861, following an edict issued by Czar Alexander II, which led to a rapid improvement in the Russian economy.

**ABOLITION OF SERFDOM IN RUSSIA, ALFONS MARIA MUCHA, 1914**

for tuberculosis. She introduced him to music by Chopin, Schumann, and other Romantic composers. Back in St. Petersburg in 1862, Borodin taught at the Medical-Surgical Academy, succeeding his mentor Nikolay Zinin as professor of chemistry. He also joined a group of musicians known as The Five or the Mighty Handful.

Borodin soon began writing his First Symphony, completing it during term breaks and summer holidays over the next three years. Then, in 1869, after abandoning one opera, he returned to the genre again, having received a scenario from

critic Vladimir Stasov based on the 12th-century "Song of the Host of Igor." He worked on *Prince Igor* for the rest of his life, but also found time to compose a Second Symphony in B minor, sketches for a third in A minor, and works such as *In Central Asia* and the final act of the opera-ballet *Mlada*.

### A new following

Because his work as a scientist was so time-consuming, Borodin's overall musical output was small. Apart from operas, he wrote three symphonies, two string quartets, chamber music, and various songs.

*Prince Igor* was unfinished at the time of his death from a heart attack in February 1887. It was completed by Glazunov and Rimsky-Korsakov and entered the international repertoire. Borodin reached new audiences in the early 1950s, when Robert Wright and George Forrest recycled several of his greatest melodies in their Broadway musical *Kismet*.

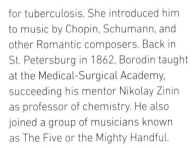

◁ **MARKET PLACE, SET DESIGN**
Created by the Russian artist Konstantin Alexandrovich Veshchilov (1878–1945) for Borodin's magnum opus, the opera *Prince Igor*, this atmospheric stage design depicts a typical marketplace scene.

△ **TITLE PAGE, STRING QUARTET**
Dedicated to his wife, Borodin's String Quartet No. 2 in D major is often said to convey a sense of serenity, triumph, and happiness. It was published in 1894.

# Johannes Brahms

## 1833–1897, GERMAN

One of the giants of 19th-century music, Brahms was a perfectionist who excelled in every major genre except opera. For most of his life, he was able to devote himself exclusively to composing.

Brahms was so brutally self-critical that he destroyed many more of his works than he published. He discarded almost all of his juvenilia and even in middle age—when he became prosperous and famous—he was still known to burn compositions that he considered unsatisfactory.

One result of this refusal to compromise is that Brahms's surviving output is almost unfailingly high in quality. His four symphonies and four concertos are mainstays of the orchestral repertoire; his two dozen chamber works, for various combinations of instruments, are almost all acknowledged masterpieces; his solo piano pieces, ranging from powerful sonatas to exquisite miniatures, are much loved; his *German Requiem* is one of the most popular of all choral pieces; and as a songwriter he had a gift for melody that perhaps ranks second only to Schubert's. He never wrote an opera.

### Youthful talent

Johannes Brahms was born in Hamburg in northern Germany, the country's largest port city. His father was a jobbing musician who played several string and wind instruments, and his mother (aged 44 at his birth, 17 years older than her husband) was a seamstress. The traditional view is that the family were wretchedly poor, living in a slum, but this is an exaggeration. Although their finances were often precarious, the family were respectable and happy, and Brahms was devoted to his parents and siblings (an elder sister and a younger brother). He was educated at good schools and his outstanding talent at the piano was nurtured by skillful and caring teachers.

Brahms first performed in public when he was ten. By his early teens, he was helping supplement the family income by playing the piano in restaurants and theaters, giving lessons to local children, and making arrangements for brass bands. According to some accounts, he also played in sleazy dockside taverns that were little better than brothels, and this experience is said to have scarred him for life, souring his relationships with women. However, many scholars now dismiss this as myth.

### Liszt and Schumann

In 1850, Brahms met a young Hungarian violinist, Eduard Reményi, whom he accompanied in several recitals. They made a concert tour of German cities in 1853, and although this was not particularly successful as a business venture, it had a profound impact on Brahms's life. During the tour he met another violinist, Joseph Joachim, who became one of his

◁ **A GERMAN REQUIEM**
Brahms's longest work is perhaps his most poignant. It was inspired in part by his grief at the death of his mother.

◁ **BRAHMS'S BIRTHPLACE**
Brahms was born in this building in the poor Gängeviertel district of Hamburg, close to the docks. It was destroyed by Allied bombs in World War II.

▷ **JOHANNES BRAHMS, c. 1890**
In his youth, Brahms had been angelic-looking, but in later life he developed into the portly, heavily bearded, almost Santa Claus-like figure familiar from many paintings and photographs.

△ **REMENYI AND BRAHMS**
In 1850, Brahms met the talented violinist Eduard Reményi (left), a Hungarian refugee who introduced him to the folk and Roma music that came to inspire works such as his *Hungarian Dances*.

▽ **OVAL PIANO**
This distinctive oval-shaped piano belonged to Brahms; it is now preserved in Detmold Castle, where the composer resided in the winters of 1857–1860.

closest friends and gave him letters of introduction to two of the most distinguished musicians of the day—Franz Liszt in Weimar and Robert Schumann in Düsseldorf.

Brahms and Liszt did not hit it off (Liszt was the supreme keyboard showman, whereas Brahms was reserved in character), but Brahms and Schumann (and his wife, Clara) were kindred spirits: on the day after they met, Schumann recorded in his diary, "Visit from Brahms. A genius."

Clara was equally enthusiastic: when Brahms played his own compositions, she thought "everything was brimming over with imagination and emotional intensity." Already, at the age of 20, he was writing music that was remarkable for its rugged strength and pulsating energy, but the Romantic fire was tempered by Classical rigor. Brahms's work grew more subtle over the years, but this balance between Romantic passion and Classical dignity did not change throughout his career.

Schumann wrote an ecstatic article about Brahms in the music magazine he edited, hailing him as the new messiah of German music, and he arranged for some of his compositions to be published. However, the support of Brahms's influential champion was

cut short by tragic circumstances. Schumann's mental health had been fragile for some time and in February 1854, after attempting suicide, he was confined to an asylum, where he was to spend the rest of his life. At this time, the Schumanns had six children and Clara was pregnant with a seventh child.

Brahms proved a great support to the distressed family. He was probably in love with Clara and after Robert died in 1856, many people, including Clara herself, expected Brahms to propose. However, he hated the idea of being tied down, and his ardor turned into a devoted lifelong friendship with Clara. Later in life, Brahms had dalliances with several other women (he was particularly attracted to beautiful singers), but he always drew back when marriage seemed likely and remained a lifelong bachelor.

### Move to Vienna
Over the next decade, Brahms moved around a good deal. He toured as a pianist and in 1857–1860 held a

part-time post as conductor of the choral society of the princely court at Detmold, but he was always able to devote much of his time to composing. In 1862, he visited Vienna for the first time and he settled there the following year when he was made director of the Singakademie, a renowned choral society; later he was director of another of the city's distinguished musical organizations, the Gesellschaft der Musikfreunde (Society of Friends of Music).

### Public success
In 1865, Brahms's mother died, and he expressed his grief in his *German Requiem*, which he had begun earlier as a tribute to Schumann. It was first performed in 1868 and established Brahms in the front rank of living composers. He also achieved success with works in a lighter vein, notably his *Hungarian Dances* for piano duet (1869). At a time when a piano was an essential feature in middle-class homes, this kind of music was hugely popular for domestic performance

> " It is **as though** he [Brahms] has been **sent by God himself!** "
>
> CLARA SCHUMANN, ON BRAHMS PLAYING HIS OWN WORK

WILH. NOWAK. 04.

and in money-making terms the *Dances* were almost the equivalent of a hit record today.

Free of the financial worries and domestic encumbrances that have afflicted many great composers, Brahms was able to devote himself to working for his own satisfaction and at his own unruffled pace. In spite of his success, he lived modestly in a rented three-room apartment. He became notorious for his brusque,

sometimes crude, behavior and sarcastic tongue, but he was also extremely generous to his family (including his stepmother after his father remarried), to friends, and to promising young musicians. Although he had detractors, who thought his work too conservative, especially compared with that of Wagner (see pp.136–139), he was generally revered, and bracketed by some with Bach and Beethoven as one of the "three Bs."

In 1896, Clara Schumann died at the age of 76 and Brahms made an arduous 40-hour journey to attend her funeral in Bonn. On his return to Vienna, he was visibly ill and he died the following year of liver cancer, mourned by music-lovers the world over. In Hamburg, his home city, the ships in the harbor flew their flags at half mast. Brahms was buried in Vienna, near the graves of two of his heroes, Beethoven and Schubert.

△ **AT HOME IN VIENNA**
This watercolor shows the interior of Brahms's apartment in Vienna, with a bust of Beethoven on the wall. Brahms lived comfortably but unostentatiously, enjoying food, wine, cigars, and the company of friends.

## KEY WORKS

**1853**
Meets Robert and Clara Schumann, who recognize his genius and promote his career.

**1859**
Premiere of Piano Concerto No. 1 in Hanover, with Brahms himself as soloist.

**1868**
Premiere of *A German Requiem* in Bremen Cathedral; the work establishes Brahms as a major composer.

**1876**
Premiere of Symphony No. 1 in Karlsruhe; Brahms had labored over the work for 14 years.

**1887**
Premiere of Double Concerto in Cologne; it was to be Brahms's last orchestral work.

**1891**
Meets clarinettist Richard Mühlfeld, whose playing inspires Brahms to compose four works for his instrument.

▷ **CAMILLE SAINT-SAËNS**
Saint-Saëns was celebrated for his virtuosity at the organ. When Franz Liszt heard him play at the Madeleine church in Paris, he pronounced him the greatest organist in the world. He wrote numerous solo compositions for the organ, and his third and final symphony incorporates the instrument to thrilling effect.

# Camille Saint-Saëns

## 1835–1921, FRENCH

In his long career, Saint-Saëns progressed from boy wonder to grand old man. He composed in virtually every genre of music known in his time and was also one of the outstanding pianists and organists of the age.

> " I produce **music** as an **apple tree** produces **apples**. "
>
> CAMILLE SAINT-SAËNS

△ **SAMSON AND DELILAH**
Saint-Saëns's most famous opera, premiered in Weimar in 1877, has many colorful scenes, including a dance of priestesses, here depicted by French artist Pierre Carrier-Belleuse.

Camille Saint-Saëns was born in Paris into a middle-class family. A piano-playing aunt gave him his first music lessons when he was three and he showed immense precocity. He gave private recitals from the age of five and made his public debut at age 10, offering, as an encore, to play from memory any of Beethoven's 32 piano sonatas—an astonishing prospect at such a young age, especially given the difficulty of many of Beethoven's sonatas. His talents were not confined to music: he excelled at Latin and mathematics, and developed serious interests in subjects ranging from archaeology to astronomy.

## Musical tours and tragedy

From 1848 to 1853, Saint-Saëns studied at the Paris Conservatoire, then became organist at the church of St. Merry. His Symphony No. 1 was successfully premiered in 1855 and by this time he was already winning golden praise from musicians of the caliber of Berlioz and Rossini. In 1858, he moved from St. Merry to take up the high-status post of organist at the Madeleine church (see box, right).

He remained at the Madeleine church for almost 20 years, until 1877, thereafter pursuing his career independently, traveling to perform as a pianist and conductor not just in Europe, but also in North and South America and the Far East.

Although he seems to have been predominantly attracted to men, Saint-Saëns married in 1875. His 19-year-old bride was half his age and the marriage was a complete disaster. The couple had two children, both of whom died as infants in 1878, one after falling from a window. In 1881, Saint-Saëns walked out on his wife and never saw her again.

## Prolific composer

Saint-Saëns's vast output included symphonies, concertos, operas (of which *Samson and Delilah* is the best known), religious and secular choral music, tone poems (notably *Danse Macabre*, which uses a xylophone to evoke rattling bones), chamber music, songs, solo compositions for piano and organ, and even music for the cinema. Ironically, his most popular work today is probably the witty and satirical *Carnival of the Animals* (1886), which was written as a joke and not published during his lifetime.

Saint-Saëns's music is notable for its elegance, refinement, and charm—qualities considered to be quintessentially French—but by the end of his life his reputation was in decline in his own country. Nevertheless, he was honored with a state funeral at the Madeleine church.

Some detractors think his music is superficial—more about style than substance—but his best works have stood the test of time and remain much-loved staples of the repertoire.

△ **DANSE MACABRE, 1874**
Saint-Saëns's tone poem opens with a note repeated 12 times, signaling midnight. A violin, representing death, calls the dead to rise from their graves and dance.

## IN CONTEXT
## La Madeleine

The church of La Madeleine (dedicated to Mary Magdalene) is one of the great landmarks of Paris. It was conceived by Napoleon as a memorial to the glory of the French army and takes the form of an enormous Roman temple. However, it was transformed into a parish church and consecrated in 1842. Its magnificent organ was designed by Aristide Cavaillé-Coll, the 19th century's most famous organ builder. Saint-Saëns held the highly prestigious post of organist there from 1858 to 1877. His successors included his pupil Gabriel Fauré, who was organist between 1896 and 1905.

THE CHURCH OF THE MADELEINE, c.1910, HAND-COLORED PHOTOGRAPH

# Georges Bizet

## 1838–1875, FRENCH

Bizet's career reads like the libretto of a tragic opera. Precociously gifted, he struggled to find fame. At the end of his life, he created *Carmen*, one of the world's most popular operas, but died believing it was a failure.

Born in Paris, the son of a singing teacher, Georges Bizet received his early musical training from his parents and uncle, all accomplished musicians. In 1848, aged nine, he was admitted to the Paris Conservatoire and was an exceptional student, winning prizes for piano, organ, and composition.

◁ **THE PEARL FISHERS**
This is the title page of a German edition of Bizet's first major opera, *The Pearl Fishers*, which tells the story of a love triangle set in a fishing village in ancient times.

### Early breaks and interests

More importantly, Bizet found favor with Charles Gounod—20 years his senior—who became his lifelong friend and mentor. Inspired by one of the latter's works, Bizet produced his first major composition, Symphony in C (1855), now recognized as one of his finest orchestral scores. It was never performed in his lifetime, only receiving its first public airing in 1935.

In 1857, he won the Prix de Rome, which financed his studies in Italy. Here, he soon lapsed into a bohemian lifestyle and his main musical offering at that time was the comic opera *Don Procopio*. This earned him disapproval from his teachers who expected a recipient of the prestigious Prix to produce a more serious work.

Bizet was a brilliant performer, but he refused to become a concert pianist. His interest lay in the theater. In this field, his first opera of real quality was *The Pearl Fishers*, which premiered in 1863. The public liked it, as did Berlioz (see pp.110–113), but the critics lambasted it. The show closed after 18 performances.

### Turbulent times

Bizet's personal life was in turmoil at this time. In 1862, he fathered an illegitimate child with the family's housekeeper, although this was hushed up (the mother only revealed the secret on her deathbed). Bizet later married Geneviève Halévy. Their union was sometimes rocky, largely due to the interference of Geneviève's mother, who was mentally unstable.

Meanwhile, his career was stalling. He was burdened with hack work—producing piano transcriptions, creating a piano course for children,

and helping other composers. His own compositions were often rushed or abandoned for lack of time. *Carmen* (1875) should have changed all that. Based on Prosper Mérimée's powerful novella (see box, below), it had hot-blooded characters, Spanish and Roma rhythms, and the mercurial Célestine Galli-Marié singing the lead. Yet Bizet's opera shocked Parisian audiences, who were appalled by the rawness of the passions, the on-stage murder of Carmen by her jealous ex-lover Don José, and scenes in which women smoked. Because it had spoken dialogue rather than recitative, it was staged at the Opéra-Comique, which normally hosted more gentle productions. Nonetheless, Bizet's masterpiece has become one of the world's most popular operas. With its brutal plot and passionate characters, it went on to influence the verismo (realism) movement (see p.187).

△ **GALLI-MARIE AS CARMEN**
Henri Lucien Doucet here depicts Célestine Galli-Marié in Spanish attire as the heroine in the title role of Bizet's thrilling opera *Carmen*. Audiences were outraged by the work's passion and violence when it premiered in 1875.

▷ **GEORGES BIZET**
Shown here bearded and bespectacled, Bizet died suddenly at the age of just 36, seemingly from a heart attack. He saw minimal success in his lifetime—his works generated far greater interest from the 20th century onward.

### IN PROFILE
## Prosper Mérimée

Mérimée (1803–1870) was a genuine polymath: a government official, man of letters, historian, and translator. In his work as the inspector-general of historical monuments, he was instrumental in founding the National Museum of the Middle Ages and restoring the citadel of Carcassonne. The Base Mérimée is the official database of French monuments. As a writer, he is best remembered as a pioneer of the novella. Published in 1845, his *Carmen* was based on a story told to him by the Countess of Montijo on his visit to Spain in 1830.

PORTRAIT OF PROSPER MERIMEE, SIMON ROCHART, 1852

> " [A] **beautiful art**, but ... a **wretched profession**. "
>
> GEORGES BIZET, ON MUSIC, 1867

# Modest Mussorgsky

## 1839–1881, RUSSIAN

One of Russia's most inventive and unconventional composers, Mussorgsky was derailed by family misfortune and his own chaotic lifestyle. His work was fully appreciated only after his death.

Modest Mussorgsky was born into a world of privilege. His father was a wealthy landowner with aristocratic roots that could be traced back to the 9th century. Unfortunately for his heirs, this wealth was dependent on the unpaid labor of the many serfs who ran his estates. When Alexander II freed the serfs in 1861, the family's fortunes were fatally undermined.

By this stage, Mussorgsky was launched on his haphazard musical career. Details of his childhood are sketchy, but he was born on the country estate in the Pskov district, about 250 miles (400 km) south of St. Petersburg, and showed great musical promise, having taken piano lessons with his mother. But after studying at a military academy, he enrolled in the Preobrazhensky regiment, and then seemed destined for an army career.

Mussorgsky's musical ambitions revived after he joined a group of avant-garde composers now known as the Mighty Handful or The Five. Led by Mily Balakirev (see box, right), this included Alexander Borodin, César Cui, and Nikolai Rimsky-Korsakov. Mussorgsky persuaded Balakirev to give him lessons in composition. These were somewhat basic but fired the young man's enthusiasm. He abandoned his army career and began work on a number of projects.

### A perfect storm

Progress was disappointingly slow. In 1858, Mussorgsky suffered some form of mental breakdown (which his family described as nerves). He recovered gradually, but was affected increasingly by financial worries, which led him to take a menial post in the civil service. He was also broken-hearted following his mother's death in 1865 and began drinking heavily, sparking the terrible alcoholism that was to darken his later years.

Mussorgsky's major works date from the late 1860s. *Night on the Bare Mountain*, his most important orchestral piece, was produced in 1867, and the initial version of *Boris Godunov*, his only completed opera, was finished two years later. Neither produced the reaction he had hoped for. The committee of the Imperial Theater, for example, was baffled by the revolutionary structure of his opera, which had no prima donna, no ballet elements, no conventional arias, and a series of tableaux rather than continuous action.

Mussorgsky produced a radically revised version of *Boris* in 1874, but this, too, met with a lukewarm response—not just from the critics but also, crucially, from fellow musicians. Mussorgsky's limited musical training gave his music a rough, unpolished quality that jarred with his contemporaries. Greatly discouraged by these setbacks, the composer became a chronic alcoholic, ending his days in a military hospital.

Most of Mussorgsky's music first became known in "smoothed-out" versions by well-meaning colleagues, including Rimsky-Korsakov. It was only in the 20th century, when these recensions were stripped away, that audiences were able to appreciate the raw, earthy genius of his work.

△ *BORIS GODUNOV*, TITLE PAGE, 1874
Mussorgsky's first version of this opera appeared in 1869 but was rejected by the committee of the Imperial Theatre. A revised version premiered in 1874 in St Petersburg. The work is now considered by many to be a masterpiece

### IN PROFILE
### Mily Balakirev

Balakirev was only two years older than Mussorgsky, but his influence was crucial. He was the leader of the Mighty Handful (who were also known as The Five), the driving force behind new Russian music. Balakirev agreed to give Mussorgsky lessons and, for a while at least, this arrangement ran smoothly. At his peak, Balakirev was a fine composer—best known for *Islamey*, a showpiece for the piano, based on a Caucasian dance—but his circumstances were as testing as those of his pupil. He had a reclusive and quarrelsome nature, which alienated many of his friends. He also suffered a mental breakdown, which cost him his job as a railroad clerk.

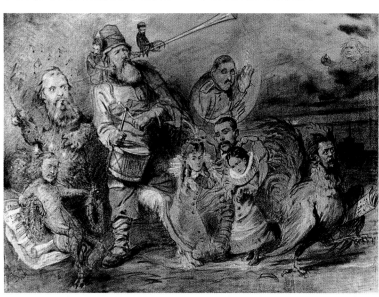

◁ *THE MIGHTY HANDFUL*, 1871
This reproduction shows the group of avant-garde composers, the Mighty Handful (or The Five), who reignited Mussorgsky's interest in music.

▷ MODEST MUSSORGSKY, 1881
Ilya Repin shows the alcoholic composer florid and in his dressing gown. He died on the eve of his final sitting, after a bottle of brandy had been smuggled in for him.

# Pyotr Ilyich Tchaikovsky

**1840–1893, RUSSIAN**

Hailed as Russia's most popular composer, Tchaikovsky mixed influences from East and West in his music. His turbulent personal life was reflected in the passionate intensity of many of his works.

### THE RUBINSTEIN BROTHERS
The Russian pianist and composer brothers Anton (left) and Nikolai Rubinstein had an important early influence on Tchaikovsky's career.

Born in Votkinsk in 1840, Pyotr Ilyich Tchaikovsky was the son of a mining engineer. A sensitive, impressionable child, when sent away to school he threw himself out of the carriage to try to run home to his mother. Her death from cholera in 1854 devastated him.

At the School of Jurisprudence in St. Petersburg, the young Pyotr sang in the choir ("My voice was a splendid soprano," he recalled), played the piano, and began to try composing.

He also developed close friendships. Both he and his younger brother, Modest, were homosexual.

### New horizons
After graduating, Tchaikovsky worked for four years as a clerk in the Ministry of Justice; but his studies with Nikolai Zaremba at the Russian Musical Society confirmed music as his true calling. When the St. Petersburg Conservatory was founded in 1862, he enrolled. His teachers included the institution's director, Anton Rubinstein, who became a major influence. Among Tchaikovsky's promising early works was an overture, *The Storm*, based on Alexander Ostrovsky's play, and a choral setting of Friedrich Schiller's poem "Ode to Joy."

Tchaikovsky moved to Moscow in 1866, having been offered a teaching post at the Moscow Conservatory by its director, Nikolai Rubinstein, brother of Anton, who championed his works and introduced him into the city's musical and intellectual circles. In 1868, Rubinstein conducted the premiere of Tchaikovsky's Symphony No. 1 ("Winter Dreams"); by this time, Tchaikovsky was hard at work on his first opera, *The Voyevoda*.

In 1869, the composer Mily Balakirev suggested Tchaikovsky should create an orchestral work based on *Romeo and Juliet* by Shakespeare; the piece premiered in 1870, but was then revised twice, reaching its final form in 1880 (which premiered in 1886). In it, Tchaikovsky achieves a synthesis of Western structure and Russian idiom: the theme linked with Friar Laurence (a monk of Renaissance Verona) is unmistakably in the musical language of the Russian Orthodox Church.

### IN CONTEXT
**Russia's first professional composer**

Tchaikovsky was the first Russian composer to be fully "professional." His five leading contemporaries, known as the Mighty Handful or The Five (see p.166), were mainly self-taught and, at best, part-timers, at worst, excellent amateurs when it came to writing music (for example, Borodin was a chemist and Rimsky-Korsakov a naval officer). Tchaikovsky was freer than them—thanks largely to the 14 years of financial support he enjoyed from Nadezhda von Meck.

### PYOTR ILYICH TCHAIKOVSKY, 1894
This portrait of Tchaikovsky near the end of his life captures the composer's troubled, melancholic disposition. It was completed the year after his death.

### DIPLOMA CERTIFICATE, 1865
Tchaikovsky's diploma certificate from the St. Petersburg Conservatory, where he enrolled in 1862, under the directorship of Anton Rubinstein.

> **"Inspiration** is a **guest** that does not willingly **visit** the **lazy."**

PYOTR ILYICH TCHAIKOVSKY

## KEY WORKS

**1866**
Symphony No. 1, Op. 13 ("Winter Dreams"), is a delicate work, imbued with sorrow and longing.

**1876**
Completes his first ballet score, *Swan Lake*, a highly dramatic, almost Wagnerian piece.

**1878**
*Eugene Onegin*, Op. 24, an opera based on Pushkin's poem, carries great personal significance for Tchaikovsky.

**1880**
Completes his rousing *1812 Overture*, Op. 49.

**1892**
*The Nutcracker*, Op. 71, Tchaikovsky's last ballet, evokes its magical tale through lyrical music.

**1893**
Symphony No. 6, Op. 74, Tchaikovsky's last symphony, seems laden with tragedy and is startlingly original.

△ **ANNA PAVLOVA, 1911**
In this detail from a painting by John Lavery, the graceful Russian ballerina is depicted in *Swan Lake*, one of Tchaikovsky's most adored works.

## ON TECHNIQUE
### Combining influences

Tchaikovsky blended, seemingly effortlessly, the European influences of Mozartian structures, Chopinesque sensibility, and Wagnerian power with distinctive Russian elements: for example, melodies influenced by the flow of the Russian language and folk song, and by the rich a cappella harmonies of Orthodox church choirs. His music is therefore often seen to bridge a gap between East and West. This, combined with his highly imaginative, colorful orchestration, creates a musical language that has virtually universal appeal.

*CHORISTERS IN THE CHURCH*, VLADIMIR EGOROVIC MAKOVSKY, 1870

Meanwhile, Tchaikovsky's personal life was strewn with tragedy. Over the years, he had relationships with a number of younger men, sometimes his pupils and, later, his own nephew. While writing *Romeo and Juliet*, he was involved with a Conservatory student, Eduard Sack, who died by suicide in 1873. Tchaikovsky wrote: "It seems to me that I have never loved anyone so strongly as him ... and his memory is sacred to me!"

New influences awaited Tchaikovsky in 1876. Visiting Paris, he attended Georges Bizet's new opera *Carmen*; its Fate motif made an impact, as much philosophical as musical. He then visited Bayreuth, Germany, as a music critic at the inaugural Wagner Festival. His favorite Wagner opera was *Lohengrin*; its influence on his *Swan Lake* was immense. On the ballet's premiere in 1877, one critic deemed Tchaikovsky's score to be

"too Wagnerian." *Swan Lake* built substantially on a little ballet that Tchaikovsky had devised some years earlier for the children of his sister, Alexandra Davydova. At her home, he could enjoy the family atmosphere that his own home lacked.

### A doomed marriage
Another crisis arose in Tchaikovsky's personal life soon after *Swan Lake*'s premiere. He decided to marry, partly to protect his family from rumors and also because, as he told Modest, "Homosexuality and pedagogy cannot abide in harmony with one another." He had fallen in love with another student, violinist Iosif Kotek, for whom he later wrote his Violin Concerto (Kotek would not give its premiere, for fear of exposing their relationship). But in 1877, Tchaikovsky received some startling letters from a former student, Antonina Milyukova, in which

she declared her love for him. It is thought that his opera *Eugene Onegin*, based on Pushkin's poem in which Tatyana approaches Onegin with a love letter, was inspired by this event. Tchaikovsky duly married Antonina.

The marriage was a disaster. In despair, the composer attempted suicide by walking into the Moscow River, intending to contract pneumonia so that it would seem he had died by natural causes. In the end, he did not even catch a cold. He did, however, experience a severe nervous breakdown. The pair soon separated, but never actually divorced.

A more rewarding relationship arrived in a similarly strange way. In 1876, Nadezhda von Meck, widow of a railroad magnate, had begun to commission music from Tchaikovsky; she went on to provide him with an annual allowance, enabling him to devote himself fully to composition. The couple agreed that they should never meet; twice, they accidentally came face to face, yet passed one another without speaking. Over 14 years, their friendship unfolded in more than 1,200 letters. Tchaikovsky secretly dedicated his Symphony No. 4—a work characterized by a powerful Fate motif—to her.

Works as popular today as the Violin Concerto, the Piano Concerto No. 1, *Eugene Onegin*, and the ballet scores

took a long time to be accepted. It was the *1812 Overture*, written in 1880 at the suggestion of Nikolai Rubinstein to commemorate Russia's victory over Napoleon, that made Tchaikovsky a household name—even though he had always hated the piece.

## International acclaim

Through the early 1880s, the now celebrated Tchaikovsky traveled widely and wrote prolifically. In 1885, he bought a house in the countryside near Klin, outside Moscow, where he declared himself "cheerful, contented and at peace." Works of this period included his operas *Cherevichki* and *The Enchantress*, plus the "Manfred" Symphony, based on Byron's poem.

The premiere of *Cherevichki* was his first attempt at conducting, which proved a splendid addition to his career. He conducted a highly successful concert of his own music in Moscow, then undertook a substantial European tour, meeting Brahms, Grieg, and Dvořák en route. In 1891, he conducted the first concert at the brand-new Carnegie Hall, New York.

In Russia, his new compositions included the Fifth Symphony and the ballet *Sleeping Beauty*—the latter was developed in close collaboration with the choreographer Marius Petipa and premiered at the Mariinsky Ballet, St. Petersburg, in 1890. Tchaikovsky was disappointed, though, by the cooler reception for his opera *The Queen of Spades*, which he regarded as one of his finest.

In his later years, Tchaikovsky became a national treasure and was celebrated abroad as one of the world's greatest living musicians. In the early 1890s, he was still full of ideas and plans, and busied himself writing the opera *Iolanta*, the ballet *The Nutcracker*, and the Symphony No. 6 ("Pathétique'"), a work he dedicated to his nephew, Vladimir ("Bob") Davydov. The young man, who was 30 years Tchaikovsky's junior, was the subject of the composer's obsessive but ultimately destructive love.

Within days of the symphony's premiere in 1893, Tchaikovsky contracted cholera during an evening at his favorite restaurant in St. Petersburg. The illness proved fatal. There is speculation that he may have drunk unboiled water on purpose in order to die by suicide. No definitive conclusion has been reached.

▷ *1812 OVERTURE*, **FRONTISPIECE**
The uncharacteristically bombastic overture—marking Russia's victory over Napoleon—was the work that placed Tchaikovsky in the spotlight.

△ *SLEEPING BEAUTY*
This photograph from 1890 shows the cast from the first ever performance of *Sleeping Beauty*, one of the greatest Tchaikovsky ballets.

" To **regret the past**, to **hope in the future,** and **never** to be **satisfied with the present**: that is what I spend my life doing. "

PYOTR ILYICH TCHAIKOVSKY, IN A LETTER TO HIS BROTHER ANATOLY, 1878

# Antonín Dvořák

## 1841–1904, CZECH

After years of struggle, Dvořák rose to become a towering composer. Fueled by diverse inspirations, from folk dance to opera, he crystallized a Bohemian national musical style, and later also created a US one.

Antonín Dvořák's music strikes a unique balance between Classical forms and folk dances, between grand-scale visions and intimacy, and between laughter and tears. Inspired by wide-ranging influences, wrapped up in a distinctive musical voice, it sometimes conceals real darkness beneath its melodic surface.

### Early talent and versatility

Born in Nelahozeves, a village near Prague, Antonín was already a fine musician by the age of 18. His chief instrument was the viola—intriguingly, the instrument of choice for many leading composers, including Mozart and Schubert. But he was also a good violinist, pianist, and organist, indeed someone to whom composition would have seemed natural.

Studying the organ in Prague, he evaded pressure to follow his father into the family business: although a fine folk musician and zither player

▷ **CERMAKOVÁ SISTERS**
This portrait shows Josefina Cermáková (standing), and her sister, Anna, later to become Dvořák's wife, sitting at the piano.

(bringing his son influence from that musical world), Dvořák senior was a butcher by trade.

For 11 years, Antonín played in the viola section in the orchestra of the Provisional Theater (later the National Theater), Prague, whose conductor was the Czech national composer in chief, Bedřich Smetana. Dvořák is believed to have taken part in a concert conducted by Wagner in 1863. He later remembered "following [Wagner] as he walked along the streets to get a chance now and again of seeing the great little man's face."

The versatile young Dvořák supplemented his income by giving piano lessons—and fell in love with one of his pupils, Josefina Cermáková. His love was sadly unrequited. This might be the point at which a sense of heartbreak began to loom under the bright surface of his music. Nevertheless, in 1873 he married Josefina's sister, Anna, and the couple soon started what became a large family.

Dvořák's financial status, though, was perilous at the time. Sending 15 substantial compositions as application for an Austrian State Stipendium for impecunious young artists in 1875, he was described as "Anton Dworak of Prague, 33 years old, music teacher, completely without means." He won the prize three times, in 1874, 1876, and 1877. On the jury were the conductor Johann Herbeck, the critic Eduard Hanslick, and the

◁ **PROVISIONAL THEATER, PRAGUE**
The Provisional Theater, where Dvořák played for several years, was built in 1862. It was an interim theater until the opening of the National Theater in 1881.

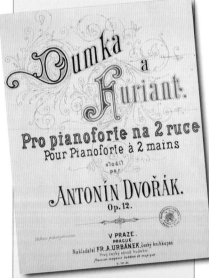

**TITLE PAGE OF DVORAK'S SLAVIC DANCE MUSIC** *DUMKA AND FURIANT*, OP. 12

▷ **ANTONIN DVORAK**
During his career, Dvořák developed an immediately recognizable musical voice. He was widely honored for his music, receiving honorary doctorates from Charles University, Prague, and the University of Cambridge, UK.

△ **RUSALKA**
This 2006 production of Antonín Dvořák's most notable opera, *Rusalka*, is from the Prague National Opera House. The work resembles Hans Christian Andersen's fairy tale *The Little Mermaid* and includes rhapsodically poetic music.

composer Johannes Brahms; the latter was "visibly overcome" by Dvořák's "mastery and talent."

Much encouraged, Dvořák left his orchestral job, redoubled his efforts, and in 1875 finished three chamber works, a song cycle, his Fifth Symphony, and the *Serenade for Strings*. Brahms befriended him and introduced him to the publisher Fritz Simrock, who commissioned his first set of *Slavonic Dances*.

### Reputation and obstacles
Soon, Dvořák began to enjoy his first taste of real recognition. Even at this time, however, his progress was occasionally checkered: in 1879, for example, he wrote a violin concerto for Brahms's friend Joseph Joachim (see p.160), Europe's most celebrated violinist. Joachim—who was known to be hard to please—refused to play the work.

The "conservative" Brahms and the "progressive" Wagner were at opposite ends of the spectrum in Romantic music. Dvořák was influenced by both. His operas, including *Rusalka* (1901), are full of Wagnerian references. Even his early chamber music and symphonies (notably No. 4) have grand Wagnerian gestures and echoes of his favorite Wagner opera, *Tannhäuser*

(1845). But some of Dvořák's works of the 1880s have strong similarities to Brahms. The first and last movements of his Symphony No. 6, for example, are evocative of Brahms's Symphony No. 2, notably in mood, key, tempo, orchestration, theme, and motif.

### British premieres
The Dvořáks' marriage, in the meantime, was happy and fruitful; six of their nine children survived. Anna was described by Dvořák's friend Tchaikovsky as "a simple, likable woman and a splendid housewife." Yet Dvořák's affection for his sister-in-law haunted him. The slow movement of his Cello Concerto (1894–1895) was a tribute to her after her death, quoting from one of his songs of which she had been fond. "If I had known it was possible to write such a concerto for the cello, I would have tried it myself," Brahms said after hearing the work.

The concerto, like his Symphony No. 7 (1885) and *Requiem* (1890), enjoyed its world premiere in Britain, where Dvořák was extremely popular and influential. Composers including Edward Elgar and Samuel Coleridge-Taylor owed him a major debt.

In 1891, Dvořák—by now a composer of eight symphonies, recipient of honorary doctorates, and professor

# "I'd give **all my symphonies** if I could have **invented** the **locomotive!**"
ANTONIN DVORAK

## ON TECHNIQUE
### Creating a Bohemian style

**It was the atmosphere, rhythms, and emotional temperature of Czech folk music that seeped into Dvořák's compositions, rather than actual folk songs, which he usually did not quote directly. The dance forms, lively rhythms, and incantatory melodies of**

Bohemian folk music became part of his language. His *Slavonic Dances* and "Dumky" Trio (1891) are prime examples: the latter's movements are all based on the alternation of slow and fast sections found in the *dumky*, a traditional folk dance.

CZECH FOLK DANCES, ENGRAVING, 19TH CENTURY

of composition at the Prague Conservatory—was offered the chance to become director of a new National Conservatory in New York. Here, his effective employer, the philanthropist Jeannette Thurber, had another task in mind. Dvořák had created a recognizably Bohemian style, a musical national identity comparable to Grieg for Norway or Liszt for Hungary. Such styles were fashionable, influential, and a source of national pride. Thurber hoped Dvořák might concoct a US equivalent.

### New and old worlds

Soon after he arrived, Thurber gave him a copy of Longfellow's epic poem *The Song of Hiawatha*, suggesting he might create from it a great US opera. Dvořák investigated suitable sources of US musical sounds. It was not long before he declared he had found what was required—African-American spirituals (although *Hiawatha* is about Indigenous Americans).

Regrettably, he needed approval for his libretto from a committee at the Conservatory, and the submitted texts failed to please them, for reasons known best to themselves. Dvořák eventually siphoned material for the opera into a different project instead: his Symphony No. 9, "From the New

## KEY WORKS

### 1875
*Serenade for Strings*, in five movements, is a lyrical work, filled with vivacity and folk-dance rhythms.

### 1878–86
*Slavonic Dances*, Book 1 and Book 2, are colorful pieces modeled on Bohemian dance forms.

### 1887
In the magnificent Piano Quintet No. 2 in A major, the piano and string quartet create a symphonic breadth.

### 1893
Symphony No. 9, "From the New World," draws on themes derived from traditional spirituals.

### 1895
Dvořák's Cello Concerto is a work on a grand scale with hints of both heroism and tragedy.

### 1901
Dvořák's magical opera *Rusalka* is heavily influenced by Wagner's operatic techniques.

World." Upon its 1893 premiere, an interview with Dvořák in *The New York Herald* quoted the composer: "The second movement ... is in reality a study or sketch for a longer work, either a cantata or an opera which I propose writing, and which will be based upon Longfellow's *Hiawatha* ... The scherzo of the symphony was suggested by the scene at the feast in *Hiawatha* where the Indians dance."

Eventually, the homesick Dvořák returned to Prague in 1895, becoming director of the city's Conservatory. During his last years he focused on composing operas and symphonic poems, among them *The Golden Spinning-Wheel* and *The Noonday Witch*. In 1897, his daughter Otilie, herself a fine musician, married his favorite pupil, the composer Josef Suk (see p.276); the family remained close until Dvořák's death in 1904,

△ **COVER, "FROM THE NEW WORLD"**
Symphony No. 9, "From the New World," blends Dvořák's distinctive dramatic style with the influence of themes from African-American spirituals.

at age 62. Tragically, Otilie died the following year, at only 27. Suk's "Asrael" Symphony paid tribute to both his wife and her father.

But Dvořák's legacy is still strong. His Czech musical heirs were Suk and Leoš Janáček. He might also have been proud to see US composers Copland, Barber, Ives, and Bernstein bring a truly national style blazing to fruition in the 20th century.

◁ **THE DVORAK FAMILY, 1892**
The Dvořáks are pictured here soon after their arrival in the US. Antonín was appointed director of the National Conservatory of Music in New York, which had been established by a patron of US music, Jeanette Thurber, in 1885.

# Edvard Grieg

## 1843–1907, NORWEGIAN

Norway's greatest composer, Grieg trained in the Romantic tradition and used folk material to foster a national identity for his country's music. He was also a concert pianist of international renown.

◁ **EDVARD GRIEG, 1891**
Grieg was first influenced by the work of Mendelssohn and Schumann, but he was later inspired by Norwegian folk tunes, which had a huge impact on his music.

Edvard Grieg's family had Scottish roots. His great-grandfather, Alexander Greig, arrived in Norway in the 1760s, when he changed the spelling of his last name to Grieg. He settled in Bergen, on the west coast, where his family soon flourished. Edvard's father, John, held the post of British consul, while his mother, Gesine, was the daughter of a provincial governor. Both parents were highly musical, so

Edvard was encouraged to develop his skills at an early age. Gesine gave him piano lessons from the age of six and he began composing in his teens.

In 1858, the Griegs received a visit from the violinist Ole Bull, one of Norway's most famous musicians. After hearing Edvard play, he advised the boy's parents to send him to the prestigious Leipzig Conservatory. Grieg claimed later that he hated the place, but he nevertheless derived some benefit from the teachings of the composer Ignaz Moscheles; he also developed a love for the music of Schumann, particularly after hearing it performed by his widow, Clara.

◁ **BERGEN, NORWAY**
This illustration of a view of the landscape at Bergen, where Grieg was born and grew up, is from the great composer's own sketchbook.

At this time, Grieg's ambition was to establish himself as a concert pianist, but he felt dissatisfied with his musical training, so, in 1863, he moved to Copenhagen for further instruction. Here, he received advice from Niels Gade, leader of the Scandinavian Romantic school. Gade gave Grieg encouragement, but also chided him for the meager number of his compositions.

On a more positive note, Grieg met and became engaged to his cousin, the singer Nina Hagerup. The couple married in 1867.

### A decisive move

Grieg's decision to move to Copenhagen was significant. The city was the cultural hub of both Denmark and Norway. Before 1814, Norway was part of the Kingdom of Denmark. After this, it entered into a political union with Sweden that lasted until 1905, although the Danish influence still remained strong. Danish, for example, was the standard written language in Norway for much of the 19th century and even the country's capital,

---

**IN CONTEXT**
**Folk music**

Grieg's interest in folk music was closely aligned to the nationalist movement that was leading his country toward independence. The initial stimulus sprang from his friendship with the composer Rikard Nordraak and was reinforced in 1869, when he came across Ludvig Lindeman's collection of folk melodies. Filled with enthusiasm, Grieg set about producing his own arrangements of these, publishing them as *25 Norwegian Folk Songs and Dances*, Op. 17. He continued to draw inspiration from this type of material for the rest of his career, culminating in the lively *Slåtter*—piano versions of peasant fiddle-tunes. In these, Grieg mimicked the double-stopping technique of the traditional Hardanger fiddle.

**HARDANGER FIDDLE: WOOD, EBONY, MOTHER-OF-PEARL, BONE; 1786**

---

" [Like] eating a **pink bonbon** stuffed with **snow**. "

CLAUDE DEBUSSY, ON LISTENING TO GRIEG'S MUSIC

## IN PROFILE
## Henrik Ibsen

Ibsen (1828–1906) was Norway's greatest playwright, renowned for groundbreaking prose dramas, such as *Hedda Gabler*, *A Doll's House*, and *The Master Builder*. Early in his career, he also wrote verse plays, inspired by his country's greatness during the Viking era, and these attracted the attention of contemporary opera composers. But it was *Peer Gynt*, written in 1867, that provided Ibsen's strongest connection with the world of music. He decided that it would benefit from some incidental music and invited Grieg to compose this before the play's stage premiere the following decade.

ILLUSTRATION FROM *PEER GYNT* OF THE TROLLS, BY ARTHUR RACKHAM, 1936.

▷ **EDVARD AND NINA GRIEG**
The couple—shown here in front of one of Edvard's pianos—married in 1867. Nina, a soprano singer, became one of the main interpreters of her husband's work.

Christiania (later Oslo), was named after a Danish king. However, attitudes were beginning to change. The growth of a Romantic nationalist movement led many Norwegians to try to formulate a distinctive cultural identity for their country. This trend affected all major branches of the arts—music, literature, and art.

In music, there were attempts to rediscover and refine the old folk songs and dances that had survived in the countryside. Grieg's interest in this was sparked by his friendship with Rikard Nordraak, whose passion for Norwegian folk music, combined with his patriotic zeal, made a deep impression on Edvard: "Suddenly, it seemed as if a mist fell from my eyes and I knew what I wanted." Nordraak died from tuberculosis at age 23—Grieg composed a funeral march in his honor—but his influence lingered.

### Piano masterworks

In 1866, Grieg returned to Norway, settling in the capital, where he took control of an amateur orchestra, the Christiania Philharmonic. His first major compositions date from this period. In 1867, he published the first volume of his *Lyric Pieces*, a collection of eight short pieces for solo piano. Often described as a miniaturist, Grieg specialized in brief, melodic compositions. Certainly, the *Lyric Pieces* were—and have remained—one of the most popular, and profitable, parts of his repertoire.

He eventually published 10 volumes, containing a total of 66 pieces. The bulk of these compositions were produced in the 1880s and 1890s; the final volume appeared in 1901.

Grieg was also engaged in more sizeable projects. In 1868, he had completed the finest of his longer works, the Piano Concerto in A minor. This bears similarities to Schumann's Piano Concerto of 1845, which Grieg had heard performed by Clara Schumann in 1858, two years after her husband's death. In addition, to Schumann's influence, Grieg's concerto contained hints of a growing interest in folk material. The third movement carried echoes of the *halling*, an energetic folk dance from rural Norway. It also featured imitations of the traditional Hardanger fiddle (see box, p.177). Edvard had already learned about this from Ole Bull, who was something of a virtuoso on the instrument. The Hardanger fiddle had eight strings—twice as many as a standard violin—which made it easier for the violinist to perform a double stop (to play two notes simultaneously).

### Literary collaborations

In the 1870s, Grieg began working with Norwegian writers. There were abortive attempts to produce an opera with Bjørnstjerne Bjørnson, but his association with Henrik Ibsen proved far more fruitful (see box, left). Grieg produced incidental music for Ibsen's extraordinary play *Peer Gynt*, which was loosely based on a fairy tale. His 90-minute score was used when the play was successfully staged in 1876. Grieg subsequently extracted eight movements from it, to form two orchestral suites (Op. 46 and Op. 55), which were added to his own concert repertoire. Including such pieces as *Morning Mood* and *In the Hall of the Mountain King* (both from Suite No. 1), these delightful compositions rapidly gained popularity and have remained firm favorites with the public.

Grieg used literary sources of a very different kind in his songs. He composed around 170 of these during his career, the majority of which were both inspired and interpreted by his wife, Nina. The most celebrated examples, however, were contained in Grieg's only song cycle, *Haugtussa*

## KEY WORKS

**1867**
Publishes the first of his *Lyric Pieces*. He will eventually complete 10 collections of these short works for solo piano.

**1868**
Finishes the best-known of his longer works, the Piano Concerto in A minor, regarded by many as his finest composition.

**1875**
Writes incidental music for Ibsen's *Peer Gynt*. This will be performed on stage the following year.

**1884**
Commissioned to celebrate the bicentenary of writer and philosopher Ludvig Holberg, and produces a remarkable five-movement dance suite.

**1895**
Begins work on his only song cycle, *Haugtussa*, Op. 67, which is based on a series of poems by Arne Garborg.

(*The Mountain Maid*, Op. 67). This was based on an epic series of poems by the Symbolist author Arne Garborg, whose work Grieg greatly admired. The composer spent three long years agonizing over exactly how to communicate the essence of this mystical love story, before eventually distilling it into an exquisite cycle of eight songs for female voice and piano. The final work was first performed by Norway's celebrated mezzo-soprano singer Eva Nansen.

By this stage, Grieg's life had settled into a familiar routine. In 1885, he and Nina moved into the house that

### ▽ MUSIC ROOM, TROLDHAUGEN

The music room and lounge at Grieg's final home, now a museum, includes his Steinway grand piano, made in 1892, and is filled with family photographs.

> " I am sure **my music** has a **taste** of **codfish** in it. "
>
> EDVARD GRIEG

they had built for themselves at Troldhaugen, on the shores of the picturesque Bergen fjord. There, Grieg spent the spring and summer working in his "composer's hut" at the water's edge or walking in the mountains, before setting off with Nina in the fall to undertake lengthy concert tours around Europe. These were great social occasions and highly successful with the public, but they were also quite grueling and eventually took their toll on the composer's frail health.

### ▷ LYRIC PIECES

Book 1 of Grieg's *Lyric Pieces*, Op. 12, shown here, was the first of 10 volumes of short works for the piano, some of which drew on folk music.

Edvard Grieg died just as he was about to embark on a tour of England. He had, at least, lived long enough to see his beloved Norway gain its independence in 1905. His ashes were buried near his home at Troldhaugen, now the Edvard Grieg Museum, in a cliff-face niche overlooking the fjord.

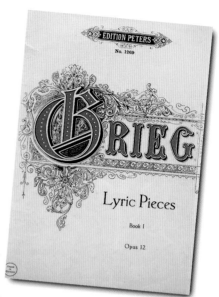

# Nikolai Rimsky-Korsakov

## 1844–1908, RUSSIAN

Propelled by Russian nationalist sentiment in the 1860s, Rimsky-Korsakov was an influential teacher as well as a composer, and became a standard-bearer for culture in late Czarist times.

Nikolai Rimsky-Korsakov belonged to the generation of Russia's "secular priesthood," as the philosopher Isaiah Berlin described the country's mid-19th-century intelligentsia, that contested and shaped ideas of Russian national identity. He was born on March 18, 1844, in the provincial town of Tikhvin to a noble family. Music played an important part in his childhood, helped by his ability to repeat overheard melodies at the piano. The boy's older brother, however, encouraged him to join the Imperial Russian Navy, and in 1856 young Nika enrolled at the College of Naval Cadets in St. Petersburg. The move introduced him to the capital city's vibrant musical scene and, above all, to its captivating opera productions.

◁ **NIKOLAI RIMSKY-KORSAKOV**
The composer, a master of orchestration who incorporated Russian folklore into his music, is portrayed here by the renowned portraitist Valentin Serov.

Private lessons in music theory and composition led to an introduction in 1861 to the composer Mily Balakirev, an ardent champion of nationalism in Russian music and leader of a select group of like-minded musicians. Balakirev became Rimsky-Korsakov's musical mentor and immediately instructed him to write a symphony. However, in 1862, midshipman Rimsky-Korsakov set sail on the clipper *Almaz* for a three-year term of service. On his return to St. Petersburg in the summer of 1865, he completed his Symphony No. 1 in E minor, Op. 1, ready for Balakirev to polish its contents and conduct its premiere at the city's Free Music School on December 31, 1865.

### Russian-flavored music

Rimsky-Korsakov's light onshore duties left ample time for composition. His *Fantasia on Serbian Themes*, first heard at the Moscow Slavonic Conference in 1867, reflected its composer's solidarity with Slavs in Russia and beyond. The critic Vladimir Stasov responded with affection by dubbing Rimsky-Korsakov and his fellow nationalist composers—namely Balakirev, Alexander Borodin, Modest Mussorgsky, and César Cui—as *Moguchaya kuchka*, or the Mighty Handful, a group that was often known outside Russia as The Five.

While completing his first opera, *The Maid of Pskov*, Rimsky-Korsakov became a professor of composition at the St. Petersburg Conservatory. He remained on the staff until his death on June 21, 1908. His composition students included Lyadov, Glazunov, Tcherepnin, and Myaskovsky; Stravinsky, meanwhile, was among Rimsky-Korsakov's private pupils.

Stasov's writings on native Russian art and folk traditions encouraged Rimsky-Korsakov to explore the legends of Russia's past. *Sadko* (1897), both as an orchestral work and as an opera, and the opera *The Tale of Czar Saltan* (1900) grew from ideas suggested by Stasov. The melodies and harmonies of works such as the symphonic suite *Scheherazade* (1888) and the operas *Mlada* (1890) and *The Golden Cockerel* (1907) were enhanced by the composer's genius for orchestration and ability to reform his style without smashing the boundaries of convention.

### IN PROFILE
### Savva Mamontov

Pre-Revolutionary Russia, although backward by the standards of Western Europe, was changing fast toward the end of the 19th century. The economy grew in harness with the expansion of the railroads, as did the cultural life of the major cities. The railroad tycoon Savva Mamontov (1841–1918) made a fortune and spent much of it on his Moscow Private Opera company. Mamontov's money bankrolled a long run of Rimsky-Korsakov operas, beginning in 1897 with *Sadko* and expanding (even after Mamontov was unjustly imprisoned for embezzlement two years later) to include such works as *The Czar's Bride*, in 1899, and *Kashchey the Immortal*, in 1902.

**PORTRAIT OF SAVVA IVANOVICH MAMONTOV, 1879**

◁ **ON THE HIGH SEAS**
Rimsky-Korsakov's (front row, right) three-year voyage on the clipper *Almaz* confirmed in him a love of the sea, which he expressed in many of his operas and symphonic works.

▷ **GABRIEL FAURE**
The US painter John Singer Sargent,
who painted this portrait in 1889, was
a great admirer of Gabriel Fauré and
helped promote his music in London.

# Gabriel Fauré

### 1845–1924, FRENCH

Fauré's mild manners concealed a passionate nature, which surfaced in his highly original piano pieces. Employed for several years as a church organist, he is best remembered for his sublime *Requiem*.

## "For me ... **music exists** to **elevate us** as **far** as possible **above everyday existence**."

GABRIEL FAURE, LETTER TO HIS SON, PHILIPPE, 1908

◁ **THE *OFFERTORY***
This sketch of the second movement of the *Requiem*, the *Offertory*, is written in Gabriel Fauré's own hand.

Gabriel Fauré was born in southern France, in the foothills of the Pyrenees. He showed great musical promise and at the age of nine was sent to the Ecole Niedermeyer in Paris, where he initially learned mainly about church music. However, in 1861, a new piano teacher, Camille Saint-Saëns (see pp.162–163), introduced Gabriel to the modern composers who would come to exert a strong influence on his style.

After leaving school, Fauré worked as a church organist while also taking on pupils. His first official post was at St. Sauveur in Rennes, where he had an extremely rocky relationship with the local priest, and was finally asked to leave after showing up for Sunday service in full evening dress, having been out all night at a ball.

### Recognition and royalties

After volunteering for service in the Franco-Prussian War and fighting in the Siege of Paris, Fauré resumed his musical career, eventually becoming the choirmaster and chief organist at the Madeleine, a famous Parisian church. Fauré saw this prestigious post as his "mercenary job" because it left him so little time to compose. Lack of time and money were perennial problems for him. He only rarely received royalties for his music, instead selling songs outright for 50 francs apiece.

In 1871, Fauré became a founder member of the Société Nationale de Musique, a body that was created by Saint-Saëns

in order to promote modern French composers, and his music was celebrated in the cultivated salons of the Princesse de Polignac and Madame de Saint-Marceaux. Wider recognition eluded him, however, until late in his career.

### Tremendous originality

Fauré's work was never truly avant-garde, but many of his critics found it challenging; even his most famous creation, the *Requiem*, was deemed insufficiently somber, and dubbed "a lullaby to death."

Fauré's style forms a clear bridge between the Romanticism of Chopin and Schumann, and the more modern approach of Impressionist composers such as Debussy. He specialized in song cycles, piano pieces, and chamber music, and many of his compositions are gentle and reflective. However, in his later years when he was going deaf, he was capable of evoking fierier moods, using mild discords and disruptive harmonies. Fauré's tremendous originality was finally recognized when he was appointed director of the Paris Conservatoire and honored with a public tribute, which was led by the French president.

▷ **CARICATURE OF SAINT-SAËNS**
Fauré captured his friend and mentor in this charming cartoon. Saint-Saëns encouraged the young Fauré to compose his own works.

**EMMA BARDAC, MISTRESS OF GABRIEL FAURE, 1903**

# Cécile Chaminade

## 1857–1944, FRENCH

Driven by financial need as well as talent, French pianist and composer Cécile Chaminade defied the expectations of her gender and class to create music that brought her international fame.

Born in Paris in 1857, Chaminade received her earliest musical training from her mother, a singer and pianist. Her musical education was limited by her father's belief that women of her social class should not enroll in the Paris Conservatoire, but he allowed her to study composition and piano with its professors privately.

The composer Georges Bizet (see pp.164–165) was a neighbor of the family, and also an early influence. Chaminade impressed him by playing her own compositions.

At the age of 20, Chaminade made her professional debut at the Salle Pleyel concert hall. Thereafter, however, she performed mainly in salon settings.

### Work and reputation

After her father's death in 1887, which created financial challenges for the family, Chaminade composed primarily in the smaller genres, such as character pieces for solo piano and arts songs, which were more commercially lucrative. Such genres were typically dominated by women and considered "feminine," in contrast to large-scale, "masculine" works, such as symphonies and operas. However, a comic opera, *La Sévillane*, was produced privately in 1882, and her *Concertstück* for piano and orchestra and *Concertino* for flute and orchestra are fairly well-known today. The latter, a demanding showpiece of technical bravura, was composed for the flute competition at the Paris Conservatoire in 1902.

Although she never spoke English, Chaminade was popular in England, even becoming one of Queen Victoria's favorite musicians. This admiration spread to the US, which she visited and toured. Professional music critics often viewed (and therefore belittled) her work and performances through the lens of gender.

### Later life

Chaminade's personal life was unconventional. She was a vegetarian, a rarity in her time, and married a much older man when she was in her early forties, reportedly on the condition of celibacy. She nursed her husband until his death in 1907, developing skills that proved useful in World War I, when she volunteered as a nurse. Following the war, she ceased composing altogether, and her final years were spent in poor health.

Chaminade's fame rests primarily on her approximately 200 piano pieces and 125 mélodies for voice and piano originally in French, but also available in English translations. Many of her works were composed specifically for publication and profit, which makes Chaminade unique among her female contemporaries.

△ **LEGION OF HONOR**
In 1913, Chaminade was accorded the Légion d'Honneur, the highest order of merit available to a French civilian.

◁ **COMIC OPERA**
Chaminade's comic opera, *La Sévillane*, was performed privately in 1882. Like Bizet's earlier opera *Carmen* and, later, the piano music of Debussy, Chaminade's opera was inspired by the perceived exoticism of Spain.

### IN CONTEXT
**Chaminade music clubs**

Musical clubs for women became popular in the US at the turn of the 20th century. Inspired by Chaminade's success, hundreds of clubs named after the French composer, who had not yet been to the US, sprang up across the country. "Chaminade Clubs" gave American women of varying musical skill a welcome outlet for socialization and performance, and contributed to the success of Chaminade's US tour in 1908. Several US cities continue to host such clubs today, including Providence, Rhode Island, and Yonkers, New York.

" This is not a **woman who composes,** but a **composer who is a woman**. "

AMBROISE THOMAS, COMPOSER

▷ **CECILE CHAMINADE, 1905**
In addition to being a composer, Chaminade was a talented pianist. From the age of 18, she performed with orchestras all over Europe, and most of her own compositions were for the piano.

# Giacomo Puccini

## 1858–1924, ITALIAN

Puccini wrote some of the most enduringly popular works in the operatic repertoire. A flamboyant, controversial personality, he led a life that, to some extent, mirrored the melodrama of his operas.

Born in the historic Tuscan town of Lucca in 1858, Giacomo Puccini was the oldest son of a family of nine. The male line in his family had been musicians through four generations, and his father's post as organist and choirmaster at Lucca's cathedral was regarded as hereditary. Giacomo was only five years old when his father died, but his family was assured he would inherit the job on reaching adulthood. With this future in view, he was taught to play the organ and sing in the choir. But inspired by seeing a performance of a Verdi opera, the young Puccini nourished higher ambitions. In 1880, with his family's backing, he left Lucca to study composition at the Milan Conservatory.

### IN CONTEXT
### Verismo

Verismo (realism) is a term for the dominant style in Italian opera in the 1890s. Puccini's *Tosca* was heavily influenced by verismo, as were, to a lesser extent, his *Madama Butterfly* and *La fanciulla del West*. The genre was founded by Pietro Mascagni's *Cavalleria rusticana* (1890) and Ruggero Leoncavallo's *Pagliacci* (1892), two short operas often performed as a double-bill. The verismo composers presented dramas that were raw, brutal, and even sordid. They required singers to adopt an emotional, declamatory style that sacrificed beauty to power of expression.

SCENE FROM *CAVALLERIA RUSTICANA* BY PIETRO MASCAGNI

### Success, failure, and scandal

Puccini was a vain and self-centered young man with an undisciplined, lazy streak that was often the despair of his teachers. Nevertheless, his talent proved indisputable. His instrumental composition *Capriccio sinfonico*, performed at his graduation from the Conservatory in 1883, attracted

◁ **GIACOMO PUCCINI**
Spoiled by his mother and sisters as a child, Puccini was arrogant and self-absorbed. Wealth and success in later life brought scandal and controversy.

the attention of Milan's musical elite. In the same year, his one-act opera *Le Villi* failed to win a competition prize, but his Milanese friends funded a revised two-act version the following year that won modest acclaim. Puccini was signed by the prominent music publisher Giulio Ricordi. Despite the crushing failure of his second opera *Edgar* when it premiered at La Scala in 1889, his career was now launched.

Meanwhile, Puccini's private life was racked by scandal. The death of his mother in 1884 brought the grieving

son back to Lucca. There he fell in love with Elvira Gemignani (née Bonturi), a married woman. Their affair was kept secret until 1886, when Elvira became pregnant with Puccini's child. Reviled as a disgrace to their town and families, the couple were forced to flee to Milan, where their son Antonio was born. Payments from Ricordi kept the composer's illicit ménage alive, but only just—an experience of poverty that Puccini was to draw on when writing his opera *La Bohème*, with its cast of impoverished would-be artists.

△ **ELVIRA BONTURI**
Puccini's affair with Elvira caused turmoil but her marriage was an unhappy one: her husband was an adulterer who was murdered in 1903 by his lover's husband.

> " I am a **mighty hunter** of **wildfowl, beautiful women**, and **good libretti**. "
>
> GIACOMO PUCCINI

## KEY WORKS

**1893**
*Manon Lescaut* premieres in Turin; Puccini's third opera is his first major popular success.

**1896**
Toscanini conducts the first performance of one of Puccini's most celebrated operas, *La Bohème*.

**1900**
*Tosca*, Puccini's brutal melodrama, is premiered in Rome, where the action of the opera is set.

**1904**
Destined to rank among Puccini's most popular works, the opera *Madama Butterfly* has a disastrous first performance.

**1910**
Toscanini premieres Puccini's "Wild West" opera, *La fanciulla del West*, at the Metropolitan Opera in New York.

**1924**
Puccini's last opera, *Turandot*, is unfinished at his death; Toscanini conducts the first performance in 1926.

In 1891, Puccini discovered a rural retreat at Torre del Lago on Lake Massaciuccoli in Tuscany. There he could work in peace on his third opera, *Manon Lescaut* (based on a novel by Abbé Prévost). Adapting Prévost's work, Puccini ran through five librettists in search of the ideal combination of drama, words, and music. The effort proved worthwhile. From its premiere in Turin in 1893, conducted by Arturo Toscanini (see box, left), this dark story of a doomed *femme fatale* was an overwhelming hit, establishing Puccini as Italy's most promising successor to Verdi.

### Making operatic history

Always working slowly, plagued by quarrels over rights to material and by struggles with librettists, over the next decade Puccini created the three works that define his place in operatic history: *La Bohème*, *Tosca*, and *Madama Butterfly*. Of these, *La Bohème* was the most rapid popular success. *Tosca*, first performed in Rome in 1900 before an upper-class audience unnerved by a threat of anarchist bombing, was criticized for its violent scenes of torture and murder, but also soon achieved international popularity. However, Puccini's Japan-set opera *Madama Butterfly* met with a hostile reception at its premiere in 1904: some critics said it was a "fiasco,"

others that there had been insufficient rehearsal time; Puccini himself was adamant that its poor reception was engineered by his rivals. But following substantial revisions, the emotional warmth and dramatic intensity of Puccini's score combined with the heartbreaking story—of a teenage Japanese bride who is abandoned by her US soldier husband and kills herself—finally met with acclaim.

### Crisis and tragedy

Success brought Puccini wealth and fame. He could indulge his taste for fast cars—then a rich man's novelty—and attractive mistresses. Often left alone at Torre del Lago, Elvira raged at Puccini's infidelities, especially his passionate affair with a young woman in Turin, who is known to history only as "Corinna."

In 1903, while he was still working on *Madama Butterfly*, Puccini was seriously injured in a car accident.

Around the same time, Elvira's husband died. His demise obliged Puccini to legitimize the relationship, although by that time he would probably have preferred a separation.

Marriage did nothing to lessen Elvira's wild outbursts of jealousy. In 1908, she became obsessed with the idea that a young maid at Torre del Lago, Doria Manfredi, was having an affair with Puccini. Her pitiless harassment and defamation of Doria drove the poor girl to suicide. A postmortem showed that Doria had not had sex with Puccini. The maid's family took legal action against Elvira, before being bought off. The incident caused an immense scandal in the press, damaging Puccini's reputation.

In 1910, the composer completed *La fanciulla del West*, which was commissioned by the Metropolitan Opera House in New York, where Puccini's friend Toscanini had become the principal conductor (see box, left).

▷ **PUCCINI'S HOUSE IN TUSCANY**
The composer's house in Lucca, now a museum, had been in his family since 1815 and is where he spent his childhood. On display here, among other things, are family photos and one of his pianos.

Although some people saw incongruity in an Italian opera that was set in the American West, the work brought Puccini his last wholehearted artistic and popular triumph during his lifetime.

In the US, Puccini was a stellar celebrity; in Italy some felt his music had become "Germanic." When Italy entered into World War I in 1915 as an enemy of Germany and Austria, he was working on a comic opera, *La rondine*, and appearing in public with a German mistress. His failure to engage with the Italian war effort was shown up by contrast with Toscanini, who played music for the troops in range of enemy artillery fire. The friendship between the composer and the conductor temporarily lapsed.

Puccini had long been working on an ambitious triptych of one-act operas. This came to fruition as *Il trittico*, first performed at the Metropolitan Opera House in 1918. Only one of these short operas, the comic *Gianni Schicchi*, showed the composer at his best.

### Final days

Ill with diabetes, living in a post-war Italy where he no longer felt at home, Puccini applied himself with fanatical determination to writing *Turandot*, his final work. Diagnosed with cancer of the throat, in 1924 he went to Belgium for radium treatment. Before leaving, he appealed to Toscanini to ensure that *Turandot* would be performed after his death. Appallingly painful and quite useless, the treatment killed him.

The composer was accorded a state funeral in Milan, with the funeral oration delivered by Italy's new fascist leader, Benito Mussolini. *Turandot*, left unfinished, was completed from Puccini's sketches by Italian composer Franco Alfano. Nevertheless, conducting the opera's first performance in 1926, Toscanini movingly laid down the baton at the point at which Puccini's writing had ceased. The great composer's body now lies in an improvised chapel in his villa at Torre del Lago.

▷ **POSTER FOR *TURANDOT***
Puccini was hopeful that his opera *Turandot* would seal his reputation for future generations. The work was unfinished at the time of his death.

△ **PUCCINI AND HIS WIFE, ELVIRA**
The composer (center) and his wife (left) are shown here in a car in Lucca. In 1903, Puccini's chauffeur swerved the car off the road; Puccini was discovered trapped beneath it, with a broken leg and almost choked to death by gasoline fumes.

# "Don't let my **Turandot** die!"

GIACOMO PUCCINI

# Gustav Mahler

## 1860–1911, AUSTRIAN

Mahler's large-scale symphonies and song cycles express neurotic emotion and an elevated spiritual vision in the German Romantic tradition. In his lifetime, he was most famous as a conductor.

### ◁ CONDUCTOR'S BATON
This ivory, ebony, and tortoiseshell baton was presented to Mahler in 1901 by Archduke Franz Ferdinand. A dedication plaque in the center reads: "To his beloved composer Gustav Mahler."

Born in 1860, Gustav Mahler grew up in the rural town of Iglau (now Jihlava) on the border between Moravia and Bohemia. Many of his early experiences were harsh. His father, a German-speaking Jewish trader who owned a liquor store, was a wife-beater. Family deaths were frequent—only 5 of Gustav's 13 siblings survived childhood. But his father made money and nurtured social and cultural aspirations. When Gustav displayed precocious talent

### ▽ STADTTHEATER, HAMBURG
Mahler was chief conductor at the Stadttheater in Hamburg between 1891 and 1897. He conducted almost 750 performances there over these six years.

at the piano, playing an instrument discovered in a loft, his parents paid for him to take lessons. He picked up his wider musical education by listening to military bands, barrel organs in the street, and folk songs sung by servants—all would find their place in his mature compositions.

### A spiritual venture
Recognized as a prodigy, Mahler was sent to the Vienna Conservatory when he was 15. During his three years there, and a further three years at Vienna University, he was inducted into the most advanced German culture of his day, absorbing the influence of Richard Wagner in music and Friedrich Nietzsche in philosophy.

He learned to see music as an epic spiritual venture, a search for meaning in a world of suffering. Hugely critical of his own work, he destroyed most of his youthful compositions. A single movement of a piano quartet, written when he was 16, has survived. At the end of his student years, he wrote an ambitious cantata, *Das klagende Lied* (*Song of Lamentation*), but it failed to win a composition prize in 1881 and went unperformed until 1901.

Needing to earn a living, Mahler embarked on a career as a conductor. A series of appointments carried him from the smallest of provincial opera houses via Kassel, Prague, and Leipzig to prestigious appointments at the Royal Opera House in Budapest in 1888 and at Hamburg's Stadttheater, where he held the baton from 1891 to 1897. A fanatical perfectionist with poor social skills and no respect for other people's feelings, he was often loathed by the musicians he directed and in open conflict with the opera management. But the quality of the performances he achieved, especially

"IN THE FOREST", FROM *DES KNABEN WUNDERHORN*, ILLUSTRATION, 1848

### ▷ GUSTAV MAHLER, 1907
Mahler is pictured here, aged 47 (four years before his death), in the year when he was diagnosed with a severe heart condition and his daughter Maria died.

## "**My time** will come."
GUSTAV MAHLER, AFTER CONDUCTING A STRAUSS OPERA IN 1902

# "Gustav **lives his life**, and **I, too,** must live **his life**."

ALMA MAHLER

## IN PROFILE
### Alma Schindler

Daughter of an Austrian landscape painter, Alma Schindler (1879–1964) was a promising composer when she married Mahler, 19 years her senior, in 1902. Marriage and motherhood suppressed her creativity. Following Mahler's death she married architect Walter Gropius, and later, after a divorce, writer Franz Werfel. Her other lovers included the composer Alexander von Zemlinsky and the artist Oskar Kokoschka. She bore four children, three of whom suffered early deaths. In 1938, when the Nazis took over Vienna, she fled with Werfel, first to France and then to the US, becoming a prominent figure among the European exiles in Los Angeles.

ALMA MAHLER AND HER DAUGHTERS MARIA AND ANNA, 1906

of Wagner and Mozart, made an overwhelming impression on critics and public alike.

## Loss and renewal
Mahler continued to compose in his spare time from conducting. His character combined an iron will with a neurotic sensibility that indulged feelings of loss and longing. This side of his personality fed into his music. Written between 1883 and 1885, his song cycle *Lieder eines fahrenden Gesellen* (*Songs of a Wayfarer*) set his own poems inspired by an unhappy love affair with a soprano at the Kassel opera house, Johanna Richter. The original five-movement version of his First Symphony, premiered in 1889, was partly stimulated by his troubled relationship with a married woman, Marion von Weber, in Leipzig.

Death seemed ever present—his mother, father, and one of his sisters died in 1889; his brother, Otto, shot himself in 1895. Mahler's Second and Third Symphonies, mostly written on holidays at Steinbach between 1893 and 1896, were programmatic pieces expressing his Nietzschean vision of death overcome by eternal renewal.

In 1897, aged 37, Mahler took up the prestigious post of musical director at the Vienna Hofoper (Court Opera). As a condition of the job, which was not open to members of the Jewish faith, he converted to Catholicism. Imposing his will upon singers, orchestra, and public alike, he transformed the opera's stagings, the quality of the

△ **COVER OF SYMPHONY NO. 2**
Mahler's Symphony No. 2 in C minor, known as the "Resurrection" Symphony, which premiered in 1895, is one of the composer's most popular works.

music, and the atmosphere in which it was performed. Although the response was generally favorable, performers resented his intolerant manner, and Vienna's antisemites mounted a damaging campaign against him on racial grounds.

Masterpieces continued to flow from his holidays, now chiefly spent at Wörthersee in southern Austria—the Fourth Symphony in 1900, the Fifth

Symphony in 1902, the song cycle *Kindertotenlieder* (*Songs on the Death of Children*) in 1904, and the Sixth, Seventh, and Eighth Symphonies between 1904 and 1906. Mahler's music was challenging, stretching the symphonic tradition to its limits. It was emotionally jarring in its ironic use of popular tunes, tonally adventurous, and formally innovative, employed unusual instruments, and often included songs and choral elements. But his works were not excessively out of step with public taste and were sometimes received with enthusiasm. However, he envied the wider fame of Richard Strauss, then celebrated as the hero of German new music.

## Marriage and tragedy
In 1902, Mahler married 22-year-old Alma Schindler. She brought him into contact with the radical artists of the Viennese Secession and the young Modernist Viennese composers grouped around Arnold Schoenberg.

Ill suited to a relationship with a liberated woman, Mahler insisted that Alma, a talented composer, renounce creative activity to act as a wife and mother. His concentration on his work left little time to satisfy her lively sexual demands. The couple had two daughters, Maria and Anna. The death of Maria in 1907 was a crushing blow. In the same year, Mahler himself was diagnosed as suffering from a life-threatening heart condition. Wearied by harassment from the antisemitic press in Vienna, he made a lucrative move to the Metropolitan Opera in New York.

▷ **COMPOSER'S HUT, STEINBACH**
Mahler often came to write at this cottage on Lake Attersee in Steinbach. It was here, on summer holidays between 1893 and 1896, that he composed parts of his Second and Third Symphonies.

## Final years

Mahler was not a success in the US, failing to ingratiate himself with a public demanding showmanship. Elbowed out by Arturo Toscanini at the Metropolitan Opera House, he became conductor of the New York Philharmonic, with no greater success. He continued to compose on holidays in Austria, producing the song cycle *Das Lied von der Erde*, often considered his finest work, and commencing his Tenth Symphony. The premiere of his Eighth Symphony in Munich in 1910 was a triumph. But his marriage was breaking down, Alma carrying on an affair with architect Walter Gropius. In his distress, Mahler consulted the psychoanalyst Sigmund Freud, to no obvious benefit. He attempted a reconciliation with Alma, even arranging for some of her songs to be performed. When he fell mortally ill in New York in spring 1911, she accompanied him on his final journey to die in Vienna. He was buried in Grinzing Cemetery, alongside his daughter Maria.

Mahler's music went through a long period of posthumous neglect. It was banned by the Nazis as "decadent" and largely ignored by everyone else. In the 1960s, however, Mahler underwent a spectacular revival, his music attaining iconic status as part of that radical decade's heterodox cultural mix. His works have since become established as a fixture in the orchestral repertoire.

▷ **"THE SYMPHONY OF A THOUSAND"**
Erich Büttner depicts Mahler's Symphony No. 8, nicknamed "The Symphony of a Thousand" because it requires a vast number of singers and instrumentalists.

## KEY WORKS

**1880**
Completes his first major work, *Das klagende Lied*, a cantata that is not performed until 1901.

**1885**
Mahler's first song cycle, *Lieder eines fahrenden Gesellen*, sets his own poems of failed love.

**1895**
Conducts the premiere of his Symphony No. 2, the "Resurrection" Symphony.

**1904**
*Kindertotenlieder*, Mahler's song cycle for voice and orchestra, sets poems by Friedrich Rückert.

**1909**
*Das Lied von der Erde*, his last song cycle, sets Chinese poems; it is not performed until after his death.

**1910**
Mahler's Symphony No. 8, "Symphony of a Thousand," is acclaimed on its first performance in Munich.

▷ **CLAUDE DEBUSSY, 1903**
Precociously gifted, Debussy drew inspiration for his music from a wide range of literary and artistic sources. This portrait, by the French painter Jacques-Emile Blanche, shows the pioneering composer in his early forties.

# Claude Debussy

### 1862–1918, FRENCH

Debussy was one of the most important pioneers of modern music, releasing composers from the straitjacket of traditional forms. He struggled with health issues and a tempestuous private life.

◁ **WORLD FAIR, PARIS, 1889**
Exciting musical forms and instruments sparked Debussy's imagination when he encountered them at the World Fair in Paris in 1889. The unfamiliar sounds suggested new possibilities to him.

The eldest of five children, Claude Debussy was born in a Parisian suburb. His immediate family had no musical links. His father drifted through various jobs—shopkeeper, salesman, soldier—and was briefly imprisoned for taking part in the Commune (an uprising in Paris). Claude's early musical education came from an aunt, who sent him for piano lessons with a woman who claimed to have been taught by Frédéric Chopin.

Claude made rapid progress and, at the age of 10, was accepted at the Paris Conservatoire. It soon became clear that he would not make the grade as a virtuoso pianist, but he performed well enough to win the Prix de Rome in 1884, which entitled him to three years' study in Italy. Before this, Claude enjoyed summer jobs working for Nadezhda von Meck, the wealthy benefactor of Tchaikovsky. She took him traveling and introduced him to Russian music, most notably Borodin and Rimsky-Korsakov.

### A rebellious streak

Debussy found many of the professors at the Conservatoire too traditional, and balked at following orthodox methods of composition, noting: "I don't think I shall ever be able to put music into a strict mold." His studies in Italy proved equally depressing. He disliked the Villa Medici and his fellow students and was bored by Rome. After two years, he returned to Paris.

### New sounds and influences

The late 1880s were lean years financially for Debussy, but it was also a time of discovery, when he absorbed the diverse influences that came to form his style. Thanks to a wealthy friend, he attended the Bayreuth Festival in 1888 and 1889 and, for a time, came under the spell of Richard Wagner. He was also swept along by the tide of excitement surrounding the World Exposition in Paris in 1889, with the newly erected Eiffel Tower as its centerpiece.

Debussy was especially fascinated by the Javanese gamelan music that he heard, performed on percussive instruments. The different melodies, rhythms, and scales of non-Western music stirred his imagination. Hints of its impact can be heard in his "Pagodes" ("Pagodas"), the first movement of *Estampes* (*Prints*). Debussy was to remain open to new or foreign influences throughout his career. This even extended to early forms of jazz. In his *Children's Corner*

△ **NADEZHDA VON MECK**
In the early 1880s, Debussy worked as a pianist for the wealthy Russian businesswoman and art-lover Nadezhda von Meck. She became famous as the patron of Tchaikovsky.

## ON TECHNIQUE
### Piano-roll recordings

**Debussy was one of the first composers to record himself performing his work. In 1913, he recorded 14 pieces on a Welte-Mignon reproducing piano, in which an electric suction pump replaces the foot bellow. This was the most sophisticated device of its kind, capturing not just the notes, but the nuances of the pianist's style for posterity, including phrasing, tempo, pedaling, and dynamics. Debussy's performance was encoded onto six piano rolls, continuous sheets of paper punched with holes, which were copied for use on player pianos.**

**DEBUSSY AT THE PIANO, SURROUNDED BY MEMBERS OF HIS FAMILY, 1893**

> "The **century of airplanes** deserves its own **music**. As there are **no precedents,** I must **create anew**."

CLAUDE DEBUSSY

△ **NOCTURNE, BLUE AND SILVER: BATTERSEA, 1872–1878**
James McNeill Whistler found fame with his atmospheric scenes of the Thames River in London—as in this view of Battersea in his *Nocturne* series. Debussy, who had met Whistler, also used the word "Nocturne" in his designation for a series of musical works and drew great inspiration from the artist's paintings in the creation of his music.

(1908), for example, he famously included a ragtime piece, the "Golliwog's Cakewalk," which had its roots in a dance performed by enslaved people. This featured a syncopated arpeggio that referred jokily to a chord from Wagner's *Tristan und Isolde* (1859) and a series of ingenious banjolike effects.

## The world of art
Debussy's style was also shaped by factors outside the world of music. From as early as 1887, his work was described as Impressionist—a label that stayed with him. The reference was initially made by one of his

assessors at the Conservatoire and was meant in a pejorative sense. But mostly it was used to denote the composer's blurred harmonies or his taste for creating sound-pictures of the same kind of natural subjects that the Impressionist painters used, such as clouds, mists, or gusts of wind. As a rule, Debussy was annoyed when critics described his music as Impressionist; the movement had, passed its heyday.

Debussy's closest affinity to any painter was with the US artist James McNeill Whistler, who produced misty scenes of the Thames River in London, Inspired by a series of Whistler's

paintings called *Nocturne*, Debussy used the same title in a musical series of Nocturnes, completed in 1899. He saw this music as "an experiment in the different combinations that can be created from a single color—what a study in gray would be in painting."

## The Symbolist movement
Debussy had closer links with the literary and artistic movement known as Symbolism than he ever had with Impressionism. Symbolists avoided formal structures, such as specific subjects or plots. Theirs was an art of nuance and suggestion, as they created moods, emotions, or ideas.

## KEY WORKS

### 1894
Completes his first orchestral masterpiece, the *Prélude à l'après-midi d'un faune*. Its striking originality is much admired.

### 1902
The premiere of Debussy's only opera, *Pelléas et Mélisande*, finally establishes his reputation.

### 1903
Debussy's taste for the exotic is revealed in *Estampes* (*Prints*). The title refers to the vogue for Japanese prints.

### 1905
One of Debussy's most popular orchestral pieces, *La Mer* (*The Sea*), is performed in Paris. It consists of three symphonic sketches.

### 1913
*Jeux* (*Games*), a ballet commissioned by Sergei Diaghilev for his Ballets Russes, is performed. The choreography is by Nijinsky.

# "Music is the arithmetic of sounds as optics is the geometry of light."

CLAUDE DEBUSSY

Debussy had important links with two Symbolist writers—the poet Stéphane Mallarmé and the dramatist Maurice Maeterlinck. He met Mallarmé in 1890 and regularly attended the famous Tuesday salons at which the writer hosted visitors including W.B. Yeats, Rainer Maria Rilke, and Paul Verlaine.

### Literary influences

Greatly inspired by Mallarmé's verses, Debussy produced *Prélude à l'après-midi d'un faune* (1894). This highly sensual symphonic poem, conjuring up the lust-filled dreams of the creature on a hot day (see box, right), made little impact at the time, but was hugely influential. Pierre Boulez saw it as a cornerstone of modern music.

In terms of career development, the link with Maeterlinck was more crucial. Debussy saw his play *Pelléas et Mélisande* in 1893 and soon decided that it would make a suitable subject for an opera. It took almost a decade before he was able to turn this into reality, and the production was almost derailed by an argument over one of its stars. Maeterlinck thought that the part of Mélisande would be sung by his mistress, Georgette Leblanc. Debussy, however, preferred the Scottish soprano Mary Garden. He had already dedicated two songs to her in his *Ariettes oubliées* (*Forgotten Songs*, 1885–1887). The composer had his way, but it created a long-lasting rift between the two men. There was talk of legal action and even a duel, but in the end the matter was resolved.

When the first performance of the opera finally went ahead, its success transformed Debussy's reputation and encouraged reviewers to start exploring the vast back-catalog of his music. In *Pelléas*, he had created a hauntingly beautiful accompaniment to Maeterlinck's enigmatic tale. By this stage, he had purged the most obvious Wagnerian influences from his style. Instead, his opera carried echoes of *Boris Godunov* (1869) by Modest Mussorgsky, whose music Debussy had discovered in the mid-1890s.

### Turbulent relations

In contrast to Debussy's successful career, his personal life was in tatters. The main issue concerned his first wife, Lily. The couple married in 1899, but their relationship ran into trouble when Debussy fell under the spell of the bewitching singer Emma Bardac. She had already been the mistress of the composer Gabriel Fauré and, in 1904, Debussy abandoned his wife to be with her. Distraught, Lily attempted suicide a few days before their fifth anniversary. She survived, but the incident left a permanent stain on the composer's reputation. Many of his friends disowned him and the press reaction was universally hostile.

Debussy's later years were clouded by illness. From 1909, he began to suffer from the cancer that would eventually kill him. As a result of the illness, he endured one of the earliest colostomy operations ever performed. He died in Paris at the end of World War I, with the sound of German shells echoing in the streets nearby.

**LEON BAKST'S DESIGN FOR NIJINSKY IN *L'APRÈS-MIDI D'UN FAUNE*, 1912**

◁ **MARY GARDEN AS MELISANDE**
The Scottish operatic soprano Mary Garden is shown here as Mélisande in Debussy's opera *Pelléas et Mélisande*. The casting of Garden caused a major row between Debussy and Maeterlinck, author of the play on which the opera was based.

# Directory

## Charles Gounod

1818–1893, FRENCH

Known primarily as the composer of the opera *Faust*, Gounod was born in Paris, his father a painter, his mother a piano teacher. After training at the Paris Conservatoire he spent three years in Rome, where he studied composers of church music. Returning to Paris, he contemplated taking religious orders, but instead turned to writing opera, producing *Sapho* in 1851. The success of *Faust*, first staged in 1859, made him the most famous composer in France. He created 12 operas, but no other achieved comparable success. In the early 1870s, Gounod lived in England, founding the amateur choir that later became the Royal Choral Society. In his later years he primarily wrote religious oratorios, including *La Rédemption* (1882) and *Mors et Vita* (1885). His setting of *Ave Maria* (1859), based on a Bach prelude, has proved to be enduringly popular.

**KEY WORKS:** *Faust* (opera), 1859; *Mireille* (opera), 1864; *Roméo et Juliette* (opera), 1867; *La Rédemption* (oratorio), 1882

## ▷ Arthur Sullivan

1842–1900, BRITISH

Most renowned for his operettas created with dramatist W. S. Gilbert, Sullivan was the son of a bandmaster and raised as a musician. He studied at the Royal Academy of Music from the age of 14, and later at the Leipzig Conservatory. A performance of his orchestral music for *The Tempest* at London's Crystal Palace in 1862 made him famous. A variety of works followed, from ballet music and cantatas to songs and hymns.

His talent for musical comedy was revealed in the one-act farce *Cox and Box* in 1866. The association with Gilbert, brokered by entrepreneur Richard D'Oyly Carte, began with *Trial by Jury* in 1875. A string of comic hits followed, staged at the purpose-built Savoy Theatre from 1881. A business dispute disrupted the Sullivan-Gilbert relationship in 1890, after which their collaboration was less successful. Sullivan's other major successes included the oratorio *The Golden Legend* and the opera *Ivanhoe* (1891).

**KEY WORKS:** *The Tempest* (incidental music), 1861; *HMS Pinafore* (operetta), 1878; *The Mikado* (operetta), 1885; *The Golden Legend* (oratorio), 1886

## Jules Massenet

1842–1912, FRENCH

The most successful French operatic composer of the Belle Epoque, Massenet was admitted to the Paris Conservatoire at the age of 11. His winning the Prix de Rome in 1863 financed a stay in Italy. Working tirelessly, he earned a living in Paris as a piano teacher while composing a stream of operas. His first stage work, *La Grand'Tante*, was produced in 1867, but he did not achieve significant commercial success until the mid-1870s. In 1878, he was appointed to a teaching post at the Conservatoire, which he held for almost 20 years. First staged in 1884, his opera *Manon* was the greatest success of his career, although many critics consider *Werther* (1892) a finer work. He continued to write tuneful operas with supreme fluency up to his death.

**KEY WORKS:** *Le Roi de Lahore* (opera), 1877; *Manon* (opera), 1884; *Werther* (opera), 1892; *Don Quichotte* (opera), 1910

△ **ARTHUR SULLIVAN**

## Hubert Parry

1848–1918, BRITISH

A key figure in the late-19th-century revival of English music, Parry was born into the landowning class. Despite showing precocious musical talent, he followed a traditional path for the sons of the upper middle classes, from schooling at Eton and the University of Oxford to a job as a Lloyds underwriter in the City of London. Learning composition in his spare time, he emerged as a recognized composer in 1880 with a piano concerto and the influential cantata *Scenes from Prometheus Unbound*. Further large-scale choral works graced English music festivals through the 1880s and 1890s. Parry joined the staff of the Royal College of Music at its foundation in 1883, becoming its head in 1894. He was appointed professor of music at the University of Oxford in 1900, and was also a prominent writer on music, producing books on J. S. Bach and music history. Failing health led to Parry's retirement from Oxford in 1908, releasing his creative energies for a late flowering that produced the much celebrated anthem "Jerusalem" and the unaccompanied Songs of Farewell, a set of six choral motets.

**KEY WORKS:** *Blest Pair of Sirens* (ode for chorus and orchestra), 1887; *Job* (oratorio), 1892; "Jerusalem" (song), 1916; *Songs of Farewell*, 1916

## Teresa Carreño

1853–1917, VENEZUELAN

Pianist, singer, and composer Carreño was born in Caracas, but left the country with her parents in 1862, spending most of the remainder of her life in the US and Europe. A child prodigy at the piano, she performed her first public concert in New York City before the age of 10. She became world famous, sometimes referred to as the "Valkyrie of the Piano." Her career as an operatic soprano began in Europe in the 1870s but was never comparable to her pianistic career. As a composer she wrote chiefly, but not exclusively, for piano. Most of her works were written by 1875, after which she composed only sporadically.

KEY WORKS: *Gottschalk Waltz* (piano solo), Op. 1, 1863; *Ballade* (piano solo), Op. 15, 1867; *La Fausse Note* (piano solo), Op. 39, 1872; *Serenade for String Orchestra*, 1895

## Ernest Chausson

1855–1899, FRENCH

Born into an affluent Parisian family, Chausson qualified as a barrister and toyed with literature and the visual arts before deciding to devote himself to music. In 1879, he entered the Paris Conservatoire, where he was taught by Massenet and came under the influence of Franck. Secretary of the Société Nationale de Musique from 1886, he hosted a salon frequented by the Parisian cultural elite, including Fauré and Debussy and the painter Monet. His compositions comprised songs and chamber pieces, as well as the opera *Le Roi Arthus* and a number of orchestral works. By the 1890s he had developed a distinctive style.

KEY WORKS: *Viviane* (symphonic poem), Op. 5, 1882; Symphony in B-flat major, Op. 20, 1890; *Poème* (violin and orchestra), Op. 25, 1896; *Chanson perpétuelle* (soprano and orchestra), Op. 37, 1898

## Isaac Albéniz

1860–1909, SPANISH

Composer and piano virtuoso Albéniz was born in Catalonia. A child prodigy, he gave his first public performance at the age of five and was toured internationally by his parents before settling to a serious musical education at the Brussels Conservatory in 1876. Studying under Spanish nationalist composer Felipe Pedrell influenced him to write music reflecting regional Spanish folksong. Many of these piano pieces, published in *Suite Española* and *Cantos de España*, are now better known in arrangements for classical guitar. Poorly received in his own country, Albéniz spent most of his later years in England and France. In the 1890s he wrote orchestral pieces, operas, and operettas, but a return to the piano brought about his finest work—the *Iberia* suite, a masterpiece of modern Spanish music.

KEY WORKS: *Suite Española* (piano solo), Op. 47, 1887; *Cantos de España* (piano solo), 1892; *Catalonia* (orchestral suite), 1899; *Iberia* (piano solo), 1906–1908

## ▷ Pietro Mascagni

1863–1945, ITALIAN

Chiefly remembered as the composer of the one-act opera *Cavalleria rusticana*, Mascagni was born in Livorno, Tuscany, the son of a baker. Choosing a musical career against his family's wishes, he began composing as a teenager. Admitted to the Milan Conservatory in 1882, he left without completing his course, working as conductor with an opera company. He won a prestigious competition for the score of *Cavalleria rusticana* in 1888. Premiered in 1890, the opera was a huge hit, establishing the earthy, melodramatic style known as *verismo*.

Mascagni wrote 14 more operas. Most were greatly anticipated—especially *Parisina*, with a libretto by poet Gabriele D'Annunzio—but none matched the success of his first. Mascagni also had a prominent career as a conductor. His last opera, *Nerone* (1935), was a tribute to Mussolini's Fascist regime.

KEY WORKS: *Cavalleria rusticana* (opera), 1890; *L'amico Fritz* (opera), 1891; *Iris* (opera), 1898; *Isabeau* (opera), 1911

## Samuel Coleridge-Taylor

1875–1912, BRITISH

Coleridge-Taylor brought African and Black American influences into classical music. Born in England and named after an English poet by his English mother, Coleridge-Taylor's paternal heritage included enslaved African Americans. A talented violinist in his youth, he studied composition under Charles Villiers Stanford at the Royal College of Music, and achieved early success with 1898's *Ballade in A Minor*, which has drawn comparisons with the music of Tchaikovsky. He followed that with his masterwork, *Hiawatha's Wedding Feast*, which combined a large orchestral sound with the poetry of Henry Wadsworth Longfellow. Two more Hiawatha-themed works followed, making a trilogy that led to international fame if not great wealth.

KEY WORKS: *Ballade in A Minor*, 1898; *Hiawatha's Wedding Feast*, 1898; *The Death of Minnehaha*, 1899; *Hiawatha's Departure*, 1900

△ PIETRO MASCAGNI, ANGIOLO TOMMASI, 1899

# EARLY 20th CENTURY

CHAPTER 5

# Leoš Janáček

## 1854–1928, CZECH

Janáček forged a musical language closely influenced by the speech patterns of his native Czech, but also by intense personal tragedy. After a long struggle for recognition, his music remains popular today.

◁ **LEOS AND ZDENKA JANACEK**
Janáček and his wife and former pupil, Zdenka Schulzová, are shown here in 1881, the year of their marriage and of the founding of his organ school in Brno.

Much like his older compatriot and friend Antonín Dvořák, Leoš Janáček was an all-around musician. Born in Hukvaldy, Bohemia, in 1854, Leoš became a choirboy at the Abbey of St. Thomas in Brno; later, he studied at the organ school in Prague and then piano, organ, and composition in Leipzig. His teachers were impressed by his talent, although some regarded him as a problematic personality. At first, he eked out a living by giving piano lessons and conducting amateur choirs, while composing on the side.

In 1881, Janáček founded an organ school in Brno, and married one of his pupils, Zdenka Schulzová. During the next few years, his interest in folk music grew. He began collecting and studying traditional songs and dances of the region and in the early 1890s he became effectively the leader of folklorist activities in Moravia and Silesia, often translating elements of this musical language into his own compositions. From about 1879, too, he started transcribing the intonations of speech. In 1909, he acquired an Edison phonograph, which he used to record folk song, much as Bartók did in Hungary (see pp. 250–253).

Janáček's influences from opera and the concert hall included Smetana, Dvořák, and Tchaikovsky—but he detested Wagner. He developed his own operas in a highly individual direction, using speech patterns (see box, below). He often based works on Russian literature; his first string quartet is modeled on Tolstoy's *The Kreutzer Sonata*, and two of his operas, *Katya Kabanová* and *From the House of the Dead*, on Ostrovsky and Dostoyevsky respectively.

## Tragedy and turmoil

A turning point came in 1903 with the tragic death of his daughter, Olga. Janáček's grief found some outlet in his piano music, including the suites *On an Overgrown Path* and *In the Mists*. The murder of a young political protester in 1905 inspired an intense and agonized piano sonata.

Janáček's marriage was now under strain, and after he had an affair with the opera singer Gabriela Horvátová, his wife attempted suicide. The married couple remained together, but were estranged. However, the relationship that made most impact on his music was an infatuated yet chiefly platonic friendship with a far younger woman, Kamila Stösslová, whom he met in 1917. Their letters provided him with great inspiration for his work; many of his finest operas and chamber works date from these years, notably *Katya Kabanová* and the string quartet *Intimate Letters*. It was only now, too, that his works began to achieve the full recognition that he had craved.

During an excursion to the countryside with Stösslová and her son, Janáček contracted a chill, which became pneumonia. He died of the illness on August 28, 1928.

◁ **HOUSE OF THE DEAD**
The handwritten score for Janáček's powerful final opera, *From the House of the Dead*, which was published 10 years after the end of World War II.

△ **FOLK DANCES IN MORAVIA**
Title page of the score for Janáček's *Folk Dances in Moravia*. The composer was inspired by Moravian traditions to produce a radically new form of music.

## ON TECHNIQUE
### Speech patterns

An interest in folklore was shared by many nationalist composers in central Europe during Janáček's lifetime, but his use of speech patterns was entirely new. He would notate the pitches and rhythms of the spoken Czech language and examine how "speech tunes" altered according to context and the speaker's state of mind. This enabled him to break free from the specter of Wagner and develop his music in a different way. The technique powers his operas such as *The Cunning Little Vixen*, but also his choral masterpiece, the *Glagolitic Mass*, and even his instrumental works, such as the *Sinfonietta*.

" I hear music **constantly** in the **empty silence**, while the **intellect** is **stilled** and all **emotional strings** are **relaxed**. "

LEOS JANACEK

# Edward Elgar

### 1857–1934, BRITISH

The most prominent English composer of the early 20th century, Elgar wrote music ranging from the dramatic, brash, and robust to the tender and lyrical. His work retains universal appeal.

Edward Elgar was born in 1857 in the village of Broadheath, outside Worcester, in the West Midlands. His family were of the modest lower-middle class. His father ran a music shop in Worcester, played the organ at a local church, and tuned pianos. His mother was an ardent Catholic and raised her children in that faith.

Elgar's musical education consisted of learning to play piano and violin from his father. As an adolescent, he aspired to study music in Germany, but his family could not afford to send him to Leipzig. Instead, he settled into a life as a musician, giving lessons, playing violin in provincial orchestras, and even organizing music at an asylum for the mentally ill.

## Early life and influences

Elgar began composing from an early age. Although often regarded as a quintessentially English composer, he had no interest in his nation's folk music and was dismissive of its musical traditions. Instead, the models he sought to emulate were the great Germans such as Brahms, Schumann, and Wagner, whose works he had heard at concerts on day trips to London and later on vacations in Bavaria. Two of Elgar's early orchestral pieces were given public performances in 1883 and 1884, without making any impact. His private life also stalled, his

### IN CONTEXT
### The Three Choirs Festival

Founded in 1715 and still flourishing today, the Three Choirs Festival rotates annually between Hereford, Gloucester, and Worcester cathedrals. It has provided great opportunities for music-making on a scale rarely seen in the English provinces.
From 1878 to 1893, the young Elgar played violin in the orchestra each time the festival was held in Worcester Cathedral. Many of his early works were written to be performed at successive festivals, including the *Froissart* overture (1890) and the cantatas *The Black Knight* (1893) and *The Light of Life* (1896).

**WORCESTER CATHEDRAL, NORTHWEST VIEW, 1836**

engagement to a Worcester girl, Helen Weaver, terminated when she emigrated to New Zealand.

The person who saved Elgar from provincial frustration was Alice Roberts. Nine years older than the composer, she was the daughter of a major-general. In 1886, Elgar was employed to give her piano lessons. An unlikely love blossomed and the couple married in 1889, to the disgust of the haughty Roberts family, who were appalled by Elgar's inappropriate age, his lowly social status, and his Catholicism. The marriage had a

profound influence on Elgar's career. Alice was intelligent and gifted: she wrote poetry and had published a novel. She gave Elgar emotional security and boosted his confidence. She also taught him to handle contacts with a higher social stratum and, importantly, had a private income that boosted his slim earnings. His first successful composition, the tuneful *Salut d'amour*, written for Alice on their engagement, premiered in 1889, the year of their marriage. Their only child was born in 1890.

Following a brief sojourn in London, the couple returned to rural Worcestershire, settling near the Malvern Hills. Through the 1890s Elgar had built a reputation as a composer of choral works, from *The Black Knight*, premiered in Worcester in 1893 (see box, above), to *Caractacus*, featured at the Leeds Festival in 1898. To the general public, however, he was a complete unknown when the first performances of the *Enigma Variations*

△ **CAROLINE ALICE ELGAR**
The accomplished Caroline Alice Roberts, known as Alice, married Edward Elgar at London's Brompton Oratory, a Catholic church, when she was 40 and he was in his thirties. The marriage met fierce opposition from her family.

◁ **ELGAR'S BIRTHPLACE**
Elgar was born in this picturesque yet simple cottage in Lower Broadheath, Worcestershire, the heart of the British countryside, in 1857. It is now the Elgar Birthplace Museum.

△ **THE MALVERN HILLS**
After spending a short period of time in London soon after their marriage, the Elgars returned to live near the Malvern Hills in rural Worcestershire, where they had both been born and brought up. The countryside remained a source of immense comfort, joy, and inspiration to Elgar throughout his life.

in 1899 brought him national renown. Dedicated to "my friends pictured within," the conceit of a series of character studies allowed the *Variations* to cover a wide emotional range, by turns grave and humorous, melancholy and exhilarating. The "enigma" referred to in the title was never explained, but no doubt aided the work's popular success.

## Criticism and acclaim

Elgar's finest choral work, *The Dream of Gerontius*, followed, but did not win easy acceptance. With a setting of a long poem by Cardinal John Henry Newman, the key figure in the Catholic revival in 19th-century England, it provoked criticism from the Protestant Church. Its first performance at the Birmingham Festival in 1900 was a poorly rehearsed shambles that reduced the composer to despair. However, the following year his stirring *Pomp and Circumstance* marches were greeted with frantic enthusiasm by patriotic audiences. The first of them soon became

an unofficial national anthem, the well-known melody of the trio section later acquiring lyrics as "Land of Hope and Glory." In 1902, *Gerontius* was performed to acclaim in Germany, and the English now realized that, for the first time since the 17th century, they had a native-born composer of international stature.

Elgar was fêted and showered with honors, culminating in a knighthood in 1904. He bought a large house in Hereford and acquired wealthy friends, concealing his neurotic, sensitive, melancholy nature behind the persona of a bluff, dog-loving, golf-playing English gentleman. Adopted by the British establishment, he always at heart felt like an outsider, because of both his Catholicism and his lowly birth. Inner stresses

▷ **THE *ENIGMA VARIATIONS***
This score from the first page of Elgar's *Enigma Variations*, Op. 36, includes the signatures of the members of the London Symphony Orchestra who played the piece at the Festival of Leeds in 1901.

revealed themselves in a spate of psychosomatic illnesses. He above all despised the British ruling classes for failing to share his belief in the transcendental value of music. Made professor of music at Birmingham University—a post created for him in 1905—he used his lectures to deliver an attack on English cultural philistinism that astonished his patriotic admirers.

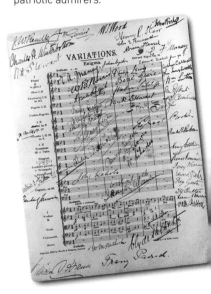

"There is **music in the air … the world** is **full of it** and you simply **take as much** as you **require.**"
EDWARD ELGAR

## KEY WORKS

**1890**

*Froissart*, a concert overture for the Three Choirs Festival, is Elgar's first well-received orchestral work.

**1899**

*Enigma Variations, Variations on an Original Theme* are performed to critical acclaim at St. James's Hall in London.

**1900**

*The Dream of Gerontius*, Elgar's choral work setting a poem by Cardinal Newman, is staged in Birmingham Town Hall.

**1908**

Symphony No. 1, premiered by the Hallé Orchestra in Manchester, is a popular and critical triumph.

**1910**

The first performance of Elgar's technically demanding and lyrical Violin Concerto is given by Fritz Kreisler.

**1919**

The Cello Concerto, Elgar's last masterpiece, is written in the aftermath of World War I.

Musical inspiration continued to flow. Elgar completed two of an intended trilogy of oratorios, *The Apostles* (1903) and *The Kingdom* (1906); he abandoned the third part. In 1908, his robust First Symphony repeated and even exceeded the triumph of *Pomp and Circumstance*, receiving almost a hundred performances in its first year. The symphony was also well received internationally, notably in the US and Germany.

The Violin Concerto, first performed by Austrian virtuoso Fritz Kreisler in 1910, was another enduring success. One of the most demanding works in the violin repertoire, it may have owed its emotional lyricism to Elgar's love for Alice Stuart Wortley, daughter of the British artist John Everett Millais and wife of an MP. If the romance did take place, there is no evidence that it disturbed Elgar's marriage.

In 1912, the Elgars moved to London. They led a life of theater-going and dinner parties. Elgar's music was then developing toward inwardness. A listening public expecting simpler

pleasures was disappointed. Elgar said of an unresponsive audience at the premiere of his Second Symphony at the Queen's Hall, London, in 1911, "they just sat there like stuffed pigs."

He reacted to the outbreak of World War I in 1914 with horror, and was appalled at the jingoistic exploitation of his "Land of Hope and Glory." In 1917, he withdrew to an isolated house in Sussex, where he wrote his Cello Concerto, a masterpiece of elegiac sadness and piercing nostalgia. It was his last finished work. Alice died in 1920; Elgar's creative drive died with her.

### Later years

Associated with the lost Edwardian prewar world, Elgar's music was derided by the young Modernists who were the trend-setters of the 1920s.

▷ **COCKAIGNE OVERTURE**
Elgar's *Cockaigne Overture* ("In London Town"), 1900–1901, written for full orchestra, offers a lively and humorous portrait of London and its inhabitants. The cover of the score is shown here.

Elgar's appointment as Master of the King's Music in 1924 only confirmed his misplaced reputation as a stuffy establishment figure. The composer remained musically active as a conductor of his own works, many of which he recorded for posterity. In 1932, a commission from the BBC led him belatedly to resume composition, working on a Third Symphony, but it was never completed. Elgar died of cancer in 1934 and was buried alongside his beloved Alice in the village of Little Malvern in Worcestershire.

### IN CONTEXT
### Orchestral recording

Elgar was a pioneer of recorded music. In the early 20th century, records of famous singers were marketed, but very few recordings of orchestras had been attempted before 1914, when the Gramophone Company signed Elgar to conduct his most popular works. In 1931, as technology began to transform the quality of recorded sound, Elgar was invited to inaugurate EMI's new Abbey Road studio, conducting the London Symphony Orchestra in his *Falstaff* suite. His most famous recording was a 1932 performance of his Violin Concerto with violinist Yehudi Menuhin, who was then just 16 years old.

**GRAMOPHONE AT ELGAR'S BIRTHPLACE MUSEUM, BROADHEATH**

# Ethel Smyth

## 1858–1944, BRITISH

Fiercely independent, Smyth defied convention to become one of the first female composers to achieve international recognition. She gained notoriety for her uncompromising support for the suffragette movement.

Ethel Mary Smyth was born in 1858 in Sidcup, Kent, at that time one of the most conservative of London suburbs. Her middle-class upbringing reflected the Victorian idea that a woman's place was in the home, but her father's career as a major general in the army had enabled the family to travel to India periodically, so Ethel's horizons were widened.

### Bold early move

At home in England, she had music lessons and, in defiance of her father, decided to pursue a career in the subject. She set off, aged 19, to study at the Conservatoire in Leipzig, where she came into contact with leading composers such as Dvořák, Grieg, and Tchaikovsky. However, she was disappointed with the tuition at the Conservatoire and left after a year to study privately under Heinrich von Herzogenberg, who introduced her to Brahms and Clara Schumann.

Her studies with von Herzogenberg gave her a solid grounding in musical theory, enabling her to progress with

Dedicated to THE WOMEN'S SOCIAL AND POLITICAL UNION.

**THE MARCH OF THE WOMEN**
( Popular Edition in F. To be sung in Unison )
By **ETHEL SMYTH**, Mus.Doc.
Price: One Shilling & Sixpence net.

⊲ **ETHEL SMYTH, c. 1925**
Although from a staunchly middle-class, conservative background, Smyth became a prominent suffragette and composed the rousing anthem of the Women's Social and Political Union.

⊲ **"THE MARCH OF THE WOMEN"**
The song sheet for Smyth's inspirational anthem—incorporating the suffragette colors of purple, green, and white—shows women and girls of the WSPU.

her composition, but, as a woman, she struggled to get her music played, until a performance of her Mass in D at the Albert Hall, London, in 1893 to an enthusiastic audience gave her the breakthrough she deserved.

Smyth then turned her attention to opera, beginning with *Der Wald*, which was premiered in Berlin in 1902, and the next year performed at the New York Metropolitan Opera. This was followed by perhaps her best-known work, *The Wreckers*, a three-act opera championed by conductor Thomas Beecham, an admirer of her music.

In 1910, Smyth put her musical career on hold after she met, and fell passionately in love with, the

campaigner Emmeline Pankhurst, founder of the Women's Social and Political Union (see box, right). Devoting all her efforts to the cause of women's suffrage, Smyth composed a stirring march that was used by the suffragettes at their rallies in London.

### Imprisonment and acclaim

After addressing a demonstration in Trafalgar Square in 1912, Smyth was arrested and imprisoned for breaking the windows of the home of the colonial secretary. While incarcerated in Holloway Prison, she was seen by Beecham—who was visiting the jail—leaning out of her cell window, conducting "The March of the Women" with her toothbrush.

During World War I, she trained as a radiographer in France, and on her return to England, enjoyed modest success from performances of her work. She was made a Dame of the British Empire in 1923. In her latter years she wrote little music, but published several entertaining books of memoirs. She died of pneumonia after a long illness in 1944, aged 86.

**EMMELINE PANKHURST, ACTIVIST AND COFOUNDER OF THE WSPU**

> " The **charms** of **seclusion** are seldom **combined** with the **conveniences** of **civilization**. "
> ETHEL SMYTH, *STREAKS OF LIFE*, 1921

# Frederick Delius

## 1862–1934, BRITISH

Although Delius studied music in Germany and lived much of his life abroad, his style was both highly individual and recognizably English, placing him among the greatest British composers of the 20th century.

Fritz Delius (he adopted the name Frederick many years later) was one of 14 children born to Julius and Elise Delius, who had moved to England from Germany. He was born in Bradford—where Julius was a successful wool merchant—and showed an early talent for music. It was, however, assumed that Fritz would follow in his father's footsteps.

After completing his education in 1880, he worked for the family business in offices in France, Sweden, and Germany. He enjoyed the cultural life of these countries, and also took lessons in music. Still opposed to his son's wish to take up a musical career, his father then sent him to Florida to manage an orange plantation. Undaunted, Fritz continued his studies in the US, and after a year moved to Danville, Virginia, where he made a living teaching music, French, and German and also composed pieces inspired by US popular songs.

### The big break

In 1886, despite his father's wishes, Fritz moved to Leipzig to study at the Conservatoire. This gave him the grounding in theory he needed, but his inspiration came from meeting Edvard Grieg, who encouraged the young composer and influenced his early style. Grieg persuaded the family

to support Fritz's developing career, and in 1888 he moved to Paris where, with financial help from his uncle, he worked full-time as a composer.

Delius mixed with artists and writers in the city, and it was probably here that he caught syphilis, which plagued his later years; but it was also where he began his relationship with German painter Jelka Rosen. She bought a house in the village of Grez-sur-Loing, just outside Paris, where the couple lived after their marriage in 1903.

Despite his German ancestry and studies in Leipzig, Delius developed a distinctive, eclectic style that owed little to German Romanticism and more to the folk-inspired nostalgia associated with English pastoral music. Surprisingly, however, his work became popular with German conductors and audiences, while comparatively unknown elsewhere.

Nonetheless, in 1907, the conductor Thomas Beecham heard some of Delius's pieces at a concert in London, and became his most ardent champion. Encouraged by Beecham, Delius produced some of his best-known music, including *Brigg Fair*, the *Mass of Life*, *In a Summer Garden*, *On Hearing the First Cuckoo in Spring*, and *A Village Romeo and Juliet*.

During World War I, he and Jelka traveled to Norway and Britain, and visited spas in France for Frederick's health, as the effects of syphilis began to take hold. During the 1920s, as his reputation peaked, he became increasingly incapable of working; by 1928, he was blind and confined to a wheelchair. However, with help from Eric Fenby (see box, below), he was able to complete and revise his unfinished works, and even start new projects before his death in 1934.

△ **DELIUS AND HIS WIFE, 1929**
Delius, in a wheelchair, is shown arriving at Queen's Hall, London, with his wife, Jelka Rosen, to attend rehearsals of his works conducted by Thomas Beecham.

▷ **FREDERICK DELIUS, 1929**
This work by Ernest Procter is a sketch of the composer listening to a rehearsal for the Delius festival held at the Queen's Hall in West London in November 1929. It is a study for a larger painting that shows the composer in his wheelchair.

### IN PROFILE
### Eric Fenby

Delius's amanuensis, Eric Fenby (1906–1997), was an organist and choirmaster, and also accompanied silent films on the piano in his local cinema. In 1928, he heard Delius's music and, learning of the composer's disabilities, offered his services as an assistant. After Delius's death, he worked with the music publisher Boosey & Hawkes, and during World War II served in the Royal Army Education Corps. He was appointed artistic director of the 1962 Delius Centenary Festival, and two years later became professor of harmony at the Royal Academy of Music.

ERIC FENBY WITH A GRAMOPHONE ONCE BELONGING TO DELIUS, LONDON, 1980

ERNEST PROCTER 29

# Richard Strauss

## 1864–1949, GERMAN

A prolific writer of songs and tone poems, Strauss is celebrated above all for his operas. Although he flirted with Modernism in *Salome* and *Elektra*, he remained essentially a (very) late Romantic to the end of his long life.

◁ **RICHARD STRAUSS**
In Strauss's long career as conductor and composer, he traveled extensively through Europe and the US, directing many of the world's greatest orchestras.

Richard Georg Strauss was born in Munich on June 11, 1864, the eldest child of Franz Joseph Strauss, principal horn in the city's court orchestra, and his second wife, Josephine Pschorr Strauss. The boy quickly proved something of a child prodigy, though his musically conservative father would not allow him to hear anything but the Austro-German classics. Wagner was beyond the pale. After composing his first song at the age of six, Strauss continued to write songs modeled on Schubert and Schumann, encouraged by his father and his flamboyant aunt Johanna, a talented mezzo-soprano.

A crucial moment in Strauss's teens was his discovery of Wagner's *Tristan und Isolde*. Defying his father's orders, he devoured the score "in a trance" and became a lifelong Wagnerian—though not yet in his own music. Before he was 20 he had composed

◁ **PAGE FROM *TRISTAN UND ISOLDE***
Strauss described the final bars of Wagner's opera *Tristan und Isolde* as "the most beautifully orchestrated B-major chord in the history of music."

fluent instrumental works modeled largely on Mozart, Beethoven, and Mendelssohn, including two symphonies and an ebullient horn concerto. At 21, Strauss published his first truly original set of songs, including the soaring "Zueignung."

### A growing reputation

*Macbeth* (1886–1888) was the first of a series of brilliant orchestral tone poems that made Strauss's international reputation. "I've arrived," he exclaimed after the 1889 triumph of the sexually explicit *Don Juan*— in effect a condensed Wagner opera minus the voices. There was, by all accounts, more than a touch of wish fulfillment in his identification with the Don's amorous exploits, as well as in the idealized self-portrait of *Ein Heldenleben* (*A Hero's Life*).

From the mid-1880s, Strauss held a series of conducting posts in Munich, Weimar, and Berlin. In 1894, he married a former singing pupil, Pauline de Ahna, a general's daughter (who once said that Strauss was "anything but a Don Juan").

**IN CONTEXT**
**Treading a thin line**

Strauss's conduct under the Nazis has been a subject of controversy. Naively apolitical, he both loathed the regime and occasionally did their bidding, as when he conducted Wagner's *Parsifal* at the 1933 Bayreuth Festival after Toscanini withdrew in protest at the Nazis' treatment of the Jews. In mitigation, Strauss was anxious to protect his Jewish daughter-in-law, Alice, and her children. He did, though, court danger with his support of the Jewish Stefan Zweig, librettist of the opera *Die schweigsame Frau*.

**A NAZI PARTY POSTER DEPICTING ADOLF HITLER, c. 1935**

> " I employ **cacophony** to **outrage** people. "
> RICHARD STRAUSS TO GUSTAV MAHLER

## ON TECHNIQUE
### Tone poems

**ALSO SPRACH ZARATHUSTRA, OP. 30, FRONTISPIECE**

Strauss's tone poems are the natural successors to Liszt's symphonic poems, though they far surpass them in vivid characterization and virtuoso use of a vast orchestra. Yet for all their late-Romantic opulence, they never lose sight of the Classical tradition in which Strauss was raised. *Ein Heldenleben* and *Don Juan* are cast in sonata form, while *Till Eulenspiegel* is a rondo. Most ambitious is the Nietzsche-inspired *Also sprach Zarathustra*, famous for its use in the 1968 film *2001: A Space Odyssey*. Its ongoing clash between the keys of B and C symbolizes the irreconcilability of nature and humankind.

Pauline was notoriously abrasive, as evident in the graphic portrait of her in the autobiographical opera *Intermezzo*. However, she was also a gifted singer: Strauss wrote four of his finest songs as a wedding present for Pauline. Published as Op. 27, these include "Morgen!," a rapt love duet for piano and voice, and the operatically extrovert "Cäcilie."

Pauline created the leading role in Strauss's first opera, *Guntram* (a failure on its premiere in 1894), and inspired his abiding love affair with the soprano voice. He once said of her: "She sang my songs with an expression and a poetry such as I have never heard since." She remained his ideal interpreter even when her voice grew more fragile and her platform manner (including shameless applause-seeking antics during her husband's piano postludes) increasingly outrageous.

### Operatic success
Between 1894 and 1906, Strauss composed some 70 songs, many of which he performed with Pauline. But in the new century, his creative life was dominated by opera. After the satirical *Feuersnot* (1901), the composer embraced Modernism with the violently compressed *Salome* (1905), to a play by Oscar Wilde, and *Elektra* (1909). Both operas probed emotional and sexual extremes by taking dissonance to a new level; and both caused a sensation. Strauss built a luxurious villa at the resort of Garmisch in Bavaria on the proceeds of *Salome*. A study in morbid hysteria, *Elektra* contains the most discordantly "advanced" music that Strauss ever composed. The opera was his first collaboration with the Viennese author Hugo von Hofmannsthal, who then also provided the libretto

△ **DER ROSENKAVALIER**
In this 1912 painting by Robert Sterl, Ernst von Schuch conducts *Der Rosenkavalier*. Schuch conducted the premieres of many of Strauss's operas.

for a very different work, the ever popular *Der Rosenkavalier* (1911). Retreating from Modernist anarchy, Strauss wrote a bittersweet comedy of manners that mingles Wagnerian techniques (including subtle thematic transformation) with a Mozartian lightness and grace. If *Figaro* has a successor, this is it.

What might be called the Mozartian and Wagnerian sides of Strauss's musical personality also intermingle in most of his later operas. *Ariadne auf Naxos* (1912, revised 1916), is a chamber opera of self-conscious

sophistication. Like *Rosenkavalier*, it contains three great soprano roles: the ardent, idealistic young composer (apparently modeled on the teenage Mozart), the death-haunted Ariadne, and the flighty coloratura soprano Zerbinetta. *Die Frau ohne Schatten* (*The Woman Without a Shadow*, 1913 ), a symbolic fairy tale that focuses on themes of human fertility and marital relationships, is Strauss's and Hofmannsthal's homage to *The Magic Flute*. Its orchestration is the most sumptuous and glittering in all of Strauss's oeuvre—which is saying something—while the Empress and the dyer Barak sing some of his most fervently lyrical music.

Inspiration burned more fitfully in Strauss's later operas, of which the two most successful are *Arabella*

> " **My wife**, my **child**, my **music**, **nature**, and **the sun**; they are **my happiness**. "
>
> RICHARD STRAUSS

## KEY WORKS

**1889**

*Don Juan* premieres in Weimar: Strauss is seen as the best German composer since Wagner.

**1905**

*Salome* uses an often discordant musical language to explore sexual and emotional extremes.

**1911**

*Der Rosenkavalier* recalls Mozart and indulges Strauss's taste for parody and pastiche.

**1933**

Strauss's final collaboration with Hofmannsthal, *Arabella* is a wry comedy of manners.

**1945**

Strauss's *Metamorphosen*, for 23 solo strings, is a response to the Allied bombing of Dresden.

**1948**

Strauss bows out with the autumnal *Vier letzte Lieder*, an evocation of a vanished Romanticism.

(1933), a comedy-cum-fairy-tale set in a faintly sleazy 1860s Vienna, and the urbane "conversation piece" *Capriccio* (1942). Essentially an opera about opera, this is Strauss's supreme act of Rococo-Romantic escapism amid the barbarism of war.

### Final creative surge

After the relatively lean decades of the 1920s and 1930s, Strauss experienced a new surge of creative energy. Having begun with *Capriccio*, his renewed flourishing continued with the second horn concerto, two wind sonatinas, and a delectable oboe concerto. All these works nostalgically refract the spirit of Mozart through a Straussian harmonic prism. Quoting the funeral march of Beethoven's "Eroica" Symphony, the elegiac *Metamorphosen* is Strauss's lament for the physical and cultural devastation of Germany. His swan song, the *Vier letzte Lieder* (*Four Last Songs*, 1948 ), is at once a consummation of his lifelong love affair with the soprano voice and a profound valediction, embracing sleep and oblivion serenely and without sentimentality. Here is the whole German Romantic tradition in its glorious death agony.

Having used his influence to protect his Jewish daughter-in-law and grandsons from the Nazis (see box, p.213), Strauss went into exile in Switzerland after the war. He was cleared by the denazification tribunal in 1948, and, already ailing, returned to Germany the following year. He died at Garmisch on September 8, 1949.

### Fame and modesty

For all his fame, Strauss never lost the aura of a down-to-earth Bavarian, at his happiest sharing a game of skat (a card game) with friends. Yet the outward nonchalance was deceptive. A meticulous professional, Strauss once remarked wryly: "I may not be a first-rate composer, but I am a first-rate second-rate composer." Coming from the creator of such works as *Elektra*, *Der Rosenkavalier*, *Metamorphosen*, and the *Vier letzte Lieder*, this might seem an unduly modest self-assessment.

▽ **FESTIVAL REHEARSAL**
Strauss plays the piano at a rehearsal for *Ariadne auf Naxos* at the Salzburg Festival in 1926. The opera was performed by the Vienna State Opera, with Lotte Lehmann in the role of Ariadne.

▷ **CARL NIELSEN, c. 1892**
Nielsen's sporadic education ended when, at the age of 13, he had a brief apprenticeship with a grocer. The following year he joined a military band, which marked the beginning of his long and successful career in music. The composer and conductor is shown here as a young man, soon after his marriage and travels in Europe.

# Carl Nielsen

## 1865–1931, DANISH

The greatest of all Danish composers, Nielsen achieved the status of a national hero. His work was highly varied, but he is chiefly renowned as one of the most powerful and original symphonists of the 20th century.

# "**Music** is **life**, whereas the **other arts** only **represent** and **paraphrase life**."

CARL NIELSEN

⊲ **MILITARY MUSICIAN**
Nielsen is shown here, instruments in hand, at the age of 14. It was at this time that he joined a military band as a regimental bugler in Odense, the capital of Funen, his homeland.

Carl Nielsen was born in Sortelung on the isle of Funen (see box, below), the seventh of 12 children in a poor family. His father was a house painter who supplemented his income by playing the violin and cornet at weddings and other events. By the age of six, Carl was learning to play his father's instruments and he wrote his earliest compositions two or three years later. He joined a military band in Odense in 1879, playing horn and trombone.

From 1884 to 1886, Nielsen studied at the Copenhagen Conservatory, and in 1889 he became a violinist in the Royal Danish Orchestra. A scholarship enabled him to spend nine months in 1890–1891 traveling around Europe, where he met (in Paris) and married (in Florence) the Danish sculptor Anne Marie Brodersen. The marriage was troubled—Nielsen resented his wife's protracted absences on work trips— but it produced three children and lasted until Nielsen's death in 1931.

In 1894, the Royal Danish Orchestra premiered Nielsen's exhilarating Symphony No. 1. Danish critic Charles Kjerulf wrote that it seemed to presage "a coming storm of genius," and described the work as "wonderfully innocent and unknowing, as if seeing a child playing with dynamite."

## Continued success
Nielsen's reputation continued to grow and in 1901 he was awarded a state pension, which gave him more time for composition. He was able to give up his violin post in 1905 (from this time, he sometimes conducted the orchestra, and was its official conductor from 1908 to 1914). In 1906, he had another resounding success with his high-spirited comic opera *Maskarade*, which remains popular in Denmark. His other work includes incidental music for the stage, chamber and choral works, and numerous songs.

## An enduring reputation
However, Nielsen's reputation rests mainly on his major orchestral works—six symphonies and three concertos (for violin, clarinet, and flute). His symphonic output begins in a late-Romantic sound-world that would have been recognizable to Brahms but becomes increasingly Modernist, encompassing violent conflict and quirky humor as well as melodic richness, all within a rough-edged, earthy vigor.

Nielsen's 60th birthday was marked by national celebration in Denmark. The next year he had a heart attack, but continued to work. In 1931, he was appointed director of the Copenhagen Conservatory, but he died nine months later. A monument to him by his wife was erected in Copenhagen in 1939. In his lifetime, his reputation was mainly confined to Denmark and neighboring Sweden, but since the 1950s it has spread worldwide.

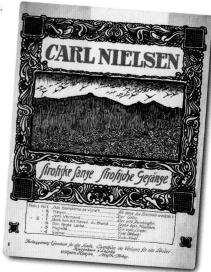

△ **SCORE COVER, *STROPHIC SONGS***
Nielsen's songs were (and still are) highly popular in Denmark. He wrote about 250, collecting the best in two volumes (1905–1907) as *Strofiske Sange* (*Strophic Songs*). This is the cover of a German edition. A strophic song is one in which each verse is sung to the same tune.

## IN CONTEXT
### Funen

Funen (known as Fyn in Danish), where Nielsen was born and grew up, is the third largest of Denmark's many islands. It is renowned for its fertile farmland and natural beauty, which has given rise to its nomination as "the garden of Denmark." Nielsen's autobiography, *My Childhood on Funen* (1927), has an honored place in Danish literature. The capital of the island is Odense, where there is a museum devoted to Nielsen and his sculptor wife.

WINDMILL IN EGESKOV, FUNEN, DENMARK

# Jean Sibelius

## 1865–1957, FINNISH

The most powerful composer ever produced by the Nordic countries, Sibelius found remarkable ways of renewing the forms of orchestral music, especially the symphony.

Johan Sibelius (he took the French version of his first name in later life) was born in December 1865 in the small town of Hämeenlinna in Finland, a region that until 1918 was a Grand Duchy of Czarist Russia. The educated classes—among them Johan's parents—were generally Swedish-speaking; the broader population spoke Finnish, which was increasingly associated with a spirit of growing national unease and restlessness at Russian political domination.

### Early struggles and success

Sibelius's father was a doctor, who died in a typhoid epidemic when Johan was only two, leaving Maria Sibelius, his pregnant young widow, a mountain of debts. Maria took her family to live with her mother elsewhere in Hämeenlinna. They could not afford to give the three children an elite, Swedish-speaking education, so Johan was sent to a local Finnish-speaking school.

In 1885, aged 20, having graduated from high school, Sibelius moved to Helsinki and studied violin at the Music Institute. During his time there, he adopted his father's feckless habits and struggled with debt and drinking issues for the next four decades.

His dream of becoming a virtuoso violinist was tempered as a result of his friendship with Ferruccio Busoni (see p.276), the master-pianist who taught at the Institute. Realizing that this level of performance would be beyond him, Sibelius spent a year as a promising student-composer in Berlin, then another in Vienna. But he could never have envisaged the astonishing success of his first major work, *Kullervo*, when he conducted its premiere in Helsinki in 1892. In this work, Sibelius tells the story of the principal character in the *Kalevala*, the Finnish folk epic, in the form of a 90-minute, five-movement "symphonic poem" for two soloists, male chorus, and orchestra.

In 1888, Sibelius had met Aino Järnefelt, the 17-year-old daughter of an aristocratic family who, unusually for their class, were Finnish-speaking nationalists. The couple were married soon after *Kullervo*'s premiere, and the first of their six daughters (one died in infancy) was born the following year.

### New directions

Sibelius now grappled with the issues of how to earn a living (part-time teaching at the Music Institute helped) and what to compose next. His first response was the symphonic poem *En Saga* (1892), commissioned by the conductor Robert Kajanus (see box, right). He also produced the first of many unaccompanied choral works, *Rakastava* (*The Lover*), a beautifully imagined small masterpiece. In 1893, his *Karelia*—incidental music written for a pageant in the town of Viipuri (now Vyborg)—celebrated the culture of the northeastern province of Finland (now part of Russia).

The composer's next major statement was a symphonic suite that was based on the exploits of Lemminkäinen, the adventurer-warrior of the *Kalevala*. The premiere in 1896 was a lukewarm success, but one of the movements, "The Swan of Tuonela," soon took on an independent life of its own;

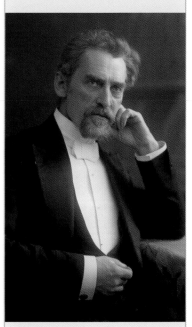

**ROBERT KAJANUS**

▷ **JEAN SIBELIUS**
This portrait, showing Sibelius brooding and with disheveled hair, is by Akseli Gallen-Kallela, a friend of the composer (see also caption p.220, left).

◁ **SCENE FROM THE *KALEVALA***
A 19th-century watercolor depicts the character in the Finnish epic the *Kalevala* on whom Sibelius based his symphonic poem, *Kullervo*. The music's surging symphonic command and ultra-vivid evocation of the Finnish landscape were instantly acclaimed.

the music's long cor anglais solo, uncoiling against a background of muted and divided strings, is one of Sibelius's great feats of imagination.

His First Symphony, strongly influenced by Tchaikovsky, premiered in 1899 and was followed by the far more individual Second Symphony, with its masterly first movement that stitches together fragmentary themes into a central development section, and then unpicks them again.

Meanwhile, the waves of Finnish nationalism were rolling high. In 1899, a Russian-imposed "February Manifesto" abolished Finnish freedom of speech and right of assembly. A pageant was organized in Helsinki to protest at the suppression of press freedom, and Sibelius composed a six-movement orchestral sequence

▷ **SCORE FOR SYMPHONY NO. 2,** The remains of Sibelius's original score for Symphony No. 2 are held in the Sibelius Museum in Turku, southwest Finland.

for the occasion; the last item, *Finland Awakes*, later revised and renamed *Finlandia*, secured his international fame.

## Growing mastery

Sibelius also began to compose incidental music for Helsinki's theater scene. *Kuolema* (*Death*), by his brother-in-law Arvid Järnefelt, was a Symbolist play in the style of Maurice Maeterlinck's *Pelléas et Mélisande*

(the source of Debussy's opera, see p.197, and Schoenberg's symphonic poem, see p.239). Sibelius supplied six musical numbers, arranging one of them as *Valse triste* and selling it to a music firm. They, in turn, sold it to his German publisher, who issued it in multiple arrangements: *Valse triste* was soon being played by hotel and salon bands all over Europe. Sibelius never quite forgave himself for missing out on a small fortune in royalty payments. His next major works were a virtuosic Violin Concerto and a Third Symphony in a leaner, more Classical style and with a quietly introspective poetic streak.

▽ **LAKE KEITELE,** 1905
This tranquil landscape was painted by Sibelius's collaborator, Akseli Gallen-Kallela, whom the composer hailed as "Finland's greatest painter." The scene's contemplative mood is evocative of Sibelius's more meditative works.

## "Music begins where the possibilities of language end."

JEAN SIBELIUS, 1919

In 1903, Sibelius took out a loan to build a family home in the village of Järvenpää, near Lake Tuusula, north of Helsinki. He financed the construction of "Ainola" (Aino's Home) with help from his annual stipend from the Finnish government (first granted in 1897) and his erratic earnings from music. The family moved into their new home in 1904.

Four years later, however, Sibelius was diagnosed with throat cancer. Painful surgery in Berlin proved successful, but the experience influenced the dark, austere mood of his Fourth Symphony in 1911.

### The war years

Next came a symphonic poem, *The Oceanides*, evoking the sea-nymphs of Greek mythology. The piece was commissioned by Carl Stoeckel, a wealthy US businessman who ran a music festival in Norfolk, Connecticut. Sibelius arrived home from an acclaimed US visit just before World War I broke out in 1914 and thereafter

△ **"AINOLA," SIBELIUS'S HOUSE**
Sibelius is shown here with members of his family in the grounds of his house, "Ainola," at the picturesque lakeside village of Järvenpää.

found himself unable to travel abroad, with royalties cut off from his German publishers, where many of his works had been placed.

Nonetheless, the composer made good progress on a Fifth Symphony for his fiftieth birthday concert in 1915. He then withdrew it for revision, conducting a new version a year later; for this, he spliced the two opening movements together, so that the first flowed into the second. Still not happy, he worked on a final revision while the Civil War (see box, right) raged around him, and his longed-for independent Finnish Republic came into being.

Two more symphonies followed in 1923 and 1924: the Sixth Symphony's quiet, poised tone and four-movement design are very different from the grandly glowing single movement of

his Seventh (which was originally named *Fantasia sinfonica*). Then a commission arrived from the New York Philharmonic Orchestra. The result was *Tapiola*, named after the forest god of Finnish mythology. It is the wildest and greatest of all Sibelius's nature evocations and is, at the same time, a supreme feat of closely worked orchestral mastery.

### A long silence

Sibelius's famous "creative silence" from then on was never complete; minor works sometimes appeared, and he revised or orchestrated some of his earlier music. Yet between *Tapiola* in 1926 and his death 31 years later, he released no major new work. In the late 1920s, he was busy with an Eighth Symphony, but no manuscript existed at his death. It is believed that Sibelius destroyed it, but the reasons for this are not known—most likely a combination of self-criticism (always extreme, in his case) and the pressures of international fame.

Following his death, Sibelius's music was increasingly regarded as old-fashioned, and today is not as widely performed in concerts as it once was. However, a huge recorded catalog indicates that his work continues to be much loved by classical music listeners throughout the world.

### IN CONTEXT
### Finnish nationhood

Although a supporter of Finnish national independence, Sibelius was hostile to the Russia-backed "Red" militia that took over the Helsinki area in 1917, following the Russian Revolution and the seizure of power there by Lenin's Communist Party. A vicious civil war broke out between the "Reds" and the anti-Communist "White" military forces. Sibelius composed his choral *Jäger March* to honor the German battalion that fought alongside the "Whites." Their victory in 1918 led to the foundation of the modern Finnish Republic.

**CARL MANNERHEIM, FINNISH "WHITE" MILITARY LEADER IN THE CIVIL WAR**

## KEY WORKS

### 1891–92
The wildly successful first performance of his choral and orchestral *Kullervo* makes Sibelius a Finnish national celebrity overnight.

### 1893–95
The orchestral suite *Four Lemminkäinen Legends* includes "The Swan of Tuonela," which draws international interest.

### 1899–1900
*Finlandia*, at first named *Finland Awakes*, becomes Sibelius's best-known orchestral work.

### 1901–02
Marking a big advance on the Tchaikovsky-influenced First Symphony, Sibelius's Second Symphony establishes him as a master of the genre.

### 1914–19
The Fifth Symphony, which needed two significant revisions to reach its final form, is recognized as a major achievement.

### 1922–24
Compressing the symphony's traditional four movements into one, Sibelius's Seventh raises his mastery of the form to a new pinnacle.

### 1926
In *Tapiola*, his last major work, Sibelius achieves a spellbinding fusion of the forms of the symphony and tone poem.

# Erik Satie

## 1866–1925, FRENCH

Best known for his hauntingly simple *Gymnopédies* for piano, Satie was a pioneer of Modernism in the early 20th century, and an iconoclastic figure whose music and writings mirrored his eccentric lifestyle.

Often referred to as the "Velvet Gentleman," sporting a dapper gray frock coat and pince-nez, Erik Satie was a familiar figure in the cafés and cabarets of Paris at the turn of the 20th century. The image he cultivated was of the quintessential Parisian gentleman, showing little evidence of his highly unconventional ideas.

He was born Eric Alfred Leslie Satie in Honfleur, Normandy, in 1866, the elder son of Alfred Satie, a translator, and his Scottish wife, Jane Leslie. The family moved to Paris in 1870, but when Jane died two years later, Eric and his brother Conrad lived with their grandparents in Honfleur until 1878, when they rejoined their father in Paris.

Satie had a conventional middle-class education, which included music lessons, and was encouraged by his new stepmother, a piano teacher, to play and compose. His efforts were not altogether successful: he enrolled at the Paris Conservatoire in 1879, but was soon dismissed for lacking the necessary talent and dedication. Rejected but not disheartened, he rejoined the Conservatoire in 1885, but met with the same criticism of his abilities, and decided to leave the following year to join the army.

### Parisian life

Enlisting with the French infantry, he discovered that he was not cut out for military life either. He found the discipline and conditions unbearable, and in order to get himself discharged found a way of intentionally catching severe bronchitis. Once out of the army, Satie returned to live with his father until he came of age in 1887, when he moved to the bohemian Montmartre district of Paris. It was here that he began composing in earnest, publishing the first of his *Gymnopédies* for piano. These works of timeless simplicity, purity, and melancholy would be his main legacy, despite his later avant-garde

▷ **ROSICRUCIAN SYMBOL**
Satie allied himself with Rosicrucianism, a set of doctrines derived from "esoteric truths of the ancient past" that also absorbed elements of other faith systems.

compositions that were arguably more significant. In Montmartre, Satie began frequenting the bars, cafés, and cabarets where the artists, writers, and musicians of Paris congregated. Among them was Claude Debussy (see pp.194–197), who was making his name as a composer of innovative music in an Impressionist style, and he and Satie struck up a friendship, and a friendly rivalry, that would last until Debussy's death in 1918.

At this time, Satie became involved with the mystical Rosicrucian Order, joining the Ordre de la Rose-Croix Catholique du Temple et du Graal, and being appointed official composer and chapel-master. He was a devoted member of the order, but later fell out with its leader Joséphin Péladan. The religious and ritual aspects of the Rosicrucians continued to influence him, inspiring a number of semi-mystical works using his own arcane system of composing (see box, right). He took to walking around in priestly robes, proclaiming himself as founder, leader, and sole member of the Eglise Métropolitaine d'Art de Jésus

## ON TECHNIQUE
### Modernism and medievalism

Many features of Satie's musical style were a reaction against the overblown Romanticism of the 19th century. He proposed an understated lightness and simplicity, which he achieved by deliberately avoiding techniques associated with emotional expression, such as harmonic progressions and development of themes. Instead, he returned to the cool austerity of medieval music, but with stark modern harmonies. Much of his music has a static, detached quality, with a dry wit that became a hallmark of his work. Its spare textures and repetition were an important influence on many subsequent composers, up to and including the Minimalists, such as Philip Glass (see pp.310–311).

◁ **MONTMARTRE**
The district of Montmartre, crowned by the basilica of the Sacré-Cœur, became a focus of artistic activity in the Belle Epoque, largely because of its low rents.

▷ **ERIK SATIE, 1891**
This portrait of Satie as a young man in his studio was made by the Catalan painter Santiago Rusiñol i Prats, who, like Satie and many other artists, established himself in Montmartre.

△ **SUZANNE VALADON, c. 1916**
This self-portrait is by Valadon, to whom Satie proposed marriage on the night they met at the Chat Noir cabaret. During their brief affair, Valadon painted Satie's portrait; he gave her necklaces that were made of sausages.

▽ *AT THE MOULIN ROUGE,*
*THE DANCE,* 1889–1890
Toulouse-Lautrec's painting captures the atmosphere of Montmartre's decadent cabaret scene, in which Satie thrived.

Conducteur (Metropolitan Art Church of Jesus the Conductor), for which he wrote a *Grande Messe* that was later known as the *Messe des pauvres* (*Mass for the Poor*). It is difficult to judge whether this was a sincere act of devotion or a prank.

At the beginning of the 1890s, Satie began cultivating his eccentric reputation, referring to himself as a "phonometrician"or "gymnopedist" rather than as a composer, initiating a series of hoaxes, and developing an interest in obscure local history, rare marine animals, and wholly impracticable machinery.

## A change of style

With funds running low, Satie moved in 1890 to a smaller apartment in Montmartre. While there, he had a passionate affair—probably the only romantic relationship in his life—with the painter Suzanne Valadon; his devastation when she left after six months was a factor in the great changes in both his lifestyle and his music that followed.

In 1895, a small inheritance marked the beginning of a new phase in Satie's life. He used some of the money to buy seven identical gray velvet corduroy suits, ditching the clerical robes and his obsession with religious cults. The money also gave him the opportunity to publish some of his humorous writings, and the time to compose.

However, funds eventually ran out and Satie was forced to move from Paris. He took a room in the suburb of Arcueil, which was his home for the rest of his life. He lived alone, never received visitors, apart from stray dogs, and to the outside world presented himself as a respectable gentleman who walked into the city every day to earn a modest living as a pianist. However, behind that exterior was an extraordinary mind and a wicked sense of humor.

## Return to study

For some years, Satie's musical output was limited to making arrangements of popular songs and composing cabaret-style pieces, which he later

dismissed as lightweight. Still intent on making composing his career, in 1905 he enrolled in the Schola Cantorum de Paris, a conservatory that stressed plainsong in its teaching, to study under Vincent d'Indy and Albert Roussel. This was a great surprise to those who knew him, because the Schola was steeped in the 19th-century tradition, and his teachers were protégés of Saint-Saëns, whose music Satie loathed. Nevertheless, he studied diligently for five years, paying his way with the earnings from his cabaret work.

This period allowed him to mature as a composer and to consolidate his ideas: he moved away from the light, evocative piano pieces for which he was best known, and formulated what can be regarded as a Modernist musical philosophy, rejecting the overblown self-indulgence and sentimentality he associated with the late 19th century. Sometimes ironic, sometimes satirical or a parody of classical ideas, he placed emphasis on clarity and simplicity.

# "I came into **the world** very **young**, in **an age** that was **very old**. "

ERIK SATIE

◁ **SATIE AND DEBUSSY, 1910**
Satie (right) is pictured with his friend and fellow composer Claude Debussy in the latter's home on the Avenue du Bois de Boulogne, Paris.

## Cryptic compositions

With his studies at the Schola Cantorum complete, Satie set about composing with renewed confidence. He published a set of piano pieces bizarrely entitled *Trois morceaux en forme de poire* (*Three Pieces in the Shape of a Pear*). He had written these prior to his studies, building on the popularity of his early piano music, but he also set about writing other works for solo piano in a more humorous and less expressive style. In these, he continued the habit he had begun in the 1890s of giving cryptic and witty instructions to the pianist (such as "think right," "wonder about yourself," and play "on the tip of the tongue"); and, again, bizarre titles appeared,

including *Préludes flasques (pour un chien)* [*Flabby preludes (for a dog)*, 1912] and *Embryons desséchés* (*Desiccated embryos*, 1913). His aim was probably to poke fun at Debussy, whose impressionistic pieces were embellished with descriptive titles and detailed expression markings.

## Influences and collaborations

As Satie gradually made his name as a composer, opinions about him became divided: the older disciples of Debussy, including Ravel, admired Satie's early pieces, while those of the younger generation latched on to the Modernism of his more recent work. He gathered around him a group of young acolytes—including Georges

Auric, Louis Durey, and Arthur Honegger—that he wished to be known as Les Nouveaux Jeunes. Although members of the group composed in a variety of styles, they shared an affinity with Satie's rejection of both Romanticism and Debussy's Impressionism. When Satie parted from the Jeunes following the success of his ballet *Parade* in 1917, the other members gathered around Cocteau and later became known as Les Six. Satie meanwhile continued to develop his own idiosyncratic style, much influenced by the artistic movements of the time (see box, right). In 1919, he completed what many regard as his masterpiece, *Socrate*, an enigmatic Modernist work scored for chamber orchestra and four sopranos who sing sections from Plato's dialogues. The composition confounded critics (used to Satie's whimsical works) with its profundity, sincerity, and intimacy.

Satie died of cirrhosis of the liver in 1925. For the last 27 years of his life, he lived alone in chaos among unopened mail, unsorted writings, and a collection of umbrellas, all invisible to the outside world.

### IN PROFILE
### Creative partners

Through his work as a cabaret pianist, Satie met many artists, writers, and musicians and from 1910 found himself at the center of the Parisian avant-garde. Among his circle of friends was the writer Jean Cocteau, with whom he collaborated on a number of projects. The most famous of these was the ballet *Parade*, which incorporated elements of modern artistic trends, such as Surrealism, Dadaism, and Futurism. The sets and costumes were designed by Pablo Picasso and the ballet was staged by Sergei Diaghilev's Ballets Russes. In his later years, Satie mixed less with musicians and more with avant-garde visual artists including Man Ray, Constantin Brâncuși, and Marcel Duchamp.

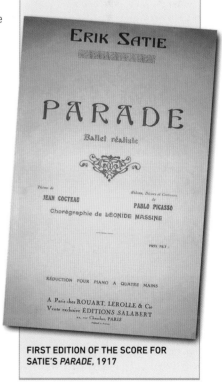

**FIRST EDITION OF THE SCORE FOR SATIE'S *PARADE*, 1917**

## KEY WORKS

**1888**
The first of the three *Gymnopédies*, works that establish his reputation, is published.

**1893**
Composes *Vexations*, a short piano piece apparently to be played 840 times in succession.

**1911**
Publication of *Trois morceaux en forme de poire* (for piano, four hands), composed around the turn of the century.

**1913**
Writes the text and incidental music of *Le Piège de Méduse*, a surreal satire of melodrama.

**1914**
Works on the humorous cycle of piano pieces *Sports et divertissements*, which is not published until 1923.

**1917**
The ballet *Parade*, a collaboration with Cocteau and with sets and costumes by Picasso, is premiered by Diaghilev's Ballets Russes.

**1918**
*Socrate* (a "symphonic drama"), scored for female vocal soloists and small orchestra, is performed privately in a version for voice and piano.

# Amy Beach

## 1867–1944, AMERICAN

A child prodigy, Amy Beach grew up to become the first American female composer to gain recognition in the US and Western Europe for symphonies, a genre previously dominated by men.

Amy Marcy Cheney Beach (later known by her married name—Mrs. H.H.A. Beach) was a native of New Hampshire. Her musical talent was discovered by her mother, a capable singer and pianist, who became her first teacher. Unlike her male contemporaries, who generally traveled to Europe for advanced music training, Beach received her entire musical education in the US.

Beach made her formal piano debut as a teenager at Boston's Music Hall in 1883. However, upper class women were not encouraged to pursue a career as a performer, and after her marriage at 18 to Dr. Henry Harris Aubrey Beach, who was 24 years her senior, she focused on composition, returning to performance only after his death in 1910

During her marriage, Beach became active in the Bostonian Episcopalian community, and her numerous sacred choral pieces reflect her spiritual devotion. Her most important large-scale works in this genre are the Mass in E flat Major and *Canticle of the Sun*, based on a text by St. Francis of Assisi.

### Operas and symphonies

Until the second half of the 20th century, women composers were encouraged to pursue salon genres such as character pieces for piano and art songs. While Beach composed prolifically in such chamber styles, she also pursued opera and symphonic works, large forms that were generally considered to be the preserve of men. She was the only female member of the Second New England School, a group of composers from the Boston, Massachusetts, area that included John Knowles Paine, Arthur Foote, George Whitefield Chadwick, and Horatio Parker.

Beach's best known work is her Symphony in E minor from the mid-1890s, nicknamed the "Gaelic," due to its incorporation of Irish folk material. It was the first symphony by an American woman to be performed, and the first American symphony to draw on folk music.

Beach died in 1944. While her works were performed frequently during her lifetime, the mid-20th century saw a decline in her popularity. However, the emergence of feminist musicology in the 1970s introduced her works to a new generation.

△ **MACDOWELL COLONY**
Beach was a regular visitor at the MacDowell Colony, an artists' retreat in Peterborough, New Hampshire. The Colony, as it was known, was founded in 1907 by composer Edward MacDowell and his wife, pianist and philanthropist Marian MacDowell (pictured).

◁ **MUSICAL SCORES**
Beach taught herself to compose through score study. In 1885, she entered into an exclusive contract with music publisher Arthur P. Schmidt, making her works more readily available.

> " We have before us ... **a musical nature** touched with **genius**. "
REVIEW OF HER *GAELIC SYMPHONY* IN THE *HAMBURGER NACHRICHTEN*, 1913

▷ **AMY BEACH, 1905**
In addition to composing, Beach wrote numerous articles on music and supported organizations dedicated to music education.

▷ **RALPH VAUGHAN WILLIAMS**
With popular classics such as *The Lark Ascending*, *The Wasps*, *Fantasia on a Theme by Thomas Tallis*, and *A Pastoral Symphony*, the work of Vaughan Williams often evokes a unique and deep sense of Englishness in the listener. His music fell out of favor following his death in the late 1950s, but has seen a significant revival in recent decades.

# R. Vaughan Williams

**1872–1958, BRITISH**

Vaughan Williams created an English national music that blended classical tradition with two home-grown cultural resources: the great composers of the Tudor and Elizabethan eras, and the world of English folk song.

# "There is **no difference** in **kind**, but only in **degree**, between **Beethoven** and the **humblest singer** of a **folk song**."

RALPH VAUGHAN WILLIAMS, IN *NATIONAL MUSIC AND OTHER ESSAYS*, 1934

The son of a country vicar, Ralph Vaughan Williams was brought up in Surrey by his widowed mother and assorted aunts in a well-to-do, progressively minded family related to Charles Darwin. Music and a wide range of reading were encouraged, and Ralph played the piano and the violin, while also making early attempts at composing. He studied at Cambridge University and the Royal College of Music, before settling in London, where he worked as a church organist and choral conductor, and as music editor of the *English Hymnal*.

## A quiet revolution

The English musical world into which Vaughan Williams was born was dominated by the cultural values of another nation, Germany—via the influences of Wagner and Brahms. But for Vaughan Williams and Gustav Holst, two young, Wagner-admiring composers who met in their student years and became lifelong friends, English music needed a fresh start.

Vaughan Williams's work as a church musician soon led to his exploration of a far older heritage— that of Thomas Tallis and William Byrd, which seemed to suggest a possible way forward with the rich invention and artistic purity of their unaccompanied choral works.

A crucial breakthrough came from another quite different area of interest. Vaughan Williams, Holst, and their fellow composer George Butterworth went out into England's villages and countryside to collect the local folk songs that they heard there, spurred on by the reality that these were literally dying out: Britain's industrialization during the 19th century had emptied the countryside of much of its population—and with it, a whole tradition of unaccompanied singing. This had sprung up on the basis that the majority of people who were living and working on the land were much too poor to own an instrument, so that in musical terms, singing was all they had.

Vaughan Williams found himself deeply drawn to folk music's sense of freedom and naturalness. The challenge was to find a successful way of bringing these qualities, and also those of English Tudor and Elizabethan church music, into the sophisticated world of the classical concert hall. The quest lasted for many years, and took in a period of study in Paris with Ravel. Although Vaughan Williams was the older of the two composers, he sensed that the chance to acquire "a little French polish," as he put it, from Ravel's technical mastery was a useful counterbalance to the German-dominated side of musical tradition.

## A breakthrough

The breakthrough came in 1910, when Vaughan Williams, now already in his late thirties, conducted the first performances of two very different masterworks. The first of these was *Fantasia on a Theme by Thomas Tallis*, which premiered in Gloucester Cathedral during the Three Choirs Festival. It is a single, 20-minute movement written for an orchestra of string instruments only—a solo quartet, a large main ensemble, and a distantly deployed smaller

△ **VAUGHAN WILLIAMS AND HOLST**
This photograph by composer William Gillies Whittaker shows Gustav Holst and Vaughan Williams—lifelong friends— walking in the Malvern Hills in 1921.

### ON TECHNIQUE
#### Folk song in classical music

Consisting of repeated verses of unaccompanied melody, folk song, by its nature, operated differently from the developmental processes of classical musical tradition, in which the young Vaughan Williams was highly trained. The same was true of the masterworks of early English choral music, whose intricate melodic workings were unlike the "symphonic" style that dominated 19th-century orchestral writing. Vaughan Williams was able to bring these different resources together, so that a folk-influenced style became the foundation of his own masterly sequence of large-scale symphonies.

◁ **LEITH HILL PLACE**
From the age of two until he left home to study at the University of Cambridge, Ralph Vaughan Williams lived at this stunning 18th-century house, Leith Hill Place, in Surrey. He gave the house to the National Trust in 1945.

ensemble. The tune is fragmented, varied, freely extended in different directions, and then eventually reassembled, all in a wholly new sound-world whose outward calm conveys great inward power.

### Poetic inspirations

The second masterwork, *A Sea Symphony*, was first heard at the Leeds Festival a few weeks after *Fantasia*. It is a large-scale, four-movement choral setting of words by the US poet Walt Whitman, whose soaring yet spiritually agnostic imaginative world was a powerful liberating influence on Vaughan

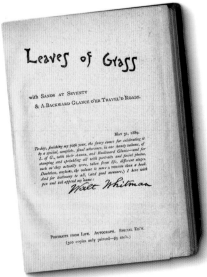

◁ **LEAVES OF GRASS, 1889 EDITION**
In *A Sea Symphony*, Vaughan Williams set verses from poet Walt Whitman's *Leaves of Grass*, first published in 1855 but with several revised editions thereafter.

Williams's generation. The composer's mastery of his choral and orchestral forces began a lifelong sequence of nine symphonies, which lie at the core of an enormous musical output.

The essence of Vaughan Williams's musical world is crystallized in *The Lark Ascending*, based on a poem by George Meredith; this describes how the flying bird's song seems to float skyward, until it drifts beyond hearing. The music was composed for violin and piano in 1914, before the composer's service in World War I, then orchestrated before the first performance in 1920. The result was another understated musical revolution. The virtuosity of the solo violin part, different from spectacular 19th-century tradition, related back to the purity of line found in the concertos of Bach. Neither of the work's two main themes is actually

a folk song, but each sounds as if it might be; and neither could have been written without the example of English folk music itself.

Army service in World War I then halted Vaughan Williams's composing for several years. His first major work afterward was *A Pastoral Symphony*, whose slow second movement features a solo trumpet imitating an army bugle, as if heard across a wide landscape in a quiet moment between relentless shellfire; and the finale is framed at its beginning and end by a solo soprano voice singing wordlessly, as if from a peaceful world that has managed to survive. Yet there were also unexpected stages in Vaughan Williams's musical journey. The Fourth Symphony's first audience in 1935 was startled by the work's ferocious dissonance and frenetic style, which were later seen as somehow prophetic of World War II, although the composer always rejected this interpretation. But he also stated privately—to Adrian Boult, who conducted the premiere—that the music's inner fury related to the situation of his wife, Adeline, crippled by arthritis from which she would not recover.

### Late love and a new life

After this musical outburst came its polar opposite, the *Serenade to Music*. This was written for the 1938 jubilee concert of the composer's longstanding supporter, the conductor Sir Henry Wood, who asked for a work involving 16 leading solo singers of the day; Vaughan Williams took the words from Shakespeare's play *The Merchant of Venice*. The music's radiant serenity had an immediate impulse:

## KEY WORKS

| 1910 | 1920 | 1922 | 1925 | 1938 | 1951 | 1958 |
|---|---|---|---|---|---|---|
| With the premieres of the *Tallis Fantasia* for strings and *A Sea Symphony*, Vaughan Williams becomes his generation's leading English composer. | Completed before World War I, *The Lark Ascending* for violin and small orchestra is now performed for the first time. | *A Pastoral Symphony* is a memorial elegy to a disappearing rural world, and to those who died in World War I. | The choral work *Sancta Civitas* (*The Holy City*) portrays the apocalyptic happenings of the biblical Book of Revelation. | Composed for the jubilee concert of conductor Sir Henry Wood, *Serenade to Music* sets words from Shakespeare's *The Merchant of Venice*. | *The Pilgrim's Progress*, an opera based on John Bunyan's story about the journey of a Christian soul toward God, is premiered at Covent Garden. | Partly inspired by Thomas Hardy's novel *Tess of the d'Urbervilles*, Vaughan Williams's Ninth Symphony is an old-age masterwork. |

# "Ralph has been **dead for over 35 years** and **every year** has seemed **as long** as the **first.**"

URSULA VAUGHAN WILLIAMS, SPEAKING OF HER HUSBAND IN THE 1990s

a meeting with Ursula Wood, a young army wife with a liking for poetry, had led to a passionate affair. Before the deaths of Ursula's husband during World War II and of Adeline in 1951, the lovers kept their relationship secret from almost everyone, except Adeline herself. In 1943, Ursula had a pregnancy terminated.

The closeness of this unlikely couple, followed by their marriage in 1953, contributed greatly to the remarkable creative energy of Vaughan Williams's final years. The Sixth Symphony of 1948 explored a turbulent yet at times also ethereally calm sound-world far removed from anything resembling traditional "Englishness." The premiere at the Royal Opera House, Covent Garden, of *The Pilgrim's Progress*, subtitled "a morality in a prologue and four acts," was the culmination of nearly half a century of on-off work on the project. The summer of 1958 saw the first performance of the powerful Ninth Symphony. The night before Adrian Boult was due to conduct the new work's first recording, the composer died—leaving a legacy that is still sometimes derided as part of the so-called "English cowpat," or pastoral, school of composers, but which continues to survive the musical world's fashion changes. Today, the range and scale of Vaughan Williams's achievement, which reach far beyond mere pastoralism, are appreciated more widely than ever before.

▽ **RALPH VAUGHAN WILLIAMS AND URSULA WOOD, 1951**
Ralph Vaughan Williams (center) and his future wife Ursula (almost 40 years his junior) are depicted here rehearsing *A Sea Symphony* with conductor and cellist John Barbirolli at the Hallé rehearsal rooms, Manchester.

# Sergei Rachmaninoff

**1873–1943, RUSSIAN**

One of the last great representatives of Romanticism, Rachmaninoff is best known for his glorious symphonies and concertos. He was also a superlative pianist and wrote memorable solo music for his instrument.

◁ **MUSIC CONSERVATORY, MOSCOW**
In 1885, after failing his exams at the St. Petersburg Conservatory, Rachmaninoff transferred to the Moscow Conservatory of Music, where he thrived.

Rachmaninoff's career has been summarized by the saying that the Revolution took him out of Russia but nothing could ever take Russia out of him. He ended his days as a US citizen, living in California, but his music remained true to the traditions he had absorbed in his youth. He was influenced by his homeland's folk songs and by the liturgical chants of the Russian Orthodox Church; and in his feeling for sweeping, soaring melody—often loaded with yearning and melancholy—he was the heir of Tchaikovsky, who encouraged and inspired him at the start of his career.

◁ **SERGEI RACHMANINOFF, 1925**
This portrait was made by Konstantin Andreyevich Somov in 1925, the year Rachmaninoff founded TAIR, a publishing company specializing in his own works and those of other Russian composers.

## Achievements and setbacks

Rachmaninoff was born near Novgorod into an aristocratic landowning family. His father gambled away his inherited wealth, and in 1882, after extensive estates had been sold to pay his debts, the family moved to a modest flat in St. Petersburg. Sergei showed musical talent, and rather than following family tradition by training for the military, in 1883, aged 10, he enrolled at the St. Petersburg Conservatory.

Although gifted, Rachmaninoff was lazy and moody, and his progress was hampered by family turmoil—his parents had separated and one of his sisters died of diphtheria. In 1885, he failed his exams and transferred to the Moscow Conservatory. His most important teacher there was the renowned piano disciplinarian Nikolai Zverev, under whose strict but enlightened guidance he flourished. In 1892, aged 19, he graduated from the Conservatory with the rarely awarded Great Gold Medal, the highest possible student distinction.

Later that year, Rachmaninoff gave the premiere of his most famous solo piano piece, the dramatic and haunting Prelude in C-sharp minor. This work became so popular he is said to have regretted writing it, as he grew weary of having it requested as an encore every time he performed. In 1893, his first opera, *Aleko*, was successfully premiered at the Bolshoi Theater in Moscow and praised by Tchaikovsky. Still only 20, Rachmaninoff seemed to be launched on a brilliant career, but in 1897 he suffered a humiliating

### IN PROFILE
### Nina Koshetz

Among the notable musicians with whom Rachmaninoff collaborated was the soprano Nina Koshetz (1891–1965). The couple are said to have had an affair, and he certainly dedicated a cycle of six love songs to her in 1916. Koshetz spent her later career in Europe and the US and had small acting roles in several Hollywood films. Numerous recordings by her survive, capturing her rich, expressive voice, but unfortunately Rachmaninoff does not accompany her in any of them.

**NINA KOSHETZ, 1916**

> " **Rachmaninoff** was made of **steel** and **gold**: **steel** in his **arms, gold** in his **heart**. "

POLISH-AMERICAN PIANIST JOSEPH HOFMANN, 1945

▷ **THE RUSSIAN REVOLUTION, 1917**
In this painting, revolutionary soldiers are shown storming a street in Moscow during the revolution in 1917. It was in December that year that Rachmaninoff and his family fled Russia for Sweden. He never returned to his homeland.

△ **PROGRAM FOR *ALEKO*, 1893**
A program for the premiere of Rachmaninoff's first opera, *Aleko*, on May 9, 1893, at the Bolshoi Theater in Moscow. The libretto, written by Vladimir Nemirovich-Danchenko, was an adaptation of Alexander Pushkin's poem *The Gypsies*.

setback when the premiere of his Symphony No. 1 was a fiasco. According to some accounts, the conductor (the composer Alexander Glazunov) was drunk; certainly, the symphony was poorly rehearsed and performed, and the critics savaged it.

## Brighter days

Rachmaninoff was badly shaken by the experience and composed almost nothing for the next three years, but he remained in demand as a pianist and also won plaudits as a conductor. He was helped out of his despondency by having hypnotherapy treatment with the music-loving Dr. Nikolai Dahl. His confidence restored, he began work on his Piano Concerto No. 2

(dedicated to Dr. Dahl), which he successfully premiered in 1901. With its achingly beautiful melodies and great waves of emotion leading to an ecstatic finale, it has become his most enduringly popular work. This triumphant resumption of his composing career was accompanied by happiness in love—in 1902, he married his cousin Natalia Satina.

As a wedding gift, his aristocratic parents-in-law (who were also his aunt and uncle) gave him a house on their country estate at Ivanovka, about 300 miles (480 km) from Moscow, which he had been visiting since 1890. This proved an ideal summer home, offering him a peaceful retreat for composing. Here, he worked on some

major pieces, including his Symphony No. 2 (premiered in 1908) and the Piano Concerto No. 3 (premiered in 1909). He continued to travel and perform widely, both in Russia and elsewhere, during this period.

After World War I began in 1914, Rachmaninoff gave numerous performances in aid of wounded soldiers and other good causes. Appropriately, his outstanding composition of the war years is a deeply serious religious work, the choral masterpiece *All-Night Vigil* (1915), often more loosely called *Vespers*. By this time, Russia was slipping into chaos and when Rachmaninoff visited Ivanovka in April 1917, he found the estate had been

## KEY WORKS

**1892**
In Moscow, premieres the Prelude in C-sharp minor, his most popular solo piano work.

**1897**
Disastrous premiere of Symphony No. 1 in St. Petersburg.

**1901**
Successful premiere of Piano Concerto No. 2 in Moscow.

**1909**
On Rachmaninoff's first visit to the US, Piano Concerto No. 3 premieres in New York.

**1915**
*All-Night Vigil*, his greatest religious work, premieres in Moscow.

**1940**
Completes his final work, the *Symphonic Dances*, premiered the following year in Philadelphia.

# "I cannot **cast out** the **old way** of **writing**, and I cannot **acquire** the **new**."

SERGEI RACHMANINOFF, 1939

hit by looting and vandalism. Later that year, the Bolshevik Revolution broke out and in December Rachmaninoff escaped Russia with his wife and two children by taking up an offer to play in Stockholm. He never saw his homeland again.

## Exile, travel, and legacy

From Stockholm, Rachmaninoff moved to Copenhagen, then in November 1918 to New York. He and his family had left Russia with nothing except what they could carry in their suitcases, and he realized that he would best be able to support them by performing as a concert pianist, especially in the lucrative US market. From this point, composing became virtually a sideline in his career: although he lived for another quarter of a century, he wrote only six new works during this period. In addition to his concerts and recitals (typically he gave about 70–80 each year), he flourished in the recording studio, leaving a rich legacy of disks, including accounts of his four piano concertos.

During his lifetime, Rachmaninoff was regarded as one of the greatest pianists who ever lived—a reputation that endures today. He mesmerized audiences with his stage presence and his extraordinary musicianship. Exceptionally tall, with hair cropped almost like a convict and a stone-faced demeanor, he was described by Stravinsky as a "six-and-a-half-foot scowl." His severe manner belied the passion and poetry of his playing and

also the warmth and wit he displayed in private. He was generous, too: after his concerts and records made him wealthy, he regularly sent money to Russia to help people in need.

For two decades, Rachmaninoff divided his time between the US and Europe, but in 1939, with war imminent, he settled permanently in the US. The life of a touring virtuoso was often exhausting and in 1942 he moved to the warm climate of California for the sake of his faltering health. After a concert in Knoxville, Tennessee, in February 1943 he collapsed and had to cancel the rest of his tour. He died of cancer at his

Beverly Hills home a month later, a few days before his 70th birthday and a few weeks after becoming a US citizen.

In spite of Rachmaninoff's enormous popularity with the public, contemporary critics were often scornful about the unabashed emotionalism of his music, dismissing it as gushing sentimentality. The entry on him in the 1954 edition of *Grove's Dictionary of Music and Musicians* predicted that his reputation would not last—a prophecy that has proved entirely misguided, as his place among the titans of music is now unquestioned.

△ **CLASSIC RECORDINGS**
Many recordings with Rachmaninoff at the piano are considered to be classics. He played alongside the great violinist Fritz Kreisler on this 1928 recording of Beethoven's Sonata in G major.

▷ **COMPOSING AT IVANOVKA**
The composer is shown here sitting at a table at his summer retreat within the family's estate at Ivanovka, Russia, working on his Piano Concerto No. 3, which premiered in 1909.

## IN CONTEXT
### Villa Senar

In 1930, Rachmaninoff bought land near Hertenstein on Lake Lucerne in Switzerland, and on it he built a substantial house, designed by the local architects Alfred Möri and Karl-Friedrich Krebs. He called the house Villa Senar (from the first two letters of his and his wife's forenames, Sergei and Natalia, and the first letter of Rachmaninoff).

He spent every summer there until moving permanently to the US in 1939. The villa and the spectacular lake on which it was situated gave Rachmaninoff the tranquility he needed for composing his music. It was here that he wrote two of his greatest works: *Rhapsody on a Theme of Paganini* (1934) and Symphony No. 3 (1935–1936).

▷ **GUSTAV HOLST, 1927**
This portrait by John Bernard Munns shows Holst in his early fifties, bespectacled, with bags under his eyes, looking tired and somewhat despondent. In the 1920s, the composer was placed under tremendous stress from overwork and the demands of his increasing fame—on doctor's orders, he retreated to the Essex countryside and significantly reduced his writing, teaching, and other work commitments.

# Gustav Holst

## 1874–1934, BRITISH

While the symphonic suite *The Planets* is Holst's most popular work, he wrote others of similar quality, creating a highly individual sound-world that was conventional in some ways, groundbreaking in others.

Gustav Holst was born in Cheltenham into a musical family of English, Scandinavian, and German ancestry. Health problems afflicted him all his life. Neuritis, which made his right arm feel like "a jelly overcharged with electricity," hampered his early promise as a pianist; he began playing the trombone at the age of 12, hoping that the activity might improve his tendency to asthma.

As a student at London's Royal College of Music, Holst met Ralph Vaughan Williams, who was to become his lifelong friend. Early in his career, he supported himself by playing the trombone in theater bands; he later joined the Carl Rosa Opera Company and the Scottish Orchestra (now the Royal Scottish National Orchestra), and worked as a church organist. While conducting the Hammersmith Socialist Choir, Holst fell in love with one of its members, the soprano Isobel Harrison. The couple married in 1901; their daughter, Imogen, later become a prominent musician in her own right.

## Diverse influences

Holst greatly admired Wagner's advanced harmonic style but was also attracted to English folk music—twin enthusiasms he shared with Vaughan Williams. A symphony subtitled "The

△ **THE "VENUS" MOVEMENT**
This is the first page of the draft score, in Holst's own handwriting, of "Venus, the Bringer of Peace," the second movement in his most famous work, *The Planets*.

Cotswolds," followed by *A Somerset Rhapsody*, drew on both areas of interest. Holst was also intrigued by Indian mythology, which inspired a set of Choral Hymns from the Hindu sacred text the *Rig Veda* and the chamber opera *Savitri*, based on a story from the Sanskrit epic *Mahabharata*. An interest in astrology steered him toward the idea of an orchestral work based on seven of the planets in Earth's solar system. He began work on *The Planets* in 1914,

at which time he was employed as a teacher at London's Morley College and St. Paul's Girls' School—positions that enabled him to buy a weekend home in the Essex village of Thaxted.

### *The Planets* and world fame

Holst completed *The Planets* in 1917. Its 1918 premiere in front of a small audience was conducted by Adrian Boult shortly before Holst left to work in Greece for several months; a second incomplete performance in 1919 (only five of the seven movements were played) was the beginning of the suite's recognition as a masterpiece of orchestral imagination. Holst was uneasy at its success, however, feeling that it drew attention away from his other works, such as the choral *Hymn of Jesus* of 1917.

Forced by overwork to take a year's rest from teaching, in 1924 Holst completed his Choral Symphony, based on poems by John Keats. His output then slowed, although he felt that *Egdon Heath*, an orchestral evocation of the bleak landscape of Thomas Hardy's novel *The Return of the Native* (1878), was his finest single achievement. The onset of a duodenal ulcer eventually led to an operation that Holst's weak heart did not survive. *The Planets* has ensured, though, that his name will live on.

### ON TECHNIQUE
### Harmonic wizardry

For its time, Holst's musical language was often strikingly advanced and unfamiliar to audiences. He was the first English composer to explore thoroughly the technique of bitonality, where two different musical tonalities (or keys) are deployed together. In "Mercury, the Winged Messenger" in *The Planets*, the melodic line flickers between two opposite tonalities as if it belongs to neither, instead speeding weightlessly through the air. In "Neptune, the Mystic," pairs of harmonies (chords) in different tonalities, each in themselves quite traditional, are played one on top of the other, creating a sound of strange, other-worldly stillness out of the simplest musical components.

▽ **THAXTED**
Holst had a country home in the picturesque village of Thaxted in northwest Essex. In 1916, he started a music festival at the village's magnificent medieval church of St. John, whose elegant spire is visible here rising above the Essex landscape.

# Arnold Schoenberg

## 1874–1951, AUSTRIAN

One of the most challenging and musically controversial 20th-century composers, Schoenberg created works of great originality and emotional power while pioneering major innovations in compositional technique.

△ **COVER OF STRING QUARTET, OP. 7**
This is the cover of the score for Schoenberg's (or, as here, Schönberg's) String Quartet, Op. 7, completed in 1905, which was the composer's first lengthy work and his first masterpiece.

Arnold Schoenberg (or Schönberg) was born in the Jewish Leopoldstadt district of Vienna in 1874. He began violin lessons at the age of eight and invented short pieces for himself and friends to play. Arnold learned the basics of composition by reading books and imitating other people's music. After his father died in 1890, he worked in a bank for five years to help support the family. He also played cello in an amateur orchestra set up by another young musician, Alexander Zemlinsky, who gave Schoenberg his only lessons in composition and became a lifelong friend.

### German cultural traditions

Schoenberg aligned himself with the great tradition of German music, from Brahms and Wagner to Mozart and Bach. In 1898, to further identify with German culture, he gave up his Jewish faith in favor of Lutheran Christianity. He adopted a Romantic view of the composer as a divinely inspired prophet with spiritual responsibilities, an attitude that precluded concern for music as entertainment.

◁ **ARNOLD SCHOENBERG, c. 1905**
The Austrian-Jewish composer, who described himself as "a conservative who was forced to become a radical," is depicted here by the artist Richard Gerstl.

His first composition performed in public was a string quartet premiered in Vienna in 1897. This was well received, but thereafter his work met with incomprehension and abuse. His *Verklärte Nacht*, originally written for a string sextet, appears in retrospect an accessible, ravishing example of late Romanticism, but in 1899 its chromaticism puzzled even open-minded Viennese music enthusiasts. Hugely ambitious, in the early 1900s Schoenberg worked on a vast Wagnerian cantata, *Gurre-Lieder*, and a large-scale orchestral tone poem, *Pelleas und Melisande*. His efforts were privately encouraged by prominent composers Richard Strauss in Germany and Gustav Mahler in Austria, but when *Pelleas* was premiered in 1905 it drew derision from both critics and public.

In 1901, Schoenberg married Mathilde Zemlinsky, the sister of his friend Alexander. The couple had two children. Dividing his time between

### IN CONTEXT
### German Expressionism

Schoenberg's atonal music formed part of the wider cultural movement of Expressionism that developed in Germany and Austria in the early 20th century. Expressionist painters such as Emil Nolde, Franz Marc, and Egon Schiele depicted tortured inner feelings, nightmares, and ecstatic visions through the use of distorted lines and lurid colors. The movement was loosely associated with the psychoanalyst Sigmund Freud's exploration of dreams, sexuality, and the unconscious, which was taking place in Vienna at the same time. Schoenberg's most overtly Expressionist works included *Pierrot Lunaire* and *Erwartung*.

**SELF-PORTRAIT WITH CHINESE LANTERN, EGON SCHIELE, 1912**

> " **If** it is **art**, it is **not for all**, and **if** it is **for all**, it is **not art**. "

ARNOLD SCHOENBERG, *STYLE AND IDEA*, 1946

▽ **GERSTL SELF-PORTRAIT, 1907**
Richard Gerstl's close relationship with Schoenberg and his tragic affair with the composer's wife, Mathilde, led to the artist's suicide in 1908, the year after he painted this piece, *Self-Portrait, Laughing*. Schoenberg made reference to the disastrous triangular relationship in a number of his works.

Berlin and Vienna, he supported his family via musical odd jobs, including teaching composition. Meanwhile, his own compositions developed in an increasingly radical direction. His *Chamber Symphony* of 1906 replaced the Romantic large-scale orchestra by a spare ensemble of 15 players. In a series of works between 1907 and 1909, including the song cycle *The Book of the Hanging Gardens* and the *Five Orchestral Pieces*, he moved toward the total abandonment of tonality. With no tonic chord to ground the music, a rootless sound-world emerged, expressive of alienation.

Schoenberg's technical innovations were fueled by heightened emotion at a troubled period in his life. Tempted to explore painting—at which he proved gifted enough to exhibit with the avant-garde Der Blaue Reiter group in 1911—he became friends with a young artist, Richard Gerstl. But in 1908, Schoenberg's wife ran off with Gerstl. After a few months, she returned to her husband and her children. Devastated, Gerstl died by suicide. These distressing events were contemporaneous with Schoenberg's development of atonality and inspired his intense music drama *Erwartung*, which he described as an "anxiety dream." Written in 17 days of furious inspiration in 1909, it tells of a woman in search of her lover who comes across his corpse.

## Drama and disarray

In the face of the hostility of critics and the public, Schoenberg was supported by a small circle—notably, the young composers Alban Berg and Anton Webern. Both had been taught by Schoenberg and became valued colleagues, forming a group known as the Second Viennese School. The first performance of Schoenberg's *Pierrot Lunaire*, an Expressionist cabaret for five instrumentalists and voice, in 1912 was described by Webern as "an unqualified success." In 1913, the belated first performance of *Gurre-Lieder* proved a triumph, but the composer refused to acknowledge the tumultuous applause, reluctantly mounting the stage only to stand with his back to the audience. He was no doubt more comfortable with what became known as the Skandalkonzert (Scandal Concert) later in the same year, when a performance of his *Chamber Symphony*, along with works by Berg, Webern, and Zemlinsky, provoked a riot, with fistfights breaking out in the audience.

These excitements of the Viennese avant-garde scene were interrupted by the outbreak of World War I in 1914. Schoenberg's first response was a

# KEY WORKS

**1899**
*Verklärte Nacht*, Schoenberg's suite for six string instruments, is rejected for performance in Vienna.

**1908**
The innovative String Quartet No. 2 includes a soprano voice part and some of Schoenberg's first atonal music.

**1912**
*Pierrot Lunaire*, a setting of poems for instrumental ensemble and singing/speaking reciter, premieres in Berlin.

**1913**
*Gurre-Lieder* receives rapturous applause at its premiere in Vienna, 10 years after it was written.

**1923**
Suite for Piano, Op. 25, a piano piece in six movements, is Schoenberg's first work using the 12-tone technique.

**1948**
*A Survivor from Warsaw* has its first performance; the cantata memorializes the victims of the Holocaust.

◁ **PIERROT LUNAIRE, 1912**
This is a poster for the Berlin premiere of Arnold Schoenberg's melodrama *Pierrot Lunaire*, which sets verses from the work of the same name by the Belgian Symbolist poet Albert Giraud.

startling expression of nationalism, denouncing French composers as "kitschmongers" and welcoming a chance to make them "venerate the German spirit." His brief spells of army service disrupted his creativity without contributing to the Austrian war effort. His only major composition begun during the war, the oratorio *Jacob's Ladder*, was never completed.

After the war, he participated in a musical turn away from the emotional excesses of Expressionism toward a more orderly Neo-Classicism. From 1921, his invention of the 12-tone method of composition (see box, right) restored structural solidity after the instinctual anarchy of atonal writing: yet the result was music that was even more impenetrable to the public. It was typical of his conservative radicalism that the movements of his first complete 12-tone work, the Suite for Piano, Op. 25, were given titles

such as *Gavotte* and *Gigue* that might have been used by Bach. In 1923, his wife Mathilde died, but he remarried, and had three children with his second wife, Gertrud Kolisch. His financial woes ended in 1926, when he began teaching composition at the Prussian Academy of Arts in Berlin.

## Refuge and change

This period of tranquility was ended by the rise to power of Adolf Hitler's antisemitic Nazi Party in 1933. Along with all other Jewish teaching staff in Germany, Schoenberg was dismissed from his post. He sought refuge abroad, settling in Los Angeles in 1934. Persecution triggered his formal readoption of the Jewish faith. His opera *Moses und Aron*, abandoned unfinished in 1932, had already

▷ **SCHOENBERG, 1950**
The composer is shown here, the year before his death, with his wife Gertrud Kolisch and other members of his family, in Los Angeles, California.

presaged this return to his religious roots with its meditation on the relationship between God and man.

Schoenberg did his best to adapt to life in the US, taking US citizenship in 1941. He taught at California universities and socialized with Hollywood movie stars at his house off Sunset Boulevard. He also wrote some notable works, including the Violin Concerto (1936) and the Piano Concerto (1942), but nothing could bridge the gap between his European elitism and US cultural populism. His declining years were darkened by knowledge of the fate of the European Jews in the Holocaust and by his own failing health. He died following a heart attack in 1951.

Schoenberg's influence on composers of the second half of the 20th century was to be immense. However, his works have never achieved the wide acceptance by concert audiences that he had always believed would one day come.

> # "**People** should know **my tunes** and **whistle** them."
>
> ARNOLD SCHOENBERG, LETTER WRITTEN IN LOS ANGELES, 1947

▷ **CHARLES IVES**
Ives came to fame late in life but was one of the first US composers to be recognized internationally. His complex compositions draw on quintessential elements of US life and culture—particularly that of New England, where he was born—and conjure up everyday sounds and familiar tunes, from hymns and patriotic songs to dances and marches.

# Charles Ives

**1874–1954, AMERICAN**

One of the 20th century's most original composers and a pioneer of experimental music, Ives was inspired by the US's democratic idealism, freedom of thought, and musical diversity.

# "The word 'beauty' is as easy to use as the word 'degenerate.' Both come in handy when one does or does not agree with you."

CHARLES IVES, 1920

Charles Ives earned a living by selling insurance but he composed music in his spare time. His liberal politics were inspired by an optimistic faith in "the people," which was reflected in the popular songs that are woven into so many of his compositions.

Charles Edward Ives was born on October 20, 1874, in Danbury, Connecticut. His father was from a prosperous local family and had served as the youngest bandmaster in the Union Army during the Civil War. Young Charlie studied piano and organ and absorbed Danbury's rich musical life, from classical concerts to rousing congregational hymn-singing. He joined his father's brass band as a drummer and, at the age of 14, became a church organist.

## Experimental works

Ives became a student at Yale University in 1894. He studied with the composer Horatio Parker, a graduate of Munich's Royal Music School, who encouraged his pupil to set German Romantic poems and master advanced contrapuntal forms. Ives supplemented his formal European-style training by running experiments with the

◁ **GEORGE IVES**
Charles Ives's father, seen here c. 1865, was the leader of a brass band in Danbury and played numerous instruments.

Hyperion Theater Orchestra, creating innovative music from hymn tunes, college songs, and dances played simultaneously in different keys and at different speeds.

After graduating in 1898, Ives spent a decade in New York working in insurance and as a part-time church organist. Unrestrained by the need to make money from composition, he experimented with daring harmonies and complex rhythmic patterns. In 1908, he married Harmony Twichell, the sister of a Yale roommate. During

their engagement, he composed a series of visionary, highly original works, *The Unanswered Question* and *Central Park in the Dark* among them. A few years after their marriage, the couple built a house near Danbury, where they spent many summers.

## Pioneering techniques

Novel combinations of classical forms and US vernacular music appealed to Ives, who pioneered techniques of polytonality, polyrhythm, and textural layering (see box, below) in works such as *Three Places in New England* (1908–1914), his Fourth Symphony (1916), and *A Symphony: New England Holidays* (c.1917–1919). In 1920, he published the "Concord Sonata," a piano work inspired by figures in the Transcendentalist movement such as Ralph Waldo Emerson and Henry David Thoreau.

Ives's life was hampered by illness, including diabetes and hand tremors. This, plus overwork, led to depression, loss of creative confidence, and dissatisfaction with his compositions. Ill health forced him to stop composing in 1927 and to retire from business three years later, but he continued to revise his scores. Ives also revisited his *Universe Symphony*, which he started in 1915 and pursued as an intellectual experiment until his death from a stroke in 1954.

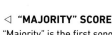

◁ **"MAJORITY" SCORE**
"Majority" is the first song in Ives's *114 Songs* (1922). At the beginning of the song, Ives notes that it is "preferably for a unison chorus; it is almost impossible for a single voice to hold the part against the score."

△ **CAPTAIN OF BASEBALL**
Ives (left) is pictured in 1894, wearing a baseball shirt with the Hopkins Grammar School initials. At school he shone on the baseball field and was captain of the Hopkins team.

## ON TECHNIQUE
## Complex innovations

Charles Ives built his radical compositions on a deep knowledge of European classical music. He explored and extended the possibilities for creative adventure in techniques used sparingly in the past for their shock value or novel effect. These included polytonality and polyrhythm, respectively the simultaneous use of two or more keys and the simultaneous use of different rhythms; the inclusion of many different musical styles within the same piece, from ragtime songs and camp-meeting hymns to complex counterpoint and echoes of Bach and Brahms; harmonic ambiguity; layering of multiple themes, textures, and timbres; and collages evoking city sounds and public occasions.

# Maurice Ravel

## 1875–1937, FRENCH

Ravel's life was devoted to the pursuit of musical perfection. A meticulous musical craftsman rather than an innovator, he produced comparatively few compositions but nevertheless developed a distinctive personal style.

Maurice Ravel was a French citizen but his father, an engineer and inventor, was Swiss, and his mother was Spanish-Basque. He was born in 1875 in Ciboure, near Biarritz, in the Basque region of France, but the family moved to Paris while Maurice was still a baby.

He and his younger brother, Edouard, were initially educated at home by their father. He gave them a solid grounding in technology and science, but also conveyed his love of the arts and music. Edouard shared his father's interest in engineering, while Maurice was drawn to his mother's love of Basque and Spanish folk culture, which was later reflected in many of his compositions.

### Emergent talent

Music played a large part in the Ravel household—both classical and the folk songs that Maurice's mother sang. Maurice showed musical talent from an early age, began piano lessons at age seven, then went on to more serious studies in music theory, including his first attempts at composing, when he was 12. In the course of his studies, he met

◁ **RAVEL AND VINES, 1905**
Lifelong friends, Ravel (left) and Viñes were both born in 1875 and first met as students. The musicians are pictured together here in their thirties.

the young Spanish pianist Ricardo Viñes, who was to become a close friend, as well as a champion of Ravel's music. The year 1889 was eventful for Ravel. He started piano lessons with Émile Decombes, a teacher at the Paris Conservatoire, who encouraged the young musician to give his first public performance. Later that year, Ravel was admitted to the Conservatoire to study piano. But it was as a composer rather than a pianist that his real talent lay, and while he was at the Conservatoire he began writing music in earnest. One of the events that inspired this change of emphasis was the 1889 Exposition Universelle in Paris, where he was exposed to exciting, new, and unfamiliar music.

Through the 1890s, Ravel focused on composition, but at the expense of his studies—his lack of progress in piano and theory obliged him to leave

### ON TECHNIQUE
**Master of orchestration**

Ravel's orchestral works are admired for his skill in handling instrumental colors, and his extraordinary aural imagination. He made a point of studying the characteristics of all the orchestral instruments in order to make the most of the palette of different instrumental timbres for expressive effect, and to give clarity to harmonies and rhythms. Surprisingly, only a handful of these works were first conceived for orchestra: most were written as piano pieces that he later orchestrated, and almost all his music was composed at the piano.

▽ **POSTER FOR PARIS EXPOSITION**
At the Exposition Universelle in 1889, Ravel was inspired by new Russian music and the exotic sounds of the Javanese gamelan.

◁ **MAURICE RAVEL**
Shown here in later life at his piano, Ravel was first introduced to the instrument when he received lessons as a young boy. He went on to study piano at the prestigious Paris Conservatoire.

△ **SET DESIGN,** *DAPHNIS ET CHLOE*
This set design was commissioned by Sergei Diaghilev for the Ballets Russes' production of Ravel's *Daphnis et Chloé*, which premiered in Paris in 1912. The set was painted by Russian artist Léon Bakst, who became famous for his magnificent costumes and bold, richly colored set designs for Diaghilev. Diaghilev also commissioned the music from Ravel for this ballet.

the Conservatoire in 1895. However, he enrolled in a composition course there two years later. His teacher, Gabriel Fauré (see pp.182–183), recognized his talent. Under his guidance, Ravel gained confidence to write his first mature works. He was also inspired by Erik Satie (see pp.222–225), whom he had met, and by his unconventional approach to composition. Ravel resolved to compose in the way he felt most comfortable, impervious to criticism.

### Progressive influences
But Ravel's progressive music, and politics, were still not acceptable at the Conservatoire and, despite Fauré's support, he was again thrown out. Undeterred, he continued to compose, and became associated with a group of young musicians known as Les

Apaches (the Hooligans), who were influenced by the composer Claude Debussy (see pp.194–197). Ravel had befriended Debussy, who was known as an "Impressionist" composer for the clear textures and subtle colors of his music. Similarly, Ravel's sensual orchestration led to his own nomination as an Impressionist. However, Debussy detested the label, and Ravel also rejected it.

Ravel had still to make his name with the concert-going public. He entered the competition for the

▷ **ALCYONE**
This score is from Ravel's *Alcyone* (1902). The cantata was the entry for one of his five unsuccessful attempts to win the Prix de Rome.

prestigious Prix de Rome each year, without success, from 1900 until 1905, when it became obvious that the musical establishment were preventing him from winning, even though he was probably the most gifted of the entrants. In the ensuing scandal, it was revealed that Théodore Dubois, director of the Conservatoire, was favoring students of one of his colleagues. Dubois was forced to

" I did my work **slowly**, drop by drop.
I **tore it out** of me by **pieces**. "

MAURICE RAVEL

△ **RAVEL'S PIANO**
Ravel's piano is on display in the small house in which he lived (now the Musée Maurice Ravel), in Montfort-l'Amaury, for the last 20 years of his life.

resign. Although Ravel had missed out on the prize, the immense publicity won him the attention he deserved.

## New avenues

This new-found celebrity inspired Ravel to revisit his earlier piano pieces and score them for orchestra to entice a wider concert-going audience. These arrangements showed that he had a flair for orchestration, revealed to brilliant effect in his first opera, *L'Heure espagnole*, and later by the ballet *Daphnis et Chloé*. The period between 1905 and the outbreak of World War I was, by Ravel's slow and meticulous standards, a productive one, and established him as a major composer in France and abroad. But by 1913 his rate of production slowed even more: he wrote almost nothing during the war and its aftermath.

When the war started, his application to join the French Air Force was turned down because of his age (he was approaching 40 years old) and health. In 1915, however, he was accepted by the army as a driver, supplying munitions to the front.

The conditions had a terrible effect on his already fragile health—he suffered dysentery and frostbite, and was deeply affected by the horrors of war. His woes increased when his mother died in 1917. But he completed the Neo-Baroque piano suite *Le Tombeau de Couperin* (*The Tomb of Couperin*) during this time, its separate movements each honoring a friend lost in war. The piece evoked the music of the Baroque composer François Couperin (1668–1733).

Ravel emerged from war exhausted and depressed, and only slowly resumed work. In contrast to his early career, Ravel was now revered by the musical establishment as the heir to Debussy, and as the foremost French composer. But this was a very different era, dominated by new ideas

from younger composers such as the group known as Les Six (see p.269), who saw Ravel's music as outdated. As always, though, he was oblivious to criticism and, after completing the richly Romantic *La Valse* (*The Waltz*) in 1920, he began a second phase of composing, developing a slightly more modern style influenced by the atonality of composers such as Arnold Schoenberg (see pp.238–241) and, especially, the harmonies and rhythms of jazz (see box, right).

## Final years

The change in musical style was accompanied by a change in lifestyle. Ravel's wartime experiences had aged him, and he found living in Paris overbearing, so he moved to Montfort-l'Amaury, west of Paris, where he lived alone for the rest of his life. Although Ravel is thought to have had one or two long-term relationships, he never married and by some accounts visited brothels from time to time. At Montfort-l'Amaury he produced, some of his finest and best-known music, concluding with *Boléro* and the two piano concertos.

Ravel's final years were marred by illness. In 1932, he suffered a head injury in a car accident, which triggered a brain condition. He began to experience symptoms of aphasia, the inability to process language. Soon, he was no longer able to play the piano, or to compose. In 1937, the condition worsened and became increasingly painful— he was then advised by a Parisian neurosurgeon to have an operation. This was initially thought to be successful, but very soon after Ravel fell unconscious and died, aged 62.

**PAUL WITTGENSTEIN**

## KEY WORKS

# Manuel de Falla

## 1876–1946, SPANISH

A leading figure in the nationalist revival of Spanish music in the early 20th century, Falla blended traditional folk melodies with modern harmony and orchestration to create vibrant works of universal appeal.

△ **EL AMOR BRUJO SCORE**
The cover of the score for Falla's work was illustrated by the Russian avant-garde artist and designer Natalia Goncharova, who captured the vibrant drama of flamenco.

Manuel María de los Dolores Falla y Matheu was born in Cádiz, Andalusia, in 1876, and studied at the Royal Conservatory of Music in Madrid. Under the influence of composer and musicologist Felipe Pedrell (1841–1922), he began exploring the diversity of Spain's musical traditions, and in particular the folk songs and dances of Andalusia, which formed the basis for his first significant work, the one-act opera *La vida breve* (*Life Is Short*), completed in 1904.

Falla aimed to establish his place in the wider European contemporary music scene and in 1907 moved to Paris, where he associated with composers such as Claude Debussy and Maurice Ravel. His output through his seven years in France was slight (a handful of songs and short piano pieces) but his musical impetus was germinating. When World War I broke out in 1914 he returned to live with his parents in Madrid, and a period of rich creativity followed.

### Music of passion

Despite his measured manner, Falla began to produce music that was flamboyant and passionate, as in *El amor brujo* (*Love, the Magician*), a ballet commissioned by the renowned flamenco dancer Pastora Imperio (see box, right). First performed in 1915, this piece included the dramatic *Ritual Fire Dance*, which became one of Falla's most enduringly popular pieces.

### International success

The sensuous *Nights in the Gardens of Spain*, described by the composer as "symphonic impressions for piano and orchestra," followed in 1916, blending French influences with distinctively Andalusian rhythms and melodies. When his colorful two-act ballet *The Three-Cornered Hat* was premiered by Sergei Diaghilev's prestigious Ballets Russes in London in 1919, Falla at last achieved international renown.

In the 1920s, Falla was a hero to a generation of Spanish Modernists such as the poet Federico García Lorca, who shared his fascination with the Andalusian Roma heritage. But Falla's music evolved in a different direction, following the contemporary trend toward Neoclassicism and the use of smaller orchestral ensembles. Works such as the Concerto for Harpsichord of 1926 harked back to a Spanish tradition of haughty pride and spiritual austerity of Catholic Castile.

Falla's creative energy declined with age. He struggled for years with a score for an oratorio, *Atlántida*, which he never completed. In the Spanish Civil War (1936–1939) he withdrew to Granada, saddened by the carnage and unable to commit to either side. After the victory of the Francoists in 1939 he left for Argentina, where he lived until his death in 1946.

▷ **MANUEL DE FALLA, 1932**
Falla was a devout Catholic, meticulous in his dress, reticent in manner, and fanatically fixed in his habits—qualities that are reflected in this portrait by Ignacio Zuloaga y Zabaleta.

## IN CONTEXT
### Flamenco and *el cante jondo*

Flamenco is a range of flamboyant singing styles and dances associated primarily with the *gitanos*, the Roma of southern Spain. It exists both as folk music and as professional entertainment. Falla was especially attracted to *el cante jondo* ("the deep song"), which was often sung without guitar accompaniment, expressing dark themes of anguish and death. Falla mounted a festival in Granada in 1922, in association with the poet Federico García Lorca, to encourage amateur singers of *el cante jondo* and stimulate public interest in authentic flamenco, which was increasingly threatened by the rise of the modern urbanized world.

*PORTRAIT OF PASTORA IMPERIO,*
*JULIO ROMERO DE TORRES, 1922*

# Béla Bartók

## 1881–1945, HUNGARIAN

Deeply rooted in Hungarian folk music, Bartók's musical language
was groundbreaking and idiosyncratic. During World War II,
he left Budapest for New York, where he struggled to survive.

# "Competitions are for horses, not artists."

BELA BARTOK

Béla Bartók was born on March 25, 1881, in the town of Nagyszentmiklós, Transylvania (then Hungary, now Sînnicolau Mare in Romania). His mother was a pianist, his father the headmaster of a local school. When Béla was seven, his father died and his bereaved family moved to Nagyszőlős, where Bartók gave his first public concert, aged 11. Later they settled in Pressburg (now Bratislava, Slovakia). A fine pianist and a composer of growing confidence and talent, Bartók elected to study at the Royal Hungarian Academy of Music in Budapest rather than taking the typical composition student's well-worn route to Vienna.

## Influences in Budapest

The move to the Hungarian capital brought the young Bartók into contact with people who would profoundly shape his future: he met Zoltán Kodály, a composer and philosopher who

◁ **LAJOS KOSSUTH**
The man to whom Bartók dedicated his tone poem *Kossuth* advocated for Hungarian independence from Hapsburg rule and became regent-president of the short-lived Hungarian Republic in 1849.

became his great friend; and he was taught by János Koessler, a friend of Brahms, and by piano virtuoso István Thoman. After he graduated in 1903, Bartók was already in great demand as a pianist (his early recordings display his distinctively clear and beautiful tone) and in 1907, he was appointed to a piano professorship at the Academy, a post that he held until 1934.

## Field studies

With the Hapsburg Empire in crisis after the suicide of Crown Prince Rudolf in 1889 destabilized the monarchy, Hungarian separatism had gained a strong following. Bartók was part of a generation inspired by the

optimism of the political activist Ferenc Kossuth and his Party of Independence. His orchestral tone poem *Kossuth* (1903) paid tribute to Ferenc's father, the reformer and national hero Lajos Kossuth. Bartók had already written prolifically for piano and chamber ensembles, but it was this work— much influenced by Richard Strauss's tone poems—that truly put him on the map. After this, his musical language developed considerably under the new influence of Debussy, whose "great service to music," according to Bartók, "was to reawaken among all musicians an awareness of harmony and its possibilities."

Around 1904, Bartók and Kodály acquired an Edison phonograph and set out into the remoter corners of the Hungarian countryside to record and catalog the folk songs that they heard there. From this time on, Bartók began to adapt traditional Hungarian

△ **EDISON PHONOGRAPH, c.1900**
Bartók and Kodály's research into folk song was made possible by the invention of sound-recording equipment, such as Edison's phonograph. From 1934 to 1940, Bartók compiled an edition of 13,000 Hungarian folk songs that he had collected, for the Hungarian Academy of Sciences.

## ON TECHNIQUE
### The value of folk song

Bartók's fascination with folk song lay not in petty nationalism, but in his belief in its fundamental importance. In an essay titled "Folk song and Art Music" in 1921, he argued that folk song had long been part of the arsenal of the most sophisticated composers, citing examples in the music of Haydn and Beethoven and— further back—in the use of Lutheran chorales in 17th-century music. He suggested that references to folk music helped listeners relate better to new works, and that composers, such as Schoenberg, who disconnected from such roots produced music that was difficult to understand. Exploring folk music, he wrote, "is a study which will refine the budding musician's taste and considerably enlarge his horizon."

BARTOK RECORDING FOLK SONGS
DURING A JOURNEY IN TRANSYLVANIA

# "I **cannot conceive** of **music** that **expresses** absolutely **nothing**."

BELA BARTOK

songs into works for the concert hall: examples include the *Six Romanian Folk Dances*, the Violin Duos, and various sets of folk songs with piano accompaniment. Folk music had a significant impact on his language— through its rhythms and harmonies and the use of quarter-tones—and is evident in all areas of his work, from string quartets to orchestral and operatic pieces. He once wrote enthusiastically, "Another completely different factor makes contemporary (20th-century) music realistic: that, half consciously, half intentionally,

it searches for impressions from that great reality of folk art, which encompasses everything."

## Love and further travel

In 1907, Bartók became infatuated with the young violinist Stefi Geyer, who inspired his Violin Concerto No. 1. Some of its themes represent Bartók's idealized image of Geyer, though she rejected his advances.

Two years later, he married Márta Ziegler, who was among his piano students and still a teenager. The pair soon had a son, also named Béla.

Meanwhile, his field research did not stop at the borders of Hungary. Over the years, he undertook many trips, visiting Turkey, the Middle East, and Algeria. The String Quartet No. 2 is one example of the results, incorporating elements from the Berber music he encountered in North Africa.

Bartók's settings of Hungarian texts reveal much about the influence of language itself upon his music. His opera *Duke Bluebeard's Castle* (1911) was steeped in the world of Symbolist poetry and set a libretto by Béla Balázs. The story, based on

▽ **STRING QUARTETS, c. 1915**
Field research into Hungarian folk songs infused Bartók's string quartets. Here Bartók and Kodály (seated, reading) pose for a photograph with members of the Waldbauer-Kerpely String Quartet.

La Barbe bleu by French writer of fairy tales Charles Perrault tells of how Bluebeard's new wife makes shocking discoveries as she opens doors in his castle. The atmospheric work shows how closely Bartók's melodic lines follow the cadences of speech.

## Mature works

Unable to leave Hungary during World War I, and disappointed by the Hungarian Fine Arts Commission's decision to reject Duke Bluebeard's Castle, Bartók devoted himself for several years to ethnomusicological research until a meeting with another alluring violinist Jelly d'Arányi (see box, right) drew him back to composition. In 1923, he and Márta were divorced; only two months later he proposed to one of his piano students, Ditta Pasztory, who was 19 to his 42, and married her 10 days afterward. The following year, their son Péter was born.

▷ **CANTATA PROFANA SCORE**
Bartók's work for chorus and orchestra, inspired by a Romanian folk tale of hunters who are transformed into stags, is rich with natural symbolism.

◁ **STEFI GEYER**
The Swiss violinist Geyer (1888–1956) was Béla Bartók's muse. Differences in age and outlook (she was a committed Catholic, he an unbeliever) confounded Bartók's romantic intentions.

The interwar years saw an upswing in Bartók's renown. He established himself on the international scene with such works as his first two piano concertos, the Cantata Profana (1930), Music for Strings, Percussion, and Celesta (1936) and the Sonata for Two Pianos and Percussion (1937). He also toured Europe, America, and the Soviet Union as a pianist. However, as right-wing politics began to take hold in Hungary, Bartók's loathing of fascist ideology put him at risk of state retribution: in Germany, his ballet The Miraculous Mandarin (written in 1918–1919) was banned for its sexually explicit content.

Bartók spent a last idyllic summer in Switzerland in 1939, working on his sixth and final string quartet and the

Divertimento for string orchestra, which had been commissioned by the philanthropist Paul Sacher. The following year, the Bartóks left Hungary and emigrated to the US.

There, holding a modest post as a "research assistant" at Columbia University, Bartók faced an uphill struggle to gain commissions and provide for his family. His health, too, was suffering. Less than two years after they arrived, he began to develop symptoms of a serious illness that turned out to be leukemia.

## American experience

A breakthrough came in 1943, when Serge Koussevitzky, the Russian-born director of the Boston Symphony Orchestra, commissioned Bartók to create a major orchestral work for a fee of $1,000. The result was the Concerto for Orchestra, a magnificent orchestral showpiece that ranges in tone from dark ferocity and despair to outright satire, mocking the use of a theme from Lehár's The Merry Widow in Shostakovich's Seventh Symphony.

The work was received with acclaim. More commissions followed, including a violin sonata written for Yehudi Menuhin, and the Viola Concerto. However, this last work was left incomplete— Bartók's illness had finally caught up with him. The composer died on September 26, 1945, aged 64. On his deathbed, he told his doctor: "What I most regret is having to leave with a full trunk."

### IN PROFILE
### Jelly d'Arányi

A great-niece of the famed Hungarian violinist Joseph Joachim, d'Arányi (1895–1966) was a legendary violin virtuoso. She was admired by many musicians including Edward Elgar, Pablo Casals, and Maurice Ravel, who dedicated his Tzigane to her in 1924. She met and enchanted Bartók in 1919, kindling in him a new phase of creativity. It was for d'Arányi that Bartók wrote both of his extremely challenging sonatas for violin and piano; however, his passion for the violinist went unrequited.

**VIOLINIST JELLY D'ARANYI**

## KEY WORKS

**1911**
Bartók's sole opera, Duke Bluebeard's Castle, is a powerful Symbolist masterpiece for two singers.

**1915**
Writes Six Romanian Folk Dances, displaying how folk songs can inspire music for the concert hall.

**1918–19**
Produces the score for The Miraculous Mandarin, a ballet so violent and explicit that it is later banned by the Nazis.

**1936**
Writes the strikingly original Music for Strings, Percussion, and Celesta.

**1909–39**
Produces some of his most personal works in his Six String Quartets.

**1943–45**
The Concerto for Orchestra traverses a great range of emotional states.

# Igor Stravinsky

## 1882–1971, RUSSIAN

Widely considered the 20th century's paramount composer, Stravinsky transformed music with his radical approach to rhythm. His compositions raised the genre of ballet to an artistic level matched only by Tchaikovsky.

Igor Fyodorovich Stravinsky was born into a musical household in Oranienbaum, on the outskirts of St. Petersburg, in June 1882. He later said that the Russian imperial capital was "dearer to my heart than any [city] in the world." Nonetheless,

◁ **IGOR STRAVINSKY, 1927**
This portrait of the composer by the celebrated Russian-born fashion photographer George Hoyningen-Huene was shot for *Vanity Fair* magazine.

he always insisted that his early years had been unhappy and his school days hopelessly lonely. Igor's father was principal bass singer at St. Petersburg's Mariinsky Opera; his mother was a pianist who seemed to adopt a severe attitude to young Igor and his three brothers. The nearest he had to a true mother-figure was his German nurse, Bertha, who brought him up to speak her language fluently, besides the French spoken by the Russian upper classes.

Igor demonstrated a musical ear from an early age, made good progress with piano lessons, and was enthralled by what he saw and heard at the Mariinsky Theater, including the great ballet scores of Tchaikovsky. Yet he was far from a prodigy: he later admitted that his father's insistence that he should study law was not unreasonable, given the absence of exceptional early talent usually needed to pursue a musical career. While he was a reluctant law student, he took private lessons in composition with Rimsky-Korsakov, which was crucial for his development into one of the supreme composers of his generation.

### Meteoric rise

Around 1908, the talk in cultural circles in Paris was of the exciting performances of Russian opera being staged there by the impresario Sergei Diaghilev, who now planned to start up a ballet company as well. Diaghilev, based in St. Petersburg, was in search of a composer for a new work, *The Firebird*. He had been impressed by Stravinsky's brilliantly written short orchestral pieces *Scherzo fantastique* and *Feux d'artifice* (*Fireworks*), which he had heard at a concert in St. Petersburg in 1909—he therefore took a chance on Stravinsky, tasking

◁ **TAMARA KARSAVINA, c. 1910**
The sensational Russian prima ballerina is shown here, in a painting by Jacques-Emile Blanche, wearing the costume of the Firebird in Stravinsky's ballet of the same name.

IN CONTEXT
**Ballet maestro**

Stravinsky's major contribution to ballet was about more than seizing the opportunity offered by Diaghilev to compose *The Firebird* as a fairy-tale spectacular, with the dance element grafted on. The tactile and rhythmic qualities in Stravinsky's music connected naturally with the technical and physical qualities of dance itself, as in *Petrushka* and *The Rite of Spring*. In 1947, he composed *Orpheus* for choreography by another Russian exile, George Balanchine, who then became artistic director of New York City Ballet. Besides choreographing many of Stravinsky's concert-hall works, Balanchine also commissioned *Agon*, premiered by NYCB in 1957.

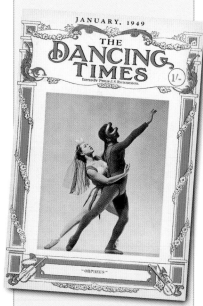

*ORPHEUS*, CHOREOGRAPHED BY GEORGE BALANCHINE, IN NEW YORK

▷ **THE RITE OF SPRING**
This is a scene from the premiere of Igor Stravinsky's controversial avant-garde ballet performed by Vaslav Nijinsky's Ballets Russes at the Théâtre des Champs-Elysées in Paris in 1913.

him to complete the ballet in just five months—Stravinsky met the deadline. *The Firebird*'s spectacularly successful premiere in Paris in May 1910 made him world-famous. The composer found himself rated as an equal by Debussy and Ravel, who were dazzled by his score's technical panache and orchestral mastery.

Immediately recommissioned by Diaghilev, Stravinsky came up a year later with *Petrushka*, a tale of fairground life, whose main character is a puppet with poignantly human feelings. Another success for its composer, the ballet also made a star of the great dancer Vaslav Nijinsky. Two years later, a third Stravinsky ballet, *The Rite of Spring*, totally rewrote the rules of what classical

▷ **PETRUSHKA, 1911**
The second draft of the score for Stravinsky's *Petrushka* is shown here. The ballet premiered in Paris in 1911; its principal character is a puppet with human sensibilities.

music could do, with its fiercely dissonant harmonic idiom and unprecedented rhythmic firepower. The famous first-night "riot" (more accurately a commotion by outraged Parisian ballet patrons in the theater's expensive seats) seems to have been sparked as much by Nijinsky's unconventional choreography as by Stravinsky's music, and was not repeated in the remaining five performances: Stravinsky's score met with increasing, if startled, admiration.

### Revolution and exile

Stravinsky's subsequent progress was directed as much by changes in his life as by his talent. The outbreak of World War I forced Diaghilev's company to close. Stravinsky took his wife Catherine and family to live in neutral Switzerland, which lacked Paris's musical resources; and the Russian Revolution in 1917 caused a lifelong exile from his native country.

Stravinsky found a positive musical response to both situations in a sequence of works that could be performed more easily on smaller budgets. The composer showed a deepening awareness of his linguistic and musical roots, particularly Russian folk song—as in the sung and danced ballet *Les Noces* (*The Wedding*), featuring an onstage chorus and an

"orchestra" of four pianos and percussion instruments, which reached its final form in 1923.

By then, Stravinsky had settled in postwar Paris. Moving beyond dissonant Modernism toward a cooler Neo-Classicism, his music now increasingly looked to adapt and transmute earlier styles. The ballet *Pulcinella* (staged by Diaghilev's revived company in 1920) was based on keyboard works supposedly by the Italian composer Pergolesi, though these are now known to be imitations. Needing to support his widowed mother, his own exiled family, and the family of his aunt (Catherine's mother), Stravinsky often appeared as a concert pianist in his own works, among them a piano concerto, and the *Capriccio* for piano and orchestra. Other major statements were a ritualized opera, *Oedipus Rex*, adapted from Sophocles' ancient Greek play *King Oedipus*, and the choral and orchestral *Symphony of Psalms*. Both works used texts in Latin, whose depersonalized, "dead language" properties appealed to Stravinsky's anti-Romantic streak. The *Symphony of Psalms*, written for the Boston Symphony Orchestra, marked the composer's return—after many years of rejection—to the Russian Orthodox faith of his upbringing.

"**Music** ... [establishes] an **order in things** including, and particularly, the **coordination** between **man** and **time**."

IGOR STRAVINSKY, 1935

## KEY WORKS

**1910**
In its first Paris season, Sergei Diaghilev's Ballets Russes company gives the first, hugely successful, performances of *The Firebird*.

**1911**
Following *The Firebird*'s success, the ballet score *Petrushka* presents the crisp rhythms and colors of Stravinsky's mature style.

**1913**
The ultra-radical dissonance and earth-stamping rhythms of *The Rite of Spring* cause an audience "riot" at the Paris premiere.

**1920**
In a shift of musical direction, the ballet *Pulcinella* combines rhythmic energy with tunefulness and roguish humor.

**1917–23**
Taking six years to complete, *Les Noces* (*The Wedding*) builds an entire ballet score out of fragments of Russian folk song.

**1930**
The statement of Stravinsky's rediscovered Russian Orthodox faith, *Symphony of Psalms* for chorus and orchestra, is premiered in Paris.

**1945**
*Symphony in Three Movements*, with prominent solo parts for piano and harp, is Stravinsky's first American-period masterpiece.

**1966**
*Requiem Canticles*, his last major work, is a concentrated, pocket-sized version of the Latin Mass for the dead.

The year 1939 brought personal tragedy: Stravinsky's mother, youngest daughter, and wife Catherine all died within a few months. For many years, he had been in a relationship with the younger Vera Sudeikina, a painter and costume designer and, like him, a Russian exile. With World War II looming, they moved to the US, married, became US citizens, and settled in Hollywood, making friends with European fellow emigrants or refugees. Earning the kind of income that Stravinsky was used to was difficult: several film-score projects fell through, but he was able to recycle music already written into his concert works. A major achievement of this kind, completed in 1945, was *Symphony in Three Movements*, with its brassy, US-influenced style and propulsive rhythmic invention.

### Late change of style
Four years of work were taken up by a full-length opera, *The Rake's Progress*, based on drawings by William Hogarth, with a libretto by English and US poets W.H. Auden and Chester Kallman. Early progress on another opera, to a projected text by Dylan Thomas, was ended a few years later by the Welsh poet's death. By now an unexpected change had taken place in Stravinsky's style.

Previously hostile to the music of Schoenberg and Webern, he now found himself increasingly stimulated by the possibilities opened up by the different kinds of "serial" or 12-note methods that these composers had evolved. The result was a sequence of late, tersely concentrated works filtering his own musical techniques through this new one. They include the ballet *Agon*, the ultra-compressed piano concerto *Movements*, and the choral and orchestral *Requiem Canticles*, which was played at the funeral service before Stravinsky's burial in the Russian Orthodox cemetery in Venice. The continuing popularity of Stravinsky's great early ballet scores has tended to deflect from wider appreciation of later masterpieces like these. No other 20th-century composer's music covered more ground with such ceaseless brilliance and inventiveness.

▽ **STRAVINSKY AT THE PIANO, 1934**
The composer is shown here at his home at rue du Faubourg Saint-Honoré in Paris, where he and his family moved the year this photograph was taken. He later said that the house was the unhappiest he had ever lived in—in 1939, while he was residing there, his mother, wife, and daughter all died. He moved to the US later the same year.

# Heitor Villa-Lobos

## 1887–1959, BRAZILIAN

The first Brazilian composer to gain international acclaim, Villa-Lobos developed a recognizably Brazilian style of composition, integrating into the classical idiom elements of indigenous folk and popular music.

FLAG OF THE REPUBLIC OF BRAZIL

Brazil gained independence from Portugal in 1822, but Portuguese influence on its culture in the ensuing Empire of Brazil remained strong. Throughout the 19th century, a nationalist movement flourished, asserting a Brazilian identity, as well as true political independence, which involved the integration of indigenous traditions and those brought by enslaved Africans into the largely European colonial culture. This started to become a reality after the establishment of the First Republic in 1889, under which creative artists such as Villa-Lobos forged a Brazilian cultural identity no longer shaped solely by European traditions.

Heitor Villa-Lobos was born in Rio de Janeiro, and was introduced to music early in life through music-making soirees at his home. With this as his inspiration, he learned to play the guitar, cello, and clarinet, but was prevented from taking further training by the death of his father in 1899, leaving him to support the family by playing in various theater and cinema orchestras, and with the *chorões*, the itinerant street musicians of Rio.

Born in 1887, a year before the establishment of the First Republic in Brazil, he grew up in a country that was anxious to shake off European influence (see box, right). Aged about 18, he began traveling around Brazil, researching its rich musical heritage.

### Striking out

In 1912, after several years traveling, he married pianist Lucília Guimarães and settled down in Rio to work as a composer. Living in this cosmopolitan city, he came into contact with some of the latest music from Europe, and through his friendship with Darius Milhaud, who was working there, he was introduced to the work of Debussy and Satie. This inspired him to make a complete break with the Germanic Romanticism that then dominated South American art music, and forge his own style.

Sadly, his efforts were not appreciated by audiences in Brazil, so he traveled to Paris, hoping to make his name as a composer. This marked a turning point in his career—he found success there and met musicians from all over the world, among them guitarist Andrés Segovia, who commissioned a study for guitar from Villa-Lobos, *Chôros*, which featured the musical styles of the Brazilian *chorões*. Villa-Lobos wrote many studies and pieces for Segovia over the years.

### Return to the homeland

On a visit home in 1930, the outbreak of a revolution prevented Villa-Lobos from returning to Paris. By the end of that year, Getúlio Vargas had seized power, declaring an end to the Old Republic. Villa-Lobos was appointed director of the Superintendência de Educação Musical e Artística in São Paulo, and until 1945 organized concerts and provided patriotic compositions for the populist leader.

In 1936, he left his wife for Arminda Neves d'Almeida, who became his muse and partner for the rest of

his life. His music, however, continued to become more propagandist and nationalist, and to appeal to a mass audience that rejected any form of Modernism. But this did bring him the recognition he sought in his home country, and prompted a prolific period of creativity, especially after Vargas was ousted. Democracy restored, Villa-Lobos traveled to the US and Europe, where he gained an international reputation.

By the mid-1950s, after Vargas's suicide, demand for Villa-Lobos's patriotic populism had waned, and as his health deteriorated, his output declined until his death in 1959.

▷ **ANDRES SEGOVIA**
The renowned Spanish classical guitarist met Villa-Lobos in Paris in the mid-1920s; Villa-Lobos went on to write a number of major works for Segovia in later years.

> " **Artists** live with **God**—but **give** their little finger to **Satan**. I **sleep** with **the angels** and **dream** of the **devil**. "
>
> HEITOR VILLA-LOBOS

▷ **HEITOR VILLA-LOBOS**
Tapping into his experience as a street musician, and the music he heard on his travels, Villa-Lobos brought the rich variety of Brazilian popular and indigenous music to the concert hall. He is shown here playing a *cuíca*, a native Brazilian friction drum.

# Sergei Prokofiev

## 1891–1953, RUSSIAN/UKRAINIAN

One of the most versatile and imaginative composers of the first half of the 20th century, Prokofiev created masterpieces in many traditional forms and also in new fields such as film music.

Prokofiev's career divides into three distinct phases. In the first phase, during the period leading up to the Russian Revolution in 1917, he was a provocative firebrand emerging as one of the country's most exciting and progressive composers. In the second, he left Ukraine following the Revolution and spent most of the next two decades abroad, establishing a worldwide reputation. The third phase saw his return to spend his later years in his homeland, where he was seen as a cultural hero but fell foul of the repressive Soviet regime.

Prokofiev was born in the village of Sontsovka, Ukraine, into a comfortable middle-class family. His father was manager of an agricultural estate and his mother was a talented amateur pianist. Two elder sisters had died as infants and he was brought up as an adored only child. He began piano lessons with his mother when he was four and within a year was writing his own pieces for the instrument. At the age of 10, he composed his first opera, performed by relatives and playmates, and in 1904 he passed the entrance examination for the St. Petersburg Conservatory.

### The early years

Prokofiev studied at the Conservatory for the next decade. He had various distinguished teachers, most notably Rimsky-Korsakov, but they left no real mark on him, as he tended to regard them as stuffy traditionalists. The most important works of his student days are his first and second piano concertos, premiered in 1912 and 1913 respectively, with himself as soloist on each occasion. Their tense, percussive muscularity contrasted sharply with the lyricism of much Russian music of the time and they provoked strong reactions—both for and against. At the premiere of the second concerto, some people are said to have booed, hissed, or walked out, but when Prokofiev played the first concerto as his graduation piece at the Conservatory in 1914, he was awarded the coveted Rubinstein Prize.

In that same year, World War I began. Prokofiev was excused military service because his father was dead

△ **SERGEI PROKOFIEV, 1900**
Prokofiev is shown here at his piano, aged nine. The following year—having already received piano lessons from his mother for six years—the young musician composed his first opera.

### IN PROFILE
### Sviatoslav Richter

Prokofiev had close links with some leading Soviet musicians, especially Sviatoslav Richter (1915–1997), widely regarded as one of the greatest pianists of the 20th century. Richter gave the first performances of several of Prokofiev's works, including the Piano Sonata No. 7 in 1943. It is one of three piano sonatas Prokofiev wrote during World War II and Richter spoke of it reflecting the anxieties of a world in which "chaos and uncertainty reign." However, he also thought it expressed a "will for victory" and affirmed "the irrepressible life force."

SOVIET MUSICIAN SVIATOSLAV RICHTER AT THE PIANO

◁ **SERGEI PROKOFIEV, 1930s**
This portrait was painted when the composer was at the height of his career. The painter, Sergei Yurievich Sudeikin, was best known as a designer of theater sets and costumes.

> "...an **unrelenting muscular exhibition** of a **completely novel** kind of **piano playing**."

COMPOSER VERNON DUKE, ON SEEING PROKOFIEV PERFORM IN 1916

## KEY WORKS

**1912**
Piano Concerto No. 1, which Prokofiev says is his "first more or less mature" work, premieres in Moscow.

**1921**
Piano Concerto No. 3 premieres in Chicago, with Prokofiev as soloist.

**1935**
Prokofiev begins *Romeo and Juliet*, his greatest ballet music, from which he also creates three orchestral suites.

**1936**
*Peter and the Wolf*, Prokofiev's charming "symphonic fairy tale for children," premieres in Moscow.

**1941**
Begins *War and Peace*, his most ambitious opera; it is not performed in full until after his death.

**1945**
Symphony No. 5, often considered the greatest of Prokofiev's seven symphonies, premieres in Moscow.

△ **LINA LLUBERA, EARLY 1920s**
Prokofiev met the Spanish singer Lina Llubera when he was living in the US. The couple married in 1923, but Prokofiev later left his wife for a younger woman.

▽ **LENIN ADDRESSES THE WORKERS**
Although sympathetic to the Revolution of 1917, Prokofiev became frustrated by the ensuing turmoil and traveled to the US, where he was based for years. This painting of the revolutionary leader Lenin at the Putilov factory is by Isaak Brodsky.

and he was his mother's only support. Thus he was able to pursue his career and continued to attract attention with his self-assured personality and brashly confident music. His compositions of this time include the savagely colorful *Scythian Suite* (premiered in 1916)—inspired by Stravinsky's *Rite of Spring* and intended to create similar outrage— and Symphony No. 1 (the "Classical" Symphony, premiered in 1918), which has a sprightly melodic charm that shows a different side to his personality. Prokofiev conducted the premieres of both these works (displaying "barbaric abandon" on the podium, according to one reviewer).

### Travel and exile

Prokofiev welcomed the Revolution, but the chaos and civil war created an unfavorable environment for a musician. In 1918, he went abroad for a concert tour, which turned into a long exile. He traveled through Siberia to Japan, performing in Tokyo and Yokohama, then went on to San Francisco and, in September 1918, to New York, where he was based for two years. His explosive pianism attracted attention (he was dubbed "the Cossack Chopin"), but reactions were mixed and he was generally unhappy in the US. He did, however, meet a young Spanish singer called Lina Llubera, who was to become his wife in 1923.

In 1920, Prokofiev visited Paris and for the next two years divided his time between Europe and the US. Two other Russian émigrés, the conductor Sergei Koussevitzky and the ballet impresario Sergei Diaghilev, helped to promote his career in Paris where, in 1921, he scored two major successes: with the *Scythian Suite* (conducted by Koussevitzky) and the music for the ballet *The Buffoon* (sometimes known as *Chout*). These helped make him one of the best-known composers of the day, and in 1922 he moved permanently to Europe (although he continued to visit the US). At first he lived at Ettal in southern Germany, where he spent much of his time

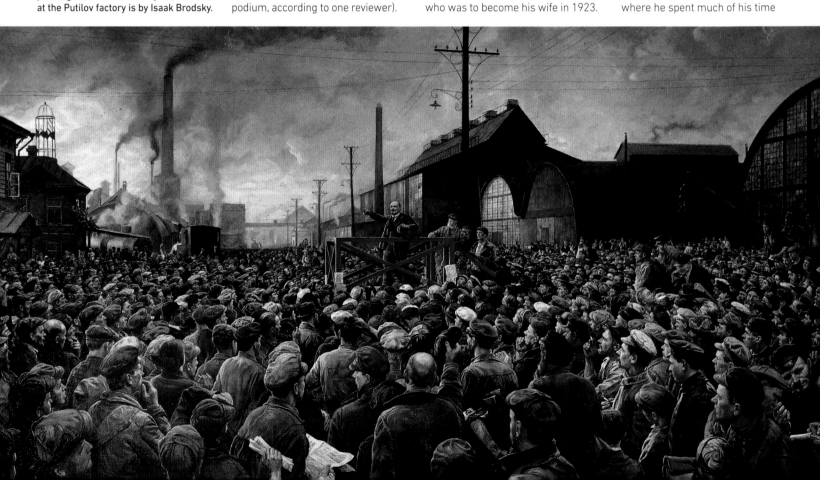

preparing his works for publication, giving him a respite from his grueling schedule of touring. Then, in October 1923, he settled in Paris.

## Recognition and acclaim

In 1927, Prokofiev made a two-month concert tour of the Soviet Union and was given VIP treatment. He also toured widely in Europe and visited the US in 1925, 1930, and 1933, the increasing lyricism of his work appealing to a wider audience than his earlier aggressiveness. Indeed, his reputation in the US was so high that he received prestigious commissions, including one from the Library of Congress for his first string quartet, premiered in 1931. As well as performing in the concert hall, Prokofiev occasionally made recordings, most notably one of his Third Piano Concerto (the most popular of the five he wrote) at London's Abbey Road Studios in 1932.

## A final return

Prokofiev visited the Soviet Union again in 1928 and 1932, before moving there permanently with his wife and two children in 1936. It was a risky decision: as a world-famous artist he could expect a privileged lifestyle, but no one was entirely safe under Stalin's tyranny. Initially, he was allowed to keep his passport and he made visits to Europe and even another tour of the US in 1938. However, he was then asked to hand in the passport, ostensibly for routine administrative purposes, and it was never returned, meaning that he was trapped in his homeland.

Prokofiev continued to produce major works, including the music for Sergei Eisenstein's celebrated film *Alexander Nevsky* (1938), but he was also obliged to create hollow

### IN CONTEXT
#### Socialist Realism

The term Socialist Realism is used to describe the officially sanctioned theory and practice of art in the Soviet Union under Stalin's rule (1924–1953). All artists, including painters, writers, and composers, were expected to glorify the state rather than to express their own ideas and personalities. This was supposed to educate and inspire the common people through instilling the principles of Communism, but typically it resulted in stereotyped and often bombastic works.

**СТАЛИН-НАШЕ ЗНАМЯ!**

"STALIN IS OUR BANNER!," SOVIET AGITPROP POSTER, 1948

pieces extolling the Soviet regime—for example, a cantata celebrating Stalin's 60th birthday (1939). During World War II he was evacuated from Moscow to keep him out of danger and was awarded the title of Honored Artist of the Soviet Union. However, in 1948, along with other composers, he was accused of showing decadent Western influence in his music and had to sign a public apology to "Dear Comrade Stalin." Soon afterward his wife Lina (whom he had abandoned for a younger woman) was arrested for alleged espionage and spent eight years in Siberian labor camps.

Several of Prokofiev's works were officially blacklisted, but he was soon rehabilitated, and in 1951 he won the last of his six Stalin Prizes. However, by this time—following a bad fall and a stroke—the composer was seriously ill.

Prokofiev died in Moscow on March 5, 1953—the same day as Stalin. Because of this coincidence, his death passed almost unremarked. It is said that every florist in Moscow was ordered to use their entire stock for Stalin's funeral, Prokofiev's mourners consequently had to make do with paper flowers.

> "I **care nothing** for **politics**—I'm a **composer first** and **last**."
>
> SERGEI PROKOFIEV, 1937

▷ **LILI BOULANGER, c. 1915**
The young composer is pictured here during World War I, at the age of 21, two years after having won the Prix de Rome for her cantata *Faust et Hélène* and just three years before her early death.

# Lili Boulanger

## 1893–1918, FRENCH

The tragically short-lived composer and pianist Boulanger was the first woman to win the coveted Prix de Rome award for composition. She is considered one of the 20th century's most talented composers.

Marie Juliette Olga Boulanger, known as Lili, was born in Paris in 1893 to a musical family: her parents were notable musicians and her sister, Nadia, went on to become a famous conductor and tutor (see box, right). Lili grew up around leading musicians and intellectuals of the age, including the composer and close family friend, Gabriel Fauré (see pp.182–183), who became her piano tutor and had a major influence on her career.

## Overcoming hardship

Lili's short life was marked by robust musical genius as well as physical frailty. At the age of two—by which time she could sing melodies by ear—she fell gravely ill with Crohn's disease, which triggered pain and sickness in her life. However, Lili was precocious in her musical talents: she sang and also learned the piano, violin, cello, harp, and organ. Her studies were steered by Nadia, Fauré and, at the Conservatoire National de Paris, other leading musicians, including the composer Georges Caussade and the harpist Alphonse Hasselmans.

The death of her father when she was six is thought to have spurred Lili to start composing. Her earliest work was the simple and poetic *Nocturne* (1911) for violin and piano. At the age of 19, she won the prestigious Prix de Rome for her cantata *Faust et Hélène* (1913), composed in just four

A towering figure in Lili's life, Nadia Boulanger (1887–1979) was a highly distinguished conductor and organist and one of the 20th century's most influential teachers of composition. Like Lili, Nadia was tutored by Gabriel Fauré at the Conservatoire de Paris. She came second in the 1908 Prix de Rome with her cantata *La Sirène*. When her father died in 1903, Nadia's teaching became a vital source of financial support for the family. She went on to instruct numerous eminent composers, many from the US, including Aaron Copland and Philip Glass. After Lili's death, Nadia was tireless in her promotion of her sister's work.

**NADIA BOULANGER CONDUCTING AN ORCHESTRA IN MANCHESTER, AGED 76**

weeks. She was the first woman to receive the award. This marked the turning point in her career, securing her a scholarship as composer-in-residence at the Villa Medici in Rome as well as a publishing contract.

The influence of Fauré, Debussy, and Wagner is evident in Boulanger's work, which also embraces religious themes (as in her psalm settings). Many of her major pieces were written during World War I, when she was often ill. Several of these are dark and brooding, as in *Poème symphonique* (1917) and Psalm 130, *Du fond de l'âbime* (*Out of the depths*, 1917–1918). By contrast, her *Vieille prière bouddhique* (1914–1917) and the sprightly *D'un matin de printemps* are more uplifting.

By 1918, although at a high point in her career, Boulanger was at a personal low, plagued by severe illness. *Pie Jesu* (for voice, strings, harp, and organ)—melancholic, sparse, beautiful—was completed on her deathbed. Her opera *La Princesse Maleine* (1916–1918) was unfinished at the time of her death at the age of 24.

◁ **VILLA MEDICI, ROME**
As a winner of the Prix de Rome, Lili was invited to spend five years composing at this magnificent 16th-century villa. Ill health and the outbreak of war cut short her tenure, but it was here that she wrote her popular *Cortège* for flute and piano.

# "**Superior morally** and **spiritually** ... She became **an example** for me."

NADIA BOULANGER, ON HER SISTER, LILI

# William Grant Still

## 1895–1978, AMERICAN

A prolific classical composer, conductor, and arranger, with roots in America's Deep South, William Grant Still produced symphonies, operas, and ballets, many infused with Black American influences and sounds.

# "It was all directed toward **one end**, and that was **learning to compose**. "

WILLIAM GRANT STILL

Born in Mississippi, Still relocated to Little Rock, Arkansas, with his mother following the death of his father. From the spirituals sung by his maternal grandmother to the opera introduced by his stepfather, he enjoyed a childhood full of music, and learned the violin, cello, and oboe.

In 1911, Still enrolled at Wilberforce University, Ohio, one of the first private historically Black colleges in the US. Later, after service in the US Navy during World War I, he attended the Oberlin Conservatory, Ohio.

Compositional studies from the early 1920s exposed Still to wildly contrasting styles by his two main teachers: George Whitefield Chadwick (1854–1931) from the New England Conservatory, who was known for his conservative style, and Edgard Varèse (see p.277) from the modernist wing. Varèse programmed Still's music, giving the young composer early exposure to audiences.

## Career develops

Still was a leading light in the Harlem Renaissance (1918–1937), an explosion of Black American art and culture

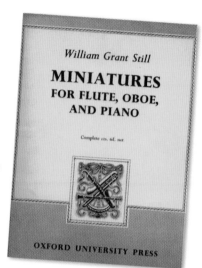

centered on Harlem in New York City. His most popular work, Symphony No. 1, "Afro-American" (1930), a traditional four-movement symphony, maintains a distinctly Black American flavor through the orchestration of a tenor banjo, blues elements, and the prefacing of each movement with a quotation from Black American poet Paul Laurence Dunbar (1872–1906), who often collaborated with Still. The symphony was conceived as part of an orchestral trilogy beginning with the suite "Africa" (1930), followed by Symphony No. 1, to represent life in the US up until Emancipation, and ending with Symphony No. 2, "Song of a New Race" (1937), depicting a racially integrated society.

Still also produced numerous vocal works, including his choral ballad of "And They Lynched Him on a Tree" (with text by American poet Katherine Garrison Chapin), composed in 1940.

◁ **INSTRUMENTALIST**
Still was a proficient performer on several instruments, including cello and violin. This knowledge informed his compositions in the string quartet genre, particularly the Little Folk Suite from the Western Hemisphere #1-6, Lyric String Quartet, and the "Danzas de Panama."

◁ *MINIATURES*, 1963
While Still's orchestral works are well-known, he also composed numerous chamber works, such as *Miniatures*, a collection of five works including "Jesus is a Rock in a Weary Land" and "Yaravi," a reference to the Inca civilization.

This dramatic, multi-movement work is scored for two separate choirs, white and Black, narrator, solo mezzo soprano, and orchestra. The theme was topical (Billie Holiday's song "Strange Fruit" had been released in 1939), because an anti-lynching law had recently passed through the US House of Representatives but failed in the Senate.

Still wrote eight operas. His opera *Troubled Island* (1937–1949), with a libretto by Langston Hughes and Still's second wife, Verna Arvey, was premiered by the New York City Opera in 1949. It was the first opera by a person of color to be produced by a major company.

## Record label

In addition to performing, composing, and arranging, Still served as music director of Black Swan Records, a company named after Black American soprano Elizabeth Taylor Greenfield (nicknamed the "Black Swan") and designed for Black Americans. Outside of classical music, he also scored for television and film.

Still died in 1978. His widely accessible, Neo-Romantic style continues to make him a favorite among audiences today.

### IN PROFILE
### W. C. Handy

Still's early career benefited from his collaboration with William Christopher Handy (W. C. Handy), widely known as the "Father of the Blues." Born in Alabama in 1873, to parents who had once been enslaved, Handy was influenced by spirituals in his early musical life. Disregarding his pastor father's ban on secular music, Handy learned to play the cornet and became involved in bands.

Still's contact with Handy began in 1915 when he played in Handy's ensemble in Memphis, Tennessee, and then worked as an arranger for Handy the following year. Still's first published arrangement was Handy's song "Hesitating Blues." In 1918, Handy relocated to New York City, where the two men continued to collaborate. They became prominent voices of the Harlem Renaissance, and the blues style remained an important aspect of Still's work, as in the "Afro-American Symphony."

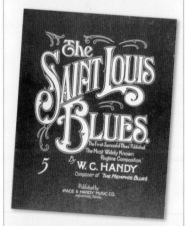

SHEET MUSIC COVER FOR HANDY'S "SAINT LOUIS BLUES," 1914

▷ **FRANCIS POULENC, 1920**
Despite Poulenc's homosexuality being an open secret that could have had him arrested by the Nazis during World War II, he remained in Paris, performing and composing patriotic and anti-German music in support of the French resistance. He is pictured here in his early twenties.

# Francis Poulenc

## 1899–1963, FRENCH

Poulenc made his name in the 1920s as one of the young composers known as Les Six, his witty, irreverent music matching his carefree life; but he later developed a more serious compositional style.

It is tempting to ascribe the two key aspects of Francis Poulenc's music, the serious and the light, to his parents: his father was a successful industrialist and a devout Catholic; his mother a bohemian amateur pianist with an eclectic taste in music. Francis was born in Paris in 1899. The expectation was that he would pursue a career in the family's pharmaceutical business, and so he had little formal musical education. However, he did take piano lessons with Spanish pianist Ricardo Viñes.

## Inspiration and early work

When Poulenc's parents died in his teenage years, Viñes became a key figure in his life. Through Viñes, he met the eccentric composer Erik Satie and his young protégés. Poulenc was also introduced to avant-garde poets such as Guillaume Apollinaire and Paul Eluard, and was inspired to try his hand at composing, despite being largely self-taught.

His first pieces, including the well-known *Trois mouvements perpétuels* for piano, showed a natural talent for attractive, melodic music with a touch of gentle parody, and established him as a composer.

◁ ROCAMADOUR
During a troubled time in his life, Poulenc visited the pilgrimage site of Rocamadour in southwestern France. It proved a turning point, reigniting his faith and inspiring him to write religious music.

▷ *LE GROUPE DES SIX*
Five of the musicians who formed Les Six are shown here, flanking female pianist Marcelle Meyer (not one of the six). Left, from the bottom: Tailleferre, Milhaud, Honegger; right: Auric (seated) and Poulenc. Also shown (in the background) are composer Jean Wiéner (top left) and writer Jean Cocteau (top right).

In 1920, at a concert of new music by some of Satie's protégés (Poulenc, Arthur Honegger, Darius Milhaud, Georges Auric, Germaine Tailleferre, and Louis Durey), the composers were dubbed by a critic as simply Les Six, a name that stuck, even though they had little in common. Poulenc was perhaps the most successful of the group in the 1920s, gaining a reputation as a *bon vivant* as well as a composer of urbane and witty music such as the ballet *Les Biches*, and a host of songs setting poems by Apollinaire and Eluard.

## Troubled times

Privately, however, Poulenc was prone to depression, especially as he tried to come to terms with his homosexuality. From 1930, in a transition that was perhaps triggered by the death of his childhood friend Raymonde Linossier, his music became more serious and reflective of a bleaker mental state.

In 1936, Poulenc visited the beautiful French pilgrimage site of Rocamadour, and rediscovered his Catholic faith. This prompted a series of religious works, beginning with the *Litanies à la Vierge Noire de Rocamadour* and the Mass in G major.

After World War II, Poulenc found success as a pianist and accompanist, but his compositions were thought by the avant-garde to be conventional and lightweight; even the profound *Stabat Mater* and dark operas such as *La Voix humaine* and *Dialogues des Carmélites*—which tells the story of Carmelite nuns who were guillotined at the end of the French Revolution for refusing to renounce their calling— did not receive the serious attention they deserved until the 21st century.

### IN PROFILE
### Pierre Bernac

Poulenc was a hugely accomplished pianist, and performed and recorded many of his own works. In the 1920s, he began a musical partnership with the young singer Pierre Bernac, who, like Poulenc himself, was born in Paris in 1899. Bernac's light baritone voice was suited to the French *chanson* (song), and early in his career he began performing Poulenc's songs, including the premiere of the *Chansons gaillardes*.

Poulenc was greatly impressed by Bernac's interpretation of his music, and in the 1930s became his accompanist in a series of recitals, tours, and recordings of the many songs that Poulenc had written for him, continuing until Bernac's retirement in 1960.

" In **Poulenc** there is something of **the monk** and something of **the rascal**. "

CLAUDE ROSTAND

# Dmitri Shostakovich

**1906–1975, RUSSIAN**

Regarded as the foremost composer of his generation, Shostakovich successfully developed an original and sometimes rebellious musical style, despite the constraints of the Stalinist establishment.

◁ **PETROGRAD, 1920**
The Communist International Congress in Shostakovich's home town (formerly St. Petersburg). The city was named Leningrad after the death of Lenin (shown left) in 1924.

## Innovation and development

This was the beginning of his uneasy relationship with the Soviet musical establishment, reflected in the development of his unique style: his desire to experiment and innovate had always to be tempered by accessibility, a hybrid of several different styles within an "acceptable," conventionally classical framework. As a result, his music is often ambiguous and unsettling, sometimes with a touch of satire, or even bitter irony in its tone. His first major composition was the Symphony No. 1, which he wrote as his graduation piece in 1926. Despite his perceived lack of commitment to the Soviet aesthetic, Shostakovich eventually graduated from the Conservatory that year, aged just 19. Intending to make his name as a concert pianist, he moved to Moscow, but in the face of fierce competition decided instead to devote his time and effort to composing.

Encouraged by the success of his Symphony No. 1, which had been performed in Germany and the US, he wrote the Second Symphony, which

Dmitri Dmitriyevich Shostakovich was born in 1906 in St. Petersburg, a city whose changing names reflected the seismic changes in Russia during his lifetime; it was renamed Petrograd in 1914, and then became known as Leningrad in 1924, reverting to its original name in 1991. His father, of Polish descent, had moved there from Siberia, as had his mother, an amateur musician. Dmitri began piano lessons with his mother at the age of nine— he soon showed remarkable talent, and a particular interest in composing.

At the age of 13, he was admitted to the Petrograd Conservatory, whose alumni included Tchaikovsky and Prokofiev. Since the revolutions of 1917, however, the Conservatory had become less tolerant of innovation, and the curriculum was prescribed by Soviet ideology. As a young composer, Shostakovich had little interest in emulating the great Russian composers, preferring the exciting new music of Stravinsky and Prokofiev, a tendency that was frowned on by his teachers.

◁ **DMITRI SHOSTAKOVICH**
The composer is pictured here as a young man in his thirties, working on a score that is believed to be to his Symphony No. 7, known as "Leningrad."

**LAVRENTIY PAVLOVICH BERIA, HEAD OF THE SOVIET SECRET POLICE, THE NKVD**

> " **Real music** is always **revolutionary**, for it **cements** the **ranks** of **the people**; it **arouses** them and **leads** them **onward**. "

DMITRI SHOSTAKOVICH, "THE POWER OF MUSIC," *MUSIC JOURNAL*, SEPTEMBER 1965

# "A **creative artist** works on his **next composition** because he is **not satisfied** with his **previous one**. "

DMITRI SHOSTAKOVICH, *NEW YORK TIMES*, OCTOBER 25, 1959

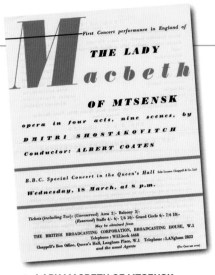

△ **LADY MACBETH OF MTSENSK**
This is the program cover for the first concert performance in England of Shostakovich's opera. It was held at Queen's Hall, London, in March 1935.

△ **THE NOSE**
Based on a satirical short story by Nikolai Gogol, Shostakovich's opera *The Nose* is performed here in 2016 by London's Royal Opera, conducted by Ingo Metzmacher and directed by Barrie Kosky, at the Royal Opera House, Covent Garden.

although pro-Soviet in its intent, was too experimental to gain full approval from the musical establishment after its first performance in 1927.

He was also working on an opera, *The Nose*, and a Third Symphony; both premiered in 1930. *The Nose* in particular attracted criticism from the authorities—who misunderstood its satirical nature—and stinging reviews condemning its incomprehensible modernity. This response was a lesson to Shostakovich in how far he could go before incurring the wrath of the establishment, and the dangers he faced in his next major project, the opera *Lady Macbeth of the Mtsensk District*, completed in 1934. The opera

was enthusiastically received by audiences as well as the authorities. But the good times were short-lived. Shostakovich's marriage to Nina Varzar ended in divorce in 1935, but they remarried shortly after when Nina discovered she was pregnant (their daughter, Galina, was born in 1936 and a son, Maxim, in 1938).

In 1936, Shostakovich was advised to attend a performance of *Lady Macbeth of the Mtsensk District* at which Stalin would be present. It soon became clear to the terrified composer that Stalin disapproved of the opera, which was then slated in the official newspaper, *Pravda*. Shostakovich was summoned by Platon Kerzhentsev, the chairman of the USSR State Committee on Culture and denounced for "Formalism"—the catch-all criticism aimed at those who ignored the tastes of the proletariat, and did not write music that sought to glorify the Soviet state.

Shostakovich thus struggled to find work as a composer. He had finished his Fourth Symphony, but withdrew it before its first performance, fearing further sanctions or even worse, as Stalin had his political opponents and their supporters summarily removed.

In a bid to restore his reputation, he completed the Fifth Symphony in 1937, which was written in a less

challenging style. Dubbed by the establishment as "a Soviet artist's creative response to just criticism," the symphony was accepted as a gesture of good faith, and Shostakovich was offered a post at the Leningrad Conservatory to teach composition.

### The war years

At the beginning of World War II, he tried to enlist in the Soviet Army, but was refused because of his very poor eyesight. He remained in Leningrad as a firefighter, leaving only when the German attack on the city turned into a lengthy siege (see box, opposite). Shostakovich and his family were evacuated to Kuibyshev, where he finished his Seventh Symphony, which he had begun in Leningrad. The siege dragged on and the symphony, seen as a symbol of resistance to the German oppressors, was given the title "Leningrad." It was premiered in Kuibyshev in March 1942, and later that year given a moving performance in Leningrad by the few surviving

# KEY WORKS

| **1925** | **1934** | **1937** | **1938** | **1942** | **1953** | **1974** |
| --- | --- | --- | --- | --- | --- | --- |
| Completes Symphony No. 1 in F minor as a graduation piece at the Petrograd Conservatory. | First performance of the opera *Lady Macbeth of the Mtsensk District*, based on a novel by Nikolai Leskov. | Symphony No. 5 in D minor, written in response to the denunciation of his experimental work, is enthusiastically received in Leningrad. | Completes the first of his 15 string quartets, which are both more personal and more adventurous than his orchestral oeuvre. | Symphony No. 7 in C major, "Leningrad," is performed in the besieged city. | Symphony No. 10 in E minor restores Shostakovich's reputation after being denounced by the establishment for a second time. | Completes his last major work, String Quartet No. 15 in E-flat minor. |

members of the Leningrad Radio Orchestra, along with whatever musicians could be found in the city.

Shostakovich was expected to produce more patriotic music to boost morale. In 1943, now living in Moscow, he completed his Eighth Symphony, but far from uplifting, it depicted the dark aspects of war. The government first saw it as anti-Soviet, but put a positive spin on it by dubbing it the "Stalingrad" symphony, as if in honor of the fallen of the Battle of Stalingrad.

In the immediate postwar years, Shostakovich's relationship with the authorities eased, although he reacted against the increase in antisemitism in Russia with works incorporating Jewish themes. But in general, he adopted a lighter, more conservative style of composition, and in 1947 was rewarded for his services by being made a deputy to the Supreme Soviet.

## Humiliation and decline

However, the following year, in a reign of terror led by Andrei Zhdanov, chairman of the RSFSR Supreme Soviet, he and a number of his fellow composers were denounced for Formalism. He was dismissed from the Conservatory and forced to make a public apology. His humiliation was compounded when he was selected as a representative to the Cultural and Scientific Congress for World Peace in

New York in 1949, and paraded before the world's press as a puppet of the Soviet state. Only after Stalin's death in 1953 did he achieve rehabilitation of his status with the Tenth Symphony, one of his most popular works.

Shostakovich's wife, Nina, died in 1954, and although it is rumored that he had affairs with at least two of his students in the 1940s and 1950s, when he remarried it was to a Leninist activist, Margarita Kainova, in 1956. The marriage ended in divorce just three years later, and he married his third wife, 27-year-old Irina Supinskaya, in 1962.

By the mid-1960s, Shostakovich was becoming increasingly ill. He was diagnosed as suffering from polio, although it seems more likely that his condition was motor neuron disease. In the final decade of his life, he gradually lost the use of most of his limbs and had a number of falls resulting in broken bones. His sight was also severely restricted, and he suffered a number of heart attacks, not helped by his lifelong heavy smoking and drinking. Nevertheless, he continued composing for as long as he was able to wield a pencil. He died of lung cancer in 1975.

△ **FIREFIGHTING, 1941**
Shostakovich is pictured with a hose on the roof of the Leningrad Conservatoire in his role as a firefighter in the first year of the siege of Leningrad (1941–1944) during World War II.

# Margaret Bonds

## 1913–1972, AMERICAN

Belonging to an esteemed group of American composers, Margaret Bonds drew on a wide range of influences, integrating Black idioms and classical musical forms, particularly solo vocal settings.

Composer, pianist, and educator Margaret Allison Bonds was born in Chicago in 1913. Her mother, Estella C. Bonds Majors was a musician and teacher, and her father, Dr. Monroe Alpheus Majors, a medical doctor, writer, and civil rights activist. Bonds studied piano and music theory with her mother, who exposed her to the work of the leading Black American composers of the time.

As a teenager, Bonds received scholarships from the Coleridge-Taylor School of Music in Chicago and began attending Northwestern University to study piano and composition. Due to racism, the library became a place of refuge, where she encountered the work of Black American poet Langston Hughes. His poem "The Negro Speaks of Rivers" became a rallying cry for her.

Bonds graduated with a master's degree in 1934. Within five years, she established The Allied Arts Academy and became the first Black American featured soloist with the Chicago Women's Symphony.

### East and West coasts

In 1939, Bonds left Chicago for New York, where she stayed for nearly 30 years. She worked at the Apollo Theater in Harlem and enrolled at the Juilliard School of Music, where she

studied composition with Roy Harris, who encouraged her interest in combining American folk music and the classical aesthetic. During this time, she wrote her first song cycle, *Five Creek Freedman Spirituals*, and *Songs of the Seasons*, settings for four poems by Hughes.

In 1967, Bonds moved to Los Angeles, hoping to work in the film industry. Although this did not happen, she became the Director of the Inner City Repertory Theater, directing musicals, and also taught piano and music theory at the Inner City Institute. Under pressure to create new works, she composed her final

◁ **SOLO RECITAL**
In addition to composing, Bonds toured as a concert pianist. She performed her debut at New York City's Town Hall on February 7, 1952, playing pieces by C.P.E. Bach, Beethoven, Coleridge-Taylor, Roy Harris, and two compositions of her own.

song cycle, *Pot Pourri*, from poems by Janice Lovoos and Edmund Penney. More than half of her works were vocal compositions. Earlier songs were influenced by Black spirituals, such as "He's Got the Whole World in His Hands," while songs after 1960 contain more complicated harmonies.

### Lasting influence

Bonds died in 1972. Her legacy for Black composers resonated well beyond her lifetime. Many of her unpublished works were discovered posthumously. A few of her surviving compositions show her commitment to social justice. They include "The Montgomery Variations" (1964), a symphonic work inspired by the racist bombing of a church in Birmingham, Alabama, that led to the deaths of four Black girls, and a large-scale choral work, "Credo," written in 1965, and featuring texts by civil rights activist W.E.B. Du Bois. Bonds' surviving works and papers are stored at Yale and Georgetown universities.

### IN PROFILE
### Langston Hughes

A central figure of the Harlem Renaissance, poet Langston Hughes inspired generations of Black American writers, musicians, and artists. His poetry demonstrated a jazz sensibility, where rhyme and rhythm reign supreme.

Bonds met Hughes in 1936 and remained close friends with him until his death in 1967. During the 1950s, she composed several works based on poems by Hughes. One of the most popular among choirs is *Three Dream Portraits*: "Minstrel Man," "Dream Variations," and "I, Too, Sing America."

**LANGSTON HUGHES, 1954**

> " Her music is **lush and full**. It has many phrases that **sound a little jazzy** and that speak to me in a **different way**. "

VERONICA CHAPMAN-SMITH, OPERA PHILADELPHIA

▷ **MARGARET BONDS, c.1940**
Bonds' move to New York City in 1939 marked the beginning of her most fruitful period, when she composed, performed, and studied, and became involved in musical theater.

# Directory

## Alexander Glazunov

1865–1936, RUSSIAN

Born in St. Petersburg, Glazunov began composing at the age of 11 and was taught by Rimsky-Korsakov. The success of his First Symphony, premiered when he was 16, won him precocious entry into the circle of composers patronized by Russian music publisher Mitrofan Belyayev. By the 1890s, he had formed his mature style, blending Romanticism with Classicism and Russian with Western influences. A stream of symphonies, concertos, ballets, and chamber works secured his place as a composer of international standing.

In 1905, Glazunov became director of the St. Petersburg Conservatory, a position he retained after the 1917 Bolshevik Revolution (when he numbered Shostakovich among his pupils), but he moved to the West in 1928. Dismissive of musical Modernism, he was sometimes criticized as old-fashioned by the time of his death in France in 1936.

**KEY WORKS:** Symphony No.4 in E-flat major, Op. 48, 1893; *The Seasons* (ballet), Op. 67, 1900; Violin Concerto in A minor, Op. 82, 1904; Concerto for Alto Saxophone, Op. 109, 1934

## Ferruccio Busoni

1866–1924, ITALIAN

A composer, pianist, and theoretician, Busoni was a major figure in the transition from Romanticism to Modernism. The son of musicians, he was a child prodigy in both piano and composition. He led a cosmopolitan life from an early age and, although born in Tuscany, was more German than Italian in culture. His spectacular performances as a virtuoso and his transcriptions of Bach for piano often overshadowed his compositions. Innovative and eclectic, his extensive oeuvre included a piano concerto with a choral finale, works based on Indigenous folksong, and experiments with atonality. Busoni's 1907 treatise *Entwurf einer neuen Ästhetik der Tonkunst* (*Sketch of a New Aesthetic of Music*) was a prophetic manifesto of 20th-century music, predicting use of microtones and electronic sounds. His later years were chiefly devoted to an opera, *Doktor Faust*, which was never completed but which generated material for over 20 "satellite" works.

**KEY WORKS:** Piano Concerto in C major, Op. 39, 1904; *Berceuse élégiaque* (orchestra), Op. 42, 1909; *Fantasia Contrappuntisca* (piano solo), 1910; *Doktor Faust* (opera, incomplete), 1924

## ▽ Enrique Granados

1867–1916, SPANISH

The son of a Spanish army officer, Granados grew up in Barcelona. He was a pupil of the composer Felipe Pedrell, who encouraged him to take an interest in Spanish folk music. After two years in France, he returned to Barcelona in 1889 and established a reputation as a piano virtuoso. His first successful compositions were the folk-influenced *Danzas españolas* (*Spanish Dances*) for piano, followed by the opera *María del Carmen*, premiered in 1898. The Goya-inspired suite of piano pieces, *Goyescas,* is considered his masterpiece. He developed the work into an opera of the same name, which premiered in New York in 1916. Returning from the US during World War I, he was drowned when his ship was sunk by a German submarine.

**KEY WORKS:** *Danzas españolas* (piano solo), 1888–1890; *María del Carmen* (opera), 1898; *Goyescas* (piano solo), 1911

△ **ENRIQUE GRANADOS, 1903.**

## Alexander Scriabin

1872–1915, RUSSIA

Composer, pianist, and mystic Scriabin was born in Moscow; his father was an aristocratic soldier, his mother a concert pianist. He studied piano alongside Rachmaninoff under Nikolai Zverev and attended the Moscow Conservatory. His early piano compositions were influenced by Chopin and Liszt. In 1897, he became a teacher at the Conservatory. His First Symphony, an ambitious work with a choral finale, appeared in 1900. From around 1903, the style of his works evolved away from conventional tonality.

In 1904, Scriabin left Russia and moved to Switzerland where, separated from his wife, he started a second family with Tatiana Schloezer. He adopted mystical ideas and pursued equivalences between colors and sounds—his *Prometheus, the Poem of Fire* (1910), had color projection as part of the score. He planned a multimedia work, *Mysterium*, which, performed in the Himalayas, would bring a blissful end to the world. After returning to Russia, he died of blood poisoning.

**KEY WORKS:** *Twelve Etudes* (piano solo), Op. 8, 1894; Piano Sonata No. 4 in F-sharp major, Op. 30, 1903; *Poem of Ecstasy* (orchestra), Op. 54, 1908; Five Preludes (piano solo), Op. 47, 1914

## Josef Suk

1874–1935, CZECH

Violinist and composer Josef Suk was introduced to music by his father, a village teacher and choirmaster. He entered the Prague Conservatory at the age of 11 and had written several of his most successful works by age 20. He became the favorite pupil of Antonin Dvořák, and married Dvořák's daughter Otilie in 1898. The happiness of this period of his life is reflected in his incidental music for the play *Radúz a Mahulena* (1898).

The deaths of both Dvořák and Otilie in 1904–1905 inspired the grief-stricken symphony *Asrael*, considered his finest work. In his later music, such as the symphonic poem *Ripening*, he adopted a more Modernist style, exploring polytonality. He played as a violinist with the Czech Quartet for 40 years. Much of his energy later in life was devoted to teaching composition at the Prague Conservatory.

**KEY WORKS:** *Serenade for Strings*, Op. 6, 1892; *Asrael* (symphony), Op. 27, 1906; *Ripening* (orchestra and chorus), Op. 34, 1917; *Epilog* (orchestra, soloists and chorus), Op. 37, 1929

## Ottorino Respighi

1879–1936, ITALIAN

One of Italy's most popular composers, Respighi was born in Bologna and studied at the city's *liceo musicale*. As an orchestral viola player he spent time in Russia, where he was taught composition by Rimsky-Korsakov, whose flamboyant orchestration he adopted. He built up his early reputation chiefly as a composer of operas and concert pieces for voice and orchestra.

From 1913, Respighi was based in Rome, where he taught at the St. Cecilia Academy. Largely indifferent to Modernism, he cultivated an eclectic interest in musical history, writing orchestral suites based on old Italian lute pieces and using Rossini melodies for his 1919 ballet *La Boutique fantasque*. He discovered his most successful genre with the symphonic poem *Fountains of Rome* in 1916. Colorful and atmospheric, his three works on Roman themes earned him wealth and fame. In later life, he was courted by Mussolini's Fascist regime but remained apolitical.

**KEY WORKS:** *Il tramonto* (voice and strings), 1914; *Fountains of Rome* (symphonic poem), 1916; *Pines of Rome* (symphonic poem), 1924; *Roman Festivals* (symphonic poem), 1928

△ PERCY GRAINGER, BY FRENCH PAINTER JACQUES-EMILE BLANCHE, 1906

## Karol Szymanowski

1882–1937, POLISH

Szymanowski was born into a Polish landowning family in Ukraine. Showing musical talent from an early age, he first attracted attention as a member of the radical Young Poland group of composers in Warsaw in 1905. His music was initially influenced by German models, notably Richard Strauss, but journeys to Sicily and North Africa stimulated a fascination with Mediterranean culture. During World War I, isolated on his family's estate in Ukraine, Szymanowski produced an impressive series of works reflecting this exotic interest, as well as the influence of contemporary French composers. Caught up by nationalist enthusiasm after Poland's declaration of independence in 1918, he sought inspiration in the folk music of the Tatra Mountains, attempting to create an authentic modern Polish music. He was appointed head of the Warsaw Conservatory in 1927, but his work was better liked outside Poland than within. From 1932, he lived mostly abroad, dying in a sanatorium in Switzerland.

**KEY WORKS:** *Myths* (violin and piano), Op. 30, 1915; Violin Concerto No. 1, Op. 35, 1916; *Król Roger* (opera), Op. 46, 1924; Symphony No. 4 (piano and orchestra), Op. 60, 1932

## △ Percy Grainger

1882–1961, AUSTRALIAN-AMERICAN

A composer, pianist, and folksong collector, Grainger was born in Melbourne, Australia, and educated by his mother at home. After attending the Hoch Conservatory in Frankfurt, he began a career as a concert pianist in London in 1901. While living in England, he collected folk songs, touring the countryside with a phonograph. His own compositions started to make an impact from 1911, consisting chiefly of short pieces and songs, which were often organized into suites. His arrangements of folk music, such as the suite *Country Gardens*, proved to be particularly successful for him.

In 1914, Grainger moved to the US, where from 1917 to 1919 he played in a US Army band. He later took US nationality. However, his creative output waned considerably after his mother's tragic death by suicide in 1922. In his later years, he argued for the democratization of music and advocated use of an electronic instrument, the theremin. He died at White Plains, New York in 1961.

**KEY WORKS:** *Hill Song No. 1* (two pianos), 1901; *Molly on the Shore* (strings), 1911; *Country Gardens* (solo piano), 1919

## Edgard Varèse

1883–1965, FRENCH

Varèse was an innovative and influential composer known for his avant-garde approach to music. He spent his early childhood in France, and studied mathematics and engineering in Turin, Italy, before focusing solely on music. Varèse moved to the US in 1915, where he worked as a conductor and composer, helping to organize the International Composers' Guild (1921–1927) and the Pan American Association of Composers (1928–1934).

As a composer, Varèse explored ways to manifest his language of "organized sound," writing music featuring dense rhythmic complexity, extensive percussion, atonality, unconventional forms, and electronic or tape-recorded sounds. In the 1950s, following a period of financial difficulties and creative stagnation, Varèse advanced his pioneering ideas through professional performances and recordings of his trailblazing pieces, most notably for percussion and stereo-panned electronic tape.

**KEY WORKS:** *Ionisation*, 1933; *Déserts*, 1954; *Poème électronique*, 1958

## Anton Webern

1883–1945, AUSTRIAN

Modernist composer Webern was born into a privileged family and studied music at the University of Vienna. His early compositions, such as the tone poem *Im Sommerwind* (1904), were in a lush late-Romantic vein. In 1904, he became a pupil of Arnold Schoenberg, who guided his evolution toward atonal music.

Webern's grief at the death of his mother in 1906 found expression in the powerful *Six Pieces for Orchestra*, first performed at the infamous "Scandal Concert" in Vienna in 1913, when the audience rioted against the music's experimentalism.

In the 1920s, as a member of the Schoenberg-led Second Viennese School, Webern adopted 12-tone serial technique, but his style was idiosyncratic in its compression, brevity, and elusive beauty. From 1922 to 1934, he conducted a workers' orchestra in Vienna. In his later years, Webern lived a withdrawn life. He was shot dead by a US soldier during the Allied occupation of Austria in 1945.

**KEY WORKS:** *Six Pieces for Orchestra*, Op. 6, 1910; *Six Bagatelles* (string quartet), Op. 9, 1913; *Variations for piano*, Op. 27, 1936; *Cantata No. 1*, Op. 29, 1939

## Alban Berg

1885–1935, AUSTRIAN

A member of the Second Viennese School, Berg's emotion-laden music harked back to late Romanticism using Modernist composition techniques. Born into a wealthy Viennese family, he had a difficult adolescence and failed at school. He began composing songs at the age of 15 but lacked any formal training until Schoenberg took him on as a pupil in 1904. One of Berg's first major works was the *Altenberg Lieder*, which premiered at the "Scandal Concert" in Vienna in 1913.

△ **FLORENCE PRICE**

After serving in the Austro-Hungarian Army during World War I, Berg completed the Expressionist opera *Wozzeck*. Performed by the Berlin State Opera in 1925, it earned him great notoriety. His music was denounced by the Nazi Party as being degenerate and was virtually banned following its rise to power in Germany in 1933. Berg's last completed work, the celebrated Violin Concerto, was written as an elegy for Alma Mahler's daughter.

At the age of 50, Berg died of septicemia following an insect bite, leaving his opera *Lulu* unfinished.

**KEY WORKS:** *Altenberg Lieder* (soprano and orchestra), Op. 4, 1912; *Wozzeck* (opera), Op. 7, 1922; *Lyric Suite* (string quartet), 1926; Violin Concerto, 1935

## △ Florence Price

1887–1953, AMERICAN

Price was the first Black American woman composer to have her works performed by major US orchestras. Born in Little Rock, Arkansas, 26 years after the end of enslavement, she left school at age 14 and enrolled at the New England Conservatory, where she studied with Benjamin Cutter and George Chadwick.

By the early 1900s, Price had already written her first compositions. She began to achieve notable success

in the 1930s, after winning the Wanamaker Foundation Award in 1932. Price wrote more than 300 works including art songs, symphonies, choral works, concertos, works for piano, violin, and organ. Her early style demonstrates a cross-pollination of Black idioms and the Classical aesthetic. Other works reflect her penchant for the Dvořákian richness and harmonic language that were prominent during the Romantic and Post-Romantic eras. In 2009, some abandoned works were discovered in her summer home in St. Anne, Illinois.

**KEY WORKS:** "Fantasie Nègre No. 2 in G minor," 1929; "Symphony in E-minor," 1931–32; "Songs to the Dark Virgin," 1935; "My Soul's Been Anchored in the Lord," 1937

## Bohuslav Martinů

1890–1959, CZECH

Prolific Czech composer Martinů was born to poor parents in a rural town in Bohemia. Impressed by his violin-playing, townspeople paid for him to attend the Prague Conservatory. His first success as a composer came with a cantata celebrating Czechoslovakia's independence, premiered in 1919. He played as an orchestral violinist and in 1923 moved to Paris, where he was influenced by the fashions for jazz and Neo-

Classicism. He survived poverty with the aid of a seamstress, Charlotte Quennehen, whom he married in 1931. He established a growing reputation with his ballets, operas, orchestral pieces, and concertos before the Nazi occupation of France in 1940 drove him to flee to the US.

Living in the US until 1953, he produced numerous works, including six symphonies, a violin concerto, and an opera commissioned for television. He returned to Europe for his final years, dying in Switzerland.

**KEY WORKS:** *La Revue de cuisine* (ballet), 1927; *Double Concerto for Two String Orchestras, Piano and Timpani*, 1938; Symphony No. 1, 1942; *The Greek Passion* (opera), 1957.

## Arthur Honegger

1892–1955, SWISS

A member of the group of Parisian composers known as Les Six, Honegger was born in France to Swiss parents. He studied at the conservatory in Zurich before moving to the Paris Conservatoire in 1911 and settling in Montmartre, where he spent most of his life.

Honegger established an early reputation with works such as the 1918 ballet *Le Dit des jeux du monde*, before his oratorio *Le Roi David* brought international renown. Associated with Les Six by friendship rather than compositional style, he produced a string of thoroughly individual works, some reflecting his extra-musical interests in sports and locomotives. As well as heavyweight orchestral and choral pieces, he wrote popular operettas and film music, including the score for Abel Gance's epic *Napoléon* (1926). His later life was darkened by illness and somber reflections on the state of the world.

**KEY WORKS:** *Le Roi David* (oratorio), 1921; *Pacific 231* (Symphonic Movement No 1), 1923; *Jeanne d'Arc au bûcher* (oratorio), 1935; Symphony No. 3 ("Symphonie liturgique"), 1946

## Paul Hindemith

1895–1963, GERMAN

Composer and musical thinker Hindemith was born in Frankfurt am Main. A gifted string player as a youth, he studied at the local conservatory and played in several orchestras and string quartets. After army service in World War I, he made his name as an avant-garde composer in the 1920s, writing chamber music for unusual combinations of instruments. He was appointed head of the Berlin music academy in 1927.

Following the Nazis' rise to power in Germany in 1933, Hindemith's music was banned and he was forced into exile. He lived in Turkey, where he reformed musical education, before moving to the US in 1940. He continued to be a prolific composer, producing larger-scale works from the 1930s onward. As a teacher and theoretician, he proposed an anti-Romantic view of composition as a practical craft. He wrote music for amateurs and children to play, as well as formal works. In his later years, he lived mostly in Switzerland.

**KEY WORKS:** *Kleine Kammermusik* (wind quintet), 1922; *Mathis der Maler* (orchestra), 1934; *Der Schwanendreher* (viola and orchestra), 1935; *Symphonic Metamorphosis of Themes by Weber*, 1943

## ▽ Carl Orff

1895–1982, GERMAN

Famous for his choral work *Carmina Burana*, Orff was born in Munich. Precociously talented, he had written ambitious works by the age of 20. He was wounded during World War I, and after the war studied Renaissance and Baroque music. He also worked on an experimental approach to teaching music through drama, rhythmic movement, and dance, first employed in a school founded by Dorothee Günther in Munich in 1924.

Orff belatedly won recognition as a composer with the performance of *Carmina Burana* in Frankfurt in 1937. His success during the period of the Hitler dictatorship in Germany led to accusations of complicity with Nazism. Many of his later works reflected his interest in classical antiquity. He wrote books of children's music for his educational method, the Schulwerk, in the 1930s and '50s.

**KEY WORKS:** *Carmina Burana* (cantata), 1937; *Catulli Carmina* (cantata), 1943; *Antigonae* (opera), 1949

## George Gershwin

1898–1937, AMERICAN

Gershwin was a renowned composer of Broadway show tunes, concertos, operas, and film scores. Born in Brooklyn to a Jewish family, he began studying piano in 1911 and was soon working as a pianist and songwriter for the popular music industry; his breakthrough came with "Swanee," recorded by Al Jolson. Gershwin collaborated with Broadway directors and formed a songwriting partnership with his brother, Ira, as lyricist. Some of his successes—such as *Rhapsody in Blue* (1924), the more classically focused *Piano Concerto in F* (1925), and the folk opera *Porgy and Bess* (1935)—blended jazz and classical styles. In recent years, *Porgy and Bess* has provoked controversy due to its racial stereotypes. Gershwin moved to Hollywood to compose for film but died less than two years later after an operation to remove a brain tumor.

**KEY WORKS:** *Rhapsody in Blue*, 1924; *Piano Concerto in F*, 1925; *An American in Paris*, 1928, *Porgy and Bess*, 1935

## Kurt Weill

1900–1950, GERMAN

A composer whose work bridged the divide between popular and serious music, Weill was born to Jewish parents in Dessau. In the early 1920s he studied composition under Ferruccio Busoni in Berlin and wrote concert works. In 1926, he turned to writing popular musical drama. His collaboration with left-wing poet and playwright Bertolt Brecht began with the satirical *Mahagonny-Songspiel* in 1927. A year later, their *Die Dreigroschenoper*, transposing John Gay's *Threepenny Opera* to modern Berlin, proved a success. Their songs such as *Mack the Knife* became popular hits. Jewish and left-wing, Weill fled Germany when Hitler took power in 1933. Living in the US, he wrote Broadway shows, from the musical comedy *Knickerbocker Glory* to the "folk opera" *Street Scene*.

**KEY WORKS:** *Die Dreigroschenoper*, 1928; *Aufstieg und Fall der Stadt Mahagonny* (opera), 1930; *Knickerbocker Holiday* (operetta), 1938

△ **CARL ORFF, c. 1978**

# LATE 20th & 21st CENTURIES

CHAPTER 6

▷ **JOAQUIN RODRIGO**
The Spanish composer stepped into the international limelight following the premiere of his *Concierto de Aranjuez* in 1940. The work's melancholy Adagio is believed to have been prompted by the tragic stillbirth of his first child.

# Joaquín Rodrigo
## 1901–1999, SPANISH

Blind from childhood, Rodrigo is best known for the enormously popular *Concierto de Aranjuez*, which established his international reputation, and also brought respect for the guitar as a concert instrument.

# "In **life** you can never be **first** in anything ... I only **aspire** to be an improved Joaquín Rodrigo."

JOAQUIN RODRIGO

Joaquín Rodrigo was born in Sagunto on St. Cecilia's day, November 22, 1901. When he was only three years old, he was one of many children in the town who contracted diphtheria, which left him permanently blind. Soon after, the family moved to Valencia, where Joaquín attended a school for the blind, and took his first music lessons on the piano and violin at the age of eight.

As a teenager, he had lessons in music theory with teachers from the Valencia Conservatoire, and began to take an interest in composition, using the Braille system of musical notation to write his music, which he then dictated to a copyist, Rafael Ibáñez. Employed by the family as Joaquín's assistant, Ibáñez shared Rodrigo's love of music and literature and became his constant companion as well as amanuensis and secretary.

## A vibrant new world

By the mid-1920s, Rodrigo's music was being performed in Valencia and Madrid. In 1927, he left Spain with Ibáñez for Paris, to study

under the composer Paul Dukas at the Ecole Normale de Musique. Here, he was also introduced to the vibrant Parisian literary and musical culture, and met the composer Manuel de Falla, who became a lifelong friend, mentor, and champion of his work.

After studying musicology at the Paris Conservatoire and the Sorbonne, Rodrigo traveled around Europe in the 1930s, composing and performing as a concert pianist. It was then that he met Turkish pianist Victoria Kamhi, whom he married in 1933. In 1941, they had a daughter, Cecilia, named after the patron saint of musicians.

Rodrigo was absent from Spain during the Spanish Civil War (1936–1939); in 1939, he and Victoria were living in Paris. But, aware of impending conflict in Europe, they moved to

◁ **CONCIERTO DE ARANJUEZ**
This is a braille manuscript for Rodrigo's *Concierto de Aranjuez*. He wrote all his music in braille, which was then transcribed into standard notation.

Madrid before World War II began. Rodrigo took with him the *Concierto de Aranjuez* for guitar and orchestra, which he had written in Paris and that secured his international reputation.

## Prominent composer

Thereafter, he became a prominent member of the musical establishment, head of music broadcasts for Spanish radio, professor of the history of music at the Complutense University of Madrid, and music critic for national newspapers. He continued to write music, including 11 concertos and orchestral and chamber works, but none of his subsequent compositions achieved the same degree of popular acclaim as the *Concierto de Aranjuez*.

Victoria died in 1997, and Rodrigo died two years later, aged 97. They were buried together in the cemetery at Aranjuez, in the south of Madrid.

IN CONTEXT
## Commissioned concertos

The *Concierto de Aranjuez* was written by Rodrigo for the Spanish guitarist Regino Sáinz de la Maza. Its success prompted other virtuoso soloists to approach him with commissions. He also arranged the work for Spanish harpist Nicanor Zabaleta, who later commissioned the *Concierto serenata* for harp and orchestra from him.

Other of Rodrigo's commissioned works include the *Concierto como un divertimento* for cello for Julian Lloyd Webber; the *Concierto pastoral* for flute for James Galway; the *Concierto Andaluz* for the Romeros Guitar Quartet; and the popular *Fantasía para un gentilhombre* for the guitarist Andrés Segovia.

▽ **GARDENS, PALACE OF ARANJUEZ**
The Palace of Aranjuez, near Madrid, was built by Philip II of Spain in the second half of 16th century. Its stunning gardens were the inspiration for Rodrigo's masterpiece, the *Concierto de Aranjuez*.

◁ **VICTORIA AND JOAQUIN RODRIGO**
Joaquín met Victoria Kamhi during his European travels; they married in 1933. She became his indispensable partner, both emotionally and professionally.

# William Walton

## 1902–1983, BRITISH

From humble beginnings, Walton rose to fame as the darling of London's musical society between the two world wars, living the life of a playboy before settling into semi-retirement on the Italian island of Ischia.

◁ **FACADE, SUITE NO. 1, 1926**
This is the front cover for Suite No. 1 of Walton's *Façade*, composed for Edith Sitwell's eccentric verses. The work brought him fame and popularity.

William Walton was born in Oldham, Lancashire, in 1902. Although not well off, his family was musical and soon recognized William's talents in this field. In 1912, he was accepted into Christ Church Cathedral School in Oxford, where he spent the next six years. It was at this choral school that he began composing.

His abilities gained him a place, aged only 16, as an undergraduate at Christ Church, a college of the University of Oxford. Although he excelled there at music, he neglected other academic subjects, repeatedly failed exams, and left the university without a degree in 1920. However, at Oxford he had become close friends with poets such as Siegfried Sassoon and Sacheverell Sitwell. The latter invited him to lodge in London with his siblings, Edith and Osbert. The Sitwells (see box, right) provided Walton with an attic in Chelsea where he could work, as well as an introduction to London society and its writers, artists, and composers.

### A different kind of music

Walton's work at this time, including an early string quartet, was in an avant-garde, experimental style. But in 1923 he created *Façade*, a new kind of music—surreal verses by poet Edith Sitwell (recited by her at the premiere through a megaphone), accompanied by Walton's jazzy and tongue-in-cheek music for small ensemble. It captured the 1920s zeitgeist, and although many were outraged, Walton had made his mark.

Trading on his reputation, he went on to write more serious orchestral works, including the massive cantata *Belshazzar's Feast* (1931), his First Symphony (1935), and concertos for viola and violin. Having drifted away from the Sitwells, whose influence was on the wane, he embarked on a series of affairs, the most lasting of which was with Alice, Viscountess Wimborne, which began in 1934. He was exempted from military service during World War II so that he could provide music for propaganda films such as *The First of the Few*, and Laurence Olivier's *Henry V*, while living on Alice's estate in Northamptonshire.

### Final movements

After the war, Walton found it difficult to return to composition, particularly after Alice died in 1948. But later that year, at a conference in Buenos Aires, he met, and soon married, Susana Gil Passo, an Argentinian woman.

By now, the composer's music was no longer fashionable, and although he was regarded highly enough to be commissioned to write the coronation march *Orb and Sceptre* for Elizabeth II, his output decreased significantly, especially after an operation for lung cancer in 1966. He and Susana moved permanently to the Mediterranean island of Ischia in 1956, where he died on their estate, La Mortella, in 1983.

◁ **WILLIAM WALTON**
The English composer burst into the limelight in 1923 with his controversial work *Façade*. He went on to become a key figure in mid-20th-century British music and was knighted in 1951.

▷ **THE GARDENS OF LA MORTELLA**
These magnificent gardens were created by Susana Walton, wife of William, at their estate on the island of Ischia, where they moved to in 1956. The gardens were opened to the public in 1991.

▷ **MICHAEL TIPPETT, 1973**
Tippett is pictured here at his piano in his late sixties, three years after he split up with his partner, Karl Hawker. It was also around this time that he moved away from an experimental period in his music to resume the lyricism that had characterized his earlier work. Despite the composer's long-held antiestablishment beliefs, his significant contribution to music was honored in 1966 with a knighthood and in 1983 with the prestigious Order of Merit.

# Michael Tippett

## 1905–1998, BRITISH

A slow and meticulous musical craftsman, Tippett achieved recognition comparatively late in life, but soon came to be regarded as one of the foremost British composers of the latter half of the 20th century.

# "**Music** is a **performance** and **needs** the **audience**. "

MICHAEL TIPPETT

Born into an upper-middle-class family, Michael Tippett was brought up in a liberal atmosphere by his freethinking parents. Soon after his birth, the family moved from Middlesex to Suffolk. Michael and his brother were privately educated by tutors at their home until 1914, when he was sent to a boarding school in Devon, and later gained a scholarship to Fettes College in Edinburgh.

This was, however, no place for a sensitive boy like Michael, who had also discovered he was gay. In 1920, he admitted he had formed a romantic relationship with another boy, and was transferred to Stamford School in Lincolnshire, which had a reputation for musical education. Here he began to flourish—but as his confidence improved, he became outspoken and was asked to leave in 1922.

## A period of development

Tippett enrolled at the Royal College of Music the following year, graduating with a music degree in 1928. His attempts at composing were unsatisfactory, so he returned to take a course in counterpoint, after which he felt ready to begin his career in

△ **FETTES COLLEGE, EDINBURGH**
Tippett was a boarder at the school from 1918 to 1920—he was a member of the choir and also studied piano and the pipe organ. The school's grandiose main building, c.1870, is shown here.

music. To support his composing, he took a job as conductor of the South London Orchestra, a publicly funded ensemble for unemployed musicians. It was a time of important personal as well as musical development: he began a serious relationship with Wilfred Franks, to whom he dedicated his first mature composition, the String Quartet No. 1; he also became more politically active, briefly joining the Communist Party.

However, Tippett's career was interrupted by a crisis of confidence. He was devastated by the end of his relationship with Franks in 1938 and struggling to come to terms with his homosexuality. Doubting his worth as a composer, he embarked on a course of Jungian psychoanalysis. This form of therapy gave him the confidence, and the inspiration, to persevere with his composition free from anxiety over his sexuality. The first work to emerge from this period was the oratorio *A Child of Our Time*.

## Taking a stand

After the outbreak of World War II, Tippett was appointed as director of music at Morley College, London (see box, right). A lifelong pacifist, he registered as a conscientious objector; in 1942, after refusing to take on civilian duties aiding the war effort, he was imprisoned for three months. Following the success of *A Child of Our Time* in 1944, his pacifism, socialism, and homosexuality—all of which were stigmatized in 1940s Britain—were overlooked, and his status so established that he was invited to present a series of talks on BBC radio.

During the 1950s, Tippett lived in Wadhurst, Sussex and in 1960 moved with his partner, Karl Hawker, to Corsham in Wiltshire, where he began to write in an experimental and dissonant style, later influenced by the jazz and blues he had heard on a trip to the US in 1965. After his breakup with Hawker in 1970, he returned to his former lyricism. Despite health issues in the 1980s and early 1990s, he traveled widely, absorbing different musical influences.

Tippett was held in remarkably high esteem, being awarded several national honors. He died in London in 1998, aged 93, following a stroke.

◁ **KING PRIAM, 2014**
The English Touring Opera company is shown here in its production of Michael Tippett's *King Priam*, directed by James Conway and conducted by Michael Rosewell, at the Linbury Studio Theatre, Royal Opera House, London, in 2014.

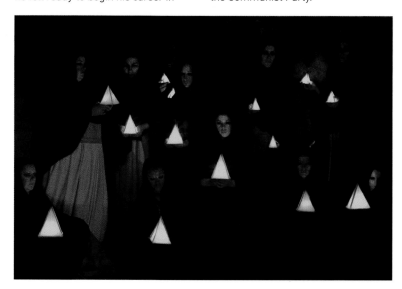

# Olivier Messiaen

## 1908–1992, FRENCH

An outstanding organist, composer, and teacher, Messiaen drew on numerous influences in his work, from Asian rhythms to birdsong, but his constant source of inspiration was his unshakable Catholic faith.

Messiaen was born in the French city of Avignon on December 10, 1908, and was baptized on Christmas Day. Both his parents were highly cultivated. His father, Pierre, was an English teacher and translator of some of Shakespeare's plays, but Olivier was closer to his mother, Cécile Sauvage, a distinguished poet. While pregnant, she wrote a collection of poems for her unborn child: *L'Ame en bourgeon* (*The Budding Soul*). Messiaen treasured them, believing some lines to be prophetic, such as: "I suffer from an unknown, distant music" and "All the Orient is singing here within me, with its blue birds."

### First steps

At the outbreak of World War I, Pierre was conscripted and Olivier moved with his mother to Grenoble. There, his musical gifts soon became apparent. He taught himself to play the rickety old piano in his uncle's house and began making up music of his own. Olivier received some private lessons, but his progress accelerated after the war, when the family moved to Paris. In 1919, aged just 10, he entered the Paris Conservatoire.

Messiaen's teachers at the Conservatoire included Paul Dukas and Marcel Dupré. Regarded as the finest organist of his generation, the latter had a particularly important influence. Under his tutelage, the organ superseded the piano as Messiaen's principal instrument, which was to play an important part in his career. In 1931, Messiaen was

◁ **BABY OLIVIER**
Messiaen is shown here as a baby, sitting on the knees of his mother, poet Cécile Sauvage. The composer later said she raised her children "in a fairy universe."

△ **MARCEL DUPRE**
An atmospheric depiction by Ambrose McEvoy of organist Marcel Dupré at the organ of Notre-Dame, Paris. Dupré was an important early influence on Messiaen.

appointed chief organist at the church of La Ste-Trinité in Paris, a great honor for one so young. He often played there over the next 60 years, although he was careful not to use it for any of his more extravagant experiments. Messiaen reassured his curate in a letter: "In music, one always has to seek what is new, but reserve that for chamber and orchestral works in which fantasy is

> "It is **possible** to **make sounds** on a **piano** that are more **orchestral** than those of an **orchestra**."
>
> OLIVIER MESSIAEN

▷ **OLIVIER MESSIAEN**
One of the most influential figures in modern French music, Messiaen poses in front of the 2,500 or so pages of the score for his opera *St. Francis of Assisi*, his last major work before his death.

△ **CONCERT OF BIRDS**
Increasingly obsessed by ornithology, Messiaen used birdsong as a model for some of his music—these innovative works are some of the most challenging in the piano repertoire. This 17th-century painting of a concert of birds led by an owl choirmaster (center) is by Flemish painter Paul de Vos (c. 1591–1678).

alternative modes in his book *La Technique de mon langage musical* (1944). Messiaen worked backward, from practice to theory. One of his friends at the Conservatoire, Jean Langlais, described how he found the sounds that he liked through improvisation and then developed a system to accommodate them: "he told me later on, he discovered his system by analyzing his own works, the scales and everything. He did not decide before—he discovered afterward."

Messiaen was equally radical in his approach to tempo. He sometimes lengthened individual notes or played them very slowly (occasionally, he marked the tempo as "infinitely slow"). *Le Banquet céleste*, for example, consists of only 25 bars, but when Messiaen performed it, the piece could last for seven or eight minutes. This helped to endow it with a solemn, meditative quality.

### Changing circumstances
Meanwhile, Messiaen's personal circumstances were changing dramatically. In 1927, his mother died. She had been suffering from depression for years, often locking herself away from the family. Shortly afterward, Messiaen met his future wife Claire Delbos, marrying her in 1932. She was a talented violinist and the pair performed a number of recitals together in the early 1930s. Their married life did not run entirely smoothly—Claire suffered a number of miscarriages, before finally giving birth to a son, Pascal, in 1937.

In the same year, Messiaen won a prestigious commission to provide music for the *Fêtes des belles eaux* (a combination of fireworks, light, and water effects) at the World Fair in Paris. For this, he opted to create

admissible." Messiaen's employment at the church did, however, dovetail with his chief source of inspiration as a composer: his faith. A devout Catholic, he often claimed that he was "born believing." Not surprisingly, this was reflected in his choice of material. His first published work was an ethereal organ piece celebrating the Eucharist (*Le Banquet céleste*, or *The Heavenly Feast*, 1928). Similarly, *La Nativité du Seigneur* (*The Nativity of the Lord*, 1935) was his first truly mature work, in which all the various components of his compositional experiments fell neatly into place.

If religion was the dominant theme of Messiaen's work, the driving force behind his creative impulse was a tireless search for new forms. While still a student, he became intrigued by the possibility of looking beyond the traditional modes of Western music—the major and minor scales.

Over the years, he explored the modes of antiquity, the forms of plainsong, and non-European modes (from India, in particular). He also defined a number of new, modern modes and later codified these as "modes of limited transposition," writing at length about the seven

> " **I give bird songs** to those who dwell **in cities** ... and **paint colors** for those **who see none.** "
>
> OLIVIER MESSIAEN

## KEY WORKS

**1935**

Messiaen creates *La Nativité du Seigneur*, his first genuine organ cycle, consisting of nine meditations.

**1941**

The celebrated *Quartet for the End of Time* is written and performed at a German prisoner-of-war camp in eastern Silesia.

**1949**

The premiere of Messiaen's *Turangalîla Symphony*, which draws inspiration from the legend of Tristan and Isolde.

**1953**

Messiaen's *Réveil des oiseaux* (*Awakening of the Birds*) conjures up the sound of birdsong between midnight and noon.

**1970–74**

*From the Canyons to the Stars* is an expansive 12-movement work celebrating the beauty of Bryce Canyon in Utah.

**1975–83**

One of Messiaen's final works is his only opera, a monumental tribute to the career of St. Francis of Assisi.

a futuristic sound by employing a sextet of ondes Martenot. Messiaen was certainly not the first composer to make use of this unusual electronic instrument, but it was to become one of his trademarks (see box, p.280).

Messiaen doubtless hoped for further commissions, but the outbreak of World War II put a brake on his career. Conscripted, he was sent to the front and was captured by the Germans at Verdun. Like thousands of his fellow prisoners, he was forced into a cattle-truck and endured a hellish four-day journey to the east with no food, water, or sanitation.

While imprisoned at Stalag VIIIA in Silesia (see box, right), Messiaen composed and performed one of the major musical landmarks of the

20th century. Played on ramshackle instruments, his *Quartet for the End of Time* was a startling chamber piece for violin, piano, cello, and clarinet— the only options that were available to him. Fittingly, given its wartime context, the theme was drawn from the Apocalypse, as described in the Book of Revelation.

### Repatriation and tragedy

Messiaen was repatriated to France in 1941. He returned to work at Trinité and was also given a teaching job at the Conservatoire. One of his pupils there was a brilliant young pianist called Yvonne Loriod. She was to become one of the leading interpreters of Messiaen's music, particularly his innovative birdsong

compositions. Together with her sister Jeanne, she was also a soloist in the *Turangalîla Symphony*.

Yvonne's personal relationship with Messiaen also grew closer, following a tragedy in his domestic situation. During the 1940s, his wife began to show signs of dementia. Claire's condition worsened after an operation, as she gradually lost her memory and most of her physical faculties. She entered a sanatorium in 1953 and died there six years later. Yvonne and Messiaen were married in 1961.

Claire's illness cast a shadow over the most successful period of Messiaen's career, when his work gained international recognition. The *Turangalîla Symphony* was a joyous affirmation of the power of love, and he followed this with an ever-deepening fascination with ornithology. Messiaen was by no means the first composer to evoke the sounds of birdsong in his music, but no other has explored the theme so thoroughly. His collections—*Le Réveil des oiseaux*, *Oiseaux exotiques*, and *Catalogue d'oiseaux*—were truly unique, even if they presented an immense challenge for the pianist concerned. Messiaen was able to combine his two great passions— religion and nature—in his last major work, *St. Francis of Assisi*, a five-hour opera on the life of the saint.

**A PERFORMANCE OF *QUARTET FOR THE END OF TIME* IN 2010**

◁ **MESSIAEN AND YVONNE LORIOD**
Pianist and composer Yvonne Loriod was Messiaen's second wife and also one of the principal interpreters of his work. The couple are shown here in 1964, three years after their marriage, examining a score of music.

# Benjamin Britten

## 1913–1976, BRITISH

An internationally respected English composer, Britten is best known for his operas and his *War Requiem*. He developed his own musical language that was distinctively modern without abandoning melody or tonality.

Edward Benjamin Britten was born in 1913 in Lowestoft, on the east coast of England. His father, a dentist, was indifferent to music, but his mother was an amateur musician, delighted to find in Benjamin a son who shared her tastes. He was sent to private schools that did nothing to encourage music, but at home he learned to play the piano and the viola. At the age of 12, he expressed enthusiasm for an orchestral piece by British composer Frank Bridge, heard at a concert. Through personal contacts his mother arranged for him to have composition lessons with Bridge, who became his musical mentor.

### Early compositions

In 1930, Britten won a scholarship to the Royal College of Music in London. While there, he produced his first compositions of note, including the choral work *A Boy Was Born*, which premiered on BBC radio in 1934. After college, he found employment writing music for the GPO Film Unit, which was then at the cutting edge

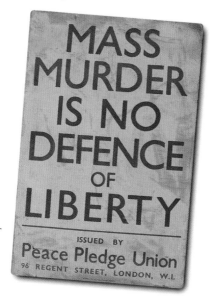

of documentary filmmaking. This brought him into contact with the poet W.H. Auden, a leading left-wing intellectual, who was writing verse voice-overs for the films. In 1936, poet and composer collaborated on the celebrated documentary *Night Mail*, as well as on Britten's first song cycle, *Our Hunting Fathers*. Both men were gay at a time when homosexual acts were illegal. Auden's influence helped Britten come to terms with his sexuality. In 1937, the composer met the tenor Peter Pears, who was to be his lifelong partner. They would often give recitals together, as Britten was a first-rate piano accompanist.

⊲ **BENJAMIN BRITTEN**
Britten is seen here conducting in Berlin's State Opera House (Staatsoper Unter den Linden) in 1968. He was a renowned conductor and pianist and performed many of his own works.

⊲ **POSTER FOR PEACE, 1930s**
An ardent pacifist and member of the Peace Pledge Union, Britten was awarded the status of conscientious objector in Britain in 1942 and unconditionally exempted from all military service.

### War and pacifism

The last years of the 1930s were dominated by the approach of World War II. Britten was an adherent of the pacifist Peace Pledge Union. In early 1939, he traveled with Pears to North America and, after the outbreak of war in September, stayed there, eventually joining Auden in New York. Self-exiles such as Britten and Auden were harshly criticized in Britain for failing to support the war effort against Nazi Germany. But the British authorities had no desire to stir up controversy by persecuting prominent conscientious objectors, and after Britten returned home in 1942—whiling away the journey by writing his choral work *A Ceremony of Carols*—he was left free to continue work as a musician.

▽ **FIRST IMPRESSIONS**
The first draft of the opera *Billy Budd* is played to writer Ronald Duncan (center) and musician Arthur Oldham. At the piano, Britten accompanies Peter Pears singing one of the arias.

> " It is **cruel** ... that **music** should be **so beautiful**. "

BENJAMIN BRITTEN (ON MAHLER'S *THE SONG OF THE EARTH*), 1937

## KEY WORKS

**1937**
*Variations on a Theme of Frank Bridge* is an international success.

**1945**
Based on a poem by George Crabbe, Britten's opera *Peter Grimes* is a critical and popular hit.

**1954**
Britten's opera based on a Henry James ghost story, *The Turn of the Screw*, premieres in Venice.

**1962**
A setting of the Requiem Mass and poems by Wilfred Owen, the *War Requiem* boosts Britten's renown.

**1964**
The first of three small-scale operas, *Curlew River*, is premiered at a church in Orford, Suffolk.

**1973**
Britten completes his final opera, *Death in Venice*, despite his failing health.

The war years were a fertile time for Britten. His output included three notable song cycles—*Les Illuminations* (1940), *Seven Sonnets of Michelangelo* (1942), and the *Serenade for Tenor, Horn, and Strings* (1943)—as well as the *Sinfonia da Requiem* (1940), one of his most successful purely orchestral works. Above all, he produced the score for the opera *Peter Grimes*. This powerful work brought together two of Britten's deepest sources of inspiration—his love of the Suffolk coast, where the opera is set, and his sense of isolation because of his homosexuality, which he expressed through the character of Grimes, who is marginalized and finally driven to his death by a repressive society.

From its first performance in London in 1945, *Peter Grimes* was hailed as a masterpiece. In a series of operas over the following decade, from *The Rape of Lucretia* (1946) and *Albert Herring* (1967) to *Billy Budd*

(1951) and *The Turn of the Screw* (1954), Britten in effect reestablished an English operatic tradition that had lapsed since the 17th century. In 1947, he set up the English Opera Group as a touring company performing chamber operas, and the following year founded the Aldeburgh Festival (see box, p.295). His status in British music was reflected by the Royal Opera House's staging his *Gloriana* to mark the coronation of Queen Elizabeth II in 1953, although the opera proved too dark and challenging to satisfy celebratory expectations.

### Popularity and innovation

Despite his growing fame, Britten's sexuality kept him nervous of the police, who were conducting a virulent campaign against high-placed homosexual people in the early 1950s. He was rendered vulnerable not only by his relationship with Pears but by the attraction he felt for adolescent

boys. The young people with whom he was most intimately associated have universally confirmed that he did not sexually abuse them. These personal tensions informed some of his best-known works, notably *Billy Budd* and *The Turn of the Screw*, which depict children and adolescents as symbols of purity and innocence menaced by evil and corrupt forces. Britten also enjoyed writing music for children, including the much-played *Young Person's Guide to the Orchestra* (1945) and the one-act opera *Noye's Fludde* (1958).

In the context of the Cold War and the nuclear arms race of the 1950s and 1960s, Britten's pacifism took on a fresh urgency and relevance. Premiered in 1962, his emotional and dramatic *War Requiem* intermingled the Latin Mass with settings of anti-war poems by Wilfred Owen. It was commissioned for performance in Coventry Cathedral, rebuilt after its destruction by aerial bombing during World War II. Appearing at a time of international crisis, when nuclear war between the Western powers and the Soviet Union seemed possible or even imminent, the work had an astonishing public impact for a piece of classical music, the first recording selling more than 200,000 copies in six months. It was partly in protest at the Cold War division of the world that Britten pursued publicized friendships

▽ **RUSSIAN FRIENDSHIP**
The Russian cellist Mstislav Rostropovich (left) grasps Britten's hand, after playing the composer's Cello Sonata in his Aldeburgh music room. Russian soprano Galina Vishnevskaya and Swiss conductor Paul Sacher applaud in the background.

with the Soviet composer Dmitri Shostakovich and Soviet cellist Mstislav Rostropovich, for whom he wrote his *Cello Symphony* in 1963.

In the 1960s, Britten was frequently denounced as a musical reactionary by avant-garde critics and composers committed to the idea that 12-tone serialism was the only valid form of contemporary music. But his work continued to be innovative in its own distinctive way, in particular integrating influences from non-European musical traditions. His exquisite sequence of small-scale music dramas written between 1964 and 1969 (*Curlew River*, *The Burning*

*Fiery Furnace*, and *The Prodigal Son*) drew inspiration from Japanese Noh theater and Balinese gamelan, among other sources. His opera *Owen Wingrave*, commissioned for television and broadcast in 1971, was far less successful, failing perhaps because of his lack of sympathy for the medium (he never owned a television set).

### Final years

From 1957 to the end of his life, Britten lived with Pears at the Red House in Aldeburgh, on the same bleak Suffolk coast where he had been born. In declining health by the 1970s, he struggled through illness to

△ **OPERA BY THE SEA**
Cast members take to the stage during the first performance of "Grimes on the Beach," a production of Britten's opera *Peter Grimes* at the Aldeburgh Festival on June 17, 2013.

finish his last major work, the opera *Death in Venice*. Thomas Mann's story of a dying artist's obsession with an idealized boy was of obvious personal significance to Britten. First performed in 1973, it is generally judged one of his finest achievements. Britten died of heart failure in 1976. He was buried in Aldeburgh churchyard, where Pears would later lie alongside him.

## " My **subject** is **War**, and the **pity** of **War**. "

WILFRED OWEN, QUOTED ON THE TITLE PAGE OF BRITTEN'S *WAR REQUIEM*, 1962

▷ **WITOLD LUTOSLAWSKI, 1992**
Lutosławski recalled that, as a boy, music "always fascinated me, and I couldn't imagine any other profession than musician, and even composer." Despite his tremendous creative talent, the repressive political situation in Poland for much of his lifetime meant that he remained virtually unknown outside his country of birth until he was more than 50 years old. The composer is pictured here in his garden two years before his death.

# Witold Lutosławski

## 1913–1994, POLISH

The young Lutosławski's musical creativity was stifled, first by the Nazi occupation, then by Stalin's Soviet regime, but in his mature works he was acclaimed as one of the finest and most original Polish composers.

# "Polish culture suffered **terrible losses** ... all **cultural activity** was **banned**."

WITOLD LUTOSLAWSKI, ON THE GERMAN OCCUPATION OF POLAND (1939–1945), 1993

Born in Warsaw in 1913, Witold Lutosławski was the son of landowning aristocrats. After the outbreak of World War I, his father, Józef, active in Polish nationalist politics, took the family to Moscow to seek safety from German invasion, but the plan soon turned sour: the Bolshevik government made peace with Germany and in 1918 Józef and his brother were executed.

## Hardship and upheaval

The family returned to Poland, where Witold learned the piano and the violin, and went on to earn diplomas in piano and composition from the Warsaw Conservatory. By the end of the 1930s, his reputation was growing, despite military service, when Poland was invaded simultaneously by Germany and Russia. In 1939, while serving as a radio operator, he was captured by German troops, but escaped and returned to Warsaw. Here, he teamed up with pianist and composer Andrzej Panufnik to make a living performing as a piano duo in cafés in the city. The pair made numerous arrangements of popular classics, as well as some original compositions, but little of this music survived the war.

Warsaw became unsafe, and Lutosławski and his mother fled the city before its complete devastation during the Warsaw Uprising in 1944, and did not return until after the war. The comparative stability of Poland as a Soviet satellite gave him the opportunity to settle down. In 1945, he

△ **FLAG OF SOLIDARNOSC**
Anti-communist feeling in Central and Eastern Europe in the 1980s led, in Poland, to the creation of the independent labor union Solidarność (Solidarity), to which Witold Lutosławski lent his support. Solidarność's flag, with its iconic red lettering, is shown here.

married Maria Danuta Bogusławska, and with her assistance started to compose in earnest. He had begun work on his first major work, the Symphony No. 1, in 1941, but with the distraction of working as a jobbing composer, only completed it in 1947. There were additional constraints: the Stalinist insistence on socialist realism in music led to Lutosławski being branded a Formalist composer, and he was denied the freedom to compose as he wished.

## A temporary freedom

With Stalin's death in 1953, official attitudes became more relaxed, and Lutosławski felt he had the freedom to explore the new musical idioms that were being developed in the West. He experimented with such techniques as serial composition, atonal harmony, and even aleatoric (chance) elements,

but incorporated them into his own, more traditional musical language, rather than attempting to emulate or adopt them completely.

His reputation as a highly original composer spread worldwide during the 1960s, but this became overshadowed once again by political unrest in Poland through the 1970s and 1980s. Although Lutosławski had long opposed the Soviet regime, his music had never been overtly political, but it was increasingly seen as symbolic of Polish nationalism. With the rise of union organizer Lech Wałęsa's Solidarność (Solidarity) movement in 1980, he became more politically involved, lending his support to Solidarność by refusing any engagements in Poland until independence. However, he carried on composing, and created many of his finest works in the last decade of his life. He died of cancer in 1994.

▷ **FESTIVAL OF MUSIC**
In this photograph, Lutosławski is seen conducting at the 16th International Festival of Contemporary Music in Poland in September 1972.

# Leonard Bernstein

## 1918–1990, AMERICAN

Known as much for his flamboyant conducting as for his own eclectic compositions, Bernstein was acclaimed worldwide for his contribution to both "serious" concert music and Broadway musicals.

Born in 1918 into a family of Ukrainian Jewish immigrants in Lawrence, Massachusetts, Leonard Bernstein showed a gift for music from an early age. At first, his father let him pursue his interest only reluctantly, but later became more supportive, arranging music lessons for his son when the family acquired a piano.

After attending the Boston Latin School—an institution that prided itself on providing a classical education to Boston's elite—Bernstein studied music at Harvard University, graduating in 1939. He studied under several distinguished academics and composers, but perhaps the most significant influence was Aaron Copland, who became a lifelong friend and mentor. After Harvard, Bernstein spent a year at the Curtis Institute of Music in Philadelphia, before settling in New York in 1940. Later that year he started his studies in conducting with Serge Koussevitzky at Tanglewood, the summer school of the Boston Symphony Orchestra.

Suffering from asthma, Bernstein was excused military service during World War II, leaving him free to compose and conduct. In 1943, he was appointed assistant conductor of the New York Philharmonic (see box, right), and two years later became music director of the newly formed New York City Symphony. He was also beginning to make his name as a composer, both of "serious" concert music and of a string of successful Broadway musicals.

### Married life

As his reputation as a conductor grew, Bernstein worried that his private life might damage his chances of taking one of the top conducting jobs. He was homosexual at a time when it was a criminal offense in many places, and certainly not something to be made public. Perhaps to counter suspicions, in 1951 he married an actress, Felicia Cohn Montealegre, with whom he at first lived happily and had three children. The marriage lasted until

1976, when Bernstein "came out" leaving his wife for his young male lover. However, the next year, Felicia was diagnosed with cancer, and Bernstein returned to nurse her until her death in 1978.

### A household name

During the 1950s, Bernstein became a household name in the US, not just from his successes on Broadway and appearances with the major orchestras, but because he presented a series of lectures on music for the television arts program *Omnibus*, with musical examples played live by the NBC Symphony Orchestra. This was a productive time for him as a composer, too, in which he wrote the operetta *Candide*, and probably his best-known musical, *West Side Story*. At the same time, he became musical director of the New York Philharmonic. His schedule with the Philharmonic left him little time for composing in the 1960s, and he did not produce any major work until the *Mass* in 1971.

He continued tirelessly conducting, composing, and presenting TV documentaries throughout the last two decades of his life, despite the emphysema he had contracted from years of heavy smoking. He eventually retired in October 1990, aged 72, and five days later died of a heart attack.

**BERNSTEIN REHEARSES WITH THE NEW YORK PHILHARMONIC, CARNEGIE HALL**

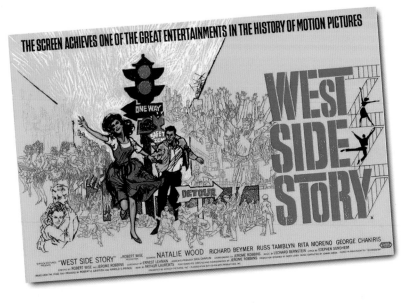

◁ **WEST SIDE STORY**
Bernstein's most famous musical, *West Side Story*, was made into a film in 1961, directed by Robert Wise and Jerome Robbins. The story is an adaptation of Shakespeare's *Romeo and Juliet*, transposed to 1950s New York.

▷ **LEONARD BERNSTEIN**
Bernstein is shown here in February 1970 at the Queen Elizabeth Hall in London. After leaving the New York Philharmonic in 1969, he performed as a guest conductor with numerous orchestras around the world.

**▷ GYÖRGY LIGETI, 1965**
During World War II, Ligeti was sent to a labor camp, his younger brother to a concentration camp, and his parents to Auschwitz. Only he and his mother survived the war. Then, in 1956, after Russia crushed the liberal government, he was forced to flee Hungary, hiding under mailbags in a train that took him close to the Austrian border. Such nightmarish events are variously worked through in his music. Ligeti is shown here in less harrowing times, in his forties, during his most productive period when his reputation as a leading composer was secure.

# György Ligeti
## 1923–2006, HUNGARIAN

One of the most original composers to emerge in the second half of the 20th century, Ligeti developed an individual style that embraced the avant-garde while still respecting musical tradition.

◁ **LE GRANDE MACABRE**
The English National Opera performs Ligeti's "anti-anti opera" *Le Grand Macabre* at the London Coliseum in 2009. It was his only opera and his longest work.

That he was born in Transylvania, with all its Gothic horror associations, later appealed to György Ligeti's dark sense of humor. He came from a Hungarian Jewish family, and was born in 1923, next to a synagogue in Dicsöszentmárton (now Târnăveni) in Romania's Transylvania region. The family later moved to the city of Cluj, where Ligeti began his studies at the local conservatory in 1941.

### Dark and fearful times

There was a great deal of political uncertainty in the region at that time: Hungary had annexed Northern Transylvania. As Hungarian speakers, the Ligetis were safe, but as Jews, they faced an increasing threat as the Nazis spread across Europe. In 1944, Ligeti was arrested and sent to a labor camp.

The following year, having survived the war, he returned to his studies, now at the Franz Liszt Academy of Music in Budapest, under the aegis of composer Zoltán Kodály. Following in the footsteps of Kodály and Bartók, Ligeti adopted a quasi-nationalist, folk-tinged style, largely because he had very limited access to new music from elsewhere in Europe. He graduated in 1949, and went on to teach at the Liszt Academy. That year he also married his first wife, Brigitte, but this ended in divorce three years later, when he married Veronika (known as Vera) Spitz—not a love match, but to prevent her deportation due to her bourgeois background. After Stalin's death in 1954, they felt it was safe to divorce, but remained friends.

Their optimism was short-lived. In 1956, the Hungarian Revolution was brutally quashed by Soviet forces, and Ligeti fled with Vera to Vienna. They then made their way to Cologne, where Ligeti was offered work with Karlheinz Stockhausen in the Electronic Music Studio, and he and Vera remarried, this time in earnest.

In Cologne he had his first real contact with current trends in music, and slowly learned to absorb these into his own compositions. One of his most productive periods was during the 1960s, when he wrote many of his best-known pieces (and achieving some popularity through their use in films by Stanley Kubrick), including *Atmosphères*, the *Requiem*, *Lux aeterna*, *Lontano*, and the Absurdist theatrical pieces *Aventures* and *Nouvelles Aventures*, which showed his darkly humorous side.

He and Vera had a son, Lukas, in 1965, and Ligeti took Austrian citizenship in 1968. By this time, his reputation had been secured and his music was being performed worldwide. After a brief period in the US, he was appointed professor of composition at the Hamburg University of Music and Theater in 1973, where he taught until 1989. During this period, his style changed from the textural blocks of sound that characterized his early mature style, to a more rhythmic and strictly structured style, influenced by US Minimalism. He also concentrated at this time on his grotesque, Absurdist "anti-anti opera" *Le Grand Macabre*.

Ligeti spent most of his last years working on three books of piano *Etudes* and concertos for various instruments and orchestra, but failing health affected his output more and more, and he withdrew into seclusion. He died in Vienna in 2006, aged 83.

△ **POEME SYMPHONIQUE, 2018**
Members of Alarm Will Sound chamber orchestra with US conductor Alan Pierson (center) perform Ligeti's *Poème symphonique* (1962)—written for 100 metronomes—in the program *This Music Should Not Exist*. In the performance at Zankel Hall, New York, Ligeti's music was interspersed with music by Anton Seifert, Stockhausen, and Charlie Chaplin.

## ON TECHNIQUE
### Micropolyphony

After World War II, a number of composers, especially in Central and Eastern Europe, adopted a technique using massive clusters of notes to form "blocks" of sound, in which texture takes precedence over the traditional parameters of harmony and melody. Not satisfied with the necessarily static nature of these cluster chords, Ligeti developed the technique a stage further, superimposing a large number of independent melodies (what he called "micropolyphony"), so that the individual parts are indiscernible, and the block is perceived as a dynamic, constantly changing whole.

LIKE LIGETI'S MICROPOLYPHONY, THESE STARLINGS APPEAR AS A SINGLE ENTITY

# Karlheinz Stockhausen

## 1928–2007, GERMAN

A towering figure of the post-World War II avant-garde, Stockhausen was an uncompromising innovator over a period of more than 50 years. His music was as controversial as it was influential.

Stockhausen was born in Mödrath, near Cologne. His early childhood was marred by the fact that his mother was admitted into a psychiatric institution in 1932. Another tragedy befell the Stockhausen family that year, when Karlheinz's younger brother, Hermann, died.

Matters did not improve when, in 1938, his father remarried. His new wife was the family's former housekeeper, a situation that the 10-year-old Karlheinz found unbearable. Then, in 1941, his mother died. The official cause of death was given as leukemia, but it is probable that she had been gassed by the Nazis.

### Continuing turmoil

In 1942, Stockhausen left home to attend college in Xanten, but his education was interrupted two years later when he was called up for military service. For the remainder of World War II, he was a stretcher-bearer—an experience that had a deep impact on the unhappy teenager. This was compounded when his father went missing in action, presumed dead, in 1945.

After the war, Stockhausen resumed studies, first at Cologne Conservatory, then at the University of Cologne. In 1952, he moved to Paris to study composition with Olivier Messiaen

and Darius Milhaud, before returning to Cologne to work with Herbert Eimert in the electronic music studio of the Nordwestdeutscher Rundfunk.

During the 1950s, Stockhausen developed a distinctive avant-garde approach to composition, which included a methodical, analytical reworking of the serialism invented by Schoenberg (see pp.238–241), to which he later introduced some elements of indeterminacy. He also explored sound's position in space and electronic music (see box, right). As his reputation as a composer grew, he became a leading figure of the Darmstadt School, a group of avant-garde and experimental composers.

◁ **KARLHEINZ STOCKHAUSEN**
The innovative composer is pictured here in a recording studio in 1965, at the height of his career. By this time, his name had almost become a byword for musical modernity.

◁ **DONNERSTAG AUS LICHT**
This is a cover of Stockhausen's opera *Donnerstag aus Licht* (*Thursday from Light*), one of a cycle of seven operas, one for each day of the week.

### International fame

By the 1960s, Stockhausen had become virtually a household name, as he continued to experiment and to develop his highly unconventional compositional techniques, while also touring internationally, as both a performer and a teacher. His major project, a massive cycle of seven operas called *Licht: Die sieben Tage der Woche* (*Light: The Seven Days of the Week*) was begun in 1977, and completed in 2003. It was followed by another cycle, *Klang* (*Sound*), which was based on the hours of the day.

Stockhausen was twice married, and twice divorced, and several of his six children have themselves become professional musicians, frequently collaborating in their father's compositions. He died at his home in Kürten of a heart attack in 2007, aged 79.

### ON TECHNIQUE
#### Pioneer of electronic music

Stockhausen was particularly noted for his groundbreaking work in electronic music in the 1950s. At that time, there was a heated debate as to whether the future lay in the purely electronically synthesized sounds produced in the German studios, or *musique concrète*, electrically modified recorded sounds, favored by the French studios. In *Gesang der Jünglinge* (*Song of the Youths*, 1955–1956), Stockhausen found ways to integrate the techniques, combining electronically generated sounds with a recorded human voice and its electronic transformations, using multiple-channel recording to explore the spatial positioning of sound as an integral parameter of the music.

▽ **STIMMUNG**
Theatre of Voices ensemble are here performing Stockhausen's *Stimmung* (*Tuning*, 1968) at Zankel Hall in New York in 2015. In this work, the performers recite erotic poems written by Stockhausen.

# Tōru Takemitsu

## 1930–1996, JAPANESE

The first Japanese composer to gain international renown in classical music, Takemitsu wrote concert pieces and film scores that achieved an unprecedented integration of Western and Japanese musical traditions.

Throughout his teens, Tōru Takemitsu had little or no contact with Western music, which was outlawed in Japan. He was born in Tokyo in 1930, but when he was only a few weeks old his family moved to Dalian, in Japanese-occupied Manchuria. He returned to Japan in 1938 to go to school, but was unable to complete his studies as he was conscripted at the age of 14 in anticipation of a US invasion—an experience he bitterly resented.

Rebelling against the Japanese establishment, Takemitsu and his friends listened clandestinely to a gramophone record of the French popular song "Parlez-moi d'amour," which he cited as a formative influence. After World War II, he worked for the US occupying forces, but his fragile health meant he spent

◁ **TORU TAKEMITSU**
Takemitsu was almost completely self-taught as a musician, but was the first Japanese classical composer to achieve worldwide acclaim.

prolonged periods in hospital, where he listened to American Forces Radio and developed a taste for Western music. Aged just 16, he decided to become a musician, even though he had no musical training. Apart from a few lessons with the composer Yasuji Kiyose in 1948, Takemitsu's skills as a composer were self-taught.

### Subverting tradition

With such an unorthodox musical upbringing, he inevitably gravitated toward the unconventional, and in 1951, he cofounded a group of avant-garde artists, writers, and musicians known as Jikken Kōbō (Experimental Workshop), who rejected the traditional academic arts. For Takemitsu, this was a conscious turning away from Japanese tradition, which for him had only negative associations. Instead, he found inspiration in Debussy's Impressionism, and in the 12-tone serial compositions of Webern and later Messiaen.

A turning point came when Stravinsky heard Takemitsu's 1957 *Requiem* for string orchestra, and his enthusiasm for it helped publicize Takemitsu in the West. Around this time, Takemitsu discovered the experimental music of John Cage. He became interested in Cage's use of indeterminacy and chance in composition, and the idea of silence as a dynamic element. Ironically, it was this US composer's work that prompted Takemitsu to reexamine Japanese traditional music, which shares many of Cage's ideals. He began studying Japanese music and its instruments, trying to find a way of integrating them into his Western musical style.

His first major work in this vein was *November Steps* for *biwa* (a traditional Japanese lute), *shakuhachi* (a flute), and orchestra, premiered in 1967. During the 1970s and 1980s, a catalog of compositions appeared in which Takemitsu refined his style, combining Japanese and Western elements to varying degrees. The aim in his later works was to create a "sea of tonality," a musical link between East and West, as in his "Waterscape" and "Dream" cycles of works.

Always physically frail, Takemitsu was diagnosed with bladder cancer in the mid-1990s; he also contracted pneumonia, and died in 1996, aged 65.

◁ **JAPANESE GARDEN**
According to Takemitsu, "Listening to my music can be compared with walking through a garden and experiencing the changes in light, pattern, and texture."

## ON TECHNIQUE
### East meets West

It was with some shock that Takemitsu recognized his own Japanese cultural identity in the 1960s, and realized its relationship with his essentially Western aesthetic ideals. He began to introduce traditional Japanese instruments into works such as *November Steps* (1967), but also found that modern indeterminate procedures of composition were compatible with traditional Japanese performance techniques, allowing for a degree of improvisation and expressive interpretation. He also discovered that the timbres and inflections of the Japanese instruments fitted well with his Debussy-inspired sound-world.

**TRADITIONAL JAPANESE BAMBOO FLUTE**

▷ **ALFRED SCHNITTKE**
Schnittke gives a masterclass in
Salzburg, Austria, in 1990. From this year,
Schnittke made his home in Hamburg,
Germany, and despite ill health enjoyed a
period of great creativity.

# Alfred Schnittke

## 1934–1998, RUSSIAN

Schnittke defied the conventions imposed by the state bureaucracy
to develop his own distinctive voice, using a technique he dubbed
"polystylism," which gained him international recognition.

◁ **GIDON KREMER**
Gidon Kremer, seen here with his chamber orchestra, the Kremerata Baltica, in 2002, performed Schnittke's work and was influential in raising his profile.

## ON TECHNIQUE
### Polystylism

Although other composers, notably Charles Ives and Luciano Berio, had adopted similar techniques of quotation, allusion, and juxtaposition of different musical styles, it was Schnittke who explicitly used the term "polystylism" to describe his music, and it became a trademark of almost all his work from the mid-1960s until around 1985. This extrovert, brash, and sometimes chaotic presentation, combining and contrasting various styles ranging from Gregorian chant to electronic experimentalism, and incorporating both classical and popular idioms, chimed with the contemporary postmodernist movement, especially in its blurring of the distinction between high and low culture, and the fragmentation and collage of disparate ideas.

Alfred Schnittke was born in Engels, a port in the autonomous Volga-German Republic of the Soviet Union, a region that retained the culture and language of its original German émigré settlers. His father was a German Jew who had moved to Engels for work, and his mother a Volga German with a Catholic background, but both had embraced communism and Alfred had a secular upbringing.

From an early age, Schnittke had a sense of being an outsider, culturally different from the country he was born into. When his father was posted to Vienna in 1945, he immediately felt at home. He fell in love with Viennese culture, and especially the music of composers such as Mozart and Schubert rather than the 19th-century Russian nationalist composers who were revered in the USSR.

The family moved to Moscow in 1948. Schnittke studied composition at the Moscow Conservatory, and completed his postgraduate studies in 1961. That year, he married the pianist Irina Kataieva, and took up a teaching post at the Moscow Conservatory. His early compositions were in the mold of Dmitri Shostakovich, who dominated the Soviet music scene, but through the 1960s he began to explore Modernist techniques in his work, including the serialism of Schoenberg and Webern.

### Prolific creativity

Unhappy with both the conventional, Soviet-approved model and much of the avant-garde, Schnittke developed a way of creating a synthesis of these, along with other styles of classical and even jazz and pop music, in what he called "polystylism." By 1972, he showed his mastery of the technique in his Symphony No. 1, which was the first of his mature works and came as he left the Conservatory to focus on composition. His main income came from composing film scores, but he also embarked on a period of prolific creativity, producing concert music in almost every genre.

However, as he was making his name in Moscow, especially among antiestablishment intellectuals, the authorities took exception to his "un-Soviet" Modernism, and in 1980 he was banned from leaving the country. Nevertheless, thanks to friends who championed his work, including Gidon Kremer, Yuri Bashmet, and Mstislav Rostropovich, he was gaining an international reputation.

The 1980s were a time of change for Schnittke. He began to take an interest in religion, and was baptized in the Catholic Church; his music became more contemplative, even mystical, in a more accessible and consonant style. In 1985, he suffered the first in a series of strokes but he continued to compose, even as his writing became almost illegible. When Soviet president Mikhail Gorbachev introduced the liberalizing policies of glasnost and perestroika, Schnittke was able to leave Moscow, and moved to Hamburg with Irina in 1990. His last work, the Ninth Symphony, was painstakingly deciphered and performed in 1998, shortly before his death.

▽ **SCHNITTKE'S GRAVE**
The musical notation on Schnittke's gravestone in Moscow comprises a rest with a pause marked fff, signifying "a long, very loud silence."

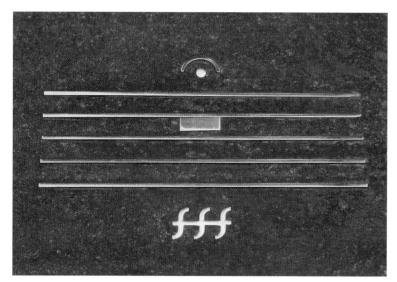

> "There are **enormous forces** lurking in **each person**, but many people **die** without having **discovered** this."
ALFRED SCHNITTKE

# Arvo Pärt

## BORN 1935, ESTONIAN

Pärt, whose works are among the most performed of any living composer, achieved international recognition for haunting, contemplative music written using his distinctive "tintinnabuli" technique.

When Arvo Pärt was born in 1935, Estonia was an independent nation state, but in 1940 it was occupied by the Soviet Red Army, and remained a part of the Soviet Union until it regained independence in 1991. Pärt was born in Paide, capital of the central Järva County; at three years old he moved with his mother to the northern town of Rakvere, where he had his first music lessons around 1942.

He showed talent, especially as a composer, and as a teenager wrote pieces in a Neo-Classical style heavily influenced by Shostakovich and Prokofiev. He had little access to anything but Soviet-approved music on which to model himself, but managed to get hold of some illicit scores and recordings, from which he learned about modern techniques such as 12-tone serialism.

### Early works

Pärt continued his musical education at the Tallinn Music Middle School and from 1958 at the Tallinn Conservatory, at the same time working as a sound producer for Estonian public radio. While still a student, he wrote his first major orchestral work, *Nekrolog*, dedicated to victims of the Holocaust.

The first piece by an Estonian composer to use the 12-tone serial technique, it was denounced by the

◁ **MUSICAL BEGINNINGS**
A piano belonging to the Pärt family, now at the Arvo Pärt Center in Laulasmaa. The composer's mother liked to start the day by playing music by Bach.

Soviet authorities. Undeterred, Pärt continued exploring avant-garde styles throughout the 1960s, and developed a sort of musical collage technique, incorporating a variety of Modernist ideas. However, he felt that he had still to find his own musical language. The turning point came in 1972. That year saw two major changes in his personal life: he got married, and he converted from Lutheranism to the Orthodox Church. This prompted him to take a break from composing, and to study medieval and Renaissance music, and more importantly the choral music of the Orthodox liturgy.

Pärt's studies elicited a radical change in his musical approach. He abandoned the complexity and intellectualism of his previous music

to create an austere and almost static sound-world. Although the simplicity of this style bore some similarities to the American minimalist composers, in his idiosyncratic technique, which he called "tintinnabuli," he had found his unique personal voice (see box, right). After early works in this style, including perhaps his best-known composition, *Spiegel im Spiegel* (1978), he has written mainly sacred works inspired by his Orthodox Christian faith, or with a spiritual theme.

### Exile and return

Pärt remained a thorn in the side of the Soviet musical establishment, and by 1980 was so pilloried by his critics that he was forced to leave Estonia with his wife and two sons. They lived at first in Vienna, moving in 1981 to West Berlin, where he was granted German citizenship. With the fall of the Soviet bloc, he renewed his contacts with his homeland, and for a while divided his time between Germany and Estonia, before moving back permanently to the coastal village of Laulasmaa, near Tallinn, in 2010.

> ## ON TECHNIQUE
> ### Tintinnabuli
>
> Since the mid-1970s, Pärt has used a compositional technique of his own invention, which he calls "tintinnabuli." The method involves setting a simple, slow-moving melody with an equally simple accompaniment drawing on the most basic three-note chord, or triad. In the short piano solo *Für Alina* (1976), for example, the melody is a rising and falling major scale, accompanied by notes of the triad of that scale. The combination of notes at any moment creates a single sound that Pärt says is "simultaneously static and in flux." Like the sound of a bell (tintinnabulation), the sounds are allowed to ring on, letting their sonorities gradually unfold.

△ **ORTHODOX CATHEDRAL, TALLINN**
The Alexander Nevsky Cathedral is an Orthodox church in Tallinn Old Town. After Pärt's conversion to Orthodox Christianity his music underwent a major change in style, often being based on sacred texts.

> ## "It is **enough** when a **single note** is **beautifully played**."
> ARVO PÄRT

▷ **ARVO PÄRT, 2014**
Pärt's music, whether orchestral or choral, has been described as "holy minimalism" and seems to strike a chord with a contemporary audience seeking spiritual connection.

# Philip Glass

## BORN 1937, AMERICAN

Considered a founding father of US Minimalism, Glass is one of the most influential composers of the late 20th century, thanks to his distinctive use of repetitive musical structures.

Although often associated with the New York arts scene, Philip Glass was born and brought up in Baltimore. His father owned a record store in the city, which stocked a wide range of classical music. As a boy, Glass played the flute, and he began composing in his teens. He studied mathematics and philosophy at the University of Chicago before moving to the Juilliard School of Music in New York where he graduated in composition in 1962.

In the mid-1960s, Glass was awarded a Fulbright Scholarship that enabled him to travel to Paris to study with the revered composition teacher Nadia Boulanger (see p.265). During

◁ **PHILIP GLASS, 2002**
Glass spent many years studying Indian and experimental music. His work has influenced musicians such as David Bowie and Brian Eno.

his two-year stay there, he came into contact with the latest European avant-garde music by the likes of Boulez and Stockhausen; he also became immersed in Indian music, working with Ravi Shankar on a film score. This, rather than modern Western music, was to be his chosen path. He was particularly attracted to the slowly evolving, repetitive nature of Indian classical music, which soon figured prominently in his work.

### Inspiration and change

Returning to New York in 1967, Glass was inspired by the music of Steve Reich, which was taking a similar Minimalist route, with works for small ensembles using static harmonies and repetitive rhythmic patterns.

Although Glass was performing his own music regularly in New York, it did not provide him with a living.

Having married in 1965, he was now starting a family, so to make ends meet he also worked as a mover, a plumber, and a cab driver.

By the mid-1970s, however, he had sufficiently established himself as a composer to concentrate on his music full-time. He embarked on a period of change in his musical style. With the series *Another Look at Harmony* (1975), he developed a more sophisticated brand of Minimalism, which he preferred to call "music with repetitive structures." He also began to write more large-scale works. The first of these was the opera *Einstein on the Beach* (on the life of Albert Einstein), one of the trilogy of "portrait" operas along with *Satyagraha* (about Nelson Mandela) and *Akhnaten* (on the Egyptian pharaoh of that name).

Glass produced a huge volume of work in the 1980s, including operas and film scores. His first marriage had ended in divorce and was followed by a brief, unsuccessful second marriage, and a tragic third, which ended in 1991 when his wife, the artist Candy Jernigan, died of cancer. During this turbulent period in his personal life, Glass began to take an interest in composing more abstract music, such as symphonies and concertos, as well as more operas—a trend that has continued to the present day.

◁ *AKHNATEN*
A scene from the English National Opera's award-winning production of Glass's *Akhnaten*, directed by Phelim McDermott at the London Coliseum.

## ON TECHNIQUE
### The Philip Glass Ensemble

After his return to New York in 1967, Glass wrote a large number of Minimalist pieces for small ensembles, usually featuring electric keyboards, amplified wind instruments, and solo voices. To perform these works, he gathered around him a group of musicians, which formally became the Philip Glass Ensemble in 1968. The number and combination of the ensemble's instruments varied from piece to piece, with a core of around 10 performers, including Glass himself. Several compositions—including the opera *Einstein on the Beach* (1975)— were written specifically with the Philip Glass Ensemble in mind.

**THE PHILIP GLASS ENSEMBLE PERFORMING LIVE**

# Judith Weir

## BORN 1954, BRITISH

Weir is best known for her operas and composition for theater, but she is also acclaimed for her orchestral and chamber music. Her work draws on folk tales and the rich cultural traditions of Scotland, India, and China.

Born to Scottish parents in Cambridge in 1954, Judith Weir spent her childhood near London. While at school, she played oboe with the National Youth Orchestra of Great Britain and studied composition under John Tavener (see p.309). Her interest in arrangement emerged in these early years, when she would think up tunes that she and her friends could play together in different instrumental combinations—writing music evolved gradually from this.

### Early years
At the University of Cambridge she was tutored by the composer Robin Holloway. Her influences were wide-ranging and included Monteverdi, Mozart, Wagner, and Verdi, whose mastery of form is as enthralling as their storytelling and sheer musical brilliance.

Weir graduated from Cambridge in 1976. Her entry into opera—which now forms the heart of her work—began three years later, when she was invited by British singer Jane Manning ("the patron saint of new vocal music," according to Weir) to write a piece for solo soprano. The result was *King Harald's Saga* (1979), which revealed her ability to compress a historical epic into less than 10 minutes and to represent a huge cast by a lone voice.

Her first work for theater came in 1985, with the creepy three-act opera, *The Black Spider*. But it was two years later that Weir drew widespread attention with the premiere of her three-act opera *A Night at the Chinese Opera*. The menacing play-within-a-play was inspired by her reading of 14th-century Chinese drama; it became one of her most popular works.

### Expressive power
This was followed by *The Vanishing Bridegroom* (1990), which draws on, and greatly enlivens, dark folk tales from the western Highlands of Scotland. Among Weir's other most successful works are *Blond Eckbert* (1994), an operatic reworking of a German folk tale about obsessive fear; her Piano Concerto (1997) for piano and strings; *The Welcome Arrival of Rain* (2001), for orchestra; and her opera *Miss Fortune* (2012).

◁ **POSTER FOR BLOND ECKBERT**
Weir's opera *Blond Eckbert*, based on an 18th-century text by Ludwig Tieck, was first staged in London in 1994.

The qualities Weir most admires in works of literature are, she says, "concision, clarity, lightness, and (hidden) wisdom"— qualities that are evident in many of her own musical creations. She is also a composer of great imaginative power, a tremendous storyteller with immense breadth of vision, whose work is lively, richly expressive, complex, and often understated and ironic. Her contribution to the field has been recognized in a string of impressive awards and appointments, including posts at Cardiff, Glasgow, Princeton, and Harvard universities, a CBE (1995), the Queen's Medal for Music (2007), and the first female Master of the Queen's Music (2014).

▷ **JUDITH WEIR**
Weir has composed many operas and written orchestral pieces for several of the world's leading orchestras. She is an important and inspiring role model for female composers.

---

## IN PROFILE
### Peter Maxwell Davies

Weir's predecessor as Master of the Queen's Music (2004–2014) was Peter Maxwell Davies (1934–2016). Initially an anti-Establishment figure, Davies attended the Royal Manchester College of Music. He and fellow students Harrison Birtwistle and Alexander Goehr were later known as the "Manchester Group."

After studying at Princeton under Roger Sessions, Davies returned to England and cofounded the Pierrot Players, a chamber ensemble, with Birtwistle. Davies's early work was modern, yet often inspired by early music. In 1971, he relocated to Scotland's Orkney Islands, where he was deeply influenced by the landscape. As he grew older, his music became more accessible.

PETER MAXWELL DAVIES, 1986

▷ **MISS FORTUNE, COVENT GARDEN**
*Miss Fortune* was staged at the Royal Opera House in London in 2012. Weir's opera brings a modern context— including a setting in a laundromat—to the Sicilian folk tale on which it is based.

# Directory

## Aaron Copland

1900–1990, AMERICAN

One of the outstanding figures in 20th-century American music, Copland was a pianist, conductor, writer, teacher, and concert organizer, as well as the composer of a large, varied, and memorable body of work. His training included a period of study in Paris with French composer and conductor Nadia Boulanger (1921–1924). Although he was sometimes influenced by various avant-garde elements, he is best known for works of wide popular appeal in an accessible, distinctively US idiom, sometimes quoting folk songs, with lively rhythms and a bracing sense of the open air. Particularly well known in this vein are his ballets *Billy the Kid*, *Rodeo*, and *Appalachian Spring*. His other work includes three symphonies, two concertos (for piano and clarinet), chamber and instrumental music, songs, choral pieces, and compositions for the stage, film, and television.

**KEY WORKS:** *Fanfare for the Common Man*, 1942; *Appalachian Spring*, 1944; Clarinet Concerto, 1948; *The Tender Land* (opera), 1954

## Aram Khachaturian

1903–1978, ARMENIAN

Although his parents were Armenian, Khachaturian was born in Georgia, spent most of his life in Moscow, and throughout his career was regarded as a Soviet composer (Armenia was part of the Soviet Union from 1922 to 1991). Nevertheless, his music was strongly influenced by Armenian folk traditions and he is now generally considered to be one of the country's leading cultural heroes. With his great contemporaries Prokofiev and Shostakovich, he was officially censured in 1948 for showing "decadent" Western influence in his work, but generally he managed to negotiate the strictures of the Soviet regime. Over the years he received many official honors in the USSR as well as international recognition. Khachaturian's diverse output includes symphonies, concertos, instrumental, chamber, and vocal music, and numerous film scores. His most famous works are probably his ballets *Gayane* (which includes the famous "Saber Dance") and *Spartacus*, which reveal his exuberant, richly colorful style.

**KEY WORKS:** Violin Concerto, 1940; *Gayane*, 1942; *Spartacus*, 1956; *Concerto-Rhapsody for Cello and Orchestra*, 1963

## Samuel Barber

1910–1981, AMERICAN

Barber came from a musical family and began composing at the age of seven. Although there are certain Modernist features in his music, essentially he worked in a fairly conservative, warmly expressive idiom that brought him acclaim and honors throughout his career. Toward the end of his life he said, "There's no reason music should be difficult for an audience to understand," and many of his works have indeed achieved broad and enduring popularity (above all, the poignant, elegiac *Adagio for Strings*, which has often been played or broadcast to accompany or commemorate solemn events). Barber's output was fairly small but highly varied, including symphonies, concertos, operas, ballets, chamber and instrumental music, and numerous songs—which were one of his favorite forms of expression. He was himself an accomplished singer and his bittersweet *Knoxville: Summer of 1915* for soprano and orchestra is often regarded as one of his masterpieces.

**KEY WORKS:** *Adagio for Strings*, 1936; Violin Concerto, 1940; *Knoxville: Summer of 1915*, 1947; Piano Concerto, 1962

## ▽ John Cage

1912–1992, AMERICAN

One of the great experimentalists in musical history, Cage was a prominent figure in avant-garde circles in New York from the early 1940s, and by the mid-1960s he had become internationally renowned: he traveled widely, performing his works, and also spread his ideas through writing and lecturing. His music is extremely unorthodox, using unconventional sound sources as well as random and chance processes. In particular, he is famous for his use of the "prepared piano," in which various small objects (of metal, rubber, or cloth, for example) are placed on or between the strings

△ JOHN CAGE, 1982

to alter the instrument's sound. His most controversial piece is *4'33"*, in which the performer or performers remain silent for 4 minutes and 33 seconds, the quiet being punctuated only by random environmental sounds. Late in life, Cage also took up drawing and printmaking.

**KEY WORKS:** Sonata for Clarinet, 1933; *The Seasons* (ballet), 1947; *4'33"*, 1952; *Cheap Imitation*, 1969

## Iannis Xenakis

1922–2001, GREEK-FRENCH

Born in Romania to Greek parents, Xenakis grew up mainly in Greece and in 1947 settled in Paris, becoming a French citizen in 1965. Before and after World War II (during which he lost an eye fighting with the Greek Resistance), he trained as an engineer, afterward working in Paris for 12 years (1948–1960) in the practice of the great architect Le Corbusier. He was largely self-taught in music. His engineering background gave him a deep understanding of mathematics, and his highly original compositions have been described as mathematical processes transformed into music of primitive power. From the early 1960s, he often used computers to help create his works. A prolific writer, he taught at universities in Europe and the US, and is widely regarded as a major figure in the creation of an experimental climate for postwar music.

**KEY WORKS:** *Metastaseis* (for orchestra), 1954; *Herma* (for piano), 1961; *Kraanerg* (ballet for orchestra and tape), 1968; *Psappha* (for percussion), 1975

## ▷ Pierre Boulez

1925–2016, FRENCH

As a composer, conductor, writer, and founder of musical institutions, Boulez was a leading figure in classical music throughout most of his long career, and was a fearsomely outspoken champion of the avant-garde. Originally, he excelled as a mathematician, and his music is complex and intellectual. He took up conducting as a way of advocating his own and other new music, but he developed into one of the foremost international conductors of his generation, performing with some of the world's leading orchestras and making many acclaimed recordings (mainly of 20th-century music, but also, for example, of Wagner's *Ring* cycle). He was also the founding director of IRCAM (opened 1978), a government-sponsored institute in Paris for research into music and technology, and for many years he toured with its instrumental group, the Ensemble interContemporain.

**KEY WORKS:** Piano Sonata No. 1, 1946; *Le Marteau sans maître* (*The Hammer without a Master*), 1955; *Pli selon pli* (*Fold by Fold*), 1962; *Dialogue de l'ombre double* (*Dialogue of the Double Shadow*), 1985

## Luciano Berio

1925–2003, ITALIAN

Berio was the leading Italian avant-garde composer of the second half of the 20th century. There had been musicians in his family for several generations, and he was composing by his early teens. Initially, he was influenced by Stravinsky, but he soon became more experimental, and in particular he explored electronic music and the use of sounds such as street noises. He also wrote in various genres for a wide range of conventional instruments and for voice (the first of his three wives was the US mezzo-soprano Cathy Berberian, a notable interpreter of his music). Although his work is intellectually complex, it has also been described as compassionately human, with strong lyrical and dramatic elements, as well as humor. Berio taught at various institutions in Europe and the US and he was regarded by many of his admirers as a kind of musical guru.

△ **PIERRE BOULEZ AT THE ROYAL FESTIVAL HALL, LONDON, APRIL 1995**

**KEY WORKS:** *Circles* (for female voice, harp, and two percussionists), 1960; *Sinfonia* (for orchestra and eight amplified voices), 1969; *Un re in ascolto* (*A King Listens*, opera), 1984; *Rendering* (for orchestra), 1990

## Hans Werner Henze

1926–2012, GERMAN

Although he worked in various genres, Henze was above all a man of the theater—the leading avant-garde opera composer of his generation. He spent his early career in Germany, then moved to Italy in 1963; he also traveled widely to supervise and conduct his work and to teach. His work was strongly influenced by his socialist political views—he said he always wanted to produce "something the masses can understand." His oratorio *The Raft of the Medusa*, was written in honor of the recently killed revolutionary Che Guevara and provoked a riot at its premiere in Hamburg in 1968. In addition to operas, ballets, and other stage works, his output included much orchestral music (notably 10 symphonies) and chamber music. Stylistically, his work is varied, influenced by jazz and Arabic music among other sources.

**KEY WORKS:** *Boulevard Solitude*, 1951; *The Raft of the Medusa*, 1968; *We Come to the River*, 1976; Symphony No. 10, 2000

## Sofia Gubaidulina

BORN 1931, RUSSIAN

The outstanding woman composer to emerge from the Soviet Union, Gubaidulina has lived in Germany since 1992, and by the turn of the century had an international reputation, winning numerous awards and attracting commissions from leading orchestras and soloists. She is deeply spiritual and her works are often informed by religious and philosophical ideas and by a sense of mystical yearning (in 1979, she was denounced by Soviet authorities for producing "noisy mud instead of real musical innovation"). Her output includes orchestral, choral, chamber and instrumental music, stage works, and film scores. She often uses unusual combinations of instruments and blends elements of the Western classical tradition with influences from Asiatic music.

**KEY WORKS:** *Offertorium* (violin concerto), 1980; *Jetzt immer Schnee* (*Now Always Snow*, cantata for voices and instruments), 1993; *St. John Passion*, 2000; *Mary Queen of Scots* (film score), 2013

## Pauline Oliveros

1932–2016, AMERICAN

Determined to become a composer from the age of 16, Oliveros is known as an accordionist, author, and central component of post-war experimental music in the US. First presented with a tape-recording deck at age 21, she was a founding member of the San Francisco Tape Music Center, where she became interested in electronic composition.

Oliveros was best known for her work in improvisation and meditation, interests that grew into the Deep Listening program in the 1980s, inspiring musicians of all skill levels to respond to environmental conditions. Since her death in 2016, Oliveros's work has continued through The Pauline Oliveros Trust.

**KEY WORKS:** *Beautiful Soop* ,1966; *Suiren*, 1989; *Four Meditations for Orchestra*, 1996

## Henryk Górecki

1933–2010, POLISH

Until he was almost 60 years old, Górecki was a respected figure in contemporary music but he was

△ KRZYSZTOF PENDERECKI IN REHEARSAL AT THE KONZERTHAUS, BERLIN, 1997

virtually unknown to the world at large. This situation changed dramatically when a recording of his Symphony No. 3, released in 1992, became an international hit, selling more than a million copies, an unprecedented figure for a serious modern work. Slow and meditative throughout, it features a soprano singing three Polish texts on the themes of suffering and war.

Górecki was a devout Catholic and some critics have linked his work with that of other spiritually minded composers of the time (notably Arvo Pärt and John Tavener), categorizing their work under the heading "holy Minimalism." The serenity of their work seems to many listeners an antidote to the harshness of much modern music.

**KEY WORKS:** Symphony No. 1, 1959; *Two Sacred Songs*, 1971; Symphony No. 3 ("Symphony of Sorrowful Songs"), 1976; Harpsichord Concerto, 1980; *Miserere*, 1981

## △ Krzysztof Penderecki

1933–2020, POLISH

Penderecki was unusual among avant-garde artists in that his work appealed to a large public from the start of his career—a reflection of the way he conveyed his humanitarian views. He came to international attention with *Threnody for the Victims of Hiroshima* for string orchestra, a characteristically somber work in which he created a harshly expressive sound-world. It won him the first of a long list of prizes and led to several prestigious composition residencies.

Penderecki's work includes operas, symphonies, concertos, choral, and chamber music, and pieces for solo instruments. He often conducted his own work, and made a reputation as a conductor of the work of others.

**KEY WORKS:** *Threnody for the Victims of Hiroshima*, 1960; *The Devils of Loudun* (opera), 1969; *Polish Requiem*, 1984; Clarinet Quartet, 1993

## Harrison Birtwistle

1934–2022, BRITISH

Born in Accrington, Lancashire, Birtwistle grew up in the world of military and brass bands, and the sounds of brass and percussion are often to the fore in his music, which is characteristically energetic and often violent (although it also has moments of humor and lyrical beauty). Initially, he excelled as a clarinetist, but from his mid-twenties he concentrated on composing.

Birtwistle was the leading British opera composer of his day, although it was not until *Gawain* (1991) that he titled a piece "opera": his first work in the field, *Punch and Judy* (1967), was called a "comical tragedy or tragical comedy." He wrote orchestral, chamber, and solo instrumental music, as well as vocal pieces.

**KEY WORKS:** *Punch and Judy*, 1967; *Earth Dances*, 1986; *Gawain*, 1991; *The Minotaur*, 2008

## Steve Reich

BORN 1936, AMERICAN

A leading Minimalist composer, Reich had a rich musical upbringing. He was an accomplished jazz drummer in his teens, before studying at the Juilliard School in New York, and with Luciano Berio at Mills College in California. His work often involves the repetition and elaboration of phrases. He began by working with tape machines, playing recorded loops, and progressed to conventional instruments combined with speech, as in *Different Trains*. This blends a string quartet with recordings of train noises and voices speaking about trains, including ones that took victims to concentration camps during the Holocaust (part of his exploration of his Jewish heritage).

KEY WORKS: *Different Trains*, 1988; *The Cave* (multimedia opera), 1993; *Three Tales* (video opera), 2002

## John Tavener

1944–2013, BRITISH

Tavener enjoyed great success with spiritual, meditative works that appealed to people who were not interested in modern music. He made an early impact with *The Whale* (admired by The Beatles and recorded on their Apple label). In 1977, he was received into the Russian Orthodox Church. His music was influenced by its traditions, using simple motifs to create a mood of contemplation. His fame soared when *Song for Athene* (written in tribute to a friend who died) was performed at the funeral of Diana, Princess of Wales, in 1997. Most of his work is choral, but *The Protecting Veil* for cello and strings is one of his most acclaimed compositions.

KEY WORKS: *The Whale*, 1966; *The Lamb*, 1982; *The Protecting Veil*, 1988; *Song for Athene*, 1993

## Alexina Louie

BORN 1949, CANADIAN

A Canadian of Chinese descent, Louie blends Eastern and Western influences in her work. She studied at the University of British Columbia and the University of California at San Diego, receiving a master's degree in composition. In the 1980s, after a decade in California, teaching piano, theory, and electronic composition, she settled in Toronto. Her first big success was *O magnum mysterium* for string orchestra, written in memory of the Canadian pianist Glenn Gould who died in 1982. The piano is her main instrument, but she has written for the orchestra, chamber groups, voice, synthesizers, and computers.

KEY WORKS: *O magnum mysterium*, 1982; *I Leap Through the Sky with Stars* (piano solo), 1991; *Triple Concerto for Three Violins and Orchestra*, 2017

## Chen Yi

BORN 1953, CHINESE-AMERICAN

Chen began studying the piano at the age of three, and was soon introduced to violin and memorizing works by classical composers. Taken to a work camp during the Chinese Cultural Revolution (1966–1967), she was only allowed to play works deemed appropriate by the government. Following the Revolution, she became concertmaster of the Peking Opera in Beijing and began a degree at the conservatory in the city. In 1986, she moved to New York City to complete her composition doctorate.

Chen has written orchestral, chamber and choral works, many of them composed for a combination of Western and Chinese instruments, and inspired by Chinese folk music.

KEY WORKS: *Xian Shi*, 1983; *Sprout*, 1986; *Chinese Folk Dance Suite*, 2001

## ◁ Eric Whitacre

BORN 1970, AMERICAN

Whitacre has achieved huge popular success, particularly with choral compositions, which his admirers find serene and uplifting. His early musical education was patchy, but he discovered a love of choral singing when he participated in a student performance of Mozart's *Requiem* and subsequently trained at the Juilliard School, New York. Since the late 1990s, he has lived mainly in Los Angeles. Whitacre's flair as a public speaker has enhanced his appeal. His work is performed by amateur as well as professional singers, and in 2009 he launched Online Choir, in which people all over the world post online videos of themselves singing his work, which are synchronized into a composite performance.

KEY WORKS: *Water Night*, 1995; *Sleep*, 2000; *Lux Aurumque* (*Light and Gold*), 2000; *Paradise Lost: Shadows and Wings*, 2003; *The River Cam*, 2011

△ ERIC WHITACRE CONDUCTING AT THE ROYAL ALBERT HALL, LONDON, 2015

# Glossary

Words in **bold** within a definition can be cross-referenced to their own entry.

**12-tone music**
Works in which each note of the **chromatic scale** is ascribed the same amount of importance, eliminating any concept of **key** or **tonality**. Developed by Arnold Schoenberg and others in the 1920s. *See also* serialism.

**a cappella**
Unaccompanied singing by a soloist or a group.

**alto**
The highest male and lowest female voice; also a term describing an instrument that is lower in **pitch** than a **treble** instrument.

**aria**
Literally "air" (Italian), a vocal piece, usually for one voice, in an **opera** or **oratorio**, more formally organized than a song. Arias written in the 17th and 18th centuries usually take the form of "da capo arias," with a three-part structure.

**arpeggio**
A **chord** in which the notes are played separately from top to bottom or vice-versa.

**atonal, atonality**
Any music without a recognizable **tonality** or **key**, such as **serial music**; the opposite of tonality.

**Baroque**
Music composed between 1600 and 1750; describes pieces from the period before the **Classical**.

**bass**
The lowest in pitch: describes the lowest male voice, the lowest part of a **chord** or piece of music, or the lowest instrument in a family.

**basso continuo**
Harmonic accompaniment, usually by a harpsichord or organ and bass viol or cello, extensively used in the **Baroque** period.

**bel canto**
Meaning "beautiful song" in Italian; an 18th- and early 19th-century school of singing characterized by a concentration on beauty of tone, virtuosic agility, and breath control.

**cantata**
A **programmatic** piece, generally for solo voices, choir, and orchestra, designed to tell a story.

**castrato (pl. castrati)**
Literally "castrated" (Italian); a male singer castrated before puberty so as to retain his high **alto** or **soprano** voice. Castrati were especially popular in 17th- and early 18th-century Italian **opera**, but castration for the purposes of art was banned by the late 18th century.

**chamber music**
Pieces composed for small groups of two or more instruments, such as duets, trios, and quartets.

**chord**
A simultaneous combination of notes. The most frequently used are called "triads," which consist of three distinct notes built on the first, third, and fifth notes of a **scale**. For example, in the **key** of C major the notes of the scale are C, D, E, F, G, A, and B; the C major triad consists of the notes C, E, and G.

**chromatic**
Literally "of color" (Latin), based on the **scale** of all 12 **semitones** in an **octave**, as opposed to **diatonic**, based on a scale of seven notes.

**Classical**
Music composed between 1750 and 1830; describes pieces from the period after the **Baroque**.

**concerto**
A large piece for solo instrument and orchestra, designed to showcase the soloist's skills; the **Baroque** *concerto grosso*, however, has a more equal interplay between the smaller orchestra (*ripieno*) and a group of soloists (*concertino*).

**concerto grosso**
*See* concerto.

**consort**
An instrumental ensemble popular during the 16th and 17th centuries in England; also used to describe the music played by these ensembles as well as the performance itself.

**contralto**
A term describing the lowest of the female voices (**alto**) in an **opera** context.

**contrapuntal**
Using counterpoint, the simultaneous playing or singing of two or more equally important melodic lines.

**counterpoint**
*See* contrapuntal.

**diatonic**
Based on a **scale** in which the **octave** is divided into seven steps, such as major and minor scales.

**dissonance**
Notes being played together to produce discord (sounds unpleasing to the ear).

**Formalism**
In the Soviet Union and Eastern Bloc countries, a catch-all criticism aimed at those who did not write music that sought to glorify the Soviet state.

**fugue**
From the Italian *fuga*, "chase" or "flight"; a highly structured **contrapuntal** piece, in two or more parts, popular in the **Baroque** era. The separate voices or lines enter one by one imitatively.

**gamelan**
The traditional ensemble music of Indonesia, featuring predominantly percussion instruments such as gongs, xylophones, and drums.

**grand opera**
French development of **opera**, characterized by historical plots, large choruses, crowd scenes, ornate costumes, and spectacular sets.

**intermezzo**
A light-hearted interlude performed between the acts of an ***opera seria***. The intermezzo developed from the intermedio, a short musical drama performed between the acts of spoken plays in the 15th and 16th centuries.

**inversion**
A **chord** or line of music is said to be inverted when its component notes have been reshuffled in a different order.

**key**
The **tonal** center of a piece of music, based on the first note of the **scale**.

**leitmotif**
Literally "leading motif" (German); a short musical phrase that recurs through a piece to indicate the presence of a character, emotion, or object.

**libretto (pl. libretti)**
The text of an **opera** or other vocal dramatic work.

**Lied (pl. Lieder)**
A traditional German song, popularized by Schubert.

**madrigal**
A secular **a cappella** song popular in Renaissance and early **Baroque** England and Italy; it was often set to a love poem.

**Mass**
The main service of the Roman Catholic Church, highly formalized in structure, comprising specific sections—known as the "Ordinary"—performed in the following order: *Kyrie, Gloria, Credo, Sanctus* with *Hosanna* and *Benedictus*, and *Agnus Dei* with *Dona nobis pacem*.

**mezzo-soprano**
Literally "half soprano"; the lowest **soprano** voice; between soprano and **contralto**.

**Minimalism**
A predominantly American school of music, favoring a sound-world involving an almost hypnotic texture of repeated short patterns.

**mode**
A type of seven-note **scale** with distinct melodic characteristics; most commonly heard in folk music and **plainsong**.

**motet**
A **polyphonic** choral composition based on a sacred text, usually unaccompanied.

**nocturne**
"Night piece." As a solo, one-movement piano piece, the nocturne originated with John Field, but was developed to a great degree by Chopin.

**octave**
The interval between one **pitch** and another with double or half its frequency; on a piano there is an octave between high C and the next-highest C note.

**opera**
A drama in which all or most characters sing and in which music is an important element; usually all dialogue is sung.

**opera buffa**
A type of comic **opera** that became popular in the 18th century; the opposite of *opera seria*.

**opéra comique**
An exclusively French type of **opera** that, despite its name, is not always comic, nor particularly light; also includes spoken dialogue.

**opera seria**
Literally "serious **opera**," the direct opposite of *opera buffa*; characterized by heroic or mythological plots, and formality in both music and action.

**operetta**
Italian for "little **opera**," sometimes known as "light opera"; a lighter 19th-century style including spoken dialogue.

**oratorio**
A sacred work for vocal soloists and choir with instrumental accompaniment; differs from an **opera** in that an oratorio is a concert piece, not a drama.

**overture**
From the French for "opening"; an instrumental introduction to an **opera** or ballet, in which some of the main musical themes are presented.

**pitch**
The position of one sound in relation to the range of **tonal** sounds—how high or low it is—which depends on the frequency of sound waves.

**plainsong**
Medieval church music also known as plainchant; consists of a unison, unaccompanied vocal line in free rhythm, like speech, with no regular bar lengths.

**pizzicato**
A style of playing stringed instruments that are usually played with a bow, by plucking the strings with the fingers.

**polyphony**
Literally "many sounds," this refers to a style of writing in which all parts are independent and of equal importance, and therefore implies **contrapuntal** music. Forms that typify this style include the **fugue** and **motet**.

**prelude**
A short piece of music generally intended as the introduction to a longer composition, although sometimes used for stand-alone pieces.

**programmatic, program music**
Any music written to describe a nonmusical theme, such as an event, landscape, or literary work.

**recitative**
A style of singing in **opera** and **oratorio** closely related to the delivery of dramatic speech in **pitch** and rhythm; often used for dialogue and exposition of the plot between **arias** and choruses.

**Romantic**
The cultural epoch heralded in music by Beethoven, which dominated the 19th century.

**rondo**
A piece of music based on a recurring theme with interspersed material; follows a form such as ABACADAE.

**scale**
A series of notes that define a tune and, usually, the **key** of the piece. Different scales give music a different feeling and "color."

**semitone**
The smallest musical interval between notes in Western **tonal** music. There are two semitones in a whole note and 12 semitones in an **octave**.

**serialism, serial music**
A system of **atonal** composition developed in the 1920s by Arnold Schoenberg and others, in which fixed sequences of music are used as a foundation to create a more complex whole work.

*Singspiel*
Literally "song play" (German), generally refers to a comic **opera** with spoken dialogue in lieu of **recitative**, as typified in Mozart's *The Magic Flute*.

**sonata**
A popular instrumental piece for one or more players; originated in the **Baroque** period, when the term referred to a short piece for a solo or small group of instruments accompanied by a *basso continuo*. The **Classical** sonata adhered to a three- or four-movement structure for one or two instruments (although the trio sonata was often popular).

**sonata form**
A structural form popularized in the **Classical** period. From this period onwards, the first movements of **sonatas**, **symphonies**, and **concertos** were mainly written in this form.

**song cycle**
A group of songs that tells a story or shares a common theme; designed to be performed in a sequence as a single entity.

**soprano**
The highest of the four standard singing voices—above **alto**, **tenor**, and **bass**; term for a female or a young boy singing in this vocal range.

**stave**
The grid of five horizontal lines on which music is written; also called a "staff."

**suite**
A multi-movement work—generally instrumental—made up of a series of contrasting dance movements, usually all in one **key**.

**symphonic poem**
An extended single-movement symphonic work, usually of a **programmatic** nature, often describing landscape or literary works. Also known as a tone poem.

**symphony**
A large-scale work for full orchestra; **Classical** and some **Romantic** symphonies both contain four movements—traditionally an allegro, a slower second movement, a scherzo, and a lively finale. The first movement is often in **sonata** form, and the slow movement and finale may follow a similar structure. Later symphonies can contain more or fewer movements.

**tenor**
The highest natural adult male voice; also a term describing an instrument in this range.

**timbre**
The particular quality (literally "stamp"), or character, of a sound that enables a listener to distinguish one instrument (or voice) from another; synonymous with "tone color."

**tonal, tonality**
A system of major and minor **scales** and **keys**; forms the basis of all Western music from the 17th century until Schoenberg in the early 20th century.

**tone poem**
*See* symphonic poem.

**treble**
The highest unchanged male voice, or the highest instrument or part in a piece of music.

**triad**
*See* chord.

**verismo**
A post-**Romantic** style of **opera** with thematic material and presentation rooted firmly in reality.

**vibrato**
The rapid, regular variation of **pitch** around a single note for expressive effect.

# Index

Page numbers in **bold** refer to main entries

# Acknowledgments

Toucan would like to thank Julie Brooke for proofreading and Vanessa Bird for indexing. The publisher would like to thank the following for their kind permission to reproduce their photographs:

(Key: a-above; b-below; c-center; l-left; r-right; t-top)

1 Dorling Kindersley: Gary Ombler / National Music Museum (c). 2 Getty Images: DEA / A. DAGLI ORTI / Contributor (c). 3 Alamy Stock Photo: Peter Horree (c). 5 Getty Images: DEA / G. DAGLI ORTI / Contributor (c). 12 akg-images: Album / Oronoz (tr). 13 Alamy Stock Photo: The Picture Art Collection (tr). aerial-photos.com (bl). 13 Getty Images: Heritage Images / Contributor (br). 14 Alamy Stock Photo: imageBROKER (c). 15 Alamy Stock Photo: Peer Marlow (tr). 15 akg-images: Erich Lessing (br). 16 Getty Images: Mondadori Portfolio / Contributor (tl). 16 Alamy Stock Photo: Niday Picture Library (br). 17 akg-images: (ca). 17 Getty Images: Heritage Images / Contributor (br). 18 Bridgeman Images: Photo © Ravenna (c). 18 Getty Images: Photo Josse/Leemage / Contributor (cr). 19 akg-images: Erich Lessing (c). 20 Alamy Stock Photo: James Hadley (tr). 21 Alamy Stock Photo: Lebrecht Music & Arts (tr). Mike Booth (bc). 21 Getty Images: DEA / G. NIMATALLAH / Contributor (br). 22 Getty Images: Education Images / Contributor (cl). 22 Bridgeman Images: © Marage Photos (bc). 23 Getty Images: DEA / A. DAGLI ORTI / Contributor (c). 24 Bridgeman Images: (c). 25 Alamy Stock Photo: Lebrecht Music & Arts (c). Peter Horree (crb). 26 Getty Images: Hulton Archive / Stringer (tr). 27 Alamy Stock Photo: World History Archive (tc). PAINTING (tr). Ian Dagnall (bl). 28 Getty Images: DEA / A. DAGLI ORTI / Contributor (c). 29 Alamy Stock Photo: Lebrecht Music & Arts (tr). Lebrecht Music & Arts (br). 30 Getty Images: Heritage Images / Contributor (tr). 31 Bridgeman Images: © British Library Board. All Rights Reserved (tl). 31 Alamy Stock Photo: ART Collection (cr). 31 akg-images: historic-maps (br). 32 Alamy Stock Photo: Photo 12 (br). 33 Alamy Stock Photo: Art Collection 2 (tl). 36 Getty Images: Heritage Images / Contributor (c). 37 Alamy Stock Photo: Tibor Bognar (tr). Hemis (br). 38 Alamy Stock Photo: UtCon Collection (tl). Westend61 GmbH (tr). 38 Getty Images: DEA PICTURE LIBRARY / Contributor (bl). 39 Getty Images: ullstein bild / Contributor (t). 40 Getty Images: DEA / A. DAGLI ORTI / Contributor (bl). DEA / G. NIMATALLAH / Contributor (cr). 41 Alamy Stock Photo: Heritage Image Partnership Ltd (c). 42 akg-images: Erich Lessing (c). 43 Getty Images: DEA PICTURE LIBRARY / Contributor (c). 43 Alamy Stock Photo: Heritage Image Partnership Ltd (br). 44 Alamy Stock Photo: The Picture Art Collection (tr). Lebrecht Music & Arts (br). 45 Alamy Stock Photo: History and Art Collection (c). 46 Getty Images: UniversalImagesGroup / Contributor (tr). 47 Getty Images: DEA PICTURE LIBRARY / Contributor (tl). 47 Bridgeman Images: (cr). 47 Alamy Stock Photo: Lebrecht Music & Arts (br). 48 Getty Images: DEA / A. DAGLI ORTI / Contributor (c). 49 Getty Images: Mondadori Portfolio / Contributor (cl). DEA / E. LESSING / Contributor (br). 50 akg-images: Fototeca Gilardi (tl). (bc). 51 Getty Images: DEA / A. DAGLI ORTI / Contributor (l). 52 Getty Images: DEA PICTURE LIBRARY / Contributor (tr). 53 Getty Images: DEA / A. DAGLI ORTI / Contributor (tr). 53 akg-images: (br). 54 Getty Images: DEA / G. DAGLI ORTI / Contributor (c). 55 Getty Images: DEA / A. DAGLI ORTI / Contributor (ca). AKSARAN / Contributor (bl). DEA / A. DAGLI ORTI / Contributor (crb). 56 akg-images: (cl). 56 Bridgeman Images: Graham Salter (cr). 57 Getty Images: Print Collector / Contributor (c). 58 Alamy Stock Photo: Lebrecht Music & Arts (tl). 58 Bridgeman Images: (tr). 58 Alamy Stock Photo: tilialucida (bc). 59 Bridgeman Images: Lebrecht Music Arts (t). 60 Getty Images: DEA PICTURE LIBRARY / Contributor (t). 61 Bridgeman Images: (tl). 61 Getty Images: DEA / A. DAGLI ORTI / Contributor (cr). Heritage Images / Contributor (cb). 62 Getty Images: Heritage Images / Contributor (cl). DEA PICTURE LIBRARY / Contributor (cr). 62 Alamy Stock Photo: age fotostock (br). 63 Getty Images: DEA PICTURE LIBRARY / Contributor (c). 64 Getty Images: Leemage / Contributor (c). 65 Alamy Stock Photo: dpa picture alliance (cla). 65 Getty Images: DEA PICTURE LIBRARY / Contributor (crb). 66 Bridgeman Images: (tc). 66 Alamy Stock Photo: ART Collection (bl). 67 Alamy Stock Photo: Artokoloro Quint Lox Limited (bl). 67 Getty Images: Leemage / Contributor (cra). 68 Getty Images: Heritage Images / Contributor (tr). 69 Getty Images: DEA / A. DAGLI ORTI / Contributor (tc). 69 Alamy Stock Photo: Lebrecht Music & Arts (cr). dpa picture alliance (bl). 70 akg-images: De Agostini Picture Lib. / A. Dagli Orti (bl). 70 Alamy Stock Photo: Heritage Image Partnership Ltd (br). 71 Getty Images: Leemage / Contributor (c). 72 akg-images: Erich Lessing (t). 72 TopFoto: Granger, NYC (cb). 73 Getty Images: Imagno / Contributor (clb). 74 Alamy Stock Photo: Art Collection 3 (c). 74 Dreamstime.com: Vvoevale (r). 75 Alamy Stock Photo: agefotostock. 76 Getty Images: DEA PICTURE LIBRARY / Contributor (cr). DEA / A. DAGLI ORTI / Contributor (tr). 77 akg-images: (tc). 77 Getty Images: ANDREAS SOLARO / Staff (bl). Imagno / Contributor (br). 78 Getty Images: Leemage / Contributor (c). 79 Getty Images: Stringer (tr). 79 Alamy Stock Photo: filmfoto (br). 80 Getty Images: Imagno / Contributor (t). 81 Bridgeman Images: Photo © Luisa Ricciarini (cra). 81 Getty Images: Leemage / Contributor (bc). Heritage Images / Contributor (br). 82 akg-images: Marion Kalter (cl). 82 Getty Images: Heritage Images / Contributor (cr). DEA / A. DAGLI ORTI / Contributor (bl). 83 Getty Images: Photo 12 / Contributor (t). 84 Getty Images: Heritage Images / Contributor (bc). 85 Getty Images: Hulton Archive / Stringer (tc). 88 Getty Images: Heritage Images / Contributor (c). 89 Getty Images: DEA / A. DAGLI ORTI / Contributor (tr). Photo Josse/Leemage / Contributor (br). 90 akg-images: Erich Lessing (tr). 90 Alamy Stock Photo: Lebrecht Music & Arts (br). 91 Alamy Stock Photo: Ian Dagnall (c). 92-93 Getty Images: Hiroyuki Ito / Contributor (tl). 92 Getty Images: DEA / S. VANNINI / Contributor (bl). 93 akg-images: Beethoven-Haus Bonn (tr). 93 Alamy Stock Photo: Granger Historical Picture Archive (br). 94 Alamy Stock Photo: GL Archive (tr). 94 Getty Images: Imagno / Contributor (clb). 95 akg-images: Beethoven-Haus Bonn (tr). 95 Getty Images: DEA / A. DAGLI ORTI / Contributor (b). 96 Alamy Stock Photo: Heritage Image Partnership Ltd (tr). 96 Getty Images: DE AGOSTINI PICTURE LIBRARY / Contributor (tl). 97 Alamy Stock Photo: Ian Dagnall (bc). 97 Getty Images: Hulton Archive / Stringer (br). 98 Getty Images: DEA / A. DAGLI ORTI / Contributor (c). 99 Alamy Stock Photo: Lebrecht Music & Arts (cla). Heritage Image Partnership Ltd (br). 100 Alamy Stock Photo: The Picture Art Collection (bl). 100 Getty Images: DEA / A. DE GREGORIO / Contributor (br). 101 akg-images: (br). 102 Getty Images: DEA / A. DAGLI ORTI / Contributor (c). 103 Getty Images: Central Press / Stringer (cr). 103 Alamy Stock Photo: Artokoloro Quint Lox Limited (br). 104 Getty Images: Imagno / Contributor (cl). 104 Alamy Stock Photo: Granger Historical Picture Archive (bc). 105 Getty Images: Imagno / Contributor (t). 106 Getty Images: DEA / A. DAGLI ORTI / Contributor (tr). 107 Getty Images: DEA / A. DAGLI ORTI / Contributor (tl). 107 akg-images: (cr). 107 Getty Images: Hulton Archive / Stringer (br). 108 Getty Images: Stefano Bianchetti / Contributor (c). 109 Getty Images: DEA / A. DAGLI ORTI / Contributor. UniversalImagesGroup / Contributor (bl). 110 Getty Images: DEA / G. DAGLI ORTI / Contributor (tr). 110 Alamy Stock Photo: Photo 12 (br). 111 Getty Images: Heritage Images / Contributor (c). 112 Getty Images: Heritage Images / Contributor (bl). Apic / Contributor (br). 113 Getty Images: Robbie Jack / Contributor (t). DE AGOSTINI PICTURE LIBRARY / Contributor (br). 114 Getty Images: Heritage Images / Contributor (c). 115 akg-images: (cla). 115 Getty Images: Hiroyuki Ito / Contributor (bl). 115 Alamy Stock Photo: The Picture Art Collection (crb). 116 akg-images: (tr). 116 Alamy Stock Photo: Artokoloro Quint Lox Limited (br). 117 Bridgeman Images: DHM (c). 118 Alamy Stock Photo: allan wright (b). 119 Getty Images: Heritage Images / Contributor (tl). 119 Bridgeman Images: Lebrecht Music Arts (cr). 119 Alamy Stock Photo: Lebrecht Music & Arts (cb). 120 Getty Images: Photo 12 / Contributor (c). 121 akg-images: (c). Erich Lessing (br). 122 Getty Images: Universal History Archive / Contributor (tr). DEA / A. DAGLI ORTI / Contributor (bc). 123 Getty Images: Fine Art Photographic / Contributor (t). Heritage Images / Contributor (br). 124 Getty Images: DEA / A. DAGLI ORTI / Contributor (c). DEA / A. DAGLI ORTI / Contributor (bl). 124 Getty Images: Heritage Images / Contributor (cr). 125 akg-images: (c). 126 Getty Images: DEA / A. DAGLI ORTI / Contributor (tl). 127 Getty Images: DEA / A. DAGLI ORTI / Contributor (tr). Bettmann / Contributor (b). 128 Getty Images: Imagno / Contributor (tr). 129 Getty Images: Imagno / Contributor (tl). Raphael GAILLARDE / Contributor (tr). 129 Bridgeman Images: Archives Charmet (br). 130 Getty Images: DEA / A. DAGLI ORTI / Contributor (t). DEA / A. DAGLI ORTI / Contributor (bl). 131 Getty Images: API / Contributor (tl). DEA / A. DAGLI ORTI / Contributor (br). 132 Getty Images: Imagno / Contributor (bl). 133 Getty Images: Universal History Archive / Contributor (tr). 136 Getty Images: Apic / Contributor (tr). Heritage Images / Contributor (bl). 137 Getty Images: Heritage Images / Contributor (c). 138 Getty Images: DEA / A. DAGLI ORTI / Contributor (cl). 138 Alamy Stock Photo: Lebrecht Music & Arts (br). 139 akg-images: (t). 139 Getty Images: Imagno / Contributor (br). 140 Getty Images: DEA / A. DAGLI ORTI / Contributor (tr). DEA / A. DAGLI ORTI / Contributor (br). 141 Getty Images: Heritage Images / Contributor (c). 142 Alamy Stock Photo: Heritage Image Partnership Ltd (tr). 142 Getty Images: DEA PICTURE LIBRARY / Contributor (cl). 142 Alamy Stock Photo: MB_Photo (br). 143 Getty Images: Jean-Marc ZAORSKI /

Contributor (t). **144 Getty Images:** Heritage Images / Contributor (tr). **145 Getty Images:** DEA / A. DAGLI ORTI / Contributor (c). **145 Alamy Stock Photo:** Lebrecht Music & Arts (bl). INTERFOTO (br). **146 Alamy Stock Photo:** Art Collection 3 (tr). **146 Bridgeman Images:** Archives Charmet (tl). **147 Getty Images:** Bettmann / Contributor (bc). **147 Alamy Stock Photo:** Gabriele Dessì (cr). **148 Getty Images:** DEA / A. DAGLI ORTI / Contributor (ca). Imagno / Contributor (cr). **148 Alamy Stock Photo:** Marek Zuk (bl).
**149 Getty Images:** DEA / A. DAGLI ORTI / Contributor (c). **150 Getty Images:** Heritage Images / Contributor (tr). **151 Getty Images:** DEA / A. DAGLI ORTI / Contributor (cr). **151 Alamy Stock Photo:** imageBROKER (bl). **152 akg-images:** Erich Lessing (tr). **152 Getty Images:** DEA / A. DAGLI ORTI / Contributor (bl). **153 Getty Images:** Imagno / Contributor (tr). **154 Getty Images:** DEA / A. DAGLI ORTI / Contributor (c). **155 akg-images:** Fototeca Gilardi (tr). **155 Getty Images:** Heritage Images / Contributor (br). **156 Alamy Stock Photo:** Pictorial Press Ltd (tr). **157 Getty Images:** Heritage Images / Contributor (tr). **157 Alamy Stock Photo:** Heritage Image Partnership Ltd (bl). Lebrecht Music & Arts (cr). **158 akg-images:** (ca). **158 Getty Images:** ullstein bild Dtl. / Contributor (bl). Heritage Images / Contributor (crb). **159 Getty Images:** DE AGOSTINI PICTURE LIBRARY / Contributor (c). **160 Getty Images:** UniversalImagesGroup / Contributor (tl). W. and D. Downey / Stringer (tr). **160 Getty Images:** DE AGOSTINI PICTURE LIBRARY / Contributor (bl). **161 Getty Images:** Imagno / Contributor (t). **162 Alamy Stock Photo:** Heritage Image Partnership Ltd (tr). **163 Getty Images:** DE AGOSTINI PICTURE LIBRARY / Contributor (tl). DEA / A. DAGLI ORTI / Contributor (cr). ND / Contributor (br). **164 Getty Images:** DEA / A. DAGLI ORTI / Contributor (cla). **164 Alamy Stock Photo:** The Picture Art Collection (tr). **164 Getty Images:** Christophel Fine Art / Contributor (br). **165 Getty Images:** DE AGOSTINI PICTURE LIBRARY / Contributor (c). **166 Bridgeman Images:** Lebrecht Music Arts (tr). **166 akg-images:** Sputnik (bl). **167 Getty Images:** Fine Art / Contributor (c). **168 Getty Images:** Heritage Images / Contributor (c). **169 Alamy Stock Photo:** Lebrecht Music & Arts (cl). **169 Getty Images:** Heritage Images / Contributor (br). **170 Getty Images:** Imagno / Contributor (cl). **170 Bridgeman Images:** (c). **171 Getty Images:** Bojan Brecelj / Contributor (t). **171 Alamy Stock Photo:** Lebrecht Music & Arts (br). **172 Alamy Stock Photo:** Lebrecht Music & Arts (ca). **172 akg-images:** De Agostini Picture Lib. / A. Dagli Orti (crb). **172 Alamy Stock Photo:** Lebrecht Music & Arts (bl). **173 Getty Images:** DEA / A. DAGLI ORTI / Contributor (c). **174 Alamy Stock Photo:** Chris Fredriksson (tl). **174 Getty Images:** DEA / A. DAGLI ORTI / Contributor (br). **175 Alamy Stock Photo:** CBW (cr). **175 Getty Images:** ullstein bild Dtl. / Contributor (bl). **176 Getty Images:** Heritage Images / Contributor (c). **177 Getty Images:** DEA / A. DAGLI ORTI / Contributor (cla). **177 Alamy Stock Photo:** age fotostock (crb). **178 Getty Images:** Time Life Pictures / Contributor (tr). Culture Club / Contributor (cl). **179 Alamy Stock Photo:** The History Collection (tr). **179 Bridgeman Images:** Graham Salter (b). **180 Getty Images:** Universal History Archive / Contributor (c). **181 Bridgeman Images:** Lebrecht Music Arts (bl). **181 Alamy Stock Photo:** Heritage Image Partnership Ltd (br). **182 Getty Images:** Heritage Images / Contributor (tr). **183 akg-images:** (tl). **183 Getty Images:** DEA / G. DAGLI ORTI / Contributor (br). **183 Alamy Stock Photo:** Lebrecht Music & Arts (bc). **184 ECPAD:** (t). **184 Getty Images:** HUM Images / Universal Images Group (b). **185 Alamy Stock Photo:** Chronicle. **186 Getty Images:** Bettmann / Contributor (c). **187 Bridgeman Images:** A. Dagli Orti / De Agostini Picture Library (cr). **187 Getty Images:** DEA / A. DAGLI ORTI / Contributor (br). **188 Getty Images:** MPI / Stringer (bl). DEA / ARCHIVIO J. LANGE / Contributor (br). **189 Getty Images:** DEA / A. DAGLI ORTI / Contributor (t). DEA / A. DAGLI ORTI / Contributor (br). **190 Alamy Stock Photo:** INTERFOTO (tl). Painters (cr). INTERFOTO (bl). **191 Getty Images:** Imagno / Contributor (c). **192 Getty Images:** DEA / A. DAGLI ORTI / Contributor (c). Imagno / Contributor (bl). Imagno / Contributor (br). **193 Getty Images:** Heritage Images / Contributor (tr). **194 Getty Images:** DEA / G. DAGLI ORTI / Contributor (tr). **195 Getty Images:** Christophel Fine Art / Contributor (tl). **195 Alamy Stock Photo:** Granger Historical Picture Archive (tr). **195 Getty Images:** DEA / G. DAGLI ORTI / Contributor (br). **196 Getty Images:** Barney Burstein / Contributor (t). **197 Alamy Stock Photo:** Granger Historical Picture Archive (bl). **197 Getty Images:** UniversalImagesGroup / Contributor (br). **198 Getty Images:** Hulton Deutsch / Contributor (tr). **199 Getty Images:** DEA / A. DAGLI ORTI / Contributor (br). **202 Bridgeman Images:** AFC (tr). **203 Bridgeman Images:** AFC (tl). **203 Getty Images:** DEA / A. DAGLI ORTI / Contributor (tr). DEA / A. DAGLI ORTI / Contributor (bl). **204 Bridgeman Images:** (tr). **205 Alamy Stock Photo:** Heritage Image Partnership Ltd (tr). **205 Bridgeman Images:** Tully Potter (cr). **205 Alamy Stock Photo:** David Jones (bl). **206-207 Getty Images:** Laurie Noble (tl). **206 Getty Images:** DE AGOSTINI PICTURE LIBRARY / Contributor (br). **207 Alamy Stock Photo:** Lebrecht Music & Arts (cr). travelib history (br). **208 Getty Images:** Sasha / Stringer (c). **209 Getty Images:** Heritage Images / Contributor (c). **209 Alamy Stock Photo:** David Cole (br). **210 Bridgeman Images:** Lebrecht Music Arts (tr). **210 Getty Images:** Michael Ward / Contributor (br). **211 Bridgeman**

**Images:** Stefano Baldini (c). **212 Getty Images:** Bettmann / Contributor (c). **213 Alamy Stock Photo:** Lebrecht Music & Arts (cl). **213 Getty Images:** Galerie Bilderwelt / Contributor (br). **214 Getty Images:** DEA / A. DAGLI ORTI / Contributor (tl). Heritage Images / Contributor (tr). **215 Getty Images:** Imagno / Contributor (b). **216 Alamy Stock Photo:** Granger Historical Picture Archive (tr). **217 Bridgeman Images:** Lebrecht Music Arts (tl). **217 Alamy Stock Photo:** Lebrecht Music & Arts (tr). Frank Bach (br). **218 Alamy Stock Photo:** 915 collection (cr). **218 akg-images:** (bl). **219 Getty Images:** DE AGOSTINI PICTURE LIBRARY / Contributor (c). **220 Bridgeman Images:** A. Dagli Orti / De Agostini Picture Library (tr). **220 Getty Images:** Heritage Images / Contributor (b). **221 Getty Images:** DEA / A. DAGLI ORTI / Contributor (tl). **221 Alamy Stock Photo:** World History Archive (br). **222 Getty Images:** API / Contributor (tr). LL / Contributor (bl). **223 akg-images:** (c). **224 Getty Images:** Heritage Images / Contributor (tl). Print Collector / Contributor (b). **225 Alamy Stock Photo:** Lebrecht Music & Arts (tl). INTERFOTO (cr). **226 Alamy Stock Photo:** Holly Ramer / Associated Press (l). **226 Library of Congress, Washington, D.C.:** pnp-ppmsca-03000-03006v (r). **227 Alamy Stock Photo:** GRANGER - Historical Picture Archive. **228 Getty Images:** ullstein bild Dtl. / Contributor (tr). **229 Bridgeman Images:** British Library Board. All Rights Reserved (tr). **229 Alamy Stock Photo:** The National Trust Photolibrary (bl). **230 Bridgeman Images:** Lebrecht Music Arts (tc). **230 akg-images:** Fototeca Gilardi (bl). **231 Bridgeman Images:** Lebrecht Music Arts (bl). **232 Bridgeman Images:** (c). **233 Alamy Stock Photo:** Lebrecht Music & Arts (tl). **233 Bridgeman Images:** Richard Bebb Collection (br). **234 Alamy Stock Photo:** Granger Historical Picture Archive (tr). **234 Bridgeman Images:** Lebrecht Music Arts (cl). **235 Alamy Stock Photo:** Lebrecht Music & Arts (tr). **235 Getty Images:** Heritage Images / Contributor (bc). **236 Alamy Stock Photo:** Painters (tr). **237 akg-images:** (tc). **237 Alamy Stock Photo:** BRIAN HARRIS (b). **238 Getty Images:** Imagno / Contributor (c). **239 Getty Images:** DEA / A. DAGLI ORTI / Contributor (tr). Fine Art / Contributor (br). **240 Getty Images:** Heritage Images / Contributor (bl). **241 Bridgeman Images:** (tl). **241 Getty Images:** PhotoQuest / Contributor (br). **242 Bridgeman Images:** Lebrecht Music Arts (tr). **243 akg-images:** (tl). **243 Alamy Stock Photo:** Lebrecht Music & Arts (tr). **243 Getty Images:** DEA / A. DAGLI ORTI / Contributor (bc). **244 akg-images:** TT News Agency / SVT (c). **245 Alamy Stock Photo:** Lebrecht Music & Arts (cla). **245 Getty Images:** swim ink 2 llc / Contributor (br). **246 Alamy Stock Photo:** Painters (t). Lebrecht Music & Arts (br). **247 Getty Images:** DEA / G. DAGLI ORTI / Contributor (tl). **247 akg-images:** Imagno (cr). **248 Bridgeman Images:** Lebrecht Music Arts (tr). **248 akg-images:** Album / Oronoz (br). **249 Getty Images:** Heritage Images / Contributor (c). **250 Alamy Stock Photo:** Everett Collection Inc (tr). **251 Getty Images:** UniversalImagesGroup / Contributor (tl). Museum of Science and Industry, Chicago / Contributor (tr). DEA / A. DAGLI ORTI / Contributor (br). **252 Getty Images:** DEA / A. DAGLI ORTI / Contributor (b). **253 Alamy Stock Photo:** Lebrecht Music & Arts (tl). **253 Getty Images:** Sasha / Stringer (cr). DEA / A. DAGLI ORTI / Contributor (cb). **254 Getty Images:** George Hoyningen-Huene / Contributor (c). **255 Getty Images:** Photo Josse / Leemage / Contributor (bl). **255 Alamy Stock Photo:** Lebrecht Music & Arts (br). **256 Getty Images:** Keystone-France / Contributor (tr). DE AGOSTINI PICTURE LIBRARY / Contributor (clb). **257 akg-images:** (br). **258 Alamy Stock Photo:** Hale Erguvenc (tr). **258 Getty Images:** GAB Archive / Contributor (br). **259 Getty Images:** Time Life Pictures / Contributor (c). **260 Getty Images:** Heritage Images / Contributor (c). **261 Getty Images:** Bettmann / Contributor (tr). ullstein bild / Contributor (br). **262 Getty Images:** Heritage Images / Contributor (tl). Photo Josse / Leemage / Contributor (b). **263 Getty Images:** Hiroyuki Ito / Contributor (tc). Heritage Images / Contributor (br). **264 Alamy Stock Photo:** Granger Historical Picture Archive (tr). **265 Getty Images:** Erich Auerbach / Stringer (tr). **265 akg-images:** Eric Vandeville (bl). **266 Miriam Matthew photograph collection, Special Collections, Charles E. Young Research Library, UCLA. 267 Alamy Stock Photo:** Lebrecht Music & Arts (t). **267 Bridgeman Images:** Peter Newark American Pictures (br). **267 Miriam Matthew photograph collection, Special Collections, Charles E. Young Research Library, UCLA** (bl). **268 Getty Images:** Choumoff / Contributor (tr). **269 Alamy Stock Photo:** The Picture Art Collection (tr). Brian Lawrence (bl). **270 Alamy Stock Photo:** Lebrecht Music & Arts (c). **271 Getty Images:** Heritage Images / Contributor (cla). UniversalImagesGroup / Contributor (br). **272 Getty Images:** Robbie Jack / Contributor (cla). **272 Alamy Stock Photo:** Lebrecht Music & Arts (tr). **273 Bridgeman Images:** Lebrecht Music Arts (tr). **273 Getty Images:** Heritage Images / Contributor (bc). **274 Booth Family Center for Special Collections, Georgetown University Library:** (c). **274 Getty Images:** Fred Stein Archive / Archive Photos / Contributor (br). **275 Alamy Stock Photo:** Pictorial Press. **276 SuperStock:** Album / Kurwenal / Prisma / Album Archivo. **277 Alamy Stock Photo:** The Picture Art Collection (tc). **278 Special Collections, University of Arkansas Libraries, Fayetteville. 279 Getty Images:** ullstein bild / Contributor (br). **282 Getty Images:** Keystone / Staff (tr). **283 akg-images:** Album / Oronoz (tc). **283 Bridgeman**

**Images:** Rodrigo Foundation (bl). AISA (br). **282 Alamy Stock Photo:** Pictorial Press Ltd (c). **285 Alamy Stock Photo:** Lebrecht Music & Arts (tl). The History Collection (cr). Brenda Kean (br). **286 Getty Images:** Radio Times / Contributor (tr). **287 Alamy Stock Photo:** Stephen Taylor (ca). **287 Getty Images:** Print Collector / Contributor (cr). Robbie Jack / Contributor (bl). **288 Alamy Stock Photo:** Art Collection 4 (c). Lebrecht Music & Arts (bl). **288 Bridgeman Images:** Peter Forrest (br). **289 Getty Images:** Manuel Litran / Contributor (c). **290 Getty Images:** DEA / G. DAGLI ORTI / Contributor (tl). **291 Getty Images:** INA / Contributor (bl). Hiroyuki Ito / Contributor (cr). **292 Getty Images:** ullstein bild / Contributor (c). **293 Bridgeman Images:** (c). **293 Getty Images:** Kurt Hutton / Stringer (br). **294 Getty Images:** Erich Auerbach / Stringer (bl). **295 Getty Images:** Bethany Clarke / Stringer (t). **296 Alamy Stock Photo:** (tr). **297 Alamy Stock Photo:** Peter Probst (tc). **297 Getty Images:** Imagno / Contributor (br). **298 Alamy Stock Photo:** SilverScreen (bl). **298 Getty Images:** Alfred Eisenstaedt / Contributor (br). **299 Getty Images:** Fox Photos / Stringer (c). **300 akg-images:** Imagno / Otto Breicha (tr). **301 Getty Images:** Robbie Jack / Contributor (tl). Hiroyuki Ito / Contributor (tr). **301 Alamy Stock Photo:** David Tipling Photo Library (br). **302 Getty Images:** Hulton Deutsch / Contributor (c). **303 akg-images:** Fototeca Gilardi (c).

**303 Getty Images:** Hiroyuki Ito / Contributor (br). **304 TopFoto:** Clive Barda / ArenaPAL (c). **305 Alamy Stock Photo:** Jui-Chi Chan (bl). **305 TOKYO SHOSEKI:** YAMADE Takashi / courtesy of YOZAN MEI SHAKUHACHI HIKICHI Yozan (r). **306 Bridgeman Images:** Marion Kalter (tr). **307 Getty Images:** Hiroyuki Ito / Contributor (tl). Amy T. Zielinski / Contributor (br). **308 Alamy Stock Photo:** dpa picture alliance (c). Peeter Kalmet (crb). **309 Getty Images:** The Washington Post / Contributor (c). **310 Alamy Stock Photo:** Allstar Picture Library (c). **311 Getty Images:** Robbie Jack / Contributor (bl). Hiroyuki Ito / Contributor (br). **312 TopFoto:** University of Bristol / ArenaPAL (c). **312 Getty Images:** Robbie Jack / Contributor (br). **312 TopFoto:** Hanya Chlala / ArenaPAL (c). **312 Getty Images:** Tim Roney / Radio Times / Contributor (cr). **314 Getty Images:** Peter Noble / Contributor (br). **315 Getty Images:** David Levenson / Contributor (bc). **316 Getty Images:** ullstein bild / Contributor (tr). **317 Bridgeman Images:** Chris Christodoulou (bl).

All other images © Dorling Kindersley. For more information see: **www.dkimages.com**

# What will you discover next?

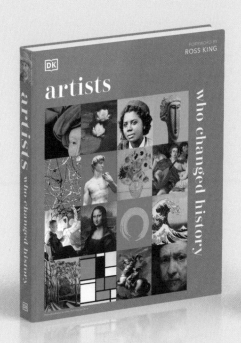

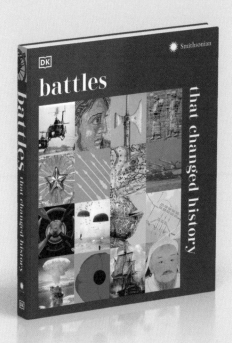

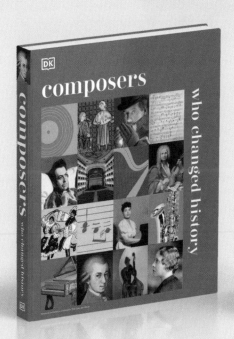

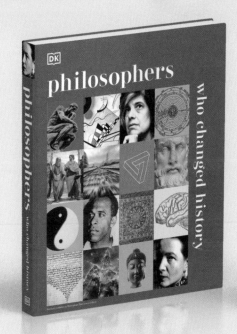

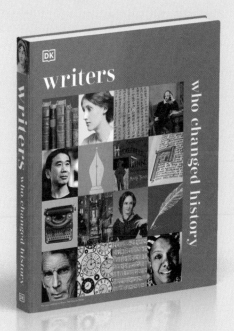